WITHDRAWN

Date Due

THREE MOZART OPERAS

Three Mozart Operas

Figaro
Don Giovanni
The Magic Flute

BY R. B. MOBERLY

DODD, MEAD & COMPANY

NEW YORK

FOR ELLY

—"Wie isset die daer singhet
Ende mi niet slaepen en laet?"
Anon, 16th Century

"Tir'd with all these, for restful death I cry,
As to behold desert a beggar born . . .
And folly—doctor-like—controlling skill,
And simple truth miscall'd simplicity . . .
Save that, to die, I leave my love alone."

CONTENTS

ILLUSTRATIONS

· ACKNOWLEDGMENTS

IT HAS BEEN a privilege to assemble, for this book, the opinions of Bernard Shaw about *Don Giovanni*. My thanks are due to the U.K. Public Trustee and Society of Authors for allowing me to print them; the quotations are from *How to Become a Musical Critic, Music in London 1890-1894* and—of course—*Man and Superman*.

We now have access to fine recent editions of most of the essential documents; and are also free to ask (if we wish) for microfilm copies of many actual originals. I am happy to acknowledge permission to include a considerable amount of copyright material, here and there, from two invaluable works: the *Mozart Documentary Biography* by Otto Erich Deutsch, translated by Eric Blom, Peter Branscombe and Jeremy Noble, published by Messrs. A. and C. Black (London) and the Stanford University Press; and *The Letters of Mozart and his family*, translated and edited by Emily Anderson, published by Messrs. Macmillan (London).

My grateful acknowledgments are also due to Ernest Benn Ltd. (London), MM. Calmann-Lévy (Paris), Editions du Seuil (Paris), Messrs. Faber and Faber (London), Alfred A. Knopf Inc., Messrs. Methuen (London), the Oxford University Press and the University of Chicago Press for quotations from the following: *Mozart on the Stage* by Christopher Benn (Benn); Gounod's *Mémoires d'un artiste* (Calmann-Levy); *La pensée de Mozart* by J.-V. Hocquard (Editions du Seuil); chapters by Gerald Abraham and Paul Hamburger in the *Mozart Companion*, edited by H. C. Robbins Landon and Donald Mitchell (Faber—from whose *Composers on Music* I took the Gounod and Berlioz English versions); *More Opera Nights* by Ernest Newman (Knopf); *Memoirs of H. Berlioz,* tr. Rachel and Eleanor Holmes, revised and annotated by Ernest Newman (Knopf); *Mozart, the Man and his Work* by W. J. Turner, edited by Christopher Raeburn (Methuen); *Mozart's Operas* by Edward J. Dent (Oxford); *Mozart, His Character, His Work* by Alfred Einstein, translated by Arthur Mendel and Nathan Broder (Oxford, New York; Messrs. Cassell, London); *Mozart in Retrospect* by A. Hyatt King (Oxford); and *Le Nozze di Figaro* by Siegmund Levarie (University of Chicago Press). Similarly, I am most grateful for permission to quote from an article by Charles Mackerras in *Opera* for April 1965; *Mozart Opera Society* notes by Walter Legge; a programme note by William Mann; and Peter Branscombe's paper (see p. 289) in the *Proceedings of the Royal Musical Association* for 1966.

In haste, I forgot to quote the most quotable of them all—Spike Hughes. This book is the poorer; I had fully intended to pillage his wonderfully evocative chapter, in *Famous Mozart Operas*, on *The Magic Flute*. My debt to him, and to the writers mentioned in the preceding paragraph, is much greater than may appear from the extent to which I happen to have quoted any of them. And my greatest debt of all is to a work that is still indispensable: Hermann Abert's *Neubearbeitete und erweiterte Ausgabe von Otto Jahn's Mozart* (seventh edition, Breitkopf und Härtel, Leipzig, 1955). I have also had invaluable help and encouragement from friends—please see the preface.

PART I

GENERAL

FOREWORD

MAY I summarize my main argument for you?

In 1785/6 Mozart came to maturity as a dramatist. His subject was a forbidden one in Vienna: *Le mariage de Figaro,* by Beaumarchais. Moreover the story was obviously much too long and complicated for operatic treatment. So what did Mozart do? He responded with what is still one of the most amazing of all musical scores; instrumentally and vocally irresistible, seamlessly continuous and coherent in meaning, highly compressed, brilliantly subtle and ironical. He did not even evade the most famous and subversive lines of the play. He put them to good use, as an F major aria. His librettist Lorenzo da Ponte hid them in Italian with a metaphor: *Se vuel ballare* . . . A clue was duly left, in the line before the aria begins.

In 1787, da Ponte suggested a Don Juan opera. The idea, we are told, pleased Mozart "infinitely." They sketched out a flawlessly coherent and logical pattern of characters (performable, too, once you accept that Mozart wanted it that way). But they soon came up against a moral and practical problem. What were they to do about the Don's legendary prowess as a seducer of women? Mozart had a realistic mind. Moreover, he was living in the century of Fiordiligi, not of Fidelio. Once again, therefore, he and da Ponte took the boldest possible course. They reported off-stage seductions of Anna and Zerlina, using music and words that could equally well be interpreted by the naive listener as showing that the Don was being foiled by indignant feminine resistance. One or two critics have tried to refute me by re-affirming the innocent meanings. But the essence of double-entendre is that *one* of the two meanings should be innocent. Competent writers do not allow passages of the consecutive double-entendre by accident. And there are a number of other clues in the score, to show which of the two meanings they intended.

In 1791, Mozart and Emanuel Schikaneder wrote a successful opera that praises Masonry. No one seems to have realized how surprising this is, as a simple matter of historical fact. The French Revolution was in progress, and liberal views were no longer acceptable in Vienna. Schikaneder had been ruined by last-minute censorship in February 1785, when Rautenstrauch's German version of *Le mariage* was forbidden. At all costs the censor had to be appeased—or fooled. There was therefore a compelling practical reason for the trivial title, the innocuous beginning, the predominant buffoonery, the lavish use of stage spectacle. But the opera, as we have it, is less incoherent than you may have supposed. The apparent change of plot was probably part of yet another bold and successful attempt at camouflaging an opera's true dramatic meaning. It is hardly surprising that, as I discovered a few days before ending my book, there is documentary evidence (p. 219) of Mozart's share in planning the libretto. And why not? The libretto plan, far more than the quality of the words, helps or hinders the dramatic quality of the completed work.

I do not know whether Mozart was wise to flout, time and time again, many of the dictates of operatic commonsense. But before we judge we must try to understand; and we cannot understand *Don Giovanni* or the *Magic Flute* without having first understood *Figaro*.

Meanwhile, Act Three of *Figaro* has again been performed in the original order (see p. 104). Anthony Besch, of Scottish Opera, has written to Christopher Raeburn and myself:—

"The new order works superbly well, and by now all of us who have been involved with the change, conductor, producer, cast, etc., are convinced that it is the only possible way to perform the Act. Everything falls more perfectly into place and all the climaxes are stronger for the revision. Particularly effective is it to have the Countess' aria immediately after the Count's, her emotion is infinitely more touching when it follows the arrogant emotion which the Count has expressed."

But on one occasion Scottish Opera were nearly caught out. Their Antonio was the understudy for Bartolo, and at one rehearsal Bartolo was ill. It then became precisely clear why the original revision had to be made!

We hope the time will come when the confused order is only used in that kind of emergency.

R. B. MOBERLY

June 18, 1968

PREFACE

I$_F$ YOU KNOW the three operas at all, you will be able to follow the commentary without a score or libretto, so long as you skip a sentence or paragraph here and there. But if you do not possess the scores, I hope that this book will persuade you to borrow or buy them. There are cross-references to them by number, or number and bar. For instance, *Figaro 1* is the opening G major duet, *1.30* is Susanna's first line, and *1A14* has secco words about "the most convenient room in the palace". References to plays are by act and scene. References to detail in the spoken sections of the *Magic Flute* libretto are by utterance, counting each change of speaker as an utterance. There are lists of section numbers at the beginning of each act, and in the index.

Vocal scores are the commonest. They give the vocal lines and a piano accompaniment. They therefore have many practical uses— for learning the notes of a voice part, for getting a rough idea of how it fits into the whole, for home performance at the piano, and above all for rehearsals. But the music of the piano reduction is wrong in tone, and incomplete. It sounds more or less right when played by some- one who knows the full score and is constantly imagining the orchestral effect. But by itself—I exaggerate, to make a point—the vocal score is not so much Hamlet as part of the corpse of the Prince of Denmark.

Yet the full-size orchestral scores are bulky and expensive. In some ways therefore the best of the existing scores are the little Eulenburg ones. They are of convenient size, except for conducting. They are surprisingly cheap. They were carefully edited, so far as the music is concerned, by scholars of the calibre of Hermann Abert and Alfred Einstein. They print the original words with tolerable care. Above all they give the elements of Mozart's dramatic art—the instrumental writing, the vocal lines, and the dance of words—as a whole. Every singer should consult them as an aid to interpretation. Every library should stock them.

The words, not being by Mozart, are carelessly given in most editions. There are minor inaccuracies in current versions of the two Italian libretti (*Figaro* and *Don Giovanni*, by Lorenzo da Ponte). As for *Die Zauberflöte*, of which the words are by Emanuel Schikaneder, editors have denied his authorship, omitted (without saying so) many of his stage-directions, and garbled the dialogue. If the spoken dialogue is to be cut or altered, we should do it for ourselves, not have other people's dialogue wished on us.

We may hope that the relevant volumes of the *Neue Mozart Ausgabe* will at long last edit the original words of all three operas properly. They are the words that Mozart saw, or wrote in his scores, or both. Once Mozart had accepted them (and whether or not they were the words that the librettist first offered him) they became *his* words. He often meant them ironically. But he always meant them fully, vividly, and precisely, with nuances and overtones. Unless the precise thoughts, as pre-acted by Mozart, are felt by the performers and put across to the audience, the impact of Mozart's intention is dimmed and blurred, as if one was hearing a symphonic performance from which one of the parts is missing. Time and again the music of a good performance comes suddenly into dramatic focus, as soon as we bother to understand the much-despised words as thoroughly as Mozart did. It is better than nothing to "enjoy the music for its own sake", provided that the singers have understood all the original words, and have had time to think about them. It is also better than nothing to hear the music sung in some free paraphrase, even if singers and audience thereby miss point after point. But until you can experience the music and the original thoughts together, you may occasionally yawn, wondering why competent judges like Bernard Shaw have said that Mozart is one of the world's great dramatists. You cannot enjoy one of these three operas fully without having done (and if possible enjoyed) your homework.

I myself have done a good thousand hours of homework, *con amore*; and I hope that this book will enable you to do a sufficient amount in a much shorter time. I shall be using my own translations; which rhyme and fit the music and are singable, but have also been kept as accurate as possible. (Why bother with the rhymes? Well, Schikaneder's rhymes are easy to match, and da Ponte's elegant Metastasian stanzas are musical as well as meaningful.) I hope my versions are in due course thought worth the effort of unlearning previous English singing versions. Meanwhile they are beginning to be thought useful for following recorded performances, and for study. In this book they tell the three stories and help to explain Mozart's intentions. *Traduttore traditore*, say the Italians. But maximum fidelity is, or should be, the aim and method of translation. Tradition—the usual way to do it, or the way in which so-and-so once sang it—has for too long been the true *traditore*.

I soon became sceptical of the apparent separateness of set-piece and secco, and have consistently ignored the arbitrary scene-divisions. I tried to identify each significant musical phrase, with or without words. One can play, sing, listen, enjoy, think, question, check, counter-check. The resultant sensation of attentive awareness is not only a whole-hearted non-verbal response to music but a precise human feeling or thought. Awareness is then amplified by similar attention to the whole series of musical and verbal facts—not just the ones we choose or remember. If the growing series seems to link oddly, we need not hasten to the strangely comforting conclusion that Mozart and his librettist were bunglers. Perhaps we bungled, by misunderstanding his intention. Perhaps we failed to use available evidence of how Mozart, in the years 1785–1791, was likely to see his problems. Patterns emerge, and provide material for further questioning and checking. Ideas have to be jettisoned, others are confirmed. After a while even the most ordinary factual additions and corrections tend incidentally to confirm or improve the emerging overall pattern—often in unexpected ways. The results, restrained and corrected all the way by the exacting disciplines of correspondence and coherence, are strangely detailed but also blindingly obvious and familiar. It all takes time, but such results are on the whole tenable—and suggestive.

There is a book list on p. 289. The books "above the line" contain primary documents which, with the scores, can help you to form your own views if you wish to do so. The ones "below the line" contain a selection of the views of men who in their generations have known and loved these operas. Those views, like mine, have no authority unless they can be confirmed by the scores and other primary documents. Though there is room for differences of attitude and interpretation, there must also be respect for ascertainable facts—just as we are entitled to hope that different pianists will play all the notes.

In writing a book like this, one can be wrong or "off beam" many times a page. One is therefore more than usually indebted to predecessors and friends. I owe a great deal to the editors and commentators, to practitioners and teachers of the crafts of music, and to men and women who taught me some of the knacks of thinking and writing. Of musician friends Julian Armitage-Smith, Eric Sams and Diana Barnham were particularly energetic and patient in saving me from dull errors of slovenliness and what Dr. Johnson called "pure ignorance, Madam"; each also threw into the pot important positive suggestions. Peter Branscombe and Christopher Raeburn allowed me to tap their scholarly expertise, suggested important out-of-the-way books, warned

me off bogus views and went out of their ways to answer questions.
Thomas Hemsley suggested translating Figaro, Livia Gollancz sug-
gested doing Don Giovanni for this book. I am indebted for other
suggestions and help to very many people including Lord Harewood,
Walter Legge, Wolfgang Plath, William Mann, Peter Stadlen, Marian
Hughes, Richard Standen, Ronald Latham, David Buglass, John
McLaughlin, Vera Wilkin, R. Lloyd Thomas and W. J. Smith; and for
various direct help to Glyndebourne, the London Library, the
Westminster Central Music and Central Reference Libraries, the Library
of Congress and the Augsburg Stadtarchiv. Jean Munro, Betty Peters,
Mary Cole and my daughter Elizabeth Moberly helped with typing;
and my wife, Elly, helped in more ways than anyone. E. C. Mitchell
did the excellent photographs.

RISING STANDARDS OF PERFORMANCE

"Until the last few decades" wrote Hyatt King in about 1955
(*Mozart in Retrospect*) "the apparent simplicity of Mozart's music has
often led to ill-considered and ill-rehearsed renderings. Even now,
when conductors, players, and soloists attain a high technical standard,
many of them still betray the most incongruous and contradictory
ideas of 'interpretation'.... Such matters as tempi, phrasing, ornamentation, the repetition of formulae, nuances, and emphasis in scale-
playing all need much study in contemporary sources before we can
claim to have recaptured some of Mozart's own standards and ideals in
performance. Meanwhile, the present variety of styles could surely be
reduced."

Let us now go back many decades, to a man who once wrote that
"in my small boy-hood I by good luck had an opportunity of learning
the Don thoroughly; and if it were only for the sense of the value of
fine workmanship which I gained from it, I should still esteem that
lesson the most important part of my education." Bernard Shaw, born
in 1856, was writing in 1891. He was not yet known as a dramatist—
Widowers' Houses was first performed in December 1892. Yet he was a
knowledgeable and articulate musician, far ahead of his time in the
understanding of Mozart's operas. I think you will believe, or at any
rate remember, the following relevant excerpts from his musical
journalism.

In 1885: "Within half a century after Bach's death, Mozart was not
only expressing emotions by means of music, but *expressing them in*

the manner of a first-class dramatist [my italics] *as they are modified by the characters of the individuals affected by them.*" In 1886: "*Don Giovanni* is certainly kept before the public; but in what plight? With fine movements omitted in the second act; with the recitative gabbled through in a manner which could not be adequately described without the employment of abusive epithets; and with most of the parts played so as to inspire a faint wonder whether ten or twenty more earnest rehearsals, followed by a run of a hundred nights, would suffice to reveal them to the players. When this is all we can do with *Don Giovanni* we had better keep it on the shelf as we now keep Shakespeare when we have not time to take due trouble with him. The actor who knows one part and consequently one play thoroughly is superior to the actor who can scramble with assistance through a dozen. The one gets into the skin of one character; the other only puts on the skin of twelve." If you or I say half as much, we are dismissed as armchair perfectionists.

In October 1887 Shaw imagined a superior person about to go to the centenary performance of "poor old Rossini's pet *dramma giocoso. . . .* I took a glance at the score and found exactly what I expected—commonplace melodies, diatonic harmonies and dominant discords, ridiculous old closes and half-closes at every eighth bar or so, 'florid' accompaniments consisting of tum-tum in the base and scales like pianoforte finger studies in the treble; and a ludicrously thin instrumentation, without trombones or clarionets except in two or three exceptionally pretentious numbers . . ." After the performance? "From Beethoven and Wagner I have learned that the orchestra can paint every aspect of nature and turn impersonal but specific emotion into exquisite sound. But *an orchestra that creates men and women as Shakespeare and Molière did* [my italics]—that makes emotion not only specific but personal and characteristic (and this, mind, without clarionets, without trombones, and without a second pair of horns): such a thing is madness: I must have been dreaming. . . ." Or, in an article on *Wagner in Bayreuth*: "Mozart is Wagner's only peer in lyric drama: he also made the orchestra envelop the poem in a magic atmosphere of sound: he also *adapted a few favorite rhythms, modulations, and harmonies* [my italics] *to an apparently infinite variety and subtlety of accent and purport.*"

Stendhal (*Rossini, II, 226*) remarked that Italian audiences saw in Mozart "pas de chant pour les voix; du chant pour la clarinette, du chant pour la basson, mais rien ou presque rien pour cet instrument admirable lorsqu'il ne crie pas, la voix humaine." Mozart's mature operas are in neither of Stendhal's "deux genres de musique dramatique; celle où la voix est toute, et celle où la voix ne fait presque que nommer les sentiments que les instruments réveillent avec une si étonnante puissance" (*Haydn*, 2). But the orchestra have at least half of the fun, and of the responsibility for musical and dramatic interpretation. "I know your style of composition" wrote Leopold Mozart anxiously to his son, during the rehearsals for *Idomeneo* in December 1780 "it requires unusually close attention from the players of every type of instrument; and to keep the whole orchestra at such a pitch of industry and alertness for at least three hours is no joke. Each performer, even the most inferior viola-player, is deeply touched by personal praise and becomes much more zealous and attentive, while a little courtesy of this kind only costs you a word or two." And they are deeply touched by the quality of the parts that Mozart wrote for them. Indeed it is the main hindrance to a full understanding of the operas today that the right shade and quality of voice, with a good orchestra, seem Paradise enough. . . .

But Shaw rightly insisted that voice and orchestra are used by Mozart to create character. Mozart did this consciously. "Let me now turn to Belmonte's aria in A major, 'O wie ängstlich, o wie feurig.' Would you like to know how I have expressed it—and even indicated his throbbing heart? By the two violins playing octaves. This is the favourite aria of all those who have heard it, and it is mine also. I wrote it expressly to suit Adamberger's voice. You feel the trembling —the faltering—you see how his throbbing breast begins to swell; this I have indicated by a crescendo. You hear the whispering and the sighing—which I have indicated by the first violins with mutes and a flute playing in unison." Note that this familiar quotation is from a letter that Mozart wrote to his father in September 1781, four whole years before he began to write *Figaro*. *Die Entführung* is glorious to sing and hear. But by 1785–7, for a number of reasons, his power of characterisation had greatly developed. In *Figaro*, as we shall see, even the minor characters come to life. In *Don Giovanni* there are no minor characters, except perhaps the Statue.

"Ever since I was a boy" (Shaw again, in May 1891) "I have been in search of a satisfactory performance of *Don Giovanni*; and I have at last come to see that Mozart's turn will hardly be in my time. . . . At the performance last Thursday, the first three acts of the four (twice too many) into which the work is divided at Covent Garden showed signs of rehearsal. . . . In the orchestra especially the improvement was marked. Not that anything very wonderful was accomplished in this department: the vigorous passages were still handled in the usual timid, conventional way; and the statue music, still as impressive as it was before Wagner and Berlioz were born, was muddled through like the vote of thanks at the end of a very belated public meeting. But the overture was at least attentively played, and in some of the quieter and simpler numbers the exhalations of the magical atmosphere of the Mozartian orchestra were much less scanty and foggy than last year, when I could not, without the risk of being laughed at, have assured a novice that *in the subtleties of dramatic instrumentation Mozart was the greatest master of them all* [my italics]. The cast was neither a very bad nor a very good one. Its weakest point was the Leporello of Isnardon. Lacking the necessary weight in the middle of his voice, as well as the personal force demanded by the character, he was quite unable to lead the final section of the great sextet *Mille torbidi pensieri* which, thus deprived of its stage significance, became a rather senseless piece of 'absolute music.' . . . In *O statua gentilissima* he hardly seized a point from beginning to end. Now if an artist has neither voice enough nor musical perception enough to interpret forcibly and intelligently such an obvious and simple dramatic transition as that which follows the incident of the statue nodding acceptance of the invitation to supper, he is not fit to meddle with Mozart. . . ." Later the same year, at the centenary of Mozart's death: "It is hard to get the most obvious dramatic points in his orchestration attended to, even the churchyard scene in *Don Giovanni* being invariably rattled through at Covent Garden as if it were a surprisingly vapid quadrille. . . . The incompetence and superficiality of Mozart's interpreters are the true and only cause of the apparent triviality of his greatest music." In 1892: "(We) have hardly yet got out of the habit of regarding Mozart's compositions as tuneful little trifles fit only for persons of the simplest taste." In 1893: "Unless you can sing those opening lines (of Mendelssohn's *Hear my prayer*) with the rarest nobility of line and the most touching depth of expression, your one duty to them is to let them alone. They are like the opening phrase of the quartet in *Don Giovanni*, '*Non ti fidar, O misera*': success in delivering them is only possible to singers who have the finest temperamental sympathy with their spirit; and anything short of success is utter failure." And: "Miss Harris . . . is not within ten years of attaining the expression and eloquence which can alone give her the right to touch in public a masterpiece like *Mi tradi*." And: "If you look at the score . . . you will find three different male voices written for on the bass clef and so treated as to leave no doubt that Mozart, as he wrote the music, had a particular sort of voice for each part constantly in his head, and that one (Masetto's) was a rough peasant's bass, another (Leporello's) a ready fluent copious basso cantante; and the third a light fine baritone, the voice of a gentleman. I have heard public meetings addressed successively by an agricultural labourer's delegate, a representative of the skilled artisans, and a university man; and they have taught me what all the treatises on singing in the world could not, about the Mozartian differentiation between Masetto, Leporello and Don Giovanni. . . . The dramatic distinction between the parts is so strong that only an artist of remarkable versatility could play one as well as the other, but there is practically no distinction of vocal range, any more than there is a distinction of physical stature or strength." In 1918: "Mozart's music is enormously more difficult than Wagner's; and his tragi-comedy is even more so. With Mozart you either hit the bulls-eye or miss, and a miss is as bad as a mile. . . ." In 1950, the year of his death, he was still writing about "*Don Giovanni*, the greatest opera in the world."

By 1950, progress had been made. Hyatt King reminds us of the efforts of Beecham, Mahler and Richard Strauss in re-educating the public towards appreciation of Mozart's operas; and, in particular, the work done in this country by the Carl Rosa Company, by E. J. Dent and Clive Carey at Sadlers Wells, and by John Christie (through giving a free hand to Fritz Busch and Carl Ebert) at Glyndebourne. Early Glyndebourne was a revelation of what can be done by concentrating on Mozart, and by adequate rehearsal.

A revolutionary development of the past decade has been the complete stereo recordings, the best of which are an enduring proof of the quality that can be achieved (with some retakes) by not having to worry about the hit-and-miss problem of filling the theatre next week; and by letting the best performers concentrate on the music and the original words. By now (1966) we have also had *Figaro* complete at Sadlers Wells, with appoggiaturas from the eighteenth-century singing manuals, discreet ornamentation from the early performing editions and real awareness of the Beaumarchais play. Scholars in several countries are busy re-editing the documents, and sifting out truth from the misleading anecdotes that were still being repeated by their predecessors. And the operatic film is at last beginning to hint at what photography will do, one day, to help reveal the lost nuances of a work like *Figaro*.

The difficulties remain. These are in the fullest sense ensemble operas. The voices (and the blend of voices, a point that happens not to be mentioned in my excerpts from Shaw but is generally accepted as essential) must be good enough. The standard of vocal artistry—singing technique, musicianship, style, emotional maturity, clarity of diction, ability to act with the singing voice—must be even higher. The singer must also be able to act (not under-act or over-act but act) with some degree of competence, and should try to look the right age. The instrumental playing cannot afford to be less than first-class. The costumes and sets and lighting need to be in period, or at any rate must not clash with the music and words. If the greater Mozart operas (not just these three famous ones) are to be done in public, they need much rehearsal and an apparently disproportionate share of the available subsidies. In order to justify the use of these scarce resources, performers as well as audiences need to have a fuller knowledge of what the operas are about. Later in this book, I shall try to offer some contributions to that knowledge.

DRAMATIC PURPOSE AND TECHNIQUE

IN GENERAL, MOZART is unsentimental and realistic about human nature—the impartial Keatsian artist who "delights in creating an Iago as much as an Imogen." Yet he is human enough to have sympathies and prejudices, and to let them appear. I suspect that he was unconsciously (and as time went on, more consciously) building up a pattern of the inner feelings of heterosexual love—much as Chaucer did, and with the same delighted mastery of a new medium of expression, in which one does not have to seek originality by being obscure or recherché. Behind (and inseparable from) the ironic precision, there is ambiguity; a quality which will become more and more evident as we achieve the historical accuracy and authenticity for which we still need to strive.

Yet we must not generalise too much. *Figaro, Don Giovanni* and the *Magic Flute* are very different works. We are still fumbling for some of the essential facts about each of them. By comparison with Shakespeare studies, Mozart studies have not yet reached the Johnson era, let alone the Bradley or Granville-Barker eras. It is a current fad to believe that, because A. C. Bradley was an academic and had his foibles, we are wrong to be interested in the characters of opera (someone should have told Mozart, or Shaw). We need to keep our minds open, and to beware of jumping to conclusions. Brigid Brophy's book *Mozart the Dramatist*, convincing or not, was a necessary protest

against our complacent narrownesses. Mozart died in 1791, less than
two hundred years ago, at the age of thirty-five. We still think of him
in formal eighteenth-century clothes, as a composer who used common
keys and traditional forms. But he did uncommon and untraditional
things with them (think for instance of the uses to which he puts C
major in these operas). He had shared the formative years of a generation of men and women who lived far into the following century,
through *Sturm und Drang*. In Vienna he was a clever young musician,
a Mason, an admirer of those dreadful English, a sympathiser with
incipient revolution in France. Yet he was above all himself, an
artist with a livelier and more creative mind than his ancestors and
contemporaries, a man who shocked (and was soon misunderstood
and despised by) his successors. *Figaro* is his whole-hearted personal
response to a particular play, itself the creation of a lively French mind.
The other two, though based on traditional material, are Mozart's
own creations. In order to understand *Don Giovanni* we need to discover, not how playwrights and composers of several countries and
two centuries had treated the subject for over a hundred and fifty
years, nor how Hoffmann and a dozen others have since reacted, but
how Mozart treated it. Similarly we shall not understand the *Flute* by
source-digging, or by assuming that the story "must have been" changed
when part of the music was already written. If a historian—even a
music historian—writes that such and such "must have" happened, we
may reasonably suspect that he has no good evidence for what he is saying.

Back to the scores! Dent said this, and many other wise things;
but was apt to wander from the point. Abert is a good and careful
guide to the music of the orchestral numbers but had less feel for the
words. Jouve and Hocquard have tended to concentrate on the edifying bits (though Jouve remarks on the bawdy bars at the end of
Madamina—see below). Gaiffe, in his book on *Le Mariage de Figaro*
(1929), is expressing a common view when he says, of the opera, that
"l'esprit de l'œuvre est entièrement modifié, transposé dans un plan
supérieur, degagé de tout ce que la verve un peu degagée de Beaumarchais y avait mis de plébéien et de matériel—l'amour surtout y
prend un tout autre aspect; ce qui était désir charnel devient chaste
besoin d'aimer, la sensibilité se transforme en tendresse." Here is a
classic example of failing to know the opera as a whole. It does indeed
modify and transcend the play—which is saying something, because
the play has endured in its own right. But the opera is full of glitter,
verve, carnal desire, etc.; for the simple reason that Mozart himself
was not such a pure and spiritual highbrow as his French (and some

of his English) admirers think. In our sex-obsessed century one is almost reluctant to have more of it thrust at us. But: "Tis dark in there, I feel!" "The darkness is ideal; as well you know, I enter for a purpose, not to read." The meaning is reinforced by a *double entendre* (28.96)—and the orchestra are delighted. The language of *Le Nozze* is constantly and cheerfully erotic, e.g.: (*18A1*)

> Look at him, doctor dearest! The happy outcome of the love that was between us!
> Let us not chatter of doings best forgotten . . .

The language of *Don Giovanni* goes further; and the music goes with it: "If she's wearing skirt and bodice, need I tell you what will pass?" These words and the music of the final word at *4.162, 164, 166* are unpardonable, from Leporello to Donna Elvira. Even Shaw could not believe that they were dramatically meant. Yet that is what the Don lived for, and it is part of the dramatic pattern that Elvira, who loves him, should find herself constantly humiliated. Similar music recurs at *13.461–2*, when Zerlina is off-stage with the Don. Even in the *Magic Flute* the language is notably candid; and we shall need to consider why Mozart made a Princess and a birdcatcher sing, in solemn innocence, a hymn to the habit of monogamy:

> He who can feel the urge of love
> Will never lack an honest heart.
> To feel the fellow-urge of love—
> That is, by Nature, woman's art.
> For joy in love our wills do strive,
> Only through love are we alive.
> It sweetens trouble, mellows neighbours;
> All living creatures love obey.
> It adds a spice to endless labours;
> To work through love is Nature's way.
> Their purpose high, by Nature's plan,
> Nobler are none than wife and man.
> Wife and man, and man and wife
> Reach to godhead here in life.

We know from Mozart's letters that he was not the man to set such lines without realising what they imply.

There is serenity and unearthly beauty in these operas—it is a poor performance that does not convey these qualities. But the earthiness is there as well, and the combination of earthy and unearthly helps to illuminate Mozart's liking for the difficult genre of tragi-comedy. W. J. Turner, who says (p. 314) that "even Professor Dent in his admirable book on Mozart's operas seems to me to have a distorted conception of *Don Giovanni*, owing perhaps to a certain moral conventionality of judgment, and a temperamental dislike to intensity of expression," has pointed out that: "What puzzles (us) is just this strange blend of the tragic and the comic. Most people like to have these elements carefully separated into different works of art so that they may feel safe. . . . When however a major dramatist like Shakespeare combines in one piece the tragic and the comic . . . not only does the auditor feel that his leg is being pulled, but he is not sure which leg, and that spoils the thing for him." Unlike life, Mozart's drama is never dull. Like life, it is apt to be funny and serious, beautiful and squalid, gay and grim—not just in rapid succession but at the same time. This is made possible because he is always working by contrasts, with characters and situations that are vividly, precisely, truthfully imagined. If you miss the joke at the end of *Madamina*, you miss much of Elvira's humiliation. If you miss her sincere and dignified credulity in *DG15*, you miss the flavour of the Don's gay charming cold-hearted irresponsibility and Leporello's dilemma. If you miss the low comedy in *Zauberflöte* you will be less forcibly uplifted by the idealistic bits. It all needs to be presented faithfully and whole-heartedly; without over-acting, and without worrying unduly whether the situation is meant to be comic or tragic or both. As Mozart had remarked when dealing with a simpler situation, six years earlier (26 Sept. 1781): "Osmin's rage is rendered comical by the use of the Turkish music. In working out the aria I have . . . allowed Fischer's beautiful deep notes to glow. The passage '*Drum beim Barte des Propheten*' is indeed in the same time, but with quick notes; but as Osmin's rage gradually increases, there comes (just when the aria seems to be at an end) the *allegro assai*, which is in a totally different tempo and in a different key . . . just as a man in such a towering rage oversteps all the bounds of order, moderation and propriety and completely forgets himself, so must the music too forget itself. But since passions, whether violent or not, must never be expressed to the point of exciting disgust, and as music, even in the most terrible situations, must never offend the ear, but must please the listener, or in other words must never cease to be *music*, so I have not chosen a key remote from F (in which the aria is written) but one related to it—not the nearest, D minor, but the more remote A minor."

Mozart can put an expressive nuance into almost any kind of detail:

the initial choice of a particular rhythm and key, a change to or from the dominant or subdominant, a move from minor to major or vice versa, a modulation to a near or relatively distant (but still common) key, the precise blend of instrumental colour and texture (counting voices as instruments), changes of tempi and dynamics, differentiation between the shape of vocal lines (or, occasionally, a deliberate lack of differentiation between them), the precise shape and timing of a particular line, the sudden use of unaccompanied voice, the emphasis given to a particular word, the way in which words are repeated with a difference of emphasis or accompaniment, the use of irony (whether or not intended as such by the speaker), the use of "tu" or "voi", the intended uses of darkness on the stage, etc. In later chapters I give instances in their contexts (for it is only in context that such meaning can be properly judged). Meanwhile, you may like to look at what is said on p. 171 about an all too precise pantomimic suggestion, in which the first violin kills the 'cello with three sforzando jabs; on p. 190, about a cackle of orchestral laughter in *DG13.129–133*; on p. 246, about the use of strings and tenor voice in E♭ (accompanied by clarinets, bassoons and horns) during the first few bars of Tamino's aria; on p. 275, about the effect of the postlude to Pamina's aria, after the way in which the instruments were used while she was still singing; on p. 111, about a quaver rest in *Fig. 19.2*; on p. 184 about a seductive change from "voi" to "tu" at *DG6A21*; on p. 92, about the entirely different effect of the same change at *Fig. 15.64*. If you know the operas, other examples may crowd into your mind.

"Rather too many notes, my dear Mozart" said the Emperor about *Die Entführung* (according to Niemetschek, who was Mozart's first biographer). It is not clear whether the Emperor was referring to the length of the piece or to its musical texture. But Mozart, who was no courtier, replied: "Exactly as many notes as are necessary, your Majesty." Mozart may err on the side of trying to say too much; but he wastes no notes in saying it. In the concluding bars of an episode one can occasionally lean back and enjoy the music for its own sake. But Mozart is often busy underlining the dramatic point that he has just been making. Even at the end of finales, when he and we are aware of imminent return to the polite nothings of life, he is apt to come out with surprises. Sometimes they are mysterious and poetic surprises, like the ecstatic fugato at *DG24.756* that seems to say:

> As you from crimes would pardon'd be,
> Let your indulgence set me free.

Sometimes they state a new fact; like the *Più stretto* in which, when the Don recovers his usual confidence, all three women at once (*DG13.624*) sing his tune. Commentators are apt to complain that there are no stage-directions in the latter part of this finale. But there could be no clearer stage-direction, in its context, than this small musical detail.

Note that this musical stage-direction, though it can only be interpreted by visible positioning or movement, is a statement of how the women instinctively feel at that moment, despite what they are trying to say. Things happen on stage, in front of our eyes. But Mozart is interested in what it feels like to be doing or suffering or seeing the thing that happens. I do not agree with those who distinguish heavily between the "exterior action" and an esoteric "interior action" which takes place in moments when Mozart is bored with the story. It is always the interior action—the nuances of the inner feelings of soliloquy and dialogue, thought and action—that Mozart's music brings to life, with a depth and precision that outranges the musicianly prose of a Shaw or the musical verse of a Shakespeare. I am not saying that Mozart is a greater dramatist; but his characteristic purpose and technique as a dramatist is to define, by little details in a large context, exactly how the inner essence of some moment is to be felt. Good Mozartian singers are not offended by this apparent lack of trust in their creative ability as interpreters. This is music whose service is perfect interpretative freedom. If singers do not obey it, they are bluffing. If they have not quite got the hang of it, they flounder; or seem like puppets, concerned with minor felicities that can only be appreciated by a few Mozart specialists. But as soon as they have mastered their briefs, the result is a direct theatrical experience—exhilarating, full-blooded, infinitely vivid and natural, not only funnier and more coherent but more moving and more beautiful than when it is done in any of the various "usual ways". Each significant musical *and verbal* detail makes dramatic sense in relation to the rest of what we are hearing and seeing at the same time. Each moment follows naturally on what went before, and merges naturally into what follows after; so that the whole of each act (or at any rate the whole of each complete scene) is as unstoppable as the finale of Act Two of *Figaro*. It is a vile mistake to treat the numbers as separate items, with rallentandi and applause; so that one yawns through the secco while waiting for the aria, and is then ecstatically oblivious to what the aria is about. In context, that famous aria is a soliloquy or chunk of dialogue, crowded with information and new developments. *Attacca subito* says the score; go straight into what follows. Secco merges into aria or duet, etc., and back into secco with barely a comma between thoughts. Wonderful though the orchestral numbers are, they are never to be regarded as oases in a dry desert. Mozart's dramatic thought runs so swiftly, and has set itself to run so far, that he needs his secco. Look more carefully at the page of secco, and you will see that pace and pitch vary as a Gielgud might vary them on the stage, if he were speaking the part. Nothing sorts out the singer-actor from the mere singer more quickly than the secco. Less of the work is done for him by the music. But Mozart is still feeling each moment in its context, still enriching it harmonically. In other words, his approach to secco recitatives is the same as his approach to the writing of accompanied solos and ensembles—they too are integral moments in a coherent composition.

It is illuminating to consider the contrast between this habit of mind and that of, say, Schubert and Wolf. It can be argued that the whole genre of the *Lied* derives from certain pages of the Mozart operas—notably Tamino's aria. But the minds of the Lieder composers were usually fired by separate situations. Mozart, on the other hand, had a mind that was more and more easily fired by (or into) long intricate stories. His operatic numbers may look self-contained, and are certainly full of miniature beauties. Yet they can be sadly misunderstood if they are considered out of context.

That is why cuts in the original score are so dangerous. It is easy to assume that some aria served only to appease a singer, or to allow the scenery to be changed. But if we do not see the dramatic point, it may be we who are at fault. If it sounds inferior as music, that also may be because we have failed to see why he wrote it in that way, i.e. for what dramatic purpose. The pages which are so often cut were part of his pattern; and Mozart does not waste pages, any more than he wastes notes. In any case cuts are apt to be futile. The performance which is full of cuts, so as not to bore a modern audience, is often slow or dramatically null or both. Artistically it is difficult to improve on Mozart's score, even by omission. When possible (and invariably, when doing our homework) we should obey the King of Hearts: "Begin at the beginning," the King said gravely, "and go on till you come to the end: then stop."

May we begin?

PART II

FIGARO

Title: Le Nozze di Figaro. *Köchel number:* 492. *First performance:*
Burgtheater, Vienna, 1st May 1786

LE NOZZE DI FIGARO

Characters in order of singing

FIGARO, aged thirty (MF 3.16) or less (see p. 114), ex-barber of Seville, principal valet at the French-looking château or palace of Aguas Frescas eight miles from Pari . . . er, I beg your pardon, Seville. He is self-educated, ambitious, and in debt.

SUSANNA, about as young as the Countess; gardener's niece, lady's maid, Figaro's bride, competent, mercurial, a born mimic.

DON BARTOLO, jeune vieillard (BS), fat (MF 1.3), nervous (BS 2.4), cliché-monger; a doctor (of medicine, not law!) at Seville; summoned to Aguas Frescas by:

MARCELLINA (pronounced Marchellina), sharp-tongued blue-stocking, in her late forties (MF 3.16) or younger (see p. 114); used to be governess to Bartolo's ward Rosina; housekeeper at the palace; dowdy, old-fashioned, rather pathetic, anti-man, hopes to force Figaro to marry her.

CHERUBINO (pronounced with a K, as Kerubino), aged thirteen (MF preface), elegant accomplished self-admiring treble; page to the Count, godson to the Countess, a charming nuisance.

COUNT ALMAVIVA, the wild and romantic young grand seigneur whose story was dear to the Europe of Mozart's day. Immensely wealthy, married for three years (MF 5.7) to his Rosina, bored, unhappy, unpopular with the tenants, fancies himself as a woman-chaser, about to go as Ambassador to London (where in December 1783 an even younger man became Prime Minister).

DON BASILIO, no longer young, music master, abbé, scandal-monger, ex-idealist, proud of his thick skin.

THE COUNTESS, aged nineteen, a gentle ingénue, devoted to her undeserving husband, well-liked by the tenants; still the Rosina (the Beaumarchais/Paisiello Rosina, not Rossini's) who helped to outwit Bartolo; the strongest character of them all.

ANTONIO, the gardener (part originally doubled by the singer of Bartolo); illiterate, but shrewd and pithy when sober.

BARBARINA, aged twelve, his daughter; gay, vivid, hopes to marry Cherubino.

DON CURZIO, solemn elderly baa–lamb judge (part originally doubled by the singer of Basilio).

Also two young girls. Chorus: young peasant lads and even younger lasses.

PROLOGUE

Le Mariage de Figaro, by Beaumarchais, was first publicly performed on 27th April 1784 in Paris. Baronne d'Oberkirch called it "possibly the most spirited piece ever written . . . a bright blaze of artifice . . . although it breaks every rule of dramatic art, and runs for over four hours, there is not a moment of boredom. It is immoral, positively indecent . . . but it will stay in the repertoire, will often be performed, will always be entertaining." It had been written in about 1778, but Louis XVI said it would never be performed. At last he relented, in the hope that it was too long to hold an audience. By then everyone wanted to see it. Beaumarchais had omitted a blatant attack on the Church. He had also sobered his account of the relation between the Countess and the pageboy (Chérubin, cherub). But Baronne d'Ober-kirch shook her head as the grands seigneurs applauded: "They have laughed at their own expense; and what is worse, have made others laugh. They will regret it, later on."

In Paris *Le mariage* ran that year for sixty-eight consecutive per-formances. On December 14th of the same year, an English version was performed in London. Thomas Holcroft wrote: "Finding it impossible to procure a Copy of the original French, though a journey to Paris was undertaken expressly for that Purpose, the copy made use of in the composing *The Follies of a Day* was taken by memory only, during eight or nine representations." According to Hazlitt, Holcroft earned £600 by it "besides a considerable sum for the copyright." The early numbers of *The Times*, then Mr. John Walter's *Daily Universal Register*, are full of announcements of it, sometimes at Drury Lane and sometimes at Covent Garden. On February 18th, 1785 it even earned an adverse review: "This piece, destitute of humour and barren of wit, owes its success to the immorality of its characters and the indecent incidents which support its flimsy meretricious fable, wherein youth is stripped of innocence and a husband is painted vicious, and a matron is cloathed with shame—Where was the good Lord Chamberlain, when this piece came into his office?" On the next day, February 19th, we read: "Nothing prevails in the sister kingdom (France) but Figaro . . . the Bird of Paradise is Figaro! her hat is Figaro! her cloaks are Figaro! her fur-below is Figaro." On February 25th: "The Follies of a Day, *of which so much has been said* [my italics], is in rehearsal (at Dublin) for the special benefit of the Manager." On April 4th, less than seven weeks

ADVERTISEMENT.   v

irritable in all bosoms, and so difficult to subdue.

To enumerate all the Obstacles encounter-ed and overcome in bringing this Comedy on the English Stage, would be to indulge this Vanity; which it is every wise Man's Pride, and every prudent Man's Interest to resist. It may, however, afford some Plea-sure to be informed, that, finding it impos-sible to procure a Copy of the original French, though a Journey to Paris was undertaken expressly for that Purpose, the Copy made use of in the composing *The Follies of a Day,* was taken by Memory, only, during eight or nine Representations; that I furnished the Plot, Incidents, Entrances, and Exits, and gave some other occasional Hints; that the remainder was the Work of a young French-man, whose Talents and whose Heart are an Ornament and an Honour to his Coun-try; and that, after it was brought to *Eng-land* and received by Mr. *Harris,* it was translated, cast, copied, recopied, studied, and, in one of its longest Parts, re-studied, and played in little more than a Month.
The

Part of a preface to the first English version, by Thomas Holcroft; Upper Mary-le-Bone St., February 21st 1785.

after condemning the story, the embryo *Times* published its own
version of a famous scene. The boy behind the chair became England's
young Prime Minister, William Pitt. The Count was Charles James
Fox. "Basil" was Charles Jenkinson, who according to Horace
Walpole "had and deserved no marked character; he was the tool of the
King, and had just parts enough to make his servility inexcusable."
Bartholo was Lord North, whom nobody loved. (Fox may have felt
flattered to be the Count; according to Horace Walpole, "nature had
not distinguished him from other young men by potency in love.")

In the same month, April 1785, the official first edition of the French
play was published in Paris. Meanwhile there had been pirated editions
in Amsterdam, from which German (and other) translations were
already in existence. On 2nd February 1785 the *Wienerblättchen*
announced: "Herr Rautenstrauch has recently translated into German
the comedy *Les Noces de Figaro*, received with such extraordinary
applause in Paris . . . this will be performed for the first time tomorrow
by the company of Messrs Schikaneder and Kumpf." Joseph Rautenstrauch was a well-known supporter of the Emperor Joseph. But the
Emperor took no chances. On 31st January he had written to Count
Pergen, President of the Lower Austrian Government: "I hear that the
well-known comedy *Le Mariage de Figaro* is said to have been proposed
for the Kärntnertor Theatre in a German translation; since the piece
contains much that is objectionable, I expect that the Censor shall
reject it altogether, or have such alterations made in it that he shall be
responsible for the performance of this play and for the impression that
it may make." On 4th February the *Wienerblättchen* reported: "The
comedy promised by Herr Schikaneder . . . was not performed
yesterday; according to the news imparted to the public by yesterday's
poster, the Censorship has authorised it to be printed but not performed." The printed text of the forbidden play, *Der Närrische Tag*,
duly appeared, with a mournful dedication by Rautenstrauch "Dem
Andenken von Zweyhundert Dukaten," to the *two* hundred ducats
[my italics] that he never received for a piece of hackwork. No doubt
the book sold well. Schikaneder, on the other hand, was ruined.

Mozart, aged twenty-nine, was riding high. "That your brother has
very fine quarters with all the necessary furniture," wrote his father,
"you may gather from the fact that his rent is 460 gulden." He had
recently "performed the six quartets for his dear friend Haydn and
other good friends, and . . . sold them to Artaria for *one* hundred
ducats" [my italics]. A few weeks later, Haydn said to Leopold Mozart:
"Before God and as an honest man I tell you that your son is the

greatest composer known to me either in person or by name. He has
taste and, what is more, the most profound knowledge of composition."
The six quartets were published on 1st September with a dedication to
Haydn; from whose genius for musical dialogue Mozart surely
learned much that is relevant to these three operas. At the end of
October Leopold Mozart met a certain Professor Lorenz Hübner who
said, "In all the announcements of musical works I see nothing but
Mozart. The Berlin announcements, when quoting the quartets, add
the following words: 'It is unnecessary to recommend these quartets
to the public. Suffice it to say that they are the work of Herr Mozart'."
Leopold Mozart reports this to his daughter and adds "I had nothing
to say as I knew nothing; it was more than six weeks since I had had a
letter from your brother. . . . My informant said something about a
new opera. . . ."

Between mid-August and early November Leopold Mozart had
heard only once from his son; who was normally a good letter-writer.
Then: "At last I have received a letter of twelve lines from your
brother, dated November 2nd. He begs to be forgiven, as he is up to
his eyes in work on his opera *Le Nozze di Figaro* . . . in order to keep
the morning free for composing, he is now taking all his pupils in the
afternoon, etc. I know the piece; it is a very tiresome play and the
translation from the French will certainly have to be altered very freely
if it is to be effective as an opera. God grant that the text may be a
success. I have no doubt about the music. But there will be a lot of
running about and discussions before he gets the libretto so adjusted as
to suit his purpose exactly. And no doubt according to his charming
habit he has kept on postponing matters and has let the time slip by."

Le barbier de Séville, by Beaumarchais, had been natural material for
comic opera—it was offered as a comic opera libretto in 1772, three
years before it became famous and popular as a stage-play. In 1782
Paisiello and Petrosellini had made a successful opera of it. But *Le
mariage* was a mammoth and unruly sequel to *Le barbier;* complicated,
controversial, nearly twice as long. Leopold Mozart, I am sure, imagined
it would be slashed and radically simplified; as Boito, a century
later, slashed and altered Shakespeare until Verdi was satisfied; and, for
that matter, as Rossini and his librettist Sterbrini gaily maltreated the
story of *Le barbier* in 1816 to provide choral opportunities. Da Ponte,
in his preface to the printed libretto of *Le nozze*, was anxious to emphasise that he had made "an adaptation or, let us say, an extract" of
the play. For reasons of prudence and practicality, he says, he "was
obliged to reduce the sixteen characters of which it consists to eleven,

two of which may be performed by a single person, and to omit, apart from an entire act, many a charming scene and a number of good jests and sallies. . . ." That is da Ponte's slant. To divide a work into four acts instead of five is not to omit. The libretto has less verbiage than the play, but is essentially faithful to the Beaumarchais story. It omits one big scene, the less important part of a garrulous soliloquy, five minor characters, and some superfluous complications. It adds important material for certain of the arias, and thereby helps to produce a somewhat different total impression. It does not effectively shorten or simplify; it compresses, a procedure contrary to all the "laws" of opera. Mozart was and is bigger than these laws. He left himself little room for expansion, and no room at all for the vocal acrobatics of his earlier and later operas. Yet da Ponte still found it necessary to remark uneasily that "the opera will not be one of the shortest to have appeared on our stage. . . . We hope sufficient excuse will be found in the variety of the threads from which the action of the play is woven, the vastness and grandeur of the same, the multiplicity of the musical numbers that had to be made in order not to leave the actors too long unemployed, to diminish the vexation and monotony of long recitatives, and to express with varied colours the various emotions that occur." Nervously da Ponte offers "a rather new kind of spectacle to the refined taste of the Viennese public."

It is easy to lose the flavour of da Ponte's writing—the preceding paragraph does less than justice to him. At irony and nuance he is in some ways better than Beaumarchais. His dialogue flows simply and meaningfully in verse and prose. A man of tact and charm, he had taken on himself the essential job of choosing the right moment to persuade the Emperor that he, da Ponte, had omitted or cut anything that "might offend good taste or public decency at a performance over which the Sovereign Majesty might preside." In this he was exaggerating, but the Tedesci would not understand what some of it was about, until the opera was an established favourite.

Da Ponte is apt to blur points for the sake of brevity (or a rhyme). Yet the music copes easily with detail after detail of action, style, costume, social distinction and verbal repartee; and adds details of a similar kind to avoid the tedium of repetition. Moreover Mozart is apt to read into da Ponte's momentary vaguenesses a precise meaning or stage-direction from the French. At the outset a stage-direction in the score corrects a stupidly casual mistranslation in the printed libretto. These little things suggest that Mozart enjoyed the French and had it in front of him when setting the Italian; also that he understood the play better than da Ponte did. Presumably they discussed a libretto plan before da Ponte began to write. But it was Mozart, according to da Ponte, who suggested the subject. It was probably Mozart who saw that a play forbidden in German prose might with luck be allowed as Italian opera. It was Mozart who had to be able to visualise a synopsis of the story in terms of an acceptable musical structure. It was Mozart who would feel the need to satisfy himself, by sketching out alternative structures, that there was no simpler way of telling the essential story of a play that he—like thousands of others, all over Europe— found exciting. It was Mozart who had to decide whether to accept the unheard-of challenge of setting so long and detailed a story, instead of altering the story radically or dropping the whole idea. It was Mozart who had to live himself into a coherent pattern of character and situation, thereby automatically verifying and allocating the detail which had to be retained and added. No wonder he seemed preoccupied, and wrote only one letter to his father between mid-August and early November. In these weeks Mozart the dramatist may have come of age. Da Ponte says in his memoirs: "I set to work, and as I wrote the words so he set them to music . . . in six weeks all was ready." If there is any truth in this flattering recollection, he is forgetting the preliminary work—or, more probably, Mozart had done most of it for him.

Or did Mozart do it all? Da Ponte recalls a conversation in which Mozart gladly agreed to set to music "a drama written for him by me" but was "certain that he would not obtain permission." This implies that Mozart had *Figaro* in mind but did not say so. Then "one day, he asked me if I could easily reduce to an opera Beaumarchais's comedy called *Le Nozze di Figaro*." Between the two conversations, had Mozart himself worked out the complete plan, exactly or almost as we now have it? If so, Leopold Mozart was wrong in guessing, from Salzburg, that there would be "a lot of running about and discussions"; Mozart had done the job himself, and da Ponte had been presented with a libretto plan that gave the content and desired length of each number. All da Ponte had to do was to write it in nice Italian. Mozart, like his father, could remember the trouble he had had with Varesco during the writing of *Idomeneo*. He like his father could see that the material would be unusually difficult to adapt—too difficult, surely, to be left to the Italian gentleman. Note that, if this is what happened, Mozart would know not only what material each number would contain, and where it would come, but roughly what keys, rhythms, and instrumentation he would use, before da Ponte even knew what the subject was to be. In his preface and memoirs da Ponte takes all the credit for the *Figaro* libretto. It serves him right that commentators have blamed him for alleged defects in the plan of Acts Three and Four.

For all we know, more than one text of the play was used. Mozart probably read and enjoyed the play in Rautenstrauch's German version. If so, *Non so più* may owe something to a crude picture (see facing p. 64) of the boy Liebetraut alone in the park. But I am fairly sure that the libretto plan was not made from the Rautenstrauch version; and I am certain that the detailed libretto was not written from it. One could further narrow the field by eliminating any other translation or pirated French edition, or other very early version of *Le mariage*, which departs further than the libretto at any point from the French text as we now have it. Other French and German editions were published too late in the year 1785, or too far from Vienna (or both; e.g. at Kehl in December). Mozart and da Ponte may even have used (and marked?) a copy of the handsome Paris edition, published in April, which was the first to contain the Beaumarchais preface. But in two libraries in London alone I have seen four Paris 1785 editions; not all of which include the preface or the splendid 1785 illustrations. One gets an overwhelming impression of the excitement of that year in capital city after capital city, town after town. One must also remember the risks and penalties. Schikaneder was ruined—and I hope to show later that Mozart and he had not forgotten the fact in 1791, when they gave to

Soon, dawn a better light will kindle;
The golden sun will rise.
Dark superstition soon will dwindle,
And rulers will be wise . . .

an innocuous title and beginning. In 1784 in England the Lord Chamberlain (Lord Salisbury, the seventh Earl, later to become first Marquis) had the sense not to forbid Holcroft's play. But in 1792, when people were scared by the Parisian violence that Mozart did not live to witness, Holcroft was indicted for high treason. The charge was an absurd one —he was discharged without a trial, after making his accusers look foolish. But one suspects that his reputation as a Figaro man had something to do with the charge. So do not laugh when you read in da Ponte's memoirs that "I *courageously* [my italics] dared to take upon myself" the task of obtaining permission for the staging of the opera. He probably saw the risks more clearly than Mozart, for whom *Le Nozze di Figaro* was a supreme gesture of artistic courage and unworldly confidence. From the worldly point of view it was mistimed, misplaced, misunderstood, unremunerative. It had nine performances in 1786 and soon took second place to Martin y Soler's *Cosa Rara* (with libretto by da Ponte). What were nine performances, compared with what Beaumarchais—and even Holcroft—won for their more traditional antics? Yet it is Mozart's *Figaro* that "lives on the stage, and in every musical circle; youth is nourished on it, age delights in it with ever-increasing delight . . . it is the pulse-beat of our own life that we feel, the language of our own heart that we catch, the sound of the irresistible witchery of immortal beauty which enchains us." That was how Jahn put it in 1855 (translated, Pauline Townsend). We say the same in 1966. They will be saying it, somewhere in the world, in 2076 and 2186.

In the latter year, they will be giving quatercentenary performances and it may still be the most detailed story that a great composer will have dared to tell in music; the story of the day of Figaro's wedding, the topsy-turvy day of his marrying (marry*ing*, not marri*age*). Before we consider it in detail, let me remind you briefly of a previous day. Figaro is on the way to his barber's shop. It is early morning. He passes the house of a local doctor, Don Bartolo. Outside it, watching a barred window, is a very young nobleman, the Count. Count Almaviva is tired of easy successes with Madrid women who are tempted by his money and title. He wants to be loved for himself. Here he is in Seville, disguised as a poor student and trying to attract the attention of Don Bartolo's wife. He and Figaro recognise each other—Figaro had once been his valet in Madrid. Figaro tells him that the girl is the doctor's ward, not his wife; and that she is being kept in her room, shut away from young men, until the doctor himself can marry her. Within the usual twenty-four hours, Figaro enables the Count to enter the house three times—to meet the sixteen-year-old Rosina, to woo her under Bartolo's nose, and finally to be married to her by the notary who had been summoned to the house to marry her to Bartolo. Bartolo's servants, and his housekeeper Marcellina, have been put out of action—by Figaro. A needy abbé and singing-teacher, Don Basilio, has twice been bribed at Figaro's suggestion. The doctor's precautions were useless.

ACT ONE

Overture

1, Cinque, dieci	*6, Non so più*
1A, Cosa stai misurando	*6A, Ah, son perduto* (or *Taci, vien*
2, Se a caso Madama	*gente*)
2A, Or bene; ascolta e taci	*7, Cosa sento!*
3, Se vuol ballare	*7A, Basilio, in traccia tosto*
3A, Ed aspettaste il giorno	*8, Giovani liete*
4, La vendetta	*8A, Cos' è questa commedia*
4A, Tutto ancor non ho perso	*8B, Giovani liete*, repeated.
5, Via, resti servita	*8C, Evviva!*
5A, Va là, vecchia pedante	*9, Non più andrai*

The OVERTURE, WITH Acts One and Two, should be performed without an interval.

D major, the key of the overture, is the key in which the opera will end; the key of the *allegro assai* when the topsy-turvy day is over. In between, it is the key in which the Count (*17*) and Bartolo (*4*) swear ineffective vengeance. Mozart seems to have associated it with *Idomeneo*, the king of his opera seria in D.

Mozart wrote down the overture some weeks or months after the opera itself. The MS. score is dated April 29th, 1786. By then the opera was not only written but copied, learned and rehearsed, for a first performance on May 1st.

The *Figaro* overture seems to have less connection with its opera than the overtures of *Don Giovanni, Così fan tutte* and *Die Zauberflöte*. Read into it what you like; the tempo and general mood of the topsy-turvy day; a deliberate slant away towards the *commedia per musica* that Mozart was claiming to have written; homage by Mozart to the gaiety of Beaumarchais ("Un homme constamment gai; aimant avec une égale passion l'étude et le plaisir; enclin à la raillerie, mais sans amertume"); the intrigue of *17.30–33:* the youth, the impatience, the excitement, the impudence. I do not regard it as that kind of music. I have always enjoyed the kind of music that is written with meaningful words. But this is music uncluttered. I am going to listen—if they play it well enough.

Figaro measures, Susanna tries a hat. Figaro is persuaded (with a little difficulty, as if they had been married for two or three years) to admire the hat. Then the vocal lines go into parallel thirds (tenths). A wedding morning is no time for original thought. There they are, Figaro and Susanna, arm in arm. There is an intense physical affection between them.

The climax of the duet is marked by a change of verse rhythm, from the tum-ti of

Now at last I am contented (*1.30*)

to the ti-ti-tum rhythm of *1.67–73*:—

> Tis the morning of Figaro's wedding,
> And his bride has a virginal bonnet,
> With a flower bouquet to go on it;
> And she made it herself, clever she.

There is no natural stress on the first syllables of the anapaestic lines. Mozart has set both kinds of line to the same music, starting in the middle of the bar, with the important words on stronger beats. There is a natural crescendo through both kinds of line. Even so, the singers must float gently into the new verbal current. If they give it the *Cinque, dieci* treatment, they find themselves swimming unhappily against a current.

But what kind of a Figaro have we here? Is he the proud lively opportunist of the Beaumarchais plays? Or is he a slow-witted fumbling character, dominated by Susanna and unable to do anything right unless she does it for him? A man who laboriously measures and remeasures bedspace with a ruler? A man unaccountably slow to respond to Susanna's reasonable request? A man who will be even slower on the uptake, when Susanna begins to explain what the Count intends to do? Surely any ordinary man—let alone a man with the energy and abilities that Figaro has in the French plays—would measure bedspace at a glance, or with a few strides each way?

Think for a moment of Rossini's Figaro. A few la la la lerà's off-stage, a shattering C major noise in the orchestra, and there he is; full of himself, bursting with self-confidence. Figaro, Figaro, Figaro, Figaro; Figaro qua, Figaro là, Figaro giù, Figaro su; ah bravo Figaro, bravo bravissimo. Rossini wrote him thirty years later, in 1816. Mozart could not know that his Figaro was going to have to compete with a walking self-advertisement. But Mozart knew the French plays, and the Paisiello setting of *The Barber*. No dramatic purpose is served by having a fumbling character in the title role of this opera. What is more, Figaro is sympathetically presented in the rest of the opera.

It is therefore a relief to find from study of the French and the music that there is nothing wrong with Figaro himself in these opening numbers except a libretto that has not quite got into its stride. According to Beaumarchais, Figaro is measuring the floor, i.e. the room. It is a large room (see the 1785 illustration, p. 65). In French, it measures 19 × 26 *feet*. Feet, pieds, piedi! The metric system has not yet been introduced. As no other unit of measurement is indicated by da Ponte, presumably his Figaro is also measuring in feet. As a fellow-translator I can see only too easily why da Ponte did not specify the unit in which Figaro is measuring. It does not fit the rhyme. Da Ponte, I suspect, wanted "trenta", thirty, at the end of the line, to rhyme with "contenta". So he has to have significantly more than thirty by the end of the next line—forty-*three* to fit the next rhyme. Da Ponte's Figaro is measuring one side of an ever larger room.

In Mahler's pre-1914 Vienna production, we are told, panels of once-beautiful damask hung in tattered strips from the walls, and unwanted pieces of furniture had been dumped there. It is not difficult to follow the reasoning. Much of the story is about differences between master and servant before the French Revolution. Therefore it has seemed appropriate that Figaro and Susanna should be shown living in squalor—the sort of squalor that might be a contributory cause of proletarian revolution in the early twentieth century.

Yet Beaumarchais, a careful dramatic craftsman, says that the room is half-*un*furnished; and so does the score (mezzo-*s*mobiliata, an interesting correction of the original printed libretto). It has to be a grand room in order to make sense of Figaro's behaviour. Why should Figaro think it generous (1A7) of the Count to let him have the room if it is a junk room? It was (2A18) generosity with an ulterior motive. But it seemed generous.

A half-unfurnished room is a room that is being vacated, a room that has been in use for another purpose, a room whose purpose is being changed. Audiences in Paris and Vienna knew that valets did not have grand bedrooms. It would seem all the more amusing that so fine a room should be vacated for Figaro. It is the ante-room on the first floor, leading to the even grander apartments of the Countess and Count. Figaro is a man who believes (17A16) that he has noble parents. Like Beaumarchais he is an able man, climbing to wealth and position (note that the opera was written during the one brief phase of Mozart's life when he too could hope for affluence). Figaro claims for Susanna's benefit that the room is "convenient" (*1A14*), and that he is measuring the room to see (*1A3*) if the bed will look well (of course it will). In fact, his bearing should tell us that he is bursting with delight and pride at being the prospective occupant of so stately an apartment. He is going up in the world. It is the grandeur of the room that preoccupies him; and that later makes him reluctant to take a hint abut the Count's intentions. His instinctive order of priorities is revealing!

Figaro entered from the door that leads to the Count's apartments. He sized up the room with quick gestures. He had nine bars in which to measure out the short side of the room. Then the music changed. He stood there, looking contented. At the same time, in bustled Susanna from another door. She was holding the virginal bonnet, complete with flower bouquet. She went to a mirror. It was not quite as she would like it. Busily she began to make a minor alteration. By *1.20* the earlier music had returned, and Figaro was measuring the longer side of the room "avec une toise."

The toise is not a ruler. The ordinary dictionaries tell us that it is 1 metre 949 millimetres, or a graduated rod used for measuring conscripts. But conscription came in with égalité during the French revolution, and millimetres seem too Napoleonic. Let us try one of the earlier, less precise, meanings of the word:

> Et d'une corde d'une toise
> Saura mon col que mon cul poise.

From a fathom of rope, says Villon, my neck shall hang; feeling my backside drag and swing. Less gruesome but equally apt are the words of Petit Jean in Racine's *Plaideurs 3.3*:

> Ils me font dire aussi des mots long d'une toise;
> De grands mots qui tiendroient d'ici jusqu'à Pontoise.

The longer words stretch from here to Pontoise. The shorter ones are a mere armstretch wide; like the fish that got away, as described in the evening over Beaujolais or best bitter.

The word "toise" comes from late Latin "tesa", a corruption of "tensa" which means a stretching. Likewise a fathom, once defined as the length of a sailor's arms round the object of his affections, is properly the stretch of a man's arms in a straight line to their full length; a convenient nautical method of paying out rope, a good rough six-foot measure. Racine was offering a better and funnier version of Horace's sesquipedalia verba; Horace's words are merely as long as a hexameter.

What has all this got to do with the performance of Mozart's *Figaro*? That Figaro is measuring the room for status-thrill with armstretches, or by expansive glance and gesture; not with anything so laborious as a rod, let alone a ruler. He is quick, elated, confident. "Ten foot, twenty, thirty! Splendid! Thirty-six foot (or less or more, to suit the size of stage) by forty-three" (or more or less, so long as it ends in a three to rhyme with "me").

Numerous other points could be made about this little dialogue in G. But let them pass. It ends without a rallentando or pause (other than the crotchet and quaver rests that are marked) and at once Susanna is asking why, on his wedding morning, Figaro's attention was being given to the size of the ante-room. Figaro is disconcerted at the tone of her question; there is an unexpected B♭ at *1A5*. He was seeing whether the bed, one of several presents from the Count, would look good in this room. Susanna, who is entitled to feel that she was being taken too much for granted while he was measuring, abruptly refuses it. Figaro, a male, asks why. She refuses to tell him. Soon she is flaring up, with an unexpected C♯ and a crotchet rest. "Are you my servant, or not?" Figaro is astonished and embarrassed at this feminine tantrum. Why refuse the most convenient room in the palace? "Why, because I am Susanna"—la Susanna, a prima donna—"and you are an idiot." "Thank you" says Figaro "I'm truly flattered" (with a B♭ again). He is not yet much upset, for (as Marcellina says in *MF1.4*) he is jamais fâché, toujours en belle humeur, donnant le présent à la joie, et s'inquiétant de l'avenir tout aussi peu que du passé.

"Tu prends de l'humeur contre la chambre du château la plus commode, et qui tient le milieu des deux appartements. La nuit, si Madame est incommodée, elle sonnera de son côté; zeste! en deux pas tu es chez elle. Monseigneur veut-il quelque chose? Il n'a qu'à tinter du sien; crac! en trois sauts me voila rendu." "Fort bien!" says Susanna "mais quand il aura tinté le matin pour te donner quelque bonne et longue commission, zeste! en deux pas il est à ma porte, et crac! en trois sauts . . ." "Qu'entendez-vous par ces paroles?" asks Figaro. "Il faudrait m'écouter tranquillement" says Susanna.

A convenient room? Convenient for what and whom? To judge by what happens in the rest of this Act, there is no privacy in this room—a general thoroughfare—for purposes marital or extramarital. But Figaro was thinking of status, and we are in an era in which to go to bed (or get up) in public was a mark of noble or royal status. In any case Figaro was committed. Not only had most of the previous furniture been removed but good old-fashioned bells had been installed. Figaro points to the bells. Susanna had not previously noticed them and is taken aback. He explains, in B♭ major, why the room is so convenient. "My lady may well pull . . . by night at the bellpull; tingaling, you are only two paces away."

In the dominant, Figaro warms to his special pleading. "I too can the faster . . . attend on the master; bom bom, in three strides I am there to obey." Even Stendhal, who felt that Mozart had disfigured the play— "In Mozart, the true expression of the French piece is nowhere to be found"—admitted that there is a feeling of the play about this duet. The music tells us that Figaro is still in high spirits. The "sensibility of the musician" has not yet "led him to convert into serious passions the transient inclinations which in the piece of Beaumarchais amuse the agreeable inhabitants of the château of Aguas Frescas." The duet sparkles; at this stage Mozart wanted it to sparkle. Figaro and Susanna are mercifully unaware of the darkness and despair that each of them, and their noble master and mistress, will feel before the topsy-turvy day is over.

With seeming innocence the oboes prepare Susanna's comment; in G minor. "Suppose that one morning without any warning he kindly —without any warning—doth ring tingaling so that you into Seville can rush, tingaling BOM BOM . . ." So far we have had the high flute and oboe juxtaposed with unaccompanied high voice, and the low horn and bassoon with low voice. But Susanna's soprano voice is now followed by horns and bassoons. The Aristophanic unexpectedness of the new and jarring juxtaposition makes us laugh. It is not just a joke, but a warning of trouble to come. These are the horns of cuckoldry. From now on they will blow often. "Bom bom, he is knocking, the doorway a-blocking" Susanna almost shouts. "Three strides, and the devil . . ." The word "devil" coincides with a sforzando horn entry.

Figaro looks nervously towards the Count's room, and hushes her furiously. I will explain, she says quietly, a little later on: "If you wish to hear it, dispel your suspicions, they wrong me, I vow." "I do wish to hear it," says Figaro, low in the voice; thereby spoiling a good duet according to Stendhal, because "he is too much in earnest." Figaro does not promise to trust Susanna, but she wisely trusts him, all the same. Much heartache would have been saved if she had remembered to keep up the same tactic after writing the letter to the Count in Act Three.

During the next recitative Figaro appears to be slower than ever in the uptake. Mozart and da Ponte, after two duets, are still faced with the dramatist's problem of explaining the situation. But Figaro knows what Susanna is getting at. His interjections are mechanical, off-hand.

He is looking round the magnificent bedroom, cursing himself for a fool—and getting angry.

We are told the story. Count Almaviva has been unfaithful to his Rosina, time and again, at a discreet distance from the château. Now he has his eye on Susanna. The dowry he has said that he will give Susanna is not a disinterested present; nor has the Count any compunction about deceiving a man who has served him well. He had promised the Countess, when they married, that he would abolish his droit du Seigneur—a right which in drama has only one, inexhaustibly comic, meaning. He now wants to buy it back, on the occasion of the first wedding since he announced its abolition. His Pandarus is—who else, in such a plot, but the resident abbé and musician, Don Basilio? Basilio is now singing teacher to Susanna as well as Rosina. Daily during the singing lesson (one must in fairness admit that his soprano pupils do him credit) he tries to persuade Susanna of the worldly wisdom, and probable pleasure, of accepting the Count as a lover.

The high-pitched bell rings. Susanna goes to the Countess, with a parting injunction to Figaro to use a bit of that brain of his—implying, to Figaro, that this is a commodity which he possesses and she does not. His anger begins to rumble formidably (2A41) in the simple-seeming notes of the 'cello and basses. He has been fooled; fooled by a man whose natural abilities are less than his own, fooled by a nobleman. It is now clear why the Count, who has been appointed Ambassador to London—a post for which he possesses no qualification by experience or natural ability—is proposing to take the concierge of his château as courier: "Me crottant, m'échinant pour la gloire de votre famille; vous, daignant concourir à l'accroissement de la mienne." Susanna . . . At the thought of her the 'cellos are no longer rough but have a pleading legato akin to some of the recitative that precedes Figaro's Act Four aria. "Ambassadress in secret? No, you shan't! No, you shan't!"

"Non, Monsieur le Comte, vous ne l'aurez pas . . . vous ne l'aurez pas. . . . Parce que vous êtes un grand seigneur, vous vous croyez un grand génie! . . . Noblesse, fortune, un rang, des places, tout cela rend si fier! Qu'avez-vous fait pour tant de biens? Vous vous êtes donné la peine de naître, et rien de plus; du reste, homme assez ordinaire." (MF5.3).

These are the famous subversive words of Le Mariage, that Napoleon later described as the revolution in action. Da Ponte assured the Emperor that he had omitted or cut anything that might offend good taste or public decency. But the essential scene (MF5.3) was not omitted, or significantly cut. Mozart and da Ponte retained part of it in Act Four, and have prefaced an aria in Act One with the first sentence of the political section of the monologue. This is not the action of men who are glad to take the politics and crudities out of Beaumarchais. They are sailing as close to the wind as they dare; obeying the advice given by Beaumarchais in *MF1.2*—"dissimulons avec eux." "Et puis dansez, Monseigneur" (*MF2.2*). The meaning of *Se vuol ballare* runs on from "Non, Monsieur le Comte, vous ne l'aurez pas, vous ne l'aurez pas."

Unless we realise this, *Se vuol ballare* is apt to be a disappointing aria. It often gets less applause than Bartolo's aria (*4*). Ulibishev felt that "Figaro est philosophe et bel-esprit français d'avant la révolution; deux malheurs auxquels tout le talent du musicien ne pouvait remédier. . . . Mozart le fait danser, il lui donne des mélodies de 3/4 quasi rossiniennes, mais sans caractère et sans charme." Yet it is only if this song is sung at its tame face value that it can lack character and charm—and good singers make much of it in any case. Mozart had himself been the musician who sat at the lower table below the Archbishop's valets; the man who referred to the Archbishop ("a very fine-looking man, particularly gallant and attentive to the ladies") as an archbooby; the man who swore to fool the Archbishop to the top of his bent; the man who was literally booted out of the Archbishop's service by young Count Arco. The Mozart letters in 1781 are unedifying but relevant.

Figaro vows in F major to outwit little mister nobleman. The word *contino*, little nobleman, retains the impertinent irony with which Susanna had used it in *2.46–7*. With the prefix *signor* (sir, mister, citoyen, comrade) it acquires an aggressive, indeed subversive, tone. "You, my dear master, wish to go dancing! You, mister noble, were born to go dancing! I'll have you prancing to my choice of tune. With my guitar I shall pick out your step, yes. New-fangled step, yes. I'll call the tune."

Figaro was known to opera-goers in Vienna as a guitarist, in Paisiello's *Barbiere*. The Count had to borrow his guitar, in order to sing "Saper bramate, bella, il mio nome." In the play the words go as follows (*BS1.6*)

> *Figaro:* Et prenez ma guitare.
> *Le Comte:* Que veux-tu que j'en fasse? j'en joue si mal!
> *Figaro:* Est-ce qu'un homme comme vous ignore quelque chose? Avec le dos de la main; from, from, from.

Mozart begins the aria as a minuet—the appropriate dance for a *signor contino*. But the minuet has a surprise ending. "With my guitar

I shall pick out your . . ." It should have been a step down from G to a nice tame crotchet on F. Instead what have we? A step up? An interjected Yes? Good God, he is doing it again, with a high F for the second "Yes." Rude. Very rude. Abert says there is malice in the two interjections. Levarie calls it an unruly extension of minuet form. Modern audiences will notice the joke if the singer jolts them by emphasis on the two crotchets. *Step, yes.* New-fangled *step, yes.* "I'll call the tune" says Mozart/Figaro.

He calls it with a variation that goes faster and more freely. So far the horns have been accompanying (with pizzicato strings which represent the guitar and do not oblige the singer to sing staccato) in the same simple minuet movement as the voice. Now the horn music begins to move in quavers, and the violins are trilling. "I caper faster, I am your teacher." (In the *Barber*, the Count was happy to describe himself as Lindor, dit l'écolier.) "Arrogant creature, I call the tune." An imagined Count is being danced along, quicker than he expected. "You wish to caper into my room, sir? I shall be there, sir! I'll make you skip, yes." Again there is the unorthodox ending, but this time the musical interval is a skip. "Let me see thee caper" cried Sir Toby Belch to Sir Andrew Aguecheek. "Ha, higher; ha, ha! excellent."

"I call the tune." Minuet rhythm disappears. There is a rushing and syncopation in the strings, with long wind chords and a grim, almost wordlessly gleeful soliloquy. "Indeed . . . I do . . . Oh yes . . . indeed . . . I do . . . I'm also very, very, very, very, very patient." The horns are still blaring. Figaro shakes his head as he thinks of the Count's advantages of position and wealth. "Secret and patient dissimulation shall win this day." Dissimulons avec eux; as underdogs have done before and since. Mozart was writing this aria for Benucci, a first-rate actor/singer with the reputation of being able not to exaggerate (Jahn, referring to the Berl. Mus. Zeit. 1793, p. 138).

Now comes a *presto*—it is like another Folle Journée in which the Queen cried "Faster, faster." Abert says that the *presto* section is Italian in rhythm, melody, and accompaniment. Levarie gives evidence to show that the rhythm of the section is akin to fashionable English dance tunes of the period. We have moved a long way from the minuet that was symbolising the *ancien régime*. "Parrying, thrusting, artfully twisting; not at all trusting, never desisting; any manoeuvre that you may essay, I'll turn away, I'll turn your way, I shall repay."

Figaro returns with pensive glee to the problem that confronts him. Then he bustles off the stage to the orchestral accompaniment of *3.96–103*. These are important bars in Figaro's mind; we hear him singing them to *La* outside the Countess' room in Act Two. Levarie describes the postlude as "irregular in technical, and insubordinately rebellious in psychological, terms." It makes a good rousing exit, if played with the venom that this suggests.

Bartolo, a doctor of medicine, lives seven or eight miles away, in Seville. He and Marcellina are "old"—to the young. He lost Rosina to the Count three years ago; but retained, as the price for his signature on the wedding-contract, her fortune. He has not come to Aguas Frescas of his own accord; he was summoned by Marcellina. As he drove along the country road, he wondered who needed his services. Has the Count had an accident? La Rosine, sa trompeuse comtesse, est-elle incommodée, Dieu merci? He is surprised to find that Marcellina wants him to help her prove that an IOU given by Figaro to Marcellina (in the form of a promise to marry her, if he does not repay 2,000 crowns that she has lent him) is valid in law.

The libretto omits about three pages of the play and has left it unclear, at first sight, whether Bartolo is a formidable or feeble adversary. Either interpretation fits the Bolognese *Commedia dell'arte* doctor from whom Bartolo derives. Either way he is related to the Bartolo of the *Barber*. On the stage, he is usually applauded for singing his aria in a bluff, forthright way. But Abert and Levarie have pointed out that the music is less 'D-majorish' than it looks; and the story points strongly to a feeble Bartolo.

Of his timidity, there was never much doubt. "J'aime mieux craindre sans sujet que de m'exposer sans précaution. Tout est plein de gens entreprenants, audacieux" (*BS2.4*). He was the kind of man who never feels secure except behind his own locked doors. "Rentrez, rentrez," he says to Rosina when she accompanies him to the door, "je ne suis pas timide." Therefore he *is* timid; just as he has a yawning servant called L'Éveillé, an aged servant called La Jeunesse, and is made to say things like "Nous ne sommes pas ici en France, où l'on donne toujours raison aux femmes" (*BS2.15*).

As he enters, he is raising an objection. "You wait till now, the very day that is appointed for the wedding, before bringing this to my attention?" Marcellina, who is "toujours amère et provocante" (*MF1.4*), is made by da Ponte to reply acidly that *she* does not lose her courage yet. She advances an obscure and futile plan for inducing Susanna to resist the Count. Despite her sharp tongue she is a weak woman and cannot imagine that Susanna will resist the Count's charms and money without being shamed into doing so. However, the conclusion of her involved reasoning is that Figaro will have to marry her. This cheers Bartolo up.

> *Marceline:* Ne le devez-vous pas? Où est le souvenir de vos engagements? Qu'est devenu celui de notre petit Emmanuel, ce fruit d'un amour oublié qui devait nous conduire à des noces?
>
> *Bartholo, ôtant son chapeau:* Est-ce pour écouter ces sornettes que vous m'avez fait venir de Séville? et cet acces d'hymen qui vous reprend si vif ...
>
> *Marceline:* Eh bien, n'en parlons plus. Mais, si rien n'a pu vous porter à la justice de m'épouser, aidez-moi donc du moins à en epouser un autre.
>
> *Bartholo:* Ah! volontiers; parlons.

The egoist will arrange it all for her. "Tell *me*" (there is a whole crotchet in *3A17* on the important word) "all about it." In an aside he relishes the thought of seeing his old mistress married off to the rascal who deprived him of the young and beautiful Rosina.

"Oh for vengeance!" It is a fine empty D from Bartolo, with Ds from trumpets, drums and every instrument in the orchestra pit except the clarinets. "Oh for some vengeance!" *La vendetta ... è un piacer serbato ai saggi.* Bartolo is fat, and could easily get out of breath. But he does not need a bar and a half to recover his breath, in the middle of so short a sentence. There is no such pause when we reach the recapitulation, at *4.73.* Bartolo is already regretting his bombastic promise to help; or is wondering whether Marcellina overheard his tactless aside; or both. He hesitates. "Er ..." The orchestra rush on.

The repetitions in this aria have a special, relentlessly inane flavour. "Il ne faut pas me dire deux fois les choses: il ne faut pas me les dire deux fois" is his exit line in BS 3.3.

> Oh for vengeance!
> Oh for some vengeance!
> Brains achieve that satisfaction,
> Brains achieve that satisfaction.
> To ignore gross malefaction,
> To ignore gross malefaction,
> Would be foolish and weak of me,
> Would be foolish and weak of me,
> And weak of me.

The music is suited to a foolish and weak man. If one ignores the characterisation, it is (despite the charming chuckle in the second violins at *4.23* and elsewhere) the dullest thing in the opera—until we reach Marcellina's aria in Act Four.

4.29 has a fermata, marked over a minim rest for evident hesitation. Bartolo plucks up courage again, with an E. "I'll outwit him." He has a four-beat rest, to recover. "Gently twit him . . . I'll be brilliant . . . and imperious, . . ." Back comes the orchestral chuckle, giving warmth and colour to the music. "Yes, I could be." The bassoons join in. In a moment he is repeating his words in patter, with disproportionate emphasis on the words *si potrebbe*, yes I could be, if I can be, underlined by a *crescendo*. Is this man self-confident? He says "'tis very serious, very serious, very serious" with the whole orchestra. He is uttering the platitude of the "éternel Docteur! toujours si grave et compassé, qu'on pourrait mourir en attendant vos secours" (*MF 1.4*). As he finishes the third "very serious", the violin line comes tumbling down in anti-climax, as it does at the end of the great quarrel in the finale of Act Two. He hesitates, then with soft light orchestration (ignored by those who sing Bartolo bluffly) continues: "But you can rely on me, but you can rely on me." He is in utter gulping panic; looking nervously at Marcellina, bitterly regretting his promise to help.

But he does not want to marry her himself. Desperately therefore he imagines learning all about the law of contract (which was not in his black bag) before the hearing of Marcellina's case, at which he has undertaken to act as her advocate. "I will be master of every reference, even the judge will be nodding in deference. Oh what ability, verbal agility! What a surprise the hearing will be." Again the orchestra chuckle (*4.66*). For indeed there will be "a big surprise, all due to me." He will discover his son.

In *4.72* Mozart again puts a fermata over a minim rest. Bartolo tries to convince himself. "All men in Seville know honest Bartolo." Everyone knows me! It is the blustering, defensive, self-justification of a foolish man. "That rascal Figaro . . ." (the words are heartfelt and perfectly accentuated, unlike *Co*nosce in the preceding phrase, and *La* vendetta at the beginning) . . . "shall bow the knee." There is yet another significant hesitation in the sentence. Bartolo would quite like to be revenged on Figaro. But he does not feel strongly about it, and does not at all fancy trying to out-argue that clever young man. He repeats the sentence, hesitantly. He repeats it twice, more confidently, with a crescendo to forte. Then it becomes a desperate "shall bow the knee, shall bow the knee, shall bow the knee" while the second violins and violas rush up and down. At the end, the orchestra peter out like a bagpipe losing air. Bartolo scuttles away to prepare his speech; leaving the stage to the doughtier female. Her remark that

"All is not yet lost" is nicely ambiguous. Hope remains—with a flattening, from C♯ to C♮, that one would not expect to find between a D major aria and an A major duet. She has not taken Bartolo at his face value. Should we?

Susanna returns, carrying a dress and nightcap that belong to the Countess. Marcellina resolves to "essay her, while feigning not to see her." She will regret the jealous instinct that makes her do so. Aloud she says "So that's the pearl of womanhood he (i.e. Figaro) wants as a wife." " 'Tis me she prates of" thinks Susanna warily. Unwarily, Marcellina proceeds. "I suppose the poor bridegroom can't afford to do better. L'argent fait tout."

Susanna is a superior palace (or château) servant in the eighteenth century. Just as Figaro is given lines that tell of considerable self-education, Susanna probably understands French. In *Così fan tutte* Despina even tries to speak some Latin—the two mistresses cannot, the maid can. But it is just as effective if Susanna does not understand French. She can react with a gesture of contemptuous, uncomprehending, indifference. An insult has missed its target, while helping to characterise Marcellina. L'argent fait tout, money is everything. Marcellina assumes that others think so. She thereby reveals something of her own outlook on life.

Tension is mounting; so is the key (now A major). Marcellina insinuates that Figaro is marrying Susanna for her dowry, and that Susanna is earning the dowry for services rendered to the Count. "She looks so unassuming, so demure and unworldly; and therefore—has such a dowry." Marcellina goes into a venomous E major (the dominant of the following duet) with the cheap sneer that Susanna is a *dear* bride. Susanna sensibly decides to go. Marcellina bars the way.

Without a second's hesitation the orchestra begin. The first two bars are still in the dominant—another clear indication of musical continuity with the recitative. At the end of 5.2 comes a first-violin tune that seems to portray the gestures and head-tossings of the women. With the second-violin triplets, it creates a feeling of excitement and tension. We are to witness an accelerating battle of icy courtesies, insincere curtseys, purring scratches, gentle venom, wounding compliments; a traditional feminine ritual, brought to formal perfection because the younger woman has a gift of shrewd, quick-witted mimicry. Couplet for couplet, line for line, half-line for half-line, tit for tat, eye for eye, tooth for tooth; effortlessly and in rhyme Susanna outdoes Marcellina.

Marcellina curtseys, and offers an opening couplet:

> Make way for a *lady*,
> A shining example.

Her action belies her words; she is barring Susanna's way. Susanna
curtseys and replies:

> Make way for a lady
> Whose *kindness* is ample.

Da Ponte says piquant madam, sharp-tongued lady; the French says
"il y a toujours quelquechose d'amer dans vos propos"; an English-
speaking Susanna can imply the same, in the insincere convention
of the duet as a whole.

"But your claim is prior" says Marcellina, curtseying. She is determined that Susanna shall neither go through the door nor marry
Figaro. "But you are my better" says Susanna, curtseying. She genuinely wants Marcellina to go out of the door. They repeat this little
interchange. The more curtseys the better, if the singers can manage
them. With or without curtseys, Susanna has already parried three
times. She is amused rather than angry.

"But *this* would be fitter" says Marcellina, politely waving the other
woman towards the door with one hand, while still barring her way.
"But *this* would be fitter" says Susanna primly, echoing Marcellina's
words with the converse gesture; sincerely meant and beautifully
mimicked. "*This* would be fitter" they both say, each waving the other
through the door. "I know what is done" they both say. For once
Susanna takes the initiative, as the episode is repeated.

Here are the violins again, first and second, tossing and tripleting.
Marcellina curtseys. "For brides, 'tis a pleasure" to make way; she
does not do so. Susanna curtseys, a little more angrily (the strings have
a forte on the fourth beat, and the wind have a fp on the first beat of
the next bar). "For ladies of honour" she says. It is more a counter-
attack than a parry. "The Count's little treasure" says Marcellina.
"A nation's madonna" says Susanna. It is a counter-attack. In context
this polite remark is a devastating insinuation; that Marcellina has been
mistress to many men, and that her lovers were of less noble birth than
the Count. The violins titter, with staccato triplets.

Marcellina is getting more than she bargained for. She becomes
flustered and inarticulate. But she persists. "So worthy of . . ." Susanna

finishes her line for her. "Smartly dressed!" The point is taken, for Marcellina is dowdy. Desperately Marcellina continues with "So high-born!" It is an ineffective insult, for Susanna is unashamed of her humble birth. She merely retorts "So young!" It is the crowning blow, the unanswerable insult; all in self-defence.

Marcellina is provoked to the edge of physical violence. "Great Bacchus, I can't resist . . ." she says. It is clear from the French that her nails are reaching for Susanna's face and hair. There is a *tutti* in the orchestra to convey Marcellina's intensified anger (and to serve as a kind of guffaw of orchestral laughter at the same time). She restrains herself, for this is civilised comedy. "Each time, each time I'm out-done." The words come through a light accompaniment with clarity. Susanna is given a soft wind accompaniment for the final couplet of triumph. "Decrepit old Latinist, you figure of fun."

Mozart has crammed this wit and repartee, this Attic stichomyth, into thirty-seven short bars. He demands our complete attention, but offers us a correspondingly complete delight—musical, verbal, visual.

During the repeat, Marcellina is less confident—she has a G♮. The first violins chuckle, as Susanna sings her first couplet back without delay. A verse is omitted, and Marcellina proceeds with "For brides, 'tis a pleasure." Susanna's retorts become more instant and devastating. Marcellina lengthens and emphasises: "The Count's little treasure." Before she has finished she is again being called a nation's madonna. Again the violins join in staccato titters. On it goes to the predestined Q.E.D., "So young." Once more Marcellina is about to become violent. Susanna merely rubs it in that her opponent is "so young, so young, so young!" Marcellina is crushed. She cannot rouse the orchestra to their tutti triplets. She succumbs. Susanna exults with "Decrepit old Latinist, you figure of fun." Her vocal line rocks with laughter, in legato triplets. Then the women repeat their final couplets for ten bars. Marcellina is meekly accompanying. As the singing ends she revives. With some final head-tossing, mercilessly mimicked by Susanna, she sweeps out of the door as if nothing had been further from her mind than to bait Susanna. The orchestra have a final guffaw, in triplets.

In the play Bartolo has no aria and therefore no chance to get away before the two women have their set-to. He is on stage, an uneasy and shocked listener who tries in vain to prevent it happening. After Marcellina's first provocative remark he laughs (such a forced and uneasy laugh!) and says "Le bon argument de femme en colère! Nous parlions, belle Suzon, du bonheur qu'il aura de vous posséder." He tries in vain to stop the verbal fight

> *Bartholo, attirant Marceline:* Adieu, jolie fiancée de notre Figaro.

but is allowed to stop it from developing into a physical fight:

> *Marceline, une révérence:* Surtout bien respectable.
> *Suzanne, une révérence:* C'est aux duègnes de l'être.
> *Marceline, outrée:* Aux duègnes! aux duègnes!
> *Bartholo, l'arrêtant:* Marceline!
> *Marceline:* Allons, Docteur, car je n'y tiendrais pas. Bonjour, madame.
>   (*Une révérence*)

Very amusing. But da Ponte's concise verse version is even more amusing. Bartolo has run away, and a feminine ritual can be observed without the presence of a male who does not understand the convention.

Susanna is left in triumphant possession of the stage. "Farewell, old madam pedant. You old arrogant school ma'am!" She hurls the dress on the chair. "With a smatter of book lore, that imposed on my lady in her youth . . ."

At that moment, in comes Cherubino—or, as we should properly call him, Cherub. The name Cherubino is not just derived from Cherub, it means Cherub; and is an accurate translation of the French word Chérubin. Rautenstrauch called him Liebetraut. Mozart, as we shall see, became increasingly fond of using names that have overtones of meaning. But this is a name identical with its meaning—more a nickname than a name.

It was Beaumarchais who thus called him Cherub, in French (though the boy is referred to in *MF 1.9* as "Cherub of love" *in Italian*). Larousse tells us that Chérubin is a term of endearment to a child or an adolescent, and that to be beautiful as a cherub is to have a charming figure with a wholly childlike grace. The Italian word Cherubino has similar associations. Cherubs are the second order of angels, supposed to excel in knowledge.

This precocious child is not a fat little baby at the bottom of a painting. But he seems better winged. He is vif, espiègle et brûlant. He is more intensely and infectiously alive than any other character in the opera; which is saying a lot. He is a personification of the tempo of the overture. He is running when he makes his first entry, he runs behind the chair, he runs round the chair, he runs into the dressing-room, he runs to the window, he takes a running jump out of the window, he runs away from the flower bed like an Olympic sprinter; he was probably running when he fell (*12A14*) and grazed his elbow. His bright eyes notice everything, from a ribbon to a fountain; the beauty of the Countess, and the habits of the Count. He gets in everyone's way, but is "aimé de tout le monde au château." He is aged thirteen. His voice is "douce et grêle." Beaumarchais said that he must be played by a woman "pour en bien sentir les finesses." The part is full of finesse, with comic and other nuances.

He is Don Chérubin, a boy of good family; godson to the Countess and first page to the Count. The Countess says that his family is "allié de mes parents" (*MF 1.10*). His parents are alive, but are shadowy figures, mentioned in passing in *MF1.9* when the Count decides to give him money and a horse, and send him back to them. How appalled his parents would have been to have their boy sent back from Aguas Frescas in disgrace; or to know of any of the events of the topsy-turvy day—including the suggestion that, in order to keep his position at the palace, he should marry the twelve-year-old daughter of a gardener.

The first Cherubino, Madame Bussani, was admired by the public for her beautiful figure and unreserved acting. Da Ponte refers to her *smorfie* and *pagliaccate*. She was later the first Despina.

The boy hurtles in, leaving the door open. "Netta dear, oh I say." This boy, who will be "timide à l'excès devant la comtesse," is revealed as "ailleurs un charmant polisson" (MF, Characters) and at the same time artlessly boyish.

Youth is relative. Susanna, who was triumphant youth a moment ago, is now the amused adult and wary maidservant. She puts him in his place with a flippant, slightly chilly remark. "You say. What do you say, sir?" Unabashed and with a grin, Cherubino calls her his heart's joy. "Oh my heart's joy, something dreadful." "Your heart's joy! What has happened?" "I am dismissed" says Cherubino, "for the Count discovered me yesterday evening with Barbarina, à qui je faisais répéter son petit role d'innocente pour la fête de ce soir. 'Sortez, m'a-t-il dit, petit . . .' Je n'ose pas prononcer devant une femme le gros mot qu'il a dit. 'Sortez, et demain vous ne coucherez pas au château.'" Later, we learn the Count's version of this incident. Meanwhile the boy continues with his story. "If the dear kind countess, if my beautiful godmother does not secure my pardon, why then . . .

I never shall see you any more, my own Susanna." "You will never see *me*? Truly? You mean that your heart is now no longer . . . no longer sighing in secret for the Countess?" "Ah but she is so very awe-inspiring." This amuses Susanna, who in the play says "C'est à dire que je ne le suis pas, et qu'on peut oser avec moi" to which Cherubino replies "Tu sais trop bien, méchante, que je n'ose pas oser." In the opera Cherubino merely hurries on to say "Oh lucky you. You're able to see her when you wish to. Every morning you dress her, you undress her each evening, and you fasten on her brooches and laces. Were I in your place. . . . What is that? Here a second." He sees a ribbon in Susanna's hand.

Susanna is enjoying the boy's self-revelation. She mocks him. "Surely 'tis . . . oh what a lucky little ribbon on the nightcap of a beautiful godmother." Cherubino snatches it. "Ah, give it me, I beg you, give it me, sister dear." "Quick, give it back, sir." "Oh gorgeous, oh beautiful fortunate lovely ribbon. I'll give it back when life shall quit this body." "Impertinence unheard of!" "Don't get excited" says the excited boy. He takes a piece of MS. music from his pocket. "Exchange is fair and therefore I am giving you the song that I have written." "Whatever use is that pray?" "Why, to be sung for the Countess. Also for you yourself. Also for Barbarina, for Marcellina. All of you, all the women in the household."

"Poor Cherubino, clean out of your senses." The practical Susanna cannot understand the boy. Il devient fou, she says in the play. We shall hear the song in Act Two. Meanwhile he pours out his soul in an E♭ major far removed from the A major of the previous duet. He is *exalté*, in ecstasy, trailing clouds of glory. "Je ne sais plus ce que je suis; mais depuis quelque temps je sens ma poitrine agitée; mon coeur palpite au seul aspect d'une femme; les mots *amour* et *volupté* le font tressaillir et le troublent."

Here perhaps is Beaumarchais, who was taken from school at thirteen and wrote a certain letter to his sisters. Many years later, when he found the letter again among the papers of one of them, after her death, he remarked that he had had a love affair when he wrote the letter. Here possibly is a bright-eyed Jewish boy, Emanuele Conegliano, soon to be baptised by the Bishop of Ceneda and renamed Lorenzo da Ponte after the bishop. Here more certainly, in the exaltation of *Non so più*, is the young Mozart. Here on the stage is a clever self-admiring young dandy (damerino, *7.102*; Narcisetto, *9.7*), pouring out a remarkable piece of self-analysis. "Un désir inquiet et vague est le fond de son caractère" says Beaumarchais; the muted violins say so too. "Unaware what I am, what I do now—'tis a fever, a shiver anew now—for all women I blush, I am burning, for all women I throb yet again." The key words "for all women" soar and soar again.

> Words, mere words in a book that I utter—
> Love or Joy—oh a heart is a-flutter,
> And I am driven to speak of love's yearning
> By desire, by desire that I cannot explain.

Words, words, words. Here is a book-fed boy, delightedly exploring life, words, and himself. He is thinking himself into a love that he has not yet found. He will find it soon; perhaps today.

The first verse is repeated; we can hardly have too much of it. Then Cherubino pauses in wonder: le besoin de dire à quelqu'un Je vous aime est devenu pour moi si pressant que je le dis tout seul, en courant dans le parc, à ta maitresse, à toi, aux arbres, aux nuages, au vent qui les emporte avec mes paroles perdues. We can imagine him roaming by day in the great park, of which a small part will be seen by us in Act Four. He is driven to speak of the unknown thing, love:

> Speak of it coming, going;
> Speak it asleep, unknowing;
> To lake, to shade, to mountain,
> To flower, to lawn, to fountain,
> To echo; yes to breezes.
> Vain word, that air so teases—
> Bears it away, is gone.

Is gone . . . Cherubino is no longer aware of Susanna. He is alone. "If nought shall stay to hear you, speak of it all alone." Suddenly he returns to earth. Through the open door he has seen the Count coming. He runs behind the chair in panic, saying (without a second's pause after the final chord of Non so più, in theory) "Oh ruination." "Why the alarm?" asks Susanna, surprised. Then she sees the Count. His Lordship? What shall she do? Enter the Count, on pleasure bent. Cherubino is behind the chair. Susanna is standing nervously in front of the chair.

"Susanna, you appear in . . . an unwonted confusion."

"My Lord, I beg your pardon. Yet . . . suppose that . . . someone found us. Please go away, please leave me."

"I am gone, in a moment." During a crotchet rest the Count sits down in the chair. He is in no hurry.

"Listen" he says. "No, no, not listen" says Susanna. He takes her hand. He begins to explain his plan of taking Figaro with him when he goes to London as Spanish ambassador: "et comme le devoir d'une femme est de suivre son mari . . ."

"Ah, si j'osais parler!" says Susanna in the play, thinking of le devoir d'un mari; the Count has a special duty of fidelity to the promises which he lavished on a woman "qu'il épousa par amour, lorsqu'il abolit pour elle un certain affreux droit du Seigneur."

"Oh if I dared ask!" says Susanna in the opera, with no clue to what she wished to ask. The Count draws her to him. "Ask me, ask me, my dearest. 'Tis your right, this day and for as long as you live, you have the right to ask me, to tell me, command me." In just such tones of life-long devotion he used to address Rosina. In just such tones perhaps, he invited a request to abolish the droit du Seigneur. "Ask me, ask me, my dearest."

"Oh master, let me go! I do not ask that, do not want it, or mean it. How you torment me!"

Gaily the Count replies. "Ah no, Susanna. I mean to make you happy. You know well how I love you; for you have heard it all from Basilio. Now listen. For a moment or two with me in the garden this evening, hidden in the shadows, ah, for such a little favour I would pay you . . ."

In the garden! We who know the opera think at once of the letter duet and *Deh Vieni*; of the *soave zefiretto*, the pines, the magical nightfall, the crowning with roses, the murmuring brook and rustling breezes that say—ah so softly—what shall befall the loved one. But the Count is requesting a more mercenary moment. It is the kind of contingency that Swift had in mind when he gave his famous Advice to the Waiting Maid:

"If you are in a great Family, and my lady's Woman, my Lord may probably like you, although you are not half as handsome as his own Lady. In this case, take care to get as much out of him as you can; and never allow him the smallest liberty, not the squeezing of your Hand, unless he puts a guinea into it; so, by degrees, make him pay accordingly for every new Attempt, doubling upon him in proportion to the Concessions you allow, and always struggling and threatening to cry out or tell your Lady, although you receive his Money: Five Guineas for handling your Breast is a cheap Pennyworth, although you seem to resist with all your Might; but never allow him the last Favour under a hundred Guineas or a Settlement of twenty Pounds a year for Life."

This is how Marcellina expects Susanna to react to the Count, a

L A

FOLLE JOURNÉE,

O U

LE MARIAGE DE FIGARO,

C O M É D I E

EN CINQ ACTES, EN PROSE.

PAR M. DE BEAUMARCHAIS.

Représentée pour la première fois, par les Comédiens français ordinaires du Roi, le mardi 27 avril 1784.

En faveur du badinage.
Faites grace à la raison. *Fond. de la pièce.*

DE L'IMPRIMERIE DE LA SOCIÉTÉ LITTÉRAIRE-TYPOGRAPHIQUE;

Et se trouve à Paris,

Chez RUAULT, libraire, au Palais-Royal, près le théâtre, n° 216.

1 7 8 5.

Der

närrische Tag,

oder die

Hochzeit des Figaro;

ein

Lustspiel in fünf Aufzügen, aus dem Französischen des

Herrn

Caron von Beaumarchais.

Gedruckte Dummheiten haben nur da einen Werth, wo man ihren freyen Umlauf hindert. Fünfter Aufzug, dritter Auftritt.

Wien, 1785.

(left) The Rautenstrauch version, published after 3rd February 1785. (Chérubin became Liebetraut.)

(right) At last! The first official edition, April 1785.

Act. I. Note the size and style of the half-*un*furnished room; the double bolster, awaiting its bed; and the male plumes worn or carried indoors. April 1785. (Designed by St Quentin, engraved by Liénard.)

Act II. "Tuez-le donc, ce méchant Page." Note the window; dressing-
room door; male ruff and cloak; guitar; and alcove (with another double
bolster). (Designed by St Quentin, engraved by Halbou.)

Act III (of the opera), engraved by Lingé. "Il vous rend chaste et pure aux mains de votre époux." Note Figaro, looking absurdly young; pairs of young girls; the tenantry dancing; and a grand entry at the back.

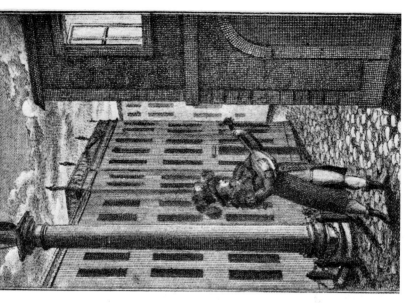

D. Giovani.   Giovane Cavaliere es-
                   tremamente licenzioso

D. Anna,   Dama promessa sposa di
D. Ottavio.
Commendatore.
D. Elvira.   Dama di Burgos abbando–
                  nata da D. Gio.
Leporello.   Serv. di D. G.
Masetto.   amante di
Zerlina.   Contadina.

The chosen characters. Note how they are described in
the first printed libretto.

(right) Luigi Bassi, a lithe and irresistible young Don,
dressed as himself. Note the narrow street to which he
can return while Zerlina comforts Masetto. Is the column
a phallic symbol? (From a contemporary engraving.)

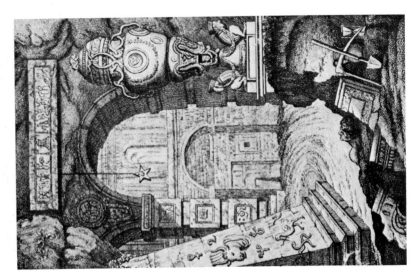

The two Alberti illustrations, from the 1791 printed libretto. *Left*, temple and forecourt; frontispiece in some copies but opposite "man sieht einen Eingang . . ." in the British Museum copy. *Right*, "Der Vogelfänger bin ich ja"; with hill and round temple.

SCENES FROM ACT ONE: two of the illustrations by Joseph and Peter Schaffer, published (in color) by a Brno journal in 1795. Not to be trusted much; naïve, careless; *facilis descensus* . . .

SCENES FROM ACT TWO: two more of the Schaffer illustrations. (Though the figures are crude, the trees and rocks are not bad!)

man of charm as well as wealth. But Susanna is incorruptible. Cherubino is listening, watching, learning the wrong moral lesson, enjoying himself hugely.

The voice of Basilio is heard from the Count's room. He is looking for the Count; who hurriedly tells Susanna to go out and stop him. "That would leave you alone here" she says. It is an incomprehensible reason to give; as the Count shows by an appropriate gesture. Basilio is at the door. He is coming from the Count's room to see if the Count is "with his lady." He is obviously going to come through the big ante-room. The Count says he will hide behind the chair. It is the only place to hide. Susanna says "Not there, not there." She bars his way, as Cherubino slips round the chair and jumps into it. She covers the boy with the dress that belongs to the Countess. (As William Mann says in his programme note, what a fragrant shelter the boy will think it!)

Basilio, in priestly garb, greets Susanna piously. "My dear, may heaven bless you." Paisiello and Rossini make him a bass. But Mozart knows that the tenor voice is more expressive for a smooth elegant hypocritical pupil of Lady Sneerwell in *The School for Scandal* ("Wounded myself in the early part of my life by the envenomed tongue of slander, I confess I have since known no pleasure equal to the reducing others to the level of my own injured reputation"). In Act Four we learn about his idealistic youth, and how he then met the Lady Patience who left him with a thick skin. In the *Barber* he is the high priest of calumny, with a penchant for using proverbial saws; a two-faced man, who will instantly change loyalties for money. No wonder the Count is glad of an opportunity to see how Basilio behaves behind his back: "I'll see how well he serves me."

At the moment no one is offering Basilio money to betray the Count, and in any case the present business is to Basilio's liking. "Have you perchance just seen his Lordship?" Note the expressive flick up to D on the last syllable. "And what would his Lordship be doing with me?" asks Susanna, to the delight of lovers of the opera. "You're rude, go away, sir." Basilio says that Figaro is looking for the Count. Susanna asks why Figaro should look for a man who "hates him almost as much as you do."

"I never feel there is any moral law that he who worships a wife must needs hate her husband. In other words, his Lordship loves you."

"Oh, go away, you cheap slave of the lust of another. I do not need you, or your horrible morals, or his Lordship, or the money."

It is a fine outburst. The Count, who is not such a logical sinner as

Don Juan, is impressed. *Onestissima Signora*, he probably thinks; less cynically than when he uses the words later. Basilio is unimpressed: " 'Twould do no harm to you." He insinuates that, like any other woman, she already has a lover to amuse her. How foolish of her to prefer Cherubino to the Count! Soon he is making insinuations about Cherubino and the Countess.

"Oh you villain!" says Susanna. "You enjoy going round and scattering horrible stories."

"I? Not a bit of it! As I buy them, I sell them. This is what they all are saying. I add no jot or tittle."

It is too much for the Count. He rises from behind the chair with an aggrieved baritone bellow. He is no longer the romantic tenor of the *Barber*. In this opera his love-making usually requires accompaniment by the bassoon.

> *Le Comte:* Courez, Bazile, et qu'on le chasse.
> *Bazile:* Ah! que je suis fâché d'être entré!
> *Suzanne, troublée:* Mon Dieu! mon Dieu!

The B♭ major trio is a masterpiece, a chameleon miracle of characterisation, humour and story-telling. Abert writes eight and a half pages about it, out of ninety pages about the opera. Ulibishev discusses it in detail, and adds sadly that he cannot devote as much space to the rest of the opera.

A fortissimo rumbling on F by second violins and violas, with long supporting Fs from the wind. Then five forthright chords. The Count is indignant. "Young seducer" splutters a man who has no right to accuse anyone, let alone a thirteen-year-old choirboy, of being a seducer. The music does the first of many changes, and becomes a set of little upward phrases like nervous flicks with the back of the hand. In jolty snatches a model of marital virtue says "I'll replace him ... go and chase him ... away from here." He gains confidence. According to Abert (German operatic tradition?) he stamps on the floor when the music reaches forte. "Go and chase, chase him, chase him out of here."

A few quavers from the first violin are all the transition that a Mozart needs, in order that strings can accompany Basilio's very different entry. Basilio is not often allowed to sing his aria in Act Four, but rarely fails to make the most of his opportunities in this trio, including this mock-anxious, unctuous, mischievous, smooth, superior, hypocritical entry. He is *so* sorry that he interrupted the Count's sport. He is not yet pretending to apologise for what he was saying about Cherubino and the Countess; first things first. "I was rude, sir, to intrude, sir." (A downward fifth, altogether.) "You were busy, it would appear!" (Another downward fifth, beginning a tone higher.)

Susanna now has D♭s, hinting at the F minor that lovers of this opera associate with Barbarina's anxious little song in Act Four. "I'm in trouble, trouble double; I am truly faint with fear." The fear is genuine, the faint is sham. Fainting, and the vapours of which we hear in Act Three, do not happen to a sturdy girl like Susanna; but she grasps at the hope that, if she fainted, the men might take her out of the room, or go for help. But for the second time in the opera men take no notice of her. She tries again, on a higher note. Still the men ignore her. Try them with a high A♭. That should do it. It does. They are all attention, as she repeats her "trouble double" with a dramatic sforzando on E♮ (7.37). All is ready for an artistic swoon with the violins. "I am truly faint with fear," she says pathetically. "I am truly . . . faint with fear."

Two chivalrous men rush to hold her, Basilio getting there first. Two chivalrous men are fairly sorry for her, in a bright dominant. "What a pity, and she so pretty." Two chivalrous men check that she is still alive. "Shall we listen? Her heart! Oh dear!" The human ear is not a good stethoscope. They check their result to make sure. "Shall we listen to her heart? Oh dear!" They check twice. The dynamics, and the less hesitant phrasing, tell us that they are doing so for pleasure. One can imagine Susanna angrily thinking, Men! It is not easy to stage-manage this little escapade, ear to breast, while singing to the audience. But da Ponte's words are wicked, precise, and amusing. By Swift's scale of charges, Susanna narrowly misses earning 30 guineas in less than ten seconds.

She soon sees the humour of it. The first violins have her fainting tune in the major (D♮, not D♭). It is an omen of recovery—Levarie suggests that she is peeping out through a half-opened eye. "Fair, with care! To the chair we bear you." They say it. They do it. Susanna has to recover hurriedly, lest Cherubino should be discovered. "Oh, where am I?" After a suitable pause she can safely vent on them her anger for their previous antics. "Sirs, how dare you? You are rogues, 'tis very clear, 'tis very clear, 'tis very clear." It is an unjust world; the men were once more being chivalrous, and can hotly protest their innocence. "We were merely, er, helping really" says Basilio, "For your honour you need not fear." "No, indeed" says the Count, beginning a little later than Basilio, "Upon my honour, we were helping, my precious dear." Even when the Count has caught up, the men do not sing with unanimity. Different words, different tunes. In his notes to the pre-war Mozart Opera Society recording of *Le Nozze*, Walter Legge drew attention to the Count's sensuous G–A♭–G. It is difficult to put across; they must both seem on the defensive for the moment.

Basilio, who is consistently quicker-witted than the Count, decides to counter-attack. He begins a new sentence, rather low in the tenor voice with string accompaniment. "As for Cherub's great ambition . . ." In mid-sentence, the voice rises more than usual in pitch; and gains a little in volume and silkiness (added oboe accompaniment). "What I said was mere suspicion." (No special emphasis on the word "mere"—yet.) If we take Basilio's words at their unctuous face value, they are a proper apology. But he did not say them like that. In the play, Bazile's apology could be genuine. But da Ponte makes Susanna implore the Count not to believe Basilio; i.e. not to believe what she and the Count know that Basilio meant. It is another instance of the ironies of meaning in this opera. "That is vicious! That is malicious! Do not trust a falsehood sheer, a falsehood sheer, a falsehood sheer." Well, well!

"I decree the boy's departure" says the Count firmly, with three more orchestral flicks of the back of the hand. "Poor young creature" mutter Susanna and Basilio (meaning it differently, compare *28.88*). The Count interrupts petulantly with a repetition of "I decree the boy's departure" and another three flicks. "Poor young creature" say Susanna and Basilio again. The Count echoes their plea sarcastically. "Poor young creature?" The first violin line trips off up into a higher octave. "Poor young creature! He was caught before, d'you hear?" "Tell us" says Susanna. She has heard part of the story from Cherubino and is human enough to want to hear the rest. "How?" says Basilio. "How?" says Susanna. "Tell us" says Basilio. "Tell us" they both say. "How?"

There is a pause. "With Barbarina" the Count explains. The orchestra titter. "Yesterday. The door was fastened." (It was the door of Barbarina's bedroom; "où Monseigneur avait sans doute affaire aussi!" as the shocked Suzanne remarks in the play.) The orchestra titter again. The Count continues gaily ("dans les moeurs de ce temps-la, les grands traitaient en badinant toute entreprise sur les femmes") "Knock, knock. I had never seen her so nervous, red, and flustered." Barbarina was blushing more than usual; so we know that she used to blush whenever the Count gave her "a nice hug and such a big kiss" *21A32*. Another orchestral titter. "So with natural suspicion . . ."

No rustle this time, but a brusque chord. "Acting on an intuition . . ." By an instinct as natural as the instinct to suspect that a twelve-year-old girl has a preferred lover hiding in the room, the Count uses Basilio's tune of malicious delight, with string accompaniment, in tempo. His hand is above his head. "Softly, softly as I was able . . ." Basilio would have started another descent but the Count's hand moves slowly and inexorably down to the dress on the chair. "I took the cloth off her bedroom table." The vocal line has come down more than an octave, and is still going down. "Cherubino . . ." At the third syllable, the wind instruments enter. The Count has finished his long descent on low A, an octave and a fourth below where he started. He grasps the dress. Pian pianino! A bar later, the bassoons help the 'cellos who help the violins who help the Count to lift the dress. At the beginning of the next bar the violins reach a crotchet C, the 'cellos reach a crotchet A, and the Count triumphantly flicks the dress aside. For a moment we are keenly aware of an interminable F on oboes, horns and violas. The Count sees . . . There is all too probably a tidal wave of audience laughter, drowning the Count's words "What do I see? No!" "Ah cruel fortune!" sings Susanna upwards, as the violins and 'cellos drop downwards. "*Doubly* delicious" says Basilio, in a seventh heaven of *School for Scandal* delight. The violins and 'cellos reach bottom. There is a pause.

The masterly simplicity, the quiet naturalism, the dramatic tension, are breathtaking. No one who has seen *Figaro* forgets this moment. All else may fade—save perhaps a memory of the Countess alone with her sadness at the beginning of Act Two. The discovery of Cherubino in the chair is unforgettable.

"You that thought us both so vicious!" exclaims the Count to Susanna; remembering *6A50*. *Onestissima signora*, impeccable bride! The accompaniment is pianissimo so that the Count's low B♭ can be audible without being loud; it rarely strikes this happy mean. "Now I understand it all."

Susanna is in panic. "Let not worse befall to me now." Worse could easily befall; the Count could prevent the wedding. There is nothing else in the opera to suggest that Susanna is religious, let alone devout. But in this extremity she prays. "God above, to Thee I call." The resident priest on the other hand points a "moral" of the situation, in words that—although Mozart did not know this at the time of composing *Figaro*—were going to have a major Mozartian future of their own. *Così fan tutte le belle*, "Women do so, 'tis their nature, it is nothing new at all." At first the words are apt to be drowned by Susanna and the Count. Then Mozart gives Basilio the words higher in the voice, in laughing quavers, with full support from the first violins. Susanna sings quietly, "Oh no! Not that" or "To Thee I call." The Count is merely accompanying. So Basilio's words should get through, if we are listening for them. And the laughing quavers recur many times in the overture of *Così fan tutte*.

After an echo (*167–174*) of the heart-beat music Basilio reminds the Count: "As for Cherub's great ambition, what I said was *mere* suspicion." His tune is back at its original level, an emphatic fifth higher than when he first used these particular words. This time it is the word "mere" that gets the emphasis, with the oboes in sixths. Susanna is too crushed to defend the Countess by denying what he still means. She continues her prayer. Basilio, man and priest, continues to moralise about what women—not, of course, men—do by nature. Soon the excitement is over, with three pianissimo chords.

So the virtuous Susanna is exposed! The Count feels unusually virtuous. Cherubino is not allowed to get out of the chair. The Count tells Basilio to fetch Figaro. "Je ne souffrirai point que Figaro, qu'un homme que j'estime et que j'aime, soit victime d'une pareille tromperie." Angrily Susanna agrees. Fetch Figaro! The Count, surprised, tells Basilio to wait. Susanna protests her innocence; innocence has no need of excuses. The Count does not believe her (we know this, because of a mischief-making remark in *8C21*). But his mind is suddenly preoccupied. How long has Cherubino been in the room? Did he . . .? A few questions, and the Count's fear is confirmed. "Oh heavens, he will have overheard what I was saying!" "Oh but" says Cherubino "I did my *best* not to hear you." "How disgraceful" says the Count. His wrath is about to descend forcibly. But Basilio hears a tramp of feet outside. People are coming. He tells his noble master to restrain himself. The Count has to be content with yanking Cherubino from the chair, as if for a breach of etiquette; but he himself had ordered the boy not to move.

Enter Figaro with the chorus; a large chorus, dressed startlingly in white. Beaucoup de valets, paysannes, paysans vêtus en blanc, says Beaumarchais. In continental countries many of them would have white clothes for processions. They troop solemnly on to the stage, to an eight-bar Tirolean prelude with flutes, bassoons and horns. There is a hint of bagpipe in the holiday music. The peasant girls are carrying white flowers. Figaro, the only one not dressed in white, is carrying a white bridal veil with white feathers and white ribbons. The essence of the French scene (*MF 1.10*) is in the words: "Monseigneur! Vos vassaux, touchés de l'abolition d'un certain droit facheux que votre amour pour Madame . . . permettez donc que cette jeune créature, de qui votre sagesse a preservé l'honneur, reçoive de votre main, publiquement, la toque virginale, ornée de plumes et de rubans blancs, symbole de la pureté de vos intentions; adoptez-en la cérémonie pour tous les mariages, et qu'un quatrain chanté en choeur rappelle à jamais le souvenir . . ."

Figaro (whose talents as a mauvais poète were displayed in *BS 1.2*) has been busy. He has organised and rehearsed a charade, and has himself written doggerel for it.

> White flowers bring we,
> Joyfully sing we.
> Praise we our master dear,
> Worthy is he.

The words are sung woodenly, with bad accentuation and a marked lack of conviction. Then music and words become more heartfelt:

> These finer flowers

(the lads point to the lasses, and the lasses point shyly to themselves)

> Graciously spares he;
> No longer shares he,
> Fresh will they be.
> Roses and lilies—
> Joyfully!—
> Lay we before our master dear.
> Worthy is he!

Levarie points out that the persistent alternation between loud phrases (usually upwards) and soft phrases (usually downwards) is intended to have dramatic significance. It is not exactly a political demonstration, although Figaro himself is aware of the political implications. He has made the peasants anxious—the girls are young (giovani liete), and this is the first wedding since the droit honteux was abolished. Are their own future nuptials to be shared? Such anxieties can be the stuff of politics, as in *Clochemerle*; but are themselves pre-political.

"What is this comedy about, pray?" asks the Count; though he has eyes, and excellent hearing. The better one gets to know this opera, the more one enjoys even individual lines of recitative. After so blatant a charade, the simple line that da Ponte gives to the Count is one that (unless the charade has been muffed) cannot fail.

"Here I come dancing" says Figaro aside to Susanna. "Follow step when I say, my dear one." She has no time to explain, but whispers that it is hopeless. Figaro can see that something has gone wrong, and that the Count is not in a mood to make any concession. But he is indomitable. "Va toujours."

Fulsomely Figaro flatters the Count for his abolition of the droit du Seigneur. Blandly mastering annoyance, the Count says that he deserves neither presents nor praises. "It was a wicked unjust right that I abolished. An unnatural right. I was doing my duty." (There is a slight hint of Rousseau here, and a strong hint of Spanish pride.)

The Count's remark is greeted with cheers and further praise. He is a magistrate—indeed, a judge (17A). But he does not perform the ceremony. He promises to perform it, er, later; with pomp, and in the presence of all his loyal subjects. Aside, he resolves to find Marcellina quickly. He tells the deputation to go. The lads and lasses repeat their song disappointedly. They hurry out in two bars—it had taken them eight bars to make their entry. Figaro starts another round of cheers. Instead of rising briskly—GGE CCG EEC—the cheers climb droopingly, falteringly; GGD, er, BBG, er, DDG. To Figaro's annoyance the third and dampest cheer comes from Basilio instead of Cherubino. Basilio is in good humour, after the failure of Figaro's amateur effort as a choral trainer. He would not cheer so damply, if he meant it for the Count. He is commiserating with Figaro, whom he hates.

"And why are you not cheering?" says Figaro crossly to Cherubino. Susanna explains that the boy is being sent home. "On such a beautiful morning?" pleads Figaro, at once forgetting his annoyance in sympathy. "On the day of our wedding?" adds Susanna hopefully. "When we are all full of your praises?" adds Figaro.

"Oh sir, please, please forgive me."

"You do not deserve it" says the Count.

"He is too young to punish" says Susanna.

"He too young? Do not believe it" says the Count. John Donne wrote a lighthearted poem in which he advised men to "love one woman, and one part in her." The Count would have thought the first part of this advice absurd; the second, self-evident. If a thirteen-year-old choirboy flirts with Barbarina or looks adoringly at the Countess or is found in a chair near Susanna, he is a seducer. "I have been foolish; but I promise that my lips are . . ." The boy is not too young to bargain. Nor is he too young to make witty remarks: Pardonner généreusement n'est pas le droit du Seigneur auquel vous avez renoncé en épousant Madame. "Very well. I will forgive you, and give you a present as well. I can dispose of a commission in my Catalonian regiment. You are a captain, sir, but go this instant." Cherubino is not too young to be a captain; younger boys than he were colonels of regiments. And commissions were valuable. The Count's decision to make Cherubino a captain is one of those absurd, impulsive, generous presents that recall the Almaviva of Le Barbier. But money is not important to the Count, and Catalonia is a long way from Aguas Frescas.

"Oh, let him stay until tomorrow" say Figaro and Susanna in thirds. "No, not a moment more" says the Count. Cherubino sadly turns to go.

Suddenly he is told that he can kiss Susanna "for the last time." Cherubino is a boy whose character and habits develop from hour to hour. He has not yet kissed Susanna—tu sais trop bien, méchante, que je n'ose pas oser. Therefore the Count's insinuation is malicious. But Cherubino moves hopefully towards Susanna; it is never too late to begin. Figaro quickly steps between them, shakes hands with Mister Captain, whispers that he wants a word with him before he goes, and bids him farewell. Adieu, mon petit Chérubin. Tu vas mener un train de vie bien différent, mon enfant. Goodbye, little page, you had not reckoned how a destiny changes in half a second.

It is clear from the French, and from the bantering good-natured music of the famous aria which follows, that Figaro, unlike the Count, is not seriously jealous of Cherubino. "Mon enfant" says Figaro. "Tu vas" says Figaro. Cherubino is too young to be a rival. In any case Figaro still trusts Susanna and is well able to discount a malicious remark from the Count. Indeed, he cannot be expected to understand its full malevolence—no one has told him what happened while he was organising the charade. Yet da Ponte has provided one or two lines, in an otherwise outstandingly good lyric, which are jealous in implication. There is perhaps a slight and instinctive undertone of jealousy. But not more.

Non più andrai begins with a cheerful C for strings and bassoons. Dame! tu ne rôderas plus au quartier des femmes (compare 6A62). Cherubino is a farfallone amoroso, an amorous butterfly. Il s'élance à la puberté, mais sans projet, sans connaissances, et tout entier à chaque événement. "You'll not flutter or twirl any more, sir." The first violins offer the voice an elegant shake at the end of the line. "Or make eyes, day and night, at the ladies." Figaro, like Basilio in *6A72*, has noticed those bright eyes gazing timidly and absorbedly at the Countess.

"Or disturb their repose as before, sir." Mozart as usual liked the bawdy implication. He gave it *tenuti* and unison accompaniment. But he meant it to be sung as a joke, in context. The women *will* adore Cherubino, says Susanna in *12.95*. On ne l'aime donc pas encore; on sent qu'on jour on l'aimera (MF, Preface). In three or four years time, says Susanna, vous serez le plus grand petit vaurien (*MF 1.7*). Meanwhile he is a "morveux sans conséquence" (*MF 1.7*), "aux premiers battements du coeur cherchant tout sans rien démêler, idolâtre, ainsi qu'on l'est a cet âge heureux, d'un objet céleste pour lui dont le hasard fit sa marraine" (Preface).

"You Adonis, you young knave of hearts." Cherubino is an elegant self-admiring little Narcissus, a beautiful little Adonis of love. There is an oboe twiddle for love. Narcissus was a lad who fell in love with his own reflection, among just such scenery as is described in *Non so più*. Adonis was loved by Aphrodite, and came to a bad end. The verbal images are therefore shrewdly relevant; Figaro is much more articulate and observant than the Count, who can only call Cherubino a *seduttor*, a *garzon malnato*. It is particularly characteristic that Figaro should use classical imagery, here and at *28.109–121*; in the eighteenth century an ambitious self-educated man would naturally smatter Latin and Greek.

The second verse is about Cherubino's costume and appearance. He is a "blue bird" (bel oiseau bleu) because of the swagger coat that hangs from his shoulders. It is this cloak that he takes off in Act Two, leaving him with an open neck. He has a feathered hat. Cloak and hat were worn indoors—see the 1785 engraving of Cherubino in the chair, and the equally early engraving of the Count wearing his hat as Susanna comes out of the dressing-room. Cherubino's costume is the ceremonial costume of a page of the Spanish court—white, embroidered with silver. The dandy (*7.102*), the little Adonis, enjoys his finery. The music goes into the dominant, the second violins and violas are in semiquavers, the first violins and flutes have a splendid bar with voluptuous upward trills. "Say good-bye to the beautiful plumage." The first violins and flutes stroke the plumage; so does Figaro. "On this elegant cap, so endearing." Figaro is holding the cap, and another trill is thrown to and fro between the violins. "See your graces and curls disappearing." Snip, snip. Figaro has been a barber. "With your blushes and womanly arts." So ends the second verse, with one of the lines which suggests that Mozart and da Ponte had an authorised edition of the play, containing the author's precise stipulation that the part of Cherubino must be played by a young and pretty woman, pour en bien sentir les finesses. Here am I, the vocal line also implies; the self-assured manly Figaro. Dame, tu ne rôderas plus. It could be cruel banter, but for the general mood of the music.

Softly the first violins begin a series of cascades. "Say goodbye . . . to pretty feathers . . . cap endearing . . . curls and graces . . . they're all disappearing." Indeed they are. Each cascade is like a doffing of finery.

Back comes the first verse, like a refrain. There it is; shakes, tenuti, oboe twiddle and all. Then there is a bigger forte, with horns, trumpets, and drums. Suddenly the orchestra have become a military band, with massed drums in their rhythm. Da Ponte too has changed his rhythm. "Gad, sir, you're with men on marches." More drumming. "Awkward packs and big moustaches." Somewhere there is a sergeant-major giving orders. Left turn! "Heavy muskets." Right turn! "Sabres dangling." Left turn! Beaumarchais gives us "de bons soldats, morbleu! Basanés, mal vêtus; un grand fusil bien lourd, tourne à droite, tourne à gauche . . ." Da Ponte adds the dangling sabre. Mozart adds the drums. "Shoulders back, sir." Right, left. "And stop them wrangling." Right, left. "Great big helmet!" Right, left. " 'Tis heavy, say you?" Right, left. "You win fame." Right, left, with a prompt omission of drums and trumpets; Figaro is singing about meritorious service, not about its recognition. "But will they pay you?" At the word "pay" the music leans into E minor. The second violins and violas are doubled by bassoons in the lower octave as they slide chromatically in quaver thirds. "What will they pay you? When will they pay you?" Another pause.

"From a ballroom hither-thither . . ." The violins briefly recall the finery of verse two. "Through the squelching mud you slither." Trumpets and drums are loud. Violins, drums, and trumpets then suddenly drop out. Cherubino is far from the ballroom, far from home, almost equally far from the glamour of the ceremonial parade. The band are just within earshot. Cherubino is on active service. "Over hill and valley going." We trudge with Cherubino. "In the heat, or is it snowing? Mortars bang, and cannon thunder, you must never knuckle under; how they miss you, 'tis a wonder; bullets whistle by your ear."

A spent bullet or piece of shrapnel whistles down. As if in a dream, it turns into another series of doffings of finery. "Say goodbye . . . to cap endearing . . . say goodbye . . . to its feathers . . . say goodbye . . . to your graces . . . they're all disappearing . . . non più andrai . . ." For

the third and last time, the *farfallone amoroso* is good-naturedly reminded that his time at Aguas Frescas is over. Souvenez vous de cette
maison où votre jeunesse a trouvé tant d'indulgence, says the Countess
in the play.

Mozart has been picturing a reluctant warrior. But he is writing a
finale, and wants a rousing finish. Insensibly we proceed, as Ulibishev
pointed out in 1840, 'de l'ironie à l'enthousiasme.' Mozart, by a com-
pulsion of musical design and psychological insight, sees that Cherubino
would make a gallant, even foolhardy, young officer. As Susanna says
in *11A3*, he is a boy who does well at everything. Beaumarchais says
in the preface: "Voyez-le à la fin de son role; à peine a-t-il un habit
d'officier, qu'il porte la main à l'épée aux premières railleries du Comte,
sur le qui pro quo d'un soufflet. Il sera fier, notre étourdi." Cherubino
would go into battle, when the time came, like little Petya in *War and
Peace*.

Softly the drumming rhythm resumes. "Cherubino, into battle."
It is still ironic. "You're a hero, never fear." Right, left. "Cherubino,
into battle, you're a hero, never fear." The trumpets are blaring, the
drums are beating. "You're a hero, never fear." The boy believes it.
He *is* a hero, never fear.

Cherubino is becoming a central character in this opera. He is
described by Figaro (*9*) and Susanna (*12*). He is abused in detail by the
Count (*7.10*, *15.1* et al.). He is anxiously and tenderly mothered by the
young Countess. He is described by Basilio (6A) and Antonio (*15.504*).
He is carefully analysed by himself (*6*, *11*). No other character in
Figaro receives half this amount of characterisation. As Paumgartner
puts it, Cherubino is a poltergeist. He darts through the plot; gay,
brilliant, unpredictable, not an embryo Don Juan or vest-pocket
Count but himself, the young winged cherub of human love. Here he
is unexpectedly, in the middle of a C major ending to the Act. The
orchestra have it, tutti and loud, as Figaro finishes his last line. We
know what they themselves thought about it at the first orchestral
rehearsal in 1786. Michael Kelly, the first Basilio and Don Curzio,
wrote in his *Reminiscences*:

"At the first rehearsal of the full band, Mozart was on the stage with
his crimson pelisse and gold-laced cocked hat, giving the time of the
music to the orchestra. Figaro's song *Non più andrai, farfallone amoroso*
Bennuci (*sic*) gave, with the greatest animation and power of voice.
I was standing close to Mozart, who, sotto voce, was repeating 'Bravo!
Bravo! Bennuci'; and when Bennuci came to the fine passage
Cherubino, alla vittoria, alla gloria militar which he gave out with

Stentorian lungs, the effect was electricity itself, for the whole of the performers on the stage, and those in the orchestra, as if actuated by one feeling of delight, vociferated Bravo! Bravo! Maestro. Viva, viva, grande Mozart. Those in the orchestra I thought would never have ceased applauding, by beating the bows of their violins against the music desks. The little man acknowledged, by repeated obeisances, his thanks for the distinguished mark of enthusiastic applause bestowed upon him."

But the Act, taken as a whole, was so intricate that only to-day are we beginning to enjoy it properly.

ACT TWO

10, Porgi, amor
10A, Vieni, cara Susanna
11, Voi che sapete
11A, Bravo! che bella voce!
12, Venite, inginocchiatevi
12A, Quante buffonerie!

13, Susanna, or via, sortite
13A, Dunque voi non aprite?
14, Aprite, presto, aprite!
14A, Oh guarda il demonietto
15, Esci, omai, garzon malnato!

Did it all happen in about thirty-six minutes? We have been conditioned to the speed and compression that were forced on Mozart by his subject. For it comes as a surprise to hear Act Two begin with seventeen leisurely bars of orchestral music; the instrumental introduction to a symphony or concerto in E♭ major.

As we get to know the opera well we realise that, unlike the play, it is about the pitfalls and power of human love. There was nothing in Act One (except *Non so più*, also in E♭) that prepared us for this way of looking at an apparently artificial comedy. The chords in *10.1* are like a compressed form of the opening bars of the overture to *The Magic Flute*. They point forward to the moment of general reconciliation at the end of Act Four.

All seventeen bars are an integral part of the aria. Not a note, not a nuance of dynamics or harmony, not a shade of colour, not a touch of lively musicianship can be spared. Mozart has deferred the entry of the Countess (she enters during Act One in the play) for maximum effect. He gives himself room to put into orchestral music the mixed, surging feelings of a beautiful, solitary, rather inarticulate young wife. Mozart is living and breathing those feelings; he makes them more individual and complex than we could have inferred from Beaumarchais and da

Ponte. There are serenity and passion, dignity and restraint, as well as sadness. It is as well that Mozart does not yet offer us the misleading help of her conscious thoughts. Listen to the gentle delicacy of the little semiquavers in bar two, and the fuller but still gentle string tone in the next four bars. A "tune" comes in the first violins; but please do not miss the sighings (followed by magical stepping and yearning) in the second violins and violas. There are calm strong bars in which the wind re-enter, voluptuous little violin trills, exquisite clarinet playing, and an arching off-beat phrase in the violins. Through it we see the Countess. She stands at the window of her bedroom (or looks at a big portrait of the Count?). She is surely in full view by bar three, in which the sighs of the second violins and violas are so unlike the music of Act One.

The Countess is a woman of moods; usually but not always shy; temperamentally apt to feel "not very well". At present her "usual vapours" (15A33) possess her, and she is using the smelling-bottle. She has reason for depression. Her husband, whom she loves so much, was lavish with promises (19) when he married her. One promise was that he would not run after other women. Another, very special, promise was that he would abolish the degrading droit du Seigneur. She has long suspected that he was breaking the first promise. Now Susanna has told her that he is trying to evade the second promise, by consent and purchase. Three years after her own wedding, the honey-moon is finally over.

"Power of love, what can restore thee? See my sorrow, and hear my sigh." The words are platitudinous. But the violins surge up, the clarinets sympathise. "Oh, bring back my treasure for me." The clarinets sound hopeful. But she is not listening. "Bring him back, or let me die!" Yes, it is slow and sad *by comparison with* the general speed and gaiety of the opera. But it is not in fact particularly slow, and must on no account be taken literally as a *lamento* aria. Our only lament need be for any inadequacy of performance. We sometimes lament for a conductor and orchestra who solemnly make a stodgy mess of *10.2–17*; like young Johnny who plays the violin at school concerts and is ever so good at fast movements. We lament, sometimes, for the poor singer as she stands or sits, or walks about a little, during those interminable bars before she is allowed to sing her crucial first long B♭; like young Mabel in the local dramatic society. We sometimes even lament for the singer as she approaches the B♭ with that slight but fatal rigidity; like Miss X. Y, facing the critics and a few friends at her Wigmore Hall recital. *Porgi amor*

is a sort of Beecher's Brook for sopranos—and none but the best are
allowed on to this particular race-course, anyway. It is all the more
admirable when the intonation of that first phrase is sure, the singing
free and expressive.

Unlike Pamina, the nineteen-year-old Countess is not really even
half in love with easeful death (and it is worth remembering that
Mozart himself, according to Nissen, took *Ach, ich fühl's* rather fast).
Although she does not yet know it, the power of her love is alive in
her first phrase and throughout. The second half of the aria is voluptuous (e.g. that bassoon G♭). "Ah, je l'ai trop aimé, je l'ai lassé de mes
tendresses, et fatigué de mon amour." He does not deserve it, but he is
her *tesoro*, her treasure. She is not a woman to use words lightly, and it
would be against her nature to parade either passion or sorrow un-
restrainedly. All is suggested, contained, in the music; a simple cavatina,
rien surtout qui dégrade aux yeux du spectateur son caractère aimable
et vertueux. We are not harrowed but ennobled.

The soliloquy has taken place in a magnificent bedroom. There is a
big bed in an alcove. The door to a small cul-de-sac dressing-room is at
the first wing on the left. The main door, leading to the big ante-
room which was the scene of Act One, is at the third wing on the right.
A third door, on one side at the back, goes chez les femmes; to the
servants' quarters, including Susanna's old room, from which she has
not moved her belongings. There is a big window on the other side at
the back. (Designers can do what they like within reason, about settings
for *Don Giovanni* and the *Magic Flute*; but at their peril do they tamper
with the precise stage stipulations for *Figaro*.)

Susanna returns, and the Countess greets her affectionately. "So he
tried to seduce you?" "Oh, but his Lordship does not pay such a
compliment to a girl of my station" replies Susanna tactfully. He had
offered a business agreement, she says. The Countess is unconvinced.
"Cruel man! He no longer loves me." (In the play, when disguised as
Susanna, the Countess asks the Count whether he does not love his
wife any more; and gets a full answer.) Again Susanna comments
tactfully: "If he no longer loves you, why is he so jealous of you?"
The Countess bursts out that nowadays all husbands are unfaithful and
jealous. Then—how like her—she regrets having said so to a nice girl
on her wedding morning. "But I am sure that Figaro loves you, and so
perhaps he . . ."

Figaro is approaching the main door. A valet may chortle "la" on
his wedding morning, even if the "la" conceals bars *88–95* of a subversive song. Some editions suggest that he enters singing. But that

would be unnecessarily discourteous to the Countess. In the play it is
when Figaro knocks that Suzanne court ouvrir, en chantant "Ah, c'est
mon Figaro." In the opera she runs to the door when she hears him
singing. It is at *Eccolo* ("Here he is") that he enters.

The Countess, who has liked and trusted Figaro since before she
met the Count, is a good listener. Figaro talks volubly, flippantly, not
very tactfully, about "a quite possible phenomenon; and only natural."
"How can you bear" asks Susanna "to be so light and flippant on a
serious matter?" "Flippant manner" Figaro replies "but, beneath it,
serious thinking." (In other words, Mozartian tragi-comedy.)

Figaro comes to the point. He has written an anonymous letter to
the Count, and has given it to Basilio to deliver; "an assignation for
tonight, at the hour of the ball, for my lady." The Countess is horrified,
and Figaro merely assures her that the Count will be so busy worrying
about the letter that he will not have time to frustrate the wedding.
The women are registering consternation. There are at least two
obvious flaws in this Machiavellian piece of reasoning. Susanna points
out the one that matters to herself and Figaro. "Aren't you forgetting
Marcellina?"

Irresistibly Figaro talks on. "Do not jump to conclusions. You tell
the Count, Susanna, that you will meet him in the garden." (More
consternation.) The little page (whom we all saw off to Seville, on the
first stage of his journey to Catalonia) has come back. I told him to do
so. You can dress him as a woman and send him to the garden in
Susanna's place. It is a golden opportunity for my lady to catch his
lordship, and shame him into doing her wishes.

Not a bad idea. The women like it (and I like Countesses who show
by a glint and a lift of the head that Rosina likes it, *before* asking
Susanna for her opinion). They settle down to detailed planning. The
Count has gone out hunting and will not be back for several hours.
Cherubino is waiting in the ante-room. "And then?" "Ah then . . ."
For a long moment Figaro seems to be singing to himself. Then he
sings aloud the rest of the first verse of *Se vuol ballare*. Off he goes.

The thoughts of a young godmother turn to the boy who is to be
dressed up as a woman. How upsetting that he was behind the chair
when his master was setting such a bad example! (Yes, and she will be
more upset when Cherubino follows the example in Act Four.) "Oh
you don't know how . . . and why did he not come straight to me . . .
and where is that song?" Susanna gives it to her, and suggests that they
should make him sing it. She hears someone coming. She goes to the
door, and opens it. "Forward march, forward march, mister officer."

Ah, says Cherubino mournfully, do not call me by that ill-fated word. "It dooms me to go away, and leave my godmother who has been so kind and good to me." "And is so beautiful?" That was Susanna, demurely recalling their conversation in Act One. Cherubino sighs. "Oh, yes! Yes, yes!" Susanna mimics him: "Oh, yes! Yes, yes! You little hypocrite! Now, quick, you can sing your song to my lady."

"The song is by . . .?" At my lady's question, he blushes. "Just look at him!" says Susanna "A pair of cheeks red-hot with blushes, all over." "Take my guitar" says the Countess "and accompany him." "I feel so very nervous" says Cherubino "but if my lady wishes . . ." "She wishes; yes, she does" says Susanna "don't go on talking."

The Countess, seated, holds the paper to follow the song. Susanna is looking over her shoulder at the music. The page-boy stands facing the Countess, eyes lowered. Beaumarchais said that the placing of the actors should follow Beauvarlet's "La Conversation Espagnole" (see Michael Levey's article in the *Journal of the Warburg and Courtauld Institutes 1959 p. 132*).

Opinions differ about the canzona which follows. Some say that *Voi che sapete* is musically perfect and deserves its enormous fame. Others feel that it is by no means above the average level of a score that is superb throughout. No one dares to say that the song is overrated, but a number of good judges admit to preferring *Non so più*. Professor Dent felt it necessary to remind us that it tends to "upset the balance of an opera if music is introduced as 'music', i.e. as an abnormal mode of expression, when the whole principle of opera is that music should be the one mode of expression which is consistently normal." Moreover the verses are not as vivid as usual, even in Italian. It is true that they seem to begin with an echo of *La Vita Nuova* XIX ("Donne ch' avete intelletto d'amore") as Greither and others have pointed out. But all those abstract nouns and platitudes seem rather too obviously a remarkable effort by a clever thirteen-year-old boy who has read Dante. They are on the same topic as *Non so più*; analysis of Cherubino's own emotions on the verge of love. Yes, one is entitled to feel that *Non so più* is in some ways an improved version of *Voi che sapete*; less stilted, less tentative, more natural and ardent. And so it should be—there is no character who develops more during the course of a Topsy-Turvy Day, for better and worse. *Non so più* was sung this morning. *Voi che sapete* was written yesterday.

Am I daring to suggest that *Voi che sapete* is overrated? No, for the music remains a miracle. But we must either forget the situation, except in a very general way; or regard *Voi che sapete* as the most subtle of all Mozart's essays in dramatic irony, in the middle of some of the finest and subtlest recitative ever written.

What is the context? An impressionable boy is singing yesterday's song to a beautiful godmother, whom he may never see again after today. He stands in front of her, eyes lowered. Susanna and the orchestra play his prelude. "Love's ladies, hark ye! Ye know him best." He raises his eyes, and sees that the Countess is looking at the music; so is Susanna. Donne, vedete! They are not looking at him, they do not notice the personal urgency of his plea. "Is this, oh mark ye, love in my breast?" Hurriedly he drops his eyes. He, un morveux sans conséquence, a boy whose voice has not yet broken, is answering his own question. Yesterday an articulate sensitive young lad toyed with words and phrases of love. Now the wind instruments touch and warm some of these words. He finds himself meaning them in a new way. "I have no notion, unless 'tis he . . . numb and adaze . . . not knowing who could come as my guide . . ." He knows who! "A sigh, a stammer, I know not why . . . a sudden tremor, that is not I . . . 'tis an incessant plaguing but oh 'tis very pleasant, languishing so."

He goes back to the first verse. "Oh mark ye!" He raises his eyes again. The Countess is no longer looking at the music. Eyes meet. Rapidly his eyes drop. She continues to look; shaking her head, smiling ruefully. He has gone further than in Non so più; further than his previous reverential awe at the beauty of a young godmother; further than the intention of the words he is singing. It is donna, not donne; singular, not plural. This is no longer the childish admiration that amused Figaro and Basilio. Here is the cruel old magic itself—none the less genuine for being premature and misplaced. Mozart and da Ponte have portrayed another aspect of Amor.

"Bravo" says the Countess "and what a nice voice! I did not know that you could sing, in addition." "Oh in very truth" says Susanna gaily "all that he does is done by such a standard." Cherubino is silent.

"Hurry now, pretty soldier . . . come here and let me see. It will go perfectly. We are more or less the same height. Take your cloak off." Cherubino, the bel oiseau bleu, takes off the blue swagger cloak that hangs from his shoulders. He stands there open-necked, in the cere-monial shirt-like tunic of a page of the Spanish court—white, em-broidered with silver (the veste blanche in which Antonio saw him run away, later, after jumping from the window). "Susanna!" says the Countess, alarmed. "There's nothing to be frightened of" says

Susanna. "If someone were to come now!" "Let them! But" (Susanna runs to the door) "I'll lock it if you like."

What shall we do with his hair? "Put a nightcap over it, from my dressing-room; go and fetch one, quickly." As Susanna goes into the little room on the left, the Countess notices a paper; the commission, which Basilio had handed to Cherubino before he left for Seville. The preparation of this formal document had been quick work, in the eighteenth (or any) century. "They seem anxious to . . . in the hurry, they have not put on the seal." "The seal of what?" asks Susanna, returning. "Of the commission." "Good heavens, what a hurry! Here is the nightcap." "Hurry, then. Ah, splendid. But"—it is a remark that the Countess will make over and over again, in one way or another—"if *he* were to come, all would be ended."

Traditionally, Susanna now dresses Cherubino as a woman. But da Ponte does not say so. Beaumarchais says "Chérubin se met à genoux. Elle le *coiffe*." When the Count knocks, it is important for the plot that Cherubino should be alone with the Countess, excited and in tears, on his knees in front of her, absurdly and improperly dressed *as a man*, with a woman's *nightcap*. Meanwhile, the Countess and Susanna are merely dawdling away precious time. Note also that Cherubino has got to be dressed *as Susanna* and has been measured for Susanna's height. At *12A29* Susanna goes through the small door at the back to her distant spinster attic, chez les femmes, to fetch "a dress"; thus leaving the Countess alone with Cherubino. They would not have been sufficiently alone if Susanna had been in the dressing-room. It is at *13.3*, *after* Cherubino has gone into the dressing-room, that Susanna returns with a pile of dresses (avec des hardes). The *collet* or *colletto* of *12.63* is the collar of the page's white tunic. The *"mio"* of *12A28* is probably a slip of Mozart's pen; it makes no sense that Susanna, who went to the *dressing-room* to fetch any old nightcap belonging to the Countess, should go *chez les femmes* to fetch any old dress belonging to the Countess—Beaumarchais says "tes hardes", da Ponte says "vestito" without the "mio".

"Come here, and kneel immediately!" Susanna is singing in G; a key that in this opera is apt to follow B♭, in a way that resolves emotional tension. Nothing could be more brilliant or playful than the way in which Susanna's vocal line dances with the various instruments of a chamber-music ensemble (one can hardly call it an orchestra). Cherubino kneels in front of Susanna. He has to be told not to fidget. "Now turn your back obediently." He turns, and finds himself facing the Countess. "Yes, yes. 'Tis quite ideal." Yes it is—he gazes timidly, adoringly, at the Countess (it is not only an anachronism but a major blunder for Cherubino to "make eyes" at the Countess at this stage).

Susanna, for the third time in the opera, finds it difficult to attract someone's attention. It takes her twelve bars to get Cherubino looking at her properly. Then she tests a hypothesis. "My lady has gone out." Great excitement in the violins; Cherubino at once looks round. Once more he is told to turn his eyes to Susanna. This time the Countess tiptoes out of sight. Once more Susanna says (this time emphatically) that "my lady has gone out." Once more he cannot help looking. She *has* gone out! Sorrowfully he looks back at Susanna. He is being trained. Like a puppy he is brought to heel. "And stop the fidgeting! And turn obediently! And look at me! Yes, yes."

At last Susanna can finish coiffing him. He is in male shirtsleeves, open-necked, with a nightcap on. She adjusts his collar and gives him some tips on deportment. "His paces he can show us. Let's let him walk about." At once the orchestra walk with Cherubino. Gaily, admiringly, Susanna prattles on. "With such a roguish air, too! And wonderfully fair, too! So furtively disarming, so elegant and charming. The women will adore him. They will, without a doubt. With reason, reason, reason; I do not doubt."

Mozart and da Ponte could not know that, some years later, Beaumarchais would complete the trilogy by writing *La mère coupable*— a play in which the Countess has a child by Cherubino. But the music and the text are evidence enough that at this particular moment the Countess is not only vividly aware of Cherubino's devotion but uncomfortable at Susanna's prattle. " 'Tis but a foolish jesting" says the Countess. What she means, and what her face should convey at that moment, is something different. She realises that she could fall in love with Cherubino. Susanna makes things worse. "I do declare I am jealous myself, ma'am. Eh, little serpent!" (she takes him by the chin) "What do you mean by it, being such a beauty?" The Countess insists sharply that they should get on with the job. Hurriedly she makes the unnecessary suggestion that the sleeves of Cherubino's shirt-like tunic should be rolled up, so that Susanna's tight-sleeved amadis (not yet fetched) will be able to fit better at the wrist. "Yes, ma'am." "No, further. Like that." Then "What is that ribbon?" For lo and behold the stolen ribbon. It is in use as bandage for a graze (Cherubino, running as usual, had slipped on some pebbles). The Countess has gone white at the sight of the blood-stained ribbon. Susanna cheerfully inspects the wound. "Nothing bad; but, heavens, his arm, even whiter than my own, 'tis more like a woman's." She laughs and gives Cherubino a push. He overbalances, and lands in a kneeling position in front of the Countess; her nightcap on his head, its ribbon on his arm.

"Susanna, still so foolish?" Once more the Countess tells Susanna to drop the subject. She sends Susanna to the dressing-room again, to fetch some English sticking-plaster. She rebukes Cherubino for taking the ribbon; she liked the colour. Susanna returns with the sticking-plaster. Is English sticking-plaster, perhaps, not as sticky as French? The question is, what shall they bandage it on with? Off goes Susanna again, to fetch another ribbon and the dress. She goes through the third door at the back, away to her own attic.

Cherubino is on his knees, with eyes lowered. He says that this ribbon would heal him more quickly. "Why? The new one will do it better." "But if a ribbon . . . was on the hair of . . . if it has touched the skin of . . . a person . . ." "Of a . . . stranger, 'tis good for injured elbows, you are thinking? A property I have never heard of." The Countess, having recovered from her moment of susceptibility to Cherubino's boyish beauty, banters gently. "My lady mocks me" says Cherubino, "and I meanwhile must leave her. "You poor boy, it's unfortunate." "I'm so unhappy" says Cherubino, and bursts into tears. The Countess is moved. But Cherubino is *exalté* (as he was when singing *Non so più*). "Oh God, I wish that I were dying. Then, yes oh then at the moment of expiring, my lips might dare to . . ." The Countess interrupts him, and wipes his eyes with her handkerchief. "Silly boy! Such wild imagination!"

Pierre Augustin Caron, better known as Beaumarchais, was a watchmaker. His plot is like the mechanism of a watch. There is therefore, at once, a knock at the door. "Who is it, who is knocking?" The Countess hears the voice of the Count, asking why the door is locked. She could have let Cherubino out by the third door. But she naturally loses her head. " 'Tis my husband! Oh heavens, I'm ruined. You here! Without a coat on . . . in such a state of . . . and he has had a letter, he is jealous by nature." "You are slow to open" comes the male voice from outside. "I am alone" she calls out in guilty panic. "Truly, I am alone." "To whom are you talking?" "To you. Yes, of course. 'Twas to you." Cherubino, also in panic, runs into the dressing-room (he would have used the third door without being told, if it led to the ante-room in which Act One took place). Cherubino closes the door, without locking it—the key is on the outside. At last the Countess does the right thing; by accident. She takes the key of the dressing-room door, without locking it. She runs to let the Count in.

The Count is not yet particularly angry. But his suspicion grows visibly, as the Countess belies excuses by her agitation. She was putting a new dress on. Susanna was with her, but has gone to her own room. "The way you look, your tone of voice, 'tis unusual" says the Count. "I pray you, read this letter." "Gracious!" thinks the Countess, "the letter that Figaro has written." She looks guiltier than ever. At that moment Cherubino knocks a chair down in the dressing-room. She pretends not to notice the noise. She evades the Count's question. She says it is Susanna. "But you said that she had gone up . . . up to her bedroom." "Or in there" says the Countess, pointing to the dressing-room; "I did not notice." "Susanna! If it is she, why are you in this confusion." "Surely" says the Countess "'tis you, not I, that are in confusion vis à vis her." "'Tis true, 'tis true—that I am *hoping* to see her!" (Note the Count's habit of saying *È vero*, 'tis true.)

The orchestra resume with one of the strangest and most turbulent of C major phrases. At the same time Susanna cheerfully pushes open the third door at the back of the stage. She comes in with a ribbon, and a pile of dresses for Cherubino to try. We hear the Count telling her to come out. "Susanna, show your face then!" A woman, unnoticed but in full view of the audience, is addressed as if she were already in the little room from which she will so soon emerge. Inside the dressing-room Cherubino shivers. The Countess, knowing that Cherubino is there, dares to stand up to her beloved bully. Impatiently he calls Susanna. "Come on, come on, come on." "Impossible" the Countess replies with a B♭. "Be patient! It would be very wrong." "They're quarrelling" thinks Susanna "Oh gracious, has Cherubino gone?" (F♯, G.)

The Count, who is not fond of being contradicted, leans past the dominant. "I need an explanation. Well?" The poor truthful Countess searches again for a fib. In the Italian, she has a slight hesitation before a suitable end of sentence occurs to her. Lo vieta . . . l'onestà. Elle est presque nue, she has got nothing on. Susanna is in full view, dressed and with a big pile of dresses. She is surprised and amused by an explanation which would not in any case decrease the Count's desire to see her. The Count finds it a familiar situation. Everyone knows what is required by the alleged practices of the well-fed men and women who were then kept in elaborate idleness at Versailles—even if the Count reveals himself as provincial and bourgeois in outlook by seeming upset about it. "Familiar situation! A lover has to hide."

In the Act One trio the characters had phrases that were, on the whole, melodically and rhythmically contrasted. Here there are some contrasts but on the whole the characters are merged in a general anxiety. Undifferentiation, in Mozart's mature operatic work, is a deliberately different way of conveying drama. The letter duet (20) is a supreme example; but the first part of the curtsey duet (5) is a more immediately relevant parallel. Ulibishev complained that Marcellina and Susanna should have been given different melodies. Yet their duet is a polite fight in which the veneer of civility is preserved. The present trio is primarily a duet between two people who have loved—and still love—each other very much. They are trying to moderate their quarrel. With the thudding anxiety and tension, there remains a desperate desire to observe the forms of politeness as far as possible. It is music which suits the drama of husband and wife telling each other in identical words to be careful, because the scandal will be embarrassing. A formal musical structure represses the quarrel, so as to have something in reserve for the finale. Abert comments on the basic minuet rhythm, which he regards as a symbol of etiquette. The 3/4 *allegro spirituoso* should not go too fast, any more than the first verse of *Se vuol ballare*. It has a lot in common with the 3/8 *molto andante* of Susanna's icily polite teasing in the finale. It is a rhythm of powerful feelings held, not always successfully, in control.

At *13.36* Susanna's thoughts lead, and are different from the agonised interjections of the Countess and the icy accusations of the Count. Then it all blends in E minor anxiety, felt as much by the Count and Susanna as by the Countess. Susanna's attitude is interesting. Abert, following an unliteral German translation, insists that she is revealing a deep and serious side of her nature; compassion and sympathy for the plight of her mistress. This seems right, according to the feel of the music. Soon the Countess has a climbing chromatic coloratura to G. This brings a dreamlike moment, in which tension is relaxed and reconciliation seems possible. Abert comments on the poetry of it. Susanna has a simple tuneful phrase, surrounded by silence. It is picked up and echoed by the Countess. In vain. Husband and wife are at it again; hammer and tong stuff, to warrant Cherubino's comment at *14.11–12*: "Oh tragedy, oh horrible, incredible affray!" This is a fire that could easily get out of control. Mozart hurriedly damps it down by recapitulation.

The Count makes a reasonable suggestion. If the naked Susanna cannot come out, she can speak. Susanna tiptoes silently to that convenient alcove behind the bed curtain. The Countess resorts to desperate defiance. "No, no, no, do not answer." It is a wonderful phrase, soaring to A. Soon husband and wife are grimly beseeching each other to be careful. Tension mounts. A section that we heard in the dominant returns in the tonic, higher in the voices. Gradually the thoughts of three anxious people merge. Susanna's unspoken thoughts are almost as strong as the spoken thoughts of husband and wife. 'Twill break my lady's heart, she thinks; the Countess soars to top C.

A footnote to the *Classiques Larousse* edition of the play says that the movements in this scene must be executed *avec souplesse et rapidité*, even at the risk of seeming improbable. This note does not go back to earlier editions but Mozart may have formed a similar opinion. There was no need to give Susanna a singing part. The play requires her to be silent, and the libretto would read as well, or better, without her lines. I cannot help wondering whether Mozart half-set the first quarrel as a duet, and then asked for some lines for Susanna in order to help moderate the passion and differentiate the two quarrels.

Charles Mackerras, who has studied these vocal lines in the autograph score, stated in *Opera* for April 1965 that Mozart definitely intended the Countess to have the higher line in ensembles and Susanna the lower line. "Later in the process of composition, Mozart altered almost every ensemble in which the two characters take part, so as to make Susanna always sing the line *above* the Countess." But in this trio "he saw that it would be nonsense for Susanna to sing a brilliant coloratura flourish (going up to high C) when she is supposed to be in hiding . . . throughout this trio one can see evidence of Mozart's alterations (by the abbreviations *Sus.* and *La Con.* in his handwriting)—but *not* at the point where such coloratura passages occur . . . Mozart evidently intended that these should be sung *fortissimo*, proudly and defiantly by the Countess."

She still has the key, and the Count assumes that the door is locked. "Will you then not unlock it?" "Why should I have to, in my private apartments?" "Very well. We will open it without the key." He shouts for a lackey. The Countess implores him not to parade suspicion in front of the servants. Very well, he will fetch the tools himself. He locks the doors, and takes the Countess with him. "If you will deign to accompany me." Raising his voice, he tells the somebody in the dressing-room, the shy Susanna, to wait. With dignity, they go.

The strings have a fluttering, a whisper. It is G major again—yes, only one sharp away from that anxious constraint in C.

There is a four-bar prelude, containing all the musical material. It is an upward swaying (twice), a staccato pattering of violins and violas in thirds, and a stagger (out of step with the 'cellos). Susanna comes out of the alcove, looks round, runs to the dressing-room and (according to Beaumarchais) bends to talk through the keyhole.

"Come out, you need not worry. Come out, it is Susanna. But hurry, but hurry; but hurry, yes oh hurry if you're to get away." (Much of this is sung at Cherubino after he comes out.) Cherubino dawdles, frittering precious bars with gossip about the horror of the scene between husband and wife. *14.13–16* are bracketed in the MS. score and are omitted in most editions. The cut, if made, leaves Susanna responding to Cherubino's ill-timed gossip with a harmonic heightening.

Susanna runs to one door. Cherubino runs to the other. They rattle the locked doors; not too loudly, but with the help of the 'cellos. They run and clasp each other. "Oh what a day, oh what a day" (in D, of course).

Cherubino now takes the matter seriously; "for hiding would be idle." "And he is homicidal" adds Susanna comfortingly. (*14.28–9*, which dwell on the comforting thought, are usually omitted with the same degree of MS. authority.)

For once the practical Susanna is defeated. She gives up hope, and is at her worst for the rest of the duet. Cherubino has more imagination. He looks out of the window. "The flower bed is waiting." "Oh no!" says Susanna. She takes the music back to the subdominant. In *14.37–40*, which make up the ten bars usually omitted, the first violins shiver with repeated top Cs, while Cherubino remarks that he will only break a flower-pot or so. He thus answers Susanna's objection. But he is not convinced by his own answer. Here is the fulfilment of *Non più andrai*. He is a hero, never fear. This is the boy who sang *Non so più*. This is the boy who said wildly "Oh God I wish that I were dying. Then, yes oh then, at the moment of expiring, my lips might dare to . . ." Indeed, they might; Cherubino is once more *exalté*. "Hands away" he says to the clinging Susanna. For love of the Countess, he will do this thing. "Not to hurt her, oh I'd go to death and torture" (G minor). "For her sake, for my lady's" he kisses a pretty substitute and goes this way. But he does not jump when he says so. The Captain draws himself up and gives a military salute. Feminam moriturus salutat. She tries to stop him. "Oh do not go to Hades, 'tis dangerous, I say." The violins go into semiquavers for the first beat of *14.54* (*44*, if your score omits ten bars). Susanna shrieks. There is a crash.

The duet must be done with precision and feathery lightness, utter clarity, apprehensive verve. It is *sempre pianissimo* until the last two bars. The tempo is *allegro assai*, not too fast for the words to be got across.

Susanna sinks to a chair, in horror. Then, quickly, she forces herself to look. At once, with a peal of laughter, she is herself again. "Look at him running! Little demon, he is miles away already." She has an idea. Purposefully she goes to the dressing-room; she will wait for the bully.

Back came husband and wife (*14A8*). All is as he left it. "Will you" he asks "open the door yourself, or must I . . .?" She timidly and tremblingly admits that there is a "he" in the dressing-room. "So it is not Susanna?" "No, nor is it a person whom you have any reason to suspect of a wrong." "Who? Tell me, and I will kill him." "It is . . . a boy. Yes, Cherubino." "Seemingly, I am fated to discover this boy in every bedroom! Here still? He disobeyed me? 'Tis a plot, then. It accounts for the letter, and your evasions, and your excuses. Ah, what an explanation." (And ah what a plot, by plotters Beaumarchais and Mozart.)

Did Cherubino think that the earlier tiff was a tragedy? What would he have thought (and what is Susanna thinking?) of the quarrel that now follows? No damper for the furnace, no shared anxiety, no mitigating artificiality, no minuet, no mutual exhortation to be careful, no concern lest the scandal might be embarrassing, no gentleman to suggest that Susanna can answer from inside if she does not want to show herself. The Count, who so anxiously fancies himself as a Great Lover, now suspects that Cherubino is preferred to him by every woman in the household, *ogni donna in ogni loco*. Two words "Si, Cherubino" produce a situation to challenge any singer's power of interpretation and acting. Somehow, within what Eric Blom called the "aristocratic art of this immaculately polished music" we must feel that a real marriage is in danger of breakdown, a real life in danger, if anyone but Susanna is in the dressing-room; we more often listen to two eminent singers in costume. Compare the libretto with the French original, and you will see that Mozart and da Ponte have gone out of their way at this point, to portray the nuances of an unhappy relationship. The gentle Countess is buffeted, dazed, stabbed by the Count's words. He becomes angrier at each well-meaning remark, each pleading gesture. The total effect at the time is one of serious drama. The more dreadful the quarrel, the funnier it will be when Susanna comes out of the dressing-room. It is one of the great quarrels of European drama; not just one of the *parti serie* of an *opera buffa*.

An E♭ chord, and we are away. This is music so unstoppable that conductor or Count or both are tempted to begin a shade too fast. It is merely *allegro*; and a vocal not an instrumental *allegro* at that. "Out you come, you misbegotten young erotic rascal, you." How tuneful by comparison is the Countess, after running to place herself between her husband and the door! "What a fury! You appal me! When he comes, what will you do?" Her repetitions are natural, cumulative.

The Count only becomes angrier. "Do you dare to interfere still?" He says it. He says it again, with a change of inflection so natural that we know that people might say the same, in the same tone of voice, in any society. Mozart wrote it for Vienna in 1785/6, but it might happen in an English, French, American or Russian city (or village) today. "No, but listen." "I can hear still" he replies, with sarcasm enough to drown the implied civil meaning. "No, but listen" she says again; with just that difference of timing and emphasis which tells us that she was going by his tone of voice, before his meaning dawned on her. Her apparent refusal of his offer makes him angrier. "I can hear still, can hear still, can hear still." He is getting louder—and she has been pushing him further and further away from the door.

"But I swear that all suspicion . . ." At once the vocal and instrumental music is tuneful again. There is desperate sincerity in her tone of voice. But she is talking to a man who has gone tone-deaf. Characteristically she peters out in mid-sentence. She anxiously emphasises a word. "*Every* suspicion . . ." She tries again. "You must not think . . ." Gulp. "that his condition . . ." Gulp. "Collar loosened . . ." Gulp. "Naked forearm . . ." (Da Ponte says "breast" but Beaumarchais says "les bras nus", and we have seen the sleeve of one arm rolled up to the elbow.)

The Countess, a bad liar, is no better at telling the truth. There is an orchestral tremolo, and the Count picks up her words. "Collar loosened? Naked forearm? Tell me more, ma'am." "'Twas to try some women's dresses" she says. It is a coherent truthful sentence. It makes him angrier still. He matches her vocal phrase with sneering words. "The unworthy wife confesses!" One can see that impatient gesture of incredulity. He was not born yesterday. He knows a lie when he hears one! "Proper vengeance is my due." "Oh 'tis shaming, 'tis defaming" she says "oh 'tis cruel, 'tis untrue."

Tension mounts again, creeping up from B♭ to E♭. "Where's that key then?" shouts the Count, only too willing to let the Countess prove her point. His downward arpeggio is like four hammer blows. The clarinets and horns offer the Countess another tuneful phrase. She is too stunned to use it. "But he did . . ." She is not allowed to finish her phrase. Down come the hammer blows again. With a different inflection she tries again. "But he did nothing—and you know it." "I don't know a thing" he shouts.

"Go, you scum, you less than human, you unfaithful wicked

woman." By a simple change from "voi" to "tu" the Italian sentence says more than the meaning of its words. The Count's abuse is vulgar, insensitive, morally retarded. The pot, that called a new kettle a misbegotten erotic rascal, calls the swan black. The Countess is being addressed as no eighteenth-century Count would address his wife. It is the end. She is divorced from him. She is scum, canaille, beneath contempt. "Yes, I . . ." Pause. "Go . . ." Pause. "But . . ." "But naught shall save you!" he shouts. "Was . . ." "Naught shall save you!" he shouts again. " . . . *not* unfaithful!" Having said what she had to say, she gives him the key. "Your face betrays you" he shouts. The nobleman draws his sword. "He shall perish" the nobleman says, brandishing the sword at the closet in which he expects to find Cherubino. "Oh his jealousy doth blind him; will it cost a human life?" "As he dies, I shall remind him that he dared to love my wife."

For nearly twenty bars the music remains on a plateau of wrath and despair. Then it tumbles away. Two and a half beats of silence. A gingerly little phrase, low down on the strings. An astonished exclamation by the Count. Another gingerly phrase, going on down. An even more astonished exclamation from the Countess. A pause.

Sword in one hand, key in the other, the Count goes towards the door. At that moment the door opens, leaving the characters well spaced out on the stage. There, a demure little Jill-in-the-box, stands Susanna. It is a moment of comic relief but must on no account be played as farce. Susanna has been listening, waiting for the bully. We know what she thought during the trio. We could guess how she reacted to this quarrel; but we do not need to guess, for we are told that she is *tutta grave*—straight-faced, thin-lipped. Instinct tells her that the most effective and devastating way to defend her mistress and deal with this man is to humiliate him by politeness. A servant re-establishes the civilised courtesies which the nobleman has betrayed.

The strings begin a simple rhythmical phrase. As Levarie says, it is really a minuet (*molto andante*, 3/8, B♭). "But, master?" The strings begin again. "You seem quite aghast, sir." Has a husband been duped? The horns mock him. "Your sword should be ready." Horns. "To slice and behead me." Horns. "The boy misbegotten" (a dramatic hornless reminder of *15.3*) "'tis I as you see." Horns. "The boy misbegotten, 'tis I as you see."

Bassoon and first violins peal down from F. "Ah, quelle école, che scola!" Lindor l'écolier (*BS2.14*) has been taught a lesson. Susanna is taking advantage of an opportunity to do what Figaro declared in *Se vuol ballare* that he intended to do (with a similar horn accompaniment). "Oh I am bewildered to see what I see" thinks the Count. "I too am bewildered" thinks the Countess. "They both are bewildered" thinks Susanna, capping their lines with a quicker-moving triplet figure.

Back come the mocking horns. "Who else is . . ." It is a natural question, and the Count is a believer in what he sees. "Go in, sir, and see what you see." Go in, yes. He knows that he must; he knows also, from her icy tone, what he will find. "Go in, sir" she insists. In goes the unhappy detective.

The tempo changes to a driving *allegro* in B♭. The Countess, believe it or not, uses the precious few seconds of privacy to make one of her too usual announcements that she is not feeling very well. It seems an odd remark to make, when the violins are leading the way with a simple motif (*15.167*) of great rhythmical vitality. But the violins are telling us that neither they nor Mozart take this next episode too seriously. Abert suggests that this motif is a secret titter.

The violins and Susanna listen amusedly to the Countess. Cheer up, says a new motif (*15.171*). It is a tuneful motif that serves all purposes, from cheering up to wheedling, from dignified rebuke to a sense of guilt, from acquiescence to reconciliation. The common factor is Mozart's amusement in the ironies of a false situation. Let me show you what happens, says Mozart, when these three characters are angry, or forgive and are forgiven, for the wrong reasons. What happens? The women begin well but are out-manoeuvred by the Count.

"Stop moaning, stop sighing" says Susanna to her mistress; unceremoniously, but time is short. "The boy got away." The best Susannas manage by a miracle to point rather late at the window without being seen by the Count when he is coming back. We hold our breath for her. The Count returns, looking confused. His feelings are richly mixed. Three loud chords, with expressive slurred sweeps on the violins, prepare us for a resentful beginning. "'Twas all an illusion" (twice). "Could eyes then deceive me?" There is always something wrong about evidence that we do not want to believe. "I stand in confusion." (True.) "I wronged you, forgive me." He sings it twice, resentfully. It is unfair of women to expect one to be a gentleman. He reveals the depth of his penitence by adding "'Tis cruel frivolity, this game that you play." The bully is sorry for himself. In brisk serene thirds the women deny the charge. "'Tis your cruel folly we reveal and repay." One up to the women; on merits.

The Countess is a long-suffering woman. But the Count now tries to wriggle out of a predicament by saying, with the proper *Voi*, that he loves her. It is too much, after what he had said during the quarrel. Does he not remember that she is scum? She reminds him. Two up to the women. The embarrassed Count asks Susanna to help him soothe her. It serves him right, Susanna replies. "Suspicion may damn the suspicious, it may. Suspicion was damning to you, sir, I say." Three up to the women.

The music is a miracle of compression. Not a second later, the Countess is complaining with desperate sincerity. "I love, and am loyal." (Yes, yes, say the orchestra.) "I care for your honour." (Yes, yes, say the orchestra.) "For this you revile and abuse me today." It is so unfair. Does he not know me at all? There are people one can trust in life, even if appearances are against them.

This little outburst remains in the Count's mind; we shall hear him thinking about it at the beginning of Act Three. But it is a false move in the present context, for it draws attention to matters which are better forgotten. The Count appeals again to Susanna for help—a mere upward fourth instead of a seventh. Susanna repeats her answer to it, lower in the voice. It is unwise of the Countess to push a bit of luck this far! Susanna turns to the Countess. She makes an urgent signal to her to calm down. Then she even takes the Count's side. "My lady!" The Count meekly follows suit. "Rosina!" He is calling the Countess by her Christian name—an unusual procedure between husband and wife in civilised society at the time, but one that serves to recall, to her and to the audience, the story of *The Barber of Seville*.

Susanna's signal had been in vain. The Countess is stung into protest. "How cruel! 'Twas she you adored so!" The key, which had only briefly touched the dominant, was already back in sub-dominant dumps; and now goes down towards A♭, below the normal key range of this opera. There is a dramatic fermata. With dignity the Countess goes on. "But I am your wife, sir, the wife you ignore so; and sad is my life, sir, since you went away." Four up to the women, in appearance. They accept the Count's plea, which runs: "Oh see my contrition at your admonition. Oh hear my petition, have mercy I pray." They all sing together. Reconciliation seems near.

Yet back come those slurred sweeps on the violins, and the Count is asking awkward questions. "The boy and the key, then?" "Were part of the testing" they say. "Your shaking, your shivering?" he asks. "Were part of the jesting" they say. "That terrible letter was . . .?" Impulsively—it is a tribute to the essential truthfulness of both women —they betray a secret; the letter "was Figaro's, you owe him that, he gave it to Basilio." Instantly the Count vows to punish both men—

Basilio as well. "The wretches! I'll show them that . . ." Oh no, say
the women; we do not forgive so that you can repay. Oh very well,
says the Count smugly. Anyway his Rosina could never be unfor-
giving. She at once throws away the advantages that she and Susanna
have won. "I cannot, Susanna, be hard and inhuman. The fury of
woman is less than they claim." Susanna disgustedly agrees. "My lady,
I know it, with men it is useless, whatever we do, it is always the same.
We flatter and threaten, we threaten and flatter; whatever we do, it is
always the same." (Would Susanna's own fury ever be "less than they
claim"?) "Oh look at me" says the Count. The Countess refuses, with
the last spark of her anger. "Oh look at me" he says a second time. She
refuses with less conviction. "Oh look at me" he says a third time. He
kneels in apparent repentance. The violins and violas begin a gently
descending series of the 15.171 motif, against long wind chords. "And
this is your sentence: today will have taught you to love her again."
Maybe. But meanwhile the reconciliation has a beautiful dreamlike
unreality (Abert). There is a pause which, says Newman, cannot be too
scrupulously observed.

Noisily the orchestra resume. They are for a moment the local band;
a nice band, whom we shall meet again at the end of Acts Three and
Four. We hear a thoroughly unexpected G major—brisk, brash, and
bright. Levarie tells us that the rhythm, which has affinities with the
choral rhythms of Acts One and Three, is taken from popular dance
music of the day.

Figaro bustles in. He creates an impression of being unaware of all
that has happened. But if so he would not be looking for the Count
here or now. We know from 15.508 that he saw Cherubino jump from
the window. In any case the great quarrel was probably audible, to a
household that would be intrigued to know why the hunt had returned. Figaro needed some pretext to come to the help of the women.
It is a bold and wary man who dares, without much hope, to repeat the
tactic that had already failed in Act One—an attempt to persuade the
Count that he will lose face with the tenantry if the wedding is not
brought forward.

"My lord, they are ready to play for the wedding." (Do you hear,
do you hear?) "The pipers are piping." (Do you hear, do you hear?)
"The fifers are fifing, your vassals are frolicking, yodelling, rollicking,
bawling, and calling us all to begin." "No, not such a hurry" says the
Count. "The people will worry" says Figaro noisily, feigning surprise.
"You'll answer a question before we begin" says the Count, with a
long trill on the violins and violas. "To talk would be awkward before

we begin" thinks Figaro. (He drops to a low G but is not yet particularly perturbed.) Meanwhile, the women were hoping that Figaro
will not feign ignorance. "To baulk would be awkward before we
begin" they think. "My ace I will place, I will play for a win" thinks
the gleeful Count. There is a short pause.

As so often, the next section begins with a simple keynote. This one
is C; 2/4 *andante*. "Here's a letter, master Figaro, you have seen before,
I know." It is an unpretentious line (in quavers, mainly) giving not much
hint of the miracles to come. And yet what about the swagger of those
few semiquavers? As the first violins step demurely up to G, the vocal
line does a gay little frolic and gets there first from C. Master Figaro!
A fig for you! The Count is confident, sarcastic. There is a preparatory
undercurrent of semiquavers in the second violins.

The violins are enjoying the situation. They trill. The Count's words
and tone of voice reveal that the women—curse them—have blabbed.
Figaro is momentarily stunned. But he expected trouble. He looks at
the document as if it were strange to him. No, he has never seen it
before. He reads it, and grins incredulously at its absurd contents. "No,
not ever." The women look agitated, and there are (says Abert) unmistakable secret winks in the orchestra. Susanna, the Countess and the
Count ask "No, not ever?" in turn. "No" Figaro says to each. They ask
together. He gives them a "No" each.

Twice the simple vocal line becomes a long daisy chain, from
Susanna to the Countess, from the Countess to the Count, from the
Count to Figaro. It is in the dominant, with more and more semiquavers, more and more daisies. The women plead and question; the
Count follows up gruffly, with loud orchestral backing; Figaro dogged-
ly denies all knowledge of the letter. "That you gave to Don Basilio?"
"To deliver?" "So you see that . . ." "Absurd, oh no." "Nor about
the pretty lover?" "In the garden, under cover?" "You can gather
that . . ." "I don't, oh no."

"No denials" says the Count, two octaves below the first violins.
"No excuses" he continues; while bassoon, viola and 'cello pick up the
tune. "Do not lie" (he and the violin over-reach the other three instruments) "for lies are useless". (Bassoon, viola, and 'cello show that they
can pick up this one too.)

"I can read them in your eyes." We are overwhelmed with music. Then
Figaro is given a simple accompaniment for his retort: "Eyes may lie,
but I not, ever." "Very clever, very clever" say the women "but it was
a vain endeavour, we have told him, do be wise." Figaro complacently
repeats his witticism, as the women sing "But it was a vain endeavour."

"You admit to . . ." "Nothing, nothing." "You confess that . . ." "No, by heaven!" Then the women give him the one important piece of information. "Silly fellow, you're forgiven, ended is our little play." At once, and without admitting that he wrote that letter, an indomitable opportunist seizes his advantage. "Then to have a happy ending in theatrical tradition we can wed with your permission, we can wed without delay." It is good straight-faced diplomacy, back in the tonic. The violin trills are for matrimony. "Oh my Lord, no more defer it" say Figaro and Susanna "we'd prefer it straight away." "Oh my Lord, no more defer it" says the Countess "they'd prefer it straight away." "Marcellina, Marcellina!" says the Count, "why oh why does she delay?"

Although Figaro has been scoring no marks for truthfulness, he has snatched victory from defeat, with an impressive display of doggedness and wit. Admittedly Marcellina is still a danger. Admittedly Antonio is coming upstairs with his broken flower-pots. But to escape one danger is to continue travelling hopefully. Va toujours, va toujours.

The tempo changes to *allegro molto*. Rumty-ti-tum go the orchestra, tutti. The rumty-ti is a C. The tum is down on A, taking us to F major. We hear a slurred violin figure. The melodic and contrapuntal beauty of the *andante* section is far away. In its place is a rhythmic excitement, expressively denuded of melody.

In bursts Antonio the gardener. He is known to all present as a habitual drunkard; mon ivrogne de jardinier, as the Count says in the play. He is already—rather early in the day, but a man should be getting ready to celebrate his niece's wedding properly—half-drunk, *demi-gris*. Indignantly, he clutches and fondles some broken pots of flowers. In an aggrieved tone of voice he addresses the Count. "Ah, moy lord, moy lord." "What's the matter?" asks the Count.

Antonio is no fool. But he is at present too fuddled and angry to express himself clearly. "Will you punish him, who was it, who?" The words are difficult to articulate clearly at such a speed, given the character and condition of Antonio; but the words must get through. "What has happened, and why do you splutter?" A patter-like precision comes more easily to Antonio's four listeners. Even so, it is hard to escape the conclusion that the *molto* of *allegro molto* must not be allowed to go too far. "Ay but listen" says Antonio. "We listen to you." "Ay but listen." "We listen anew."

We listen in patience and with amusement while Antonio gathers his boozy wits. The music settles into what Abert calls an orgy of triplets. "From this balcony into the garden, what they toss every day is unfair, sir." It is a nice glimpse into the domestic routine of Aguas Frescas; and into Antonio's daily resentments. "But a moment ago, I was there, sir, 'twas a person, a man that they threw." Nothing could be more rudimentary than Antonio's vocal line, and even the Italian words can easily get muffled and lost. They must not be lost.

The Count feels better at once. "From this window?" "And look at what he did to the . . ." "The flower-pots?" The women turn to Figaro. Like Bertie Wooster, asking Jeeves if he has been eating plenty of fish recently, they hope his wits are in good order. The Count is laboriously thinking. The women and Figaro are disconcerted, but ask: "Who allowed the old boozer up here?" "Where, where, where did he go, have you reckoned?" asks the Count. "He was off, sir, in less than a second; flew away like a bird, very near."

Antonio, as well as Susanna, has told us how quickly Cherubino was running. We are not surprised. Susanna whispers to Figaro that it was Cherubino who jumped. Figaro winks. "I saw him." He bellows with laughter; a good non-committal way of keeping one's end up while one thinks. He goes on laughing, oblivious of cries of "Shut your mouth" and "Why the bellow?" Twice he says that Antonio is drunk. The Count makes Antonio repeat his evidence. The women and Figaro try to discredit the witness. "Tell me more then" says the Count to Antonio "for surely you saw him." "No, I did not" admits Antonio. There is a ripple of relief from Susanna and the Countess. At once Figaro seizes the advantage. "What a fuss, it is out of proportion, oh you jittering blubbery toper! If it has to come into the open, it was I who came down with a bump."

"You? How could you?" Back comes the slurred violin figure, and the Count is duly incredulous. The women have a delighted aside: "A notion of genius." "You? How could you?" (Antonio, belatedly echoing the Count.) "I say you're a liar" jeers the Count. "You have grown a lot fatter and higher" jeers Antonio (with a plain fp chord in the orchestra, to help ensure that the words are heard and understood). "I say you're a liar, a liar" repeats the Count. Back come the triplets. Antonio adds triumphantly that "You were certainly not such a lump." "Doubled up? As one is, for a jump." It is a neat reply by Figaro. But Antonio has been putting two and two together. "Well, I never!" he says suddenly. The women are apprehensive. "Well, what is it?" asks the Count. "'Twas the boy, in appearance." "Cherubino?" asks the Count. The gardener nods. "Curse him" think the women. Figaro is unperturbed. Cheerfully he points out that Cherubino is riding to

Seville. "And we all saw him off, little devil. You remember? You gave him a mare." It is too much for fuddled wits. "But I never said this was a horseman, there was never a horse in the air."

"Give me patience" says the Count, raising half-clenched hands to some patron deity. "What a day!" say the women to each other. "Of course, yes of course, man" says the Count to Antonio with remarkable restraint. "'Tis a muddled affair" say the women, much relieved. The Count turns in despair to Figaro. "So 'twas you?" "That is true." "What befell?" 'Sudden fear." "Why the fear?" Figaro obliges with a story. Like Pooh-bah he adds corroborative detail to give artistic verisimilitude to an otherwise bald and unconvincing narrative. He not only admits (at last) that he wrote that letter. He adds, after a violin gesture of leaping:

> So I leapt with my heart palpitating,
> And I twisted my foot, sir, as well.

Like Pooh-bah he will regret his story. Meanwhile, it serves. Figaro is full of self-pity, as the music slides into B♭ (andante, 6/8).

There follows an episode in which, according to Abert, Mozart was leaving maximum scope for good expressive acting. Figaro holds his F on the word "well" (piè) for two long bars, while the strings lightly sketch out a new tune in B♭. It is a rhythmical fragment, admirably suited to cat and mouse games such as the Count and Figaro now proceed to play with each other. In the context of a swiftly-moving opera it is a delicious and deliberate dawdling; for just the right length of time. It is not, taken in isolation, very slow.

The illiterate Antonio holds out a paper to Figaro. "Then you'll take back this wonderful writing, that fell out of . . ." "Oh no, I will instead" says the Count, and takes it. "Now I'm trapped again" thinks Figaro. "Do not look frightened" whisper the women. The Count has been reading; and proceeds to enjoy a leisurely inquisition. "Kindly say what is this I have read." Eh bien, l'homme aux expédients, vous ne devinez pas? The admirable Figaro pulls papers from various pockets. "I-i-i-in a moment." (He drags out the "I-i-i-in" for five beats.) "So many, in my pockets." It wasn't this four-page letter from Marcellina; or this begging letter from the poor poacher in prison; or the inventory of furniture at the hunting lodge. "I should say 'tis a list of his creditors" suggests Antonio. "Or . . . of your empty bottles" comes the instant repartee. The Count wants Figaro's answer. "Go away, fellow" he says to Antonio, not unkindly. "Shut the door behind you" say the others less kindly. Antonio scowls at Figaro. "Very well then, but don't let me find you (on my flower beds again)." Precious seconds are gained; there is a short slanging match between Figaro and Antonio, punctuated by cries of "Shut the door behind you" from the Count and the women. A relatively loud climax is reached, with almost the whole orchestra. The music has gone into the dominant.

The gently insistent quavers continue, building up suspense. "Well then?" says the Count. He casually re-opens the paper. The Countess recognises it. "Oh no!" she thinks in horror "'tis the page's commission." She whispers to Susanna. Susanna whispers to Figaro. It is usually assumed that she is helping Figaro out of a difficulty. In fact, this time she is as horrified as the Countess: Tout est perdu, c'est le brevet. "No fishing" warns the Count. But it is Figaro's turn to take the initiative. At once he sees what can be made of the apparently bad news. He takes courage (as is hinted by da Ponte's ironic "Coraggio"). He plays his fish. He has an unhurried headache in G minor. "Oh my headache, oh my headache." Then with a start (dramatic art) he remembers. "It is the commission. Yes, he gave it to me when he went."

Remorselessly the dawdling quavers proceed. The Count raises a sardonic eyebrow. "For what reason?" Figaro fishes. "It needed . . ." "It needed?" prompts the Count mockingly. To his eye the document is in order. Fortunately the Countess knows it is not, and why. It needed proper sealing, she whispers to Susanna. Proper sealing, whispers Susanna to Figaro. This time she is consciously, gleefully, helping him; good teamwork is going to win a victory. "I'll hound you" says the Count, relishing his own certain victory. Figaro, with even greater relish, is master of the situation. "It is *usual* . . ." he says with heavy head-shaking tact. He pauses without saying what is usual. He is tantalising the Count. The thudding repetitive tension grows. "Oh hurry, confound you" says the Count uneasily. Like a small boy doing exactly the opposite of what he is told, Figaro drags out a simple sentence interminably—until he reaches the key words. "It is usual, surely, to . . . seal them."

The music, after an even more interminable modulation, is back in B♭. The Count had not noticed the lack of a seal. Taken by surprise, he stamps his foot on the floor and tears the commission into many pieces—a splendidly symbolic action which should be done with emphasis. "Oh my head will come off, it is reeling: I was never so puzzled before." "If I weather the storm into harbour" thinks Susanna (with a long F for the first syllable of the word harbour) "I will not go to sea any more." The Countess thinks the same. "How he stamped on the floor, 'twas a marvel" thinks Figaro "but he knows less than I do, I'm sure." Once again, we have a fairly harmonious conclusion. The lull will not last. But its harmony subtly helps to prepare the reconciliation at the end of the opera; the Count and Countess have more in common than one would yet suspect.

There is a pause. Then comes a good strong E♭ (for bassoons, first and second horns, first and second trumpets, drums, first and second violins, violas, 'cellos, first flutes, first oboes and first clarinets). The few remaining instruments (including some third violins) have a G. We are definitely back in E♭ major, the key of the Act as a whole. But this is no solemn introduction to *Porgi amor*, no chord to begin that harrowing quarrel between husband and wife. It is a brief pompous triumphal prelude, to mark the entry of Marcellina, Bartolo and Basilio. The rhythmical figure recalls the angrier, less dignified entry of Antonio; but that was *allegro molto*, and this is only *allegro assai* with scope for acceleration later.

"Give us justice, give us justice." The words of the elderly avengers ring out as a kind of antiphonal response to their orchestral prelude, thus preparing the way for a section which is largely antiphony—the old versus the young (save that the Count, himself a young man, significantly chooses to side with the old). By way of sincere subconscious flattery of the Count, the trio use a dotted crotchet rhythm.

The short prelude is repeated. "Listen, listen to our plea" say the elderly trio, again in dotted crotchets. The Count is delighted, and has an unusually melodious thought: "Marcellina is arriving at the right time to comfort me." The Countess, Susanna and Figaro are thrown into confusion. Disunitedly they contemplate the smug elderly trio. Each has the same rueful thought. "Marcellina is arriving. How embarrassing for me!" But they are soon united in resentment (dotted crotchets!).

Figaro appeals to the Count, as one young man to another. "They are muddled, old and feeble. Will you let them baffle me?" The Count walks across the stage to stand with the elderly. "I shall give these worthy people every opportunity." The mere *words* are fair and judicial; Marcellina can, without moving, hand the Count the fateful IOU. She claims that it is a formal written contract. She turns to Figaro. "You, sir, undertook to marry me." She breaks into excited patter. "So tarry not, but carry on, and marry little me." Orchestral hubbub. The young call out "Monstrous, monstrous." "Aha" says the

Count virtuously "be silent, be silent, be silent." It is the young who have to be silent. The elderly "can state their case to me."

Bartolo speaks. He echoes Marcellina. He states, with a revealing slip of the tongue, that he is the *defending* counsel. Yes, the singer of *La vendetta* is again on the defensive. "Chosen as defending counsel, I'll adopt a benchside manner, give an ipecacuanha pill of technicality." More patter. More hubbub. More protests from the young. "Aha" says the Count again "be silent, be silent, be silent, they can state their case to me."

Basilio also echoes Marcellina (and has presumably been paid to support her story). "I'm a man of known discretion" he says. ("You can tell me in confidence" he said in *6A67* "I am a friend, and will tell it to no one"). "I provide corroboration of a solemn affirmation that was overheard by me." He too has broken into patter. For the third time there is hubbub. "They are crazy" say the young. "Aha, be silent and obedient" says the Count "let me read it, let me read it; no more impropriety!"

Finally we have 150 bars or so of choral tableau; *più allegro*, then *prestissimo*. The young think "I'm bewildered, I'm dejected, disregarded, unprotected. 'Tis a very fiend incarnate who enables them to laugh." The old think "Path of roses, path of roses; yes, we have them by the noses. I believe a guardian angel has enabled us to laugh." There is fine pictorial music about the fiend incarnate, alias the guardian angel; who sings smugly with the old as he reads Marcellina's contract.

It is Susanna who feels the tragedy most deeply. As she sees Marcellina triumphant, she has heartfelt lines of misery and detestation. This is the Susanna who at the beginning of Act One was unworried by the Count's antics; who at the end of the trio in Act One was fearful lest worse befall; who has been present during the two quarrels; who, as we shall see, can hardly bear to play her pretended part in a duet with the Count in Act Three. The Countess on the other hand, her marriage in ruins, is full of sympathy for Susanna and Figaro. Angrily Figaro bides his time.

So ends the great finale. Duet, trios, quartets, quintets, quartet, septets; E♭, B♭, G, C, F, B♭, E♭; *allegro* to *prestissimo*, by way of *molto andante, allegro, allegro, andante, allegro molto, andante, allegro assai*, and *più allegro*; unstoppable from the first bar to the last. "Musically" wrote Walter Legge "this is the most masterly ensemble, not only in this opera but in all Mozart. For nearly twenty minutes the music flows unbroken, responding to every turn and twist of the complicated and fast-moving comedy, illuminating, reflecting, commenting upon the action and the widely differing emotions of the participants. Step by step with the action, the music intensifies the surprises, adds point to the subtleties, and yet casts over the whole rather sordid play of intrigue a magical cloak of the most enchanting music that, while it is always faithful to the incident, transmutes it into the purest gold of beauty."

Quite so. No wonder we are tempted to feel that Acts Three and Four may be a prolonged anti-climax.

ACT THREE

15A, Che imbarazzo	*18A, Eccovi, o caro amico*
16, Crudel, perché finora	*19A, Io vi dico, signor*
16A, E perché fosti	*20, "Che soave zeffiretto"*
17, Hai già vinta la causa	*20A, Piegato è il foglio*
⌈ *18B, Andiamo, andiam, bel paggio*	*21, Ricevete, o padroncina*
⌊ *19, E Susanna non vien!*	*21A, Queste sono, Madama*
17A, È decisa la lite	*22, Ecco la marcia, andiamo*
18, Riconosci in questo amplesso	

ACTS THREE AND FOUR, like Acts One and Two, are better performed without an interval or cuts. (Michael Kelly may have thought of Acts Three and Four as the "second act"—see p. 117).

The words of *18B* and *19*, the two episodes which do not come from the play, were written to come after *17*. I saw this, one day in 1963, when translating one of the nonsenses (*18A13*, between *18.28* and *19.1–4*) which are created by the traditional order. By itself it was a very tiny piece of literary detection—certainly correct, but of academic interest only. It became slightly larger and more important when I saw what followed from it: the general musical structure had probably also been planned as A major (the *No, no, yes* duet), D major (the Count) C major (the Countess), F major (the sextet), B♭ major (the letter duet) and G major (the village girls) *in that order*. It is a typically straightforward order; with the final jump, back to G major, which is in any case characteristic of this opera.

The discovery became more interesting still when I realised that the inferred original order of music and words would make the Act as coherent and compelling as Acts One and Two. Yet the usual order goes back to the autograph score and first printed libretto; and was almost certainly used in performances which Mozart himself conducted. There could be no mistake. The order had been deliberately changed.

The commentators—from Niemetschek to Nissen, from Stendhal to Ulibishev, from Jahn to Abert, from Dent to Newman—have occasionally asserted their independence of mind by condemning Mozart for this or that apparent blemish in one of these three operas, or in *Così fan tutte*. I was myself busy discovering that, almost without exception, they had thereby succeeded in making fools of themselves. I was therefore most unhappy to find myself toying with the hypothesis that Mozart and da Ponte had deliberately committed an artistic blunder by preferring, instead of an excellent order which they themselves had thought of using, the incoherent order which has led everyone for so long to feel that Act Three is a comparatively weak act. I have never been able to believe that da Ponte decided these things and is therefore to blame. Nor was I much consoled by Alfred Einstein's convenient dictum that Mozart's second thoughts are not always to be preferred to his first. As a fidelity hound, I did not know what to think.

In July 1964 Christopher Raeburn discovered the simple answer. (Simple, *when* you have once thought of it!) It was eighteenth-century practice to let minor parts, like Bartolo and Antonio, be doubled. At the first performance of *Le Nozze* Francesco Bussani sang both parts. Between the planning and the writing out of the music, someone realized that Bussani would have no time to change clothes after *18A*. So the order of the act was hurriedly changed, by moving the only two bits whose order is not predetermined by the play. We published the joint discovery in *Music and Letters* (April 1965) with the detailed evidence. We inferred that "it is certainly legitimate and probably preferable to go back to the original order in productions of *Figaro* that have two singers for the two parts."

Charles Mackerras, who has since put the theory into practice at Sadler's Wells, was at first hesitant for a valid musical reason. *18B* and *17A* have music written to fit the traditional order. A small musical scar is twice left, when the originally intended order is restored.

Peter Stadlen asked why, if Mozart and da Ponte had all this in mind when planning and writing Act Three, they forgot it in Act Four. They allowed Bartolo and Antonio on stage together at the final lift from B♭ major to G major in *28.335*. Did they forget? Only Antonio sings solo in this final scene (two words, *28.371*). Bartolo is needed on stage at *28.431* as the male of one of the three reconciled couples. But he could have been any portly member of the chorus, dressed in the right clothes.

The *Mozart Jahrbuch* for 1966 has republished the *Music and Letters* article in German (translated by Christel Wallbaum).

The curtain rises, and the Count is alone in a big hall. Once again the dialogue is so compressed that every phrase matters. But the crucial words in the opening soliloquy are: "to doubt her at all is to offend her . . . indeed, she has too keen a sense of self-respect and of my honour. My honour! Where the deuce do my little pleasures banish it."

The Countess and Susanna are at the back of the hall. The Countess has been urging Susanna on. "Don't be frightened, go and tell him you will meet him in the garden; I will go in your place, you will not be deceiving Figaro." The Countess has had the brightest idea of all, between Acts; Cherubino is no longer available, but even if he was still available, it is far better for the Countess to go to the bogus assignation herself. "You dare not? You need not worry. Please, please do it. For me . . ."

The Countess goes out. What she has said is sensible. Why then is Susanna so reluctant to play her part? For all her mimicry and high spirits, she is lost when it comes to the devious game of putting on an act of this kind. With a sinking heart she walks towards him. At that moment he is thinking about her. "Has she betrayed my secret? Oh, if she has!" He sees her. Like Marcellina in Act One he thinks aloud in order to be overheard. "He shall marry the duenna." Susanna gets the point. She hears her own voice—a distant, unfamiliar, breathless voice—say "My lord." "What is it?" asks the Count peevishly. "I think you are angry with me?" "What is it, what do you want?" "My lady has her usual vapours and wants to borrow your little smelling bottle." "Take it." "I will return it." "You may need it yourself." "Oh but girls of my station in life don't have the vapours." "Not even if one loses a bridegroom just before the wedding?" "I shan't lose him. We shall pay Marcellina with the dowry that you promised me." "What dowry?" "I understood that . . ." "Yes, if you had been willing to understand me." "But I know my duty; and your Excellency's wish is also my wish."

She has agreed to be his mistress, and has sensed that the Count wanted, above all, her affectionate consent. He is a strange character. In the play he has a brief and urbane reply to Susanna's declaration of love. *Pourquoi donc, cruelle fille, ne me l'avoir pas dit plus tôt?* In the opera, this is extended into a revelation of uncertainty and self pity. Melodious, yes. But also plaintive and hesitant. He is in A minor and uses the minor third (C♮) six times for a single couplet of verse; six times, and always on a strong beat. "How cruel of you to let me wait for the love I vowed." The notion of the "cruel she" inspired Shakespeare to some of his most lyric scenes. But it is richly comic that the Count should have such a tender regard for feelings—when they are his own. And how does the cruel she reply? In a simple legato phrase with string quartet. Gently she reminds him that "My lord, I am a woman, therefore the time is allowed." When she is at the top of her vocal phrase the string quartet have the kind of chord which invites her to linger a little; as they all lingered—just a little—in the previous bar. With an effort Susanna lifts her line into a confident-seeming C major.

Softly the flutes enter. The first violins revert to the quiet rising staccato quavers that accompanied the Count's hesitancies in his opening couplet. The Count, very unsure of himself, can hardly believe Susanna. He proceeds unwittingly to torment her by a series of silly questions. "You will be there to meet me?" The violins have caressing semiquavers, alternating with questioning quavers. "I will be there for you" she says. Softly the horns enter, then the bassoons; as the Count continues with "You do not mean to cheat me?" Shyly she reassures him. "No, no, I will be true." "You'll meet me?" "Yes." Her unbelievable word is supported by the crotchet dance of flutes and bassoons. The violins sigh in quavers. "You will not cheat me?" "No!" "You will not cheat me?" "I will be true, I will, I will be true." She has overcome his doubts. He has no notion of the misery she is inflicting on herself. He believes her. He pauses. There are moments when nature seems to stop.

"I feel oh so contented; joyful, yes, joyful withal." The Count is in A major at last, but Susanna has an aside that is one of two clear pieces of evidence of her misery. "I lied when I consented. Forgive me, lovers all." When a Mozart is in his prime, it is child's play to combine that misery with the Count's joy. And here are bassoon and violin, helping the Count to express the joy. "You will be there to meet me." There is no question mark now. Susanna compels herself to make an appropriate remark. Her misery increases as the Count, so peevish a few moments ago, becomes more and more like the nice young man who won Rosina's heart. Her concentration begins to fail, her attention wanders. I will be there for you, she says, more or less echoing the Count's joyful phrase. "You do not mean to cheat me." No, no, I will be true, she says, echoing the wrong phrase. We have been taken far beyond the four simple remarks in MF3.9 from which the section of the libretto is adapted.

The Count now shows a tenderness that might make any woman's heart turn over. Mozart has taken the trouble to mark *dolce* above the Count's line at *16.42*. It is an intensification that should be conveyed to every member of the audience. The violins sigh more happily than in *16.23*. "You'll meet me!" "Yes." "You will not cheat me!" "No."

Then the Count repeats his first phrase instead of (as in *16.24*) the second one. "Then you will meet me!" Susanna is no longer attending. Her mind is on the man who has the right to speak so tenderly to her. "No" she says. "No?" Viola and 'cello have a downward phrase, thrown in by Mozart from the prodigality of his genius. "Yes!" Earnestly, desperately, Susanna corrects herself. "I will be there for you."

The mistake would have been fatal, twenty bars earlier. But now the Count is as gay and serene as he would have been if Susanna had accepted his proposition in Act One, before Figaro's Machiavellian strategy began to undermine his lordly confidence. By now he simply thinks that the girl is overcome by the ardour he is condescending to bestow on her. He begins again, this time with "You will not cheat me"! Once more Susanna's wits wander. This time it is yes that she says by mistake.

In the remainder of the duet, words are relatively unimportant. We hear the misery of Susanna's "I told a lie"—her F♯ is answer enough to the Count's "I feel oh so contented". But from then on we listen to a deliberately conventional duet; much of it in parallel tenths. If it were not for these occasional passages of relaxation we could hardly hope to endure the subtleties of this opera.

The precise meanings of this duet are difficult to follow in Italian, even when one knows more than enough Italian to understand the simple meaning of the words on paper. When sung, they call for a speed of audience response which is only possible when Italian is second nature to the listener; or when it is sung in translation!

The opera has a hero, two heroines, and a villain. Figaro and Susanna, a fine manly man and a fine womanly woman, are more fallible than the conventional hero and heroine. The Countess, who is so sympathetically presented, has her failings. Conversely therefore, do not expect to find that the villain is black. Mozart has omitted surprisingly little of the sharp political and social criticism of the French play; and is quietly paying back some of his scores against men like Count Arco and the Archbishop of Salzburg. But he did not intend that the Count's final apology, at the end of Act Four, should be so perfunctory as to be unworthy of the affection that the score has lavished on the Countess. The Count's topsy turvy day is a rake's progress in more senses than one. He behaves atrociously, and forgets the privileges and responsibilities of his station in life. He is a man of limited abilities, without the strength of character of the Countess, Susanna, or Figaro. One suspects that he was badly brought up. Yet he is also disappointed with the tedium and frustration of his way of life; and there are signs, throughout Acts Three and Four, that a wild young man is growing up. He is *ein Mensch*, as will be said of Tamino.

Susanna evades him, with another revealing aside: "Oh go and wipe your mouth, you slobbering rascal." Figaro meets her at the door. "Eh? And where are you off to?" Susanna hushes him: "Quiet, now's the time to plead your case. You are certain to win it." The Count's sharp ears hear this remark. He echoes it note for note in secco. Jolty string chords announce his accompanied recitative. "Yes, she said so." The phrase is carefully placed a little higher in the voice than Figaro's "What has happened?" More jolty chords. "'Tis a trap, I am certain!" At the word trap the strings go warily, sfp. There is a pause. Then the strings (with oboes, bassoons and horns) burst out in five good presto chords of unrestrained vehemence, as in *7.2*. "Insolence!" They are all canaille, say the strings. "I'll punish . . ." Canaille, say the strings again. "I'll punish you, in suitable fashion." Aha go the orchestra in repeated notes of relish. The harmonic and melodic texture, wrote Walter Legge, is flushed with the Count's outraged pride, his savage jealousy, the calculated cruelty of his lust for revenge; we feel his gorge rising at the realisation of the deception. "A fitting sentence will be passed and upheld." Lips harden and twist, wrote Legge, in a sadistic determination. There is a pause.

Not for this man the cynical thought that Susanna has seen sense in time to save her marriage. He no longer wants—perhaps never wanted—a polite or sullen acquiescence to his rank and wealth for a single night; or an addition to a Leporello list of women. The droit du Seigneur made things too easy. If the girl is not worth having, let her go. If she is worth having, he will compete for her heart. He still wishes, as in *BS1.1*, to be loved for himself. Does Susanna prefer Cherubino *and* Figaro to the nobleman?

There is no need for the fermata in *17.13* unless it has dramatic significance. We come to a series of changes of tempi and dynamics that turn this recitative and aria from a relatively ordinary vow of revenge, by a relatively ordinary villain, into a strange and very human soliloquy by a man who half-realises the futility of what he is doing.

"Suppose he pays her! 'Twould settle the duenna!" There is hesitancy and foreboding in the words. The moment of hesitation passes, with a return to the tempo primo (*presto*, not the unstated transitional tempo of *17.1–4*). "Repay her? How can he hope to?" His words are vehement, aggressive; still not quite self-assured. "If so, Antonio could refuse to allow his niece to marry a man who is of unknown birth and background." Imagination kindles. "I can flatter the old half-wit." A gentle string chord cheers him. "He's proud enough to say it." The Count is also proud (and so is the Countess, with whom his affinities of temperament and outlook can be assessed in many ways—for instance, by comparing the orchestral phrases of their recitatives and the conventional trills with which they end their arias). Excitement grows, in bars that recall the overture. "In intrigue, he is fair game." The Count is indulging in self-justification; as the Countess will shortly do. Another fine crescendo, and the recitative ends. "Figaro is beaten!"

There is a strong chord of D. Flutes, trumpets and drums have joined the other instruments. This is the *allegro maestoso* D major of another inadequate potentate, Idomeneo; not the D major of Brandenburg Five or the Hallelujah chorus. Down it sweeps with vehemence, octave after octave; to a C♯; up to an A; down again, past a long tremolo on B, to another A. That tremolo was compared by Walter Legge to the hiss of a roused serpent, but is there not also weakness of character in the dotted quavers above and after the tremolo? "Shall I, in search of pleasure, be worsted by my servant?" It begins rather quietly, then rises; with a sense of outrage and a hint of hysteria. Then the four introductory orchestral bars are repeated. "Shall all be topsy-turvy? I not prevail, but he?" No great self-assurance. "Shall I forgo a treasure? Shall vulgar hearts be blissful? While I am unsuccessful? While she ignores my plea?" Soft violin trills accompany him as complacency disintegrates. The woodwind throw a sad yearning phrase from oboe and bassoon to flute and back. The two verses are then repeated, or restated, with new nuances of assertiveness and pessimism. The sadder it is, the finer is the moment when he brightens at *17.77* with a sudden up-turn and horn entry. He will cuckold the *vile oggetto*. "Shall vulgar hearts be blissful?" Not while he can help it! "Ah no, I mean to jog you, to bar you from contentment." The music is now *allegro assai*, with gusty alternations between soft and loud. "You were not born, you dog, you, to cause me this resentment." The first of those two lines has a dramatic emphasis on the contemptuous words "you dog, you" ("*audace*"). "Maybe, to find it laughable, yes, laughable that I live in misery!" It is not a flattering self-portrait. There is corroding unhappiness, a self-defeating hedonism. A man who has had no scruple in hurting others is himself being hurt. With a horrid glee in the orchestra he turns to the pleasant thought of hurting others. "Sweet is a thought that fills me, hope of revenge and laughter. It thrills me, oh it thrills me to thwart him utterly, my enemy. I'll punish him, yes, ah so nobleheartedly." The Countess was not the only one with vapours and a smelling-bottle. Yet what a contrast there is between the husband and wife who have so much in common! Vehement weakness is met by gentle strength; futility, by hope.

At the end of *MF3.11* the Count leaves the stage. Mozart originally meant him to do the same at the end of his aria—a token of conventionality, and another similarity between his aria and his wife's aria.

We heard so much about Barbarina in Act One that she seems an old friend when she enters with Cherubino. She is Antonio's daughter. "Come along, come along, pretty pageboy" she says "for I can promise you, if you come back to the cottage, that the prettiest girls in the neighbourhood will be there; but you will be prettier, yes by far, than any." No one explains why Cherubino has been to the château. Perhaps he went first to the gardener's cottage to find Barbarina; then back to the château, to fetch something he had left in his room. "Oh, suppose that the Count should find me again" he says. "He believes I am safely off to Seville." Barbarina titters gaily. "Oh does he? How surprising! If he should find you, it would not be the first time. Listen, we'll dress you as another village maiden, then we'll all go along to my lady to present her with the flowers. Trust little Barbarina, till all is ours." This twelve-year-old girl wishes to marry her Cherub. The dialogue helps to explain the story of Act Three, but Beaumarchais was content to manage without it. I doubt whether Mozart and da Ponte would have bothered with it, if they had not planned a short fill-in to separate the arias of the Count and Countess.

In comes the Countess. "It is taking so long" she says in secco. Then the strings begin a soft *andante*. "How I wonder . . . what he said to Susanna" (16) "about the proposition." The strings have an upward turn. "Yes, I am frightened. Is there too great a risk?" Another upward turn. "With such a husband! So impulsive . . ." Oh yes, say the strings. "and so jealous." The strings go faster and louder at the thought of it.

"Oh, it does no harm . . ." Oh no, oh no, say the strings, reverting at once to a soft yearning andante. ". . . to go into the garden . . . I, in Susanna's clothing . . . and she in my dress . . ." Wistfully, the violins agree. ". . . in the sheltering darkness." Yes, yes, say the violins.

"Oh heavens! I stoop to a lowly condition . . ." Her pride is as great as that of the husband she loves so dearly. ". . . because a husband has been cruel, yes cruel." Strings, loud. "His infidelities combine ('tis a most unheard-of assortment) . . ." Strings. ". . . with bitter jealousy, . . ." Strings. ". . . with insults." Strings. "He adored me . . ." The words are melodious, the strings do a gentle staccato. ". . . soon ignored me . . ." The strings do a loud staccato. ". . . and then betrayed me." The violins surge up two octaves to a high A; where they meet the voice. "Ah, now a mere servant alone can aid me."

Dove sono . . . We are accustomed to the words on their own, as a label for the soliloquy that follows. But Mozart puts them on their own, too; gropingly, without further preamble. "Where are . . ." The Countess seems more hesitant than ever. (But listen to the little rising phrases for oboe and bassoon—her unuttered thoughts.)

Those happy hours . . . "Those hours, where are they? Oh! those joys I share no more." The thought of them inspires the oboe to a *dolce* G; far away from the C on which the Countess began. The oboe reaches down for another broken groping phrase from the Countess. What has happened to . . . his promises? "Oh those promises! Fine words, how fare they?" Again we hear the little rising phrases. Horns have joined the oboe and bassoon. In the second little phrase the horns softly cancel optimism. "Oh those perjured lips that swore." The Countess is thinking about the lips as well as the perjury. She repeats her line.

The orchestra change the subject, after an embarrassed little "Hm, hm" from the horns. Here are oboe and bassoon with an unscripted happy memory in the dominant. But only half her next line is at all cheered—the other half relapses from dominant major to minor. "Why then, if to . . ."—it is major. ". . . tears and sadness"—it is minor, and her tone colour is appropriately changed. Thought by thought, feeling by feeling, the music goes with the Countess in her well-bred eighteenth-century reverie. "Why then, if to tears and sadness pleasure all is vanishéd . . ." The line is sung twice, with different nuances. The first is sung literally, without hope. The second reaches forward to hope. A sentence is going to be completed, the Countess is for once following a long consecutive thought. "Why then, if to tears and sadness pleasure all is vanishéd, is the memory of that gladness in my bosom not yet dead?" Yes, yes, oh yes, say oboe and bassoon. "Happy memory, so alive, so far from dead!"

With seeming abruptness the music returns to the tonic and the words of the first verse. The transition is apt to sound anxious if the

singer fails to realise that emotionally this is not a return, but a moment of hesitant progress to the partial illumination of a different sort
of C. That moment over, there is no hesitation in the line. *Dove sono i
bei momenti*? The word *bei* has come forward a beat, into its natural
place at the beginning of the bar. "Oh those wondrous, wondrous
hours, where are they?" By adding a bassoon phrase Mozart asks the
Countess for slightly fuller tone. The little oboe phrase is a shade louder.
The snows of yesteryear were not going to return. But here is a living
memory, a gathering hope of renewal.

Oh those promises, oh those perjured *lips*. We pause with the
Countess on an F. The double fermata heralds a change of tempo and
feeling in mid-phrase. There is complete continuity of thought and
phrasing, as the vocal line goes on from the same F. It is a quickening
of the reverie. There are little hesitations still; the slight hesitations of a
shy excitement. "But my heart . . . is faithful ever." The soft string
chords are like heart-beats; rhythmic, not melodic, in interest.

When Mozart wishes, he can be as sensitive to the obedient daughterly
words of his libretto as any of the self-denying composers who have
fancied that vocal music has to be, in some strange way, subordinate to
words. The music and the words are dancing partners; the music leads,
but each obeys the other. Da Ponte has presented Mozart with the word
"languish". It is an awkward present, at a moment of quickening C
major. He promptly leans into C minor, using longer notes. "Though
I languish, still I love."

The power of her love brings back hope of moving the Count's
false ardent heart; *di cangiar l'ingrato cor*. She repeats the crucial line,
with oboe help. All at once the music achieves yet another kind of C
major; the long-delayed orchestral forte. Oh yes this is better, say the
frolicking oboe and bassoon. Yes, thinks the Countess, my heart is
faithful ever. Yes yes, say the orchestra. Oboe and bassoon frolic.
"Yes, my heart is faithful ever. Though I languish, still I love." This
time Mozart has to lean even harder into C minor, because the orchestra
have established the C major feeling so strongly. The rest is triumph,
with a conventional trill near the end.

It is one of the crucial moments in the opera. After the buffeting of
Act Two the Countess was less despondent than the tough plebeian
couple whom she is protecting. She has had the bright idea of going into
the garden herself, and is looking for Susanna to give her the two
thousand crowns that are needed to absolve Figaro from his foolish
bond. As it turns out the money is not needed. But that does not
diminish the initiative and generosity of the gentle young woman who

is emerging as the strongest of the characters in this opera. Despite the continuing humiliation of subterfuge, the worst is over. She knows the power of her love. We who know the rest of the story can see her coming out of the right hand arbour at *28.399*. "But you will forgive them, at my wifely plea." It will not be her words alone that will evoke the Count's abject "Forgive me, forgive me, forgive me." Nor will it be the Count's realisation that he has been a fool. It will be the power of her love—the way she says the words, and what she does not say; and the way in which she holds out her hands to him during the nineteen bars in which four men mutter. "Do eyes then deceive me, oh who will believe me, how can I believe what I see"; while violin quavers run up and down, staccato. It would be wrong to say that she is rehearsing *28.399*, here at the end of *Dove sono*. But she is living the same redemptive emotion, in approximately the same time span. We, our awareness heightened by the music that Mozart lavishes on his Countess, are to sense the continuity with the final scene, as well as with *Porgi Amor*. We are to feel the essential unity and coherence of the dramatic pattern.

The Countess still needs to find Susanna. Off she goes, and in come the Count, Figaro, Marcellina, Bartolo and a new character; Don Curzio. Don Curzio is a solemn forthright foolish man, loud and self-assured. He has the "bonne et franche assurance des bêtes qui n'ont plus leur timidité". His famous stutter, usually sung as a quick-fire consonant stutter, is not indicated in the Italian libretto but was carefully written out in the French play (*MF3.12, 3.13*) as a vowel stammer of the woolly baa-lamb variety. It was intended as part of the characterisation: "son bégaiement n'est qu'une grâce de plus, et doit être à peine sentie; et l'acteur se tromperait lourdement et jouerait à contresens, s'il y cherchait le plaisant de son rôle. Il est tout entier dans l'opposition, de la gravité de son état, au ridicule du caractère; et moins l'acteur le chargera, plus il montrera de vrai talent." (See also the note on p. 117.)

In the play there is a long trial scene, in which the verdict is pronounced by the Count. In the opera, the case has been heard by Don Curzio in another room (during *17, 18B, 19*), and the Count is a court of appeal.

"The ca-ase is decided" says Don Curzio as they all enter. "He must marry her or pay her. Silence in court."

"I'm a new woman" says Marcellina, sitting down. "I'm an old wreck" says Figaro, two octaves lower. "At last!" says Marcellina "I shall be married to the man that I adore." "I appeal to your Lordship" says Figaro, relying on the tip-off that Susanna gave him in *16A17*. "The sentence is judicious" says the Count "you can marry, or pay:

well said, Don Curzio." "'Tis kind of your Lordship to say so" says Don Curzio, delighted at his own prowess (in pleasing the Count and understanding the IOU). "A superb, a superb sentence" says Bartolo. "Superb in what, pray?" asks Figaro. "That we are all revenged on you." Bartolo speaks for the Count, for Basilio, for Antonio. They nod in agreement. The Count goes towards the door.

"Marry her, I will not" says Figaro. "Oh but you will" says Bartolo. "You will marry her or pay her" says Don Curzio. "The lady lent you two thousand silver pieces." "I am a gentleman" says Figaro "I cannot marry without the consent of my noble parents." The Count turns, incredulous but interested. "But who are they, and where?"

Indomitable and impudent, Figaro replies that if the Count allows him the time he will find them. "For fifteen, fifteen years I have been looking for them everywhere." Da Ponte says ten years, and it is possible that Mozart and he wish to imply that Figaro is only about twenty or twenty-five; in which case Marcellina might be in her late thirties or early forties. But I think Mozart took it for granted that Figaro is thirty (Mozart's own age in 1786) as stated by Beaumarchais in *MF3.16*. If so, fifteen years is not likely to be an over-estimate.

"He is a common foundling!" sneers Bartolo. Figaro is stung as usual to instant repartee. "Lostling, doctor; a precious thing that was stolen." "Stolen?" asks the Count. "Stolen?" asks Marcellina. "Can you prove it?" asks Bartolo. "What is the evidence?" asks Don Curzio. "Lace on the napkins; the cloth was all embroidered; and there was gold, there were jewels. Yes, that is why the robbers noticed the baby. If that is not proof abundant that I was high-born and precious, at any rate I have on my arm a very special hieroglyph."

Marcellina listens agitatedly, then gets up. "Not a spatula, here on the upper right arm?" "Did someone tell you?" asks Figaro, without a notion of the reason for which Marcellina is asking the question. "Oh heavens! 'Tis he then" says Marcellina. "Yes, it is I still" says Figaro impatiently. "Who?" "Who?" "Who?" ask the others, in a neat D–F♯–A sequence. "Little Raphael!" says Marcellina with a B♭.

Bartolo intervenes. "You say that you were stolen?" "Not far from a castle" says Figaro proudly. "Here is your mother" says Bartolo, pointing to Marcellina. "My nursemaid!" hopes Figaro, clinging to the illusion of noble birth. "No, your mother" says Bartolo. Figaro begins to see what this means: "Do I hear aright?" Marcellina points at the doctor: "Here is your father!"

Bottom F from the 'cellos and basses; we begin the sextet (*18*). Michael Kelly said in his memoirs that it was Mozart's favourite piece in the opera. (Constanze Nissen told Vincent and Mary Novello in 1829 that he particularly liked *Non so più* as well.)

Marcellina embraces Figaro. "Let these arms recall a mother; not your wife, your parent rather." The string accompaniment is simple, joyful, soft. "Father, father!" says Figaro, turning to Bartolo with wind support. "You, not another! Kiss me then paternally." In the play Bartolo is still reluctant, but that is a minor complication which Mozart and da Ponte omit: "Conscience pricks me, this will fix me, but to kiss you I agree." Each of the couplets has a different accompaniment.

The Count and Don Curzio are aghast. "He the father? And she the mother? Then the wedding cannot be" says Don Curzio. "'Tis confusing, 'tis bemusing, oh I do not wish to see" says the Count. "My beloved son!" sings Marcellina. Mother, father, and son greet each other.

Enter Susanna, with a purse given to her by the Countess (*MF3.17*). The tonic harmony of the family reunion fades almost into G major. "Master, master, wait a minute. Here's a purse with money in it. I will pay the debt for Figaro, I have come to set him free." Her vocal line is full of tender devotion. Bartolo begins a softer round of family greetings, which must not drown the new couplet: "As the clue to this is missing, I will merely wait and see."

Susanna erupts with anger. "He and Marcellina kissing? God above, what perfidy! What perfidy! I renounce you!" "Do not shout so" says Figaro. "Doubt not, my dear one. Doubt not! Doubt not!" "What's to doubt?" says the enraged Susanna "So . . ." There is a resounding crotchet smack, in strict time (*18.53*, mid-bar).

Columbine has slapped Harlequin. But never perhaps was there so individual a realisation of the two stock characters. "Ah, she loves me fondly, purely" thinks Figaro "that is loving repartee, as all can see." Marcellina and Bartolo have similar words. The Count, nervously observed by Don Curzio, sings: "I'm beside myself with fury. What a freak of destiny!" Susanna feels much the same as the Count. "I'm beside myself with fury. Can the hag do this to me?"

After eighteen bars of this, we go back to the tonic. Marcellina explains that she is Figaro's mother. Her vocal line is a sedative, unerringly suited to the sincere bathos of what she is trying to say. At the same time she has somehow blended her opening line in this sextet with the first *two* vocal lines of the battle—was it only this morning?— with Susanna. "You now have a mother, dear daughter, in me." "His mother?" The incredulous orphan asks Bartolo, the Count, Curzio and

Marcellina in turn. Each one says she is his mother. "Your mother!" she says to Figaro.

Figaro points to Bartolo. "And this is my father; the testimony is that it is he." Once more Susanna has to seek confirmation from the other four in turn. Once more they confirm it. "Your father!" she says to Figaro. "And this is my mother" says Figaro, infuriating the Count by maudlin repetition. "The testimony is that it is she. My mother, he says it is she. My father, she says it is he."

As Figaro finishes, the Count begins a *sotto voce* expression of fury. "Oh fierce is the torment of this fatal moment." The words mean what they say. The Count is popping with anger, as we shall be reminded in *18A17* and *19A15*. As usual Don Curzio echoes his words.

"Oh perfect, oh perfect enjoyment" sing Marcellina and Bartolo, *sotto voce*. "Oh perfect enjoyment" sing Susanna and Figaro, *sotto voce*. "Oh wonderful moment" sing the happy family quartet. "This heart cannot bear all the joy, all the glee." (On the word "joy" Susanna soars an octave and a sixth with her emotion.)

Another moment of torment for the Count and Don Curzio. "Oh perfect enjoyment" for the others. "A moment of torment" for two. "Oh wonderful moment" for four. "Oh I cannot bear all the heart's misery" says the Count, with Don Curzio to help him. "Oh I cannot bear all the joy, all the glee" say the others. It goes on like that for a while. Then out goes the Count, still popping with anger. Don Curzio follows him.

Marcellina is thinking of Figaro: "Look at him, doctor dearest, the happy outcome of the love that was between us." "Let us not chatter of doings best forgotten; as we have found him . . ." With an ungracious cliché Bartolo offers to make Marcellina an "honest woman" whenever she wishes. "Today! We'll have a double wedding."

Marcellina gives Figaro his useless IOU—he had a generous wedding present in advance. "Here, catch!" says Susanna, throwing him the purse the Countess had given her. A more exciting wedding present. Not to be outdone, Bartolo throws him his purse (having checked that it is not too heavy?). Figaro, whose love of money is one of his strongest instincts, is delighted. "Thank you, thank you! I'll gladly go on catching all you throw me." Susanna says they had better go and tell the Countess and Antonio. "Who so content as I am? Who so content as I am?" "I am" says Figaro. "I am" says Bartolo. "I am" says Marcellina. Out they go, cocking (as William Mann puts it) a four-part *a cappella* snook at the Count. "Go pop, my Lord, with anger. I say 'tis high time."

Michael Kelly wrote that "In the sestetto, in the second act (which was Mozart's favourite piece of the whole opera) I had a very conspicuous part, as the Stuttering Judge. All through the piece (*sic!*) I was to stutter; but in the sestetto, Mozart requested I would not, for if I did I should spoil his music. I told him, that although it might appear very presumptuous in a lad like me to differ with him on this point, I did; and was sure, the way I intended to introduce the stuttering would not interfere with the other parts but produce an effect; besides it certainly was not in nature, that I should stutter all through the part and when I came to the sestetto, speak plain; and after that piece of music was over, return to stuttering (*sic!*); and, I added (apologising at the same time, for my apparent want of deference and respect in placing my opinion in opposition to that of the great Mozart) that unless I was allowed to perform the part as I wished, I would not perform it at all."

Kelly goes on to say, with equal garrulity, that the audience liked his stutter, and that Mozart said "Bravo! Young man, I feel obliged to you; and acknowledge you to have been in the right, and myself in the wrong." He concludes that "I have seen the opera in London and elsewhere; and never saw the Judge portrayed as a stutterer and the scene was often totally omitted: I played it as a stupid old man, though at the time I was a beardless stripling."

In come Antonio and the Count. Antonio is telling the Count that Cherubino is still at Aguas Frescas. "Yes, and here is his regimental cap!" "This I can hardly credit! When he ought to be arriving in Seville." "Beg pardon, sir, but my cottage, today, is Seville. There they dressed him as a woman; and there ay there he has left his other clothes." Again the Count pops with anger. He goes to see the clothes for himself.

Enter Rosina and Susanna (*19A13*). For different reasons each is elated. Two excited teenage girls discuss how the Count went pop with anger during the sextet. Then Rosina reverts to a more important subject. "And where have you appointed that he shall come to meet you?" In the garden; no suburban rectangle but (as we shall see) something like the grounds of an eighteenth-century English nobleman "jogging along on £40,000 a year" as one of them once said. Rosina, the dropper of letters to Lindor, would have managed better. Rosina the Countess takes charge. "Write to him." "A letter? But, my lady!"

Well might Susanna hesitate. There was no great harm in talking to the Count. But a letter! Good sense and candour, two of Susanna's main characteristics, require that she should tell Figaro. She hesitates.

What does it matter? Everything has turned out well. Nothing can stop the wedding. Her ladyship, to whom she owes so much, is speaking. "Come, write, I tell you; I take the whole responsibility." The moment of hesitation passes. Susanna shrugs gaily. She sits on a low B♭. She takes a pen. The Countess dictates the heading of a poem to be sung on the breezes. So the letter is to be in verse! Susanna writes the heading and echoes part of it. Her mistress, who has been collecting her thoughts, dictates the first line: "Soon, soon, Zephyr will be playing . . ." Impeccably considerate, the Countess pauses. Susanna writes, and repeats part of the line. "In the twilit hour serene" She writes and repeats it. "Where the willow trees are swaying." "Where the willow . . .?" Her mistress repeats the line. Of course. "Where the willow . . . trees are swaying." "He will know the place I mean." No need to write more. She puts down her pen. They agree; he will understand. They read it together. They agree joyfully that he will understand. Oh yes he will understand. Susanna folds the letter. What shall she fasten it with? A pin. "Oh, and write on the back of it, will you send back the seal pin." The seal. It reminds them of the unsealed commission. They laugh.

It is subtle, gentle comedy. At the same time it is profound and imaginative. Mozart, who enjoys differentiating characters in music, has deliberately gone naïve, by undifferentiating his two heroines. They are blended. Both are Rosina, enjoying traditional rituals. Both are the Countess, in the new-found confidence of *Dove sono*. Both are the Susanna of *Deh vieni*. It is one of the big moments in the serious inner meaning of Mozart's opera; a shared lyrical moment, tending towards the great moments of forgiveness and general reconciliation at the end of Act Four. It is the supreme eighteenth-century billet doux; serenely sensuous.

The 6/8 *allegretto* grew out of recitative in the middle of the sense. It faded into recitative in the middle of a bar. There were two equal fiddle parts supporting the melody with a lulling unison. Viola and 'cello were in octaves most of the time, marking the beat. During the dictation a douce oboe kept the melody unbroken, helping to blend the thoughts. So that the oboe should not be the odd one out, oboe tone was supported and modified by the bassoon. One voice demurely followed or led the other, with a perfect blending of tone and emotions.

The musical analysis can be carried much further. But one does not parse poetry while listening. *Che soave zeffiretto*! It blends, it flows. Yes, the two singers are doing it superbly. The magic has worked again.

(Goethe, writing to Eckermann on 13th February 1829, said that only Mozart could have composed a Faust opera. One wonders how the composer of the letter duet would have set *Das ewig Weibliche zieht uns hinan.*)

Once more the music has come from B♭ major to G major. Enter the village maidens, to simple 6/8 *grazioso* Tirolean music. It is music that has affinities with the music of the chorus in Act One, and with Figaro's "My lord, they are ready to play for the wedding" in the finale of Act Two. But it is feminine, and perfectly follows the letter duet. "Lady whom we love so dearly, pray excuse our want of art. Here are flowers gathered early, for a lady set apart. We are poor and simple peasants, we are bringing simple presents, but our little we are bringing with a singing from the heart." Once more Mozart reveals his special affection for the Countess. Here is no sulky anxious flattery, such as we enjoyed when the lads and lasses sang Figaro's doggerel in Act One.

Barbarina makes a little speech. (Was it this that she had been rehearsing all week with Cherubino?) The Countess thanks them all with evident warmth. Susanna adds a complimentary remark to please them. Meanwhile the Countess notices a girl she does not know; a girl who in some performances is absurdly awkward at curtseying; a girl who is looking devotedly at the Countess. Barbarina says it is "another cousin" who has come to stay for the wedding. Susanna, her real cousin, looks surprised. The Countess decides to be kind to the pretty little stranger. "Come here, my child, give me your bunch of flowers. Look at her blushes! Susanna, do you not find that she resembles a person?" The smiling Susanna primly agrees.

Unseen, the Count and Antonio have entered. Antonio comes up behind the pretty little stranger, snatches off a bonnet and plonks a regimental cap on Cherubino's head. "Just as I said, sir, one little army officer." The Countess is much put out. She assures the Count that she knows nothing of this latest escapade. This time, her manner is in her favour. The Count threatens Cherubino. "You shall be punished, severely and condignly."

Barbarina intervenes. "Master, master, you remember what you said, every time you have given me a nice hug, and such a big kiss? *Barbarina, if you love me, I will grant all your wishes.*" There is a titter from the village maidens. The Countess looks grim. The embarrassed Count makes a feeble response. "You say I said that?" "Yes you did! So, master, I say, let me marry Cherubino and I will love you as I love my little kitten." The Count is speechless. Barbarina takes her Cherub to the back of the stage. The Countess comments, with dignity and restraint; the Count's moments of humiliation occur in public, where a woman like the Countess would not dream of making a scene. The Count, dimly aware that he is the puppet of a plotting playwright, has an aside. "Is it a man, the devil, or the Almighty who turns each new event so as to spite me?"

Enter Figaro. He does not notice Cherubino. He is anxious to start the festivities, so that they can all have a good dance. The Count reminds him that his foot is twisted. Figaro says it is not hurting so much now. He turns to the village maidens and tells them to come along. The Count turns him back. "You were lucky that the pots were only earthenware." "You are right, sir." Figaro turns again to the girls: "Come on, my dears, come on then." Antonio turns him back: "And while you were jumping, Cherubino was galloping on that horse of his to Seville?" "Galloping, trotting, walking, who cares? A good riddance, I say. Come on, my pretty ones." Once again he turns to the girls. Once again the Count turns him back: "And yet he left the commission in your pocket?" "As I told you" says Figaro "What is this inquisition?" (He is a little apt to drop polite language in moments of stress.) Susanna is signalling to him. In vain, for Antonio triumphantly points to a girl who can prove "Sir future nephew" to be a liar. Cherubino!

The Count and Antonio have enjoyed their minute. It is the last minute they are allowed to enjoy. The Count bluffs. Cherubino, he says, has confessed to jumping out of the window. Figaro looks pityingly at him. "Oh, does Cherubino say so? I suppose he could have jumped too. I do not offer an opinion, I do not know."

The Count, who would not have had the inclination or the wit to make such a claim, is not listening to Figaro. Whatever his mental limitations he is, as we know, sharp of hearing. He, then the audience, hear the very distant sound of an approaching band. (He is the only one to hear the three missing notes at the beginning of the first phrase.) Then Figaro hears. "They are beginning" he cries. He is wrong; they are half way through, in the dominant. "Away, then! Go to your places, my beauties, take your places." This time no one turns him back. He offers his arm to Susanna. She takes it. An oboe entry accompanies her radiant smile. This annoys the Count. The Countess shivers. The bassoon enters. The Count turns to the Countess. He is about to say or explain something. The Countess checks him. Hurriedly—very hurriedly—she changes the subject. "Let us receive them smiling." The distant band are a little closer, and have got back to the beginning of their C major tune. Drums and trumpets are just audible. "The double wedding, now. You should look gay, sir. She was your protegée, sir.

We'll sit then." She goes to sit on one of the two thrones that have been brought in by menservants. Sulkily the Count follows; to plan revenge in comfort.

Unless the production is carefully managed, the dramatic tension is now finally broken. A prematurely happy ending? A musical spectacle, following a bit of meaningless recitative? A weakish Act, on the whole? Even Mozart can't keep it up for ever. Funny, how operatic comedy fades off towards the end. Shall we stick it out for *Deh Vieni*? We shall just about catch the last train. And so on. To prevent such thoughts, it is important that the production should spread the available action evenly and thinly, like butter on a large slice of bread; and should maintain as close a connection as possible between the music and the action. To this end one should probably keep to the elaborate order of procession laid down by Beaumarchais. The band are getting closer. Six bars after the Count's last remark the tune starts again, forte. Enter gamekeepers with guns (*28*). Enter Don Curzio (*30*). Enter the peasants (*32*). At *36* there enters a strange little sub-procession; two young girls carrying a toque, closely followed by two more young girls carrying a veil, and two young girls carrying a pair of gloves and bouquet. At *39* there enter another six young girls, two by two, with similar impedimenta.

For the fourth and final time, the march begins (*42*). Enter Marcellina and Figaro (who will give Marcellina away). Enter Susanna and her uncle (*44*). Enter Bartolo (*46*). Musically there is an entry to spare at this point (*48*). Does Barbarina bring in Cherubino to see the fun, while the others bow or curtsey? At *50* and *53* the young girls come forward, two by two, to hand their impedimenta to valets standing by the Count. Figaro leads the older bride to the Count. Marcellina kneels before the Count (not the Countess, whatever your edition of the score may say).

I cannot prove that Mozart meant the procession to enter in the way I have described. But I think that my reconstruction follows naturally, once one accepts a more important, and more provable, point—that Susanna gives the Count the letter "pendant les derniers vers du duo." Beaumarchais says so, and Mozart chooses the second couplet of the duo for some prominent horn-writing. Unfortunately, da Ponte has misled us for generations by a muddled recollection in his memoirs that the letter was handed over during the fandango.

A 2/4 *allegretto* begins, still in C major. The Count gives Marcellina the toque. He places the veil on her. He gives her the bouquet and gloves. She rises and makes a deep curtsey. There is just time for all this before the two young girls start singing "*Amanti costanti, seguaci d'onor.*" Faithful, honourable lovers—like Bartolo who is coming forward, thirty-one years too late, to be given Marcellina's hand. "He's royally loyal, the groom we applaud. He knows what he owes that intelligent lord." Yes, he knows. After glancing at Rosina, he takes Marcellina to the other side of the stage.

Antonio brings Susanna forward. "A dutiful beauty, the bride we applaud. Be glad, miss, you had this intelligent lord." We know how glad Susanna has been. "The right he surrenders . . . that shocks and offends you . . . a virgin he sends you to husband adored." The horns entered with the words of the second couplet. There were pauses; significant pauses, not to be found in any other part of the duo or its repeat. The horns blew during the pauses. At "a virgin he sends you" there is a tutti unison, with the first horn on a blaring high G. There can, I think, be no doubt that Mozart wrote these bars to go with the action so precisely described by Beaumarchais. Susanna has plucked the Count's sleeve. She has shown him the letter in her hand. She has lifted her hand to the side of her head. The Count has hurriedly pretended to adjust her toque. She has given him the letter. The horns were blaring. Figaro came proudly forward to receive her. Susanna shivers, gets up, makes a deep curtsey. The Count gives her to Figaro. The Count makes a gesture of goodwill. Figaro and Susanna go off to the other side of the stage, near Bartolo and Marcellina. Antonio is left alone in the middle of the stage, looking awkward (until Barbarina beckons him to the side with a bottle?). The chorus, with orchestral tutti, sing "Be glad, miss, you had this intelligent lord."

The dancing begins. The first—and, as it proves, the only—dance is a fandango. The A minor tonality tells of a constraint in the atmosphere. The tune does not sound very Spanish but is almost the only piece of genuine local colour in the opera. The original Andalusian fandango melody is printed by Abert on p. 16 of the *Noten-Beilagen* at the end of his Vol. II, with the version that Mozart more probably knew from Gluck's 1761 Don Juan ballet music. Mozart has kept Gluck's key and has made good use of a characteristic capering rhythm which is to be found at bar 7 of the Gluck version. But it is Mozart who divided the music into four main sections.

In the first section the principals politely watch an exhibition dance. In the second section, which is prolonged by Gluck's capering rhythm from eight to twelve bars, Figaro gets restless, nudges Susanna, takes her out on to the floor and dances nimbly, without a trace of a twisted foot. He may even shake it at the Count; a kind of Greek *hybris*, which provokes the Count to look at that letter.

The third section has a special two-bar false start. The Count comes forward to the edge of the stage and takes the letter from his breast. As he opens it, the third section restarts. He makes the gesture of a man whose finger has been cruelly pricked. He sucks, shakes and squeezes the finger, declaiming "Ugh, women! Why, of course, as usual! In anything, a needle or pin they poke, yes." He throws the pin away. He opens the letter. "Ha, ha! I see the joke, yes." The horns enter at "joke, yes." Flute has joined bassoon and violins in the capering rhythm. Figaro is muttering to Susanna: "Do you see? He has got a billet doux from a woman going past him. I wager it was fastened with a pin. It pricked him, look, he seems to mind it." More capering. Now the Count has read the postscript. "Do you see, he is even trying to find it!"

As soon as the fandango is over, the Count breaks up the party. The dancing will be resumed this evening, when all the preparations are completed. If they are not completed Figaro has after all, at the third attempt, managed to get the wedding hour advanced. But in truth there was no reason—except one—why the dancing should not continue from now until the peasants are exhausted. The Count wants to look for the pin. And so, in words that are an echo of *8A32*, he promises a truly magnificent occasion—later—to show how he treats those who are dear to him. The chorus are surprised, but politely sing their little song. "We're glad that we had that intelligent lord, intelligent lord, intelligent lord."

Away they go, leaving the intelligent lord to search for a pin.

ACT FOUR

Act Four takes place on a lawn, or glade, in the grounds of Aguas Frescas. It is late evening. The stage is often shown in moonlight throughout. That is wrong; but illumination, mental and physical, is certainly a problem. The action is all more or less in the dark, and that is where the audience are apt to remain, following obscure pieces of apparent anticlimax in an unfamiliar language. Yet it is possible to have lighting that is consistent with, and helps to explain, the dramatic situation. It is clear from a sentence in *MF5.2* (la lune devrait être levée) that the moon will rise *during* the Act. In other words something like complete darkness was wanted for Figaro's monologue of anguish and protest; a dark night of Figaro's soul. It is wanted in the opera for Figaro's recitative and aria (*Buja è la notte*) and *Deh vieni* (*Finchè non splende in ciel notturna face*).

The period of almost complete symbolic blackness sets in, I feel, during the second verse of Basilio's funny but degrading story. During the period of blackness, there is slight illumination from the windows of the hall in which the vassals are eating and dancing, enhanced fitfully by the light of a bonfire (with torch flares and fireworks) on a terrace in front of the palace, off stage. Before Basilio's aria, twilight. In the course of the finale, the moon gradually comes out.

If the dramatic situation is to be convincing, it is also important to have suitable scenery. Beaumarchais tells us that the décor is a cross between the park of an English stately home and the Trianon garden at Versailles; in which, even today, all sound of traffic is too distant to be heard. Imagine Hyde Park, Regent's Park, Kew Gardens and Richmond Park thrown together; you will get the right idea. In this vast garden, the trees of the rendezvous are silhouetted on the side of the stage further from the hall. (Pines and willows, unlike the "marroniers" of the play, have a characteristic silhouette.) There are flowers in a large flower bed, which ought to be visible during *Deh vieni*; they can be silhouetted against light from the windows of the hall. There are supposed to be two small pavilions, kiosks, temples or arbours, one to the left and one to the right. But there is a harmless tradition of letting the Countess appear from the château—if so, only one pavilion is needed. There is a faint sound of running water when everything is still (*Deh vieni*); from a brook. Optional extras from *Non so più* are mountains in the background, one or more fountains, and a lake beyond the willow trees.

But it is above all essential that the words should be heard and understood. If one wishes to make sense of Act Four in Italian, one must probably do or revise ones homework first.

As the curtain rises we hear a sonorous pizzicato from 'cello and bass. We see Barbarina. She is alone in the twilight. She has a lantern, and is searching for something on the ground. The violins, muted, sigh for her in F minor. "Look again then! 'Tis in vain then. Have you lost it, foolish miss? Have you lost it, foolish miss?" Like Alice, she talks to herself. There is anxiety in her musical question. She and the violins sigh. "Vain endeavour!" Another sigh. "You will never, never find it, no, not ever; you have lost it, foolish miss." She stops searching. "Gone for ever! 'Twas vain endeavour. You will never, never find it. You have lost it, foolish miss." It sounds like the end of her song, but a more dreadful question emerges. "What will my cousin—and the Count, yes and the Count!—say after this?"

It is a twelve-year-old who, with the help of F minor tonality and muted violins, tells us that the triumphant comedy of *18–22* has been prelude to a phase of darkness and despair. It was a twelve-year-old who sang it at the first performance; Anna Gottlieb, who was the first Pamina in 1791.

Along come Marcellina and Figaro. "What is wrong, little cousin?" "It is something I lost." "What thing?" "The pin that the master did give me to take to Susanna."

It is presumably three or four hours after the wedding. The hour of the rendezvous is approaching. One has to assume that Barbarina was given the message just after the wedding, as in the play. Then she forgot about it—she was so excited at the hope of marrying Cherubino that she went straight back to the cottage where he was changing back into his own clothes. Some hours later, she remembered the message. Oh tragedy! And she can't even find the pin. She must have dropped it, between the château and the gardener's cottage. It is getting dark. She runs back with a lantern. The search was hopeless from the start. Who can find a pin on a lawn at dusk?

The pin that his Lordship gave her to take to Susanna! One has to be sorry for Figaro. It is easy to say that he should have known better; Susanna was not that sort of girl. But he actually saw the billet doux, during his wedding. He was no longer on his guard but elated and lulled by triumph. His half-correct inference hurts him all the more. Normally Susanna would have told him about the letter. But she herself had been light-headed with delight when the Countess suggested the letter. Her error of judgment (not telling Figaro) led to his error of judgment. In such a way—for this is the fiction of life, not of a fairy story—misunderstandings grow.

"To Susanna? The pin? You are young, very young, miss, for the business of go-be . . ." Figaro the ex-barber, the man of humble birth, has more self-control than the Count. He pulls himself together. He completes his sentence skilfully. "You are going to be a clever woman."

Gently he wheedles the information from Barbarina. He is rightly treating her as an innocent child, whether she is one or not. Gaily

Barbarina mimics what the Count had said to her. "Here, little Barbarina, take this pin for me to the beautiful Susanna, and tell her it is the seal of the willows." "Aha! the willows!" "Of course he also told me not to let anyone see me. You promise not to tell, that you saw me?" "Of course, yes, of course, child." "'Tis no concern of yours." "Of course not, of course not." "So long as only we know. Now to Susanna; and then to Cherubino." Off she goes, with a pin that Figaro borrowed (from Marcellina) and "found". As she goes, she is skipping like—a twelve-year-old. It is a charming piece of dialogue. How many opera-goers are aware of its nuances, when it is sung in Italian in the dark? It is lost, as sculptured detail in the upper reaches of cathedrals was lost until the days of photography.

Marcellina urges Figaro to be calm: "Patience, patience, and still more patience." It is admirable advice from a middle-aged mother. But this is an opera of impatient youth. When we meet the Lady Patience in Basilio's aria, her recipe for life is to have a thick skin. Figaro has not met the Lady Patience. He is unimpressed. "'Tis very serious" his mother says "you are right to be worried, but are you sure that you know on whom she is playing the joke?" Figaro knows one thing for certain. It is under the willows! "Yes but . . . oh, I implore you." "I am about to avenge all husbands, I assure you." Off he goes.

Marcellina is left alone in the lessening twilight. We hear her thinking: "I am sure he can trust her—such a modest, such an honest face." Da Ponte brings out, more pointedly than Beaumarchais, the change in Marcellina's attitude to Susanna. Was it only this morning that Susanna was *accused* of being "demure and unworldly"? In *Figaro* words are vehicles of nuance, meaning what the dramatic situation requires.

Although Marcellina's mother love is strong, she possesses an emotion that is stronger. Having been seduced as a teenager, she is anti-man. "Ah! quand l'intérêt personnel ne nous arme point les unes contre les autres, nous sommes toutes portées à soutenir notre pauvre sexe opprimé contre ce fier, ce terrible (*en riant*) et pourtant un peu nigaud de sexe masculin." In the play, this sentence is intended to remind the audience of Marcellina's outburst in *MF3.16*. "Dans l'âge des illusions, de l'inexpérience et des besoins, où les séducteurs nous assiègent; pendant que la misère nous poignarde, que peut opposer une enfant à tant d'ennemis rassemblés? . . . Hommes plus qu'ingrats, qui flétrissez par le mépris les jouets de vos passions, vos victimes . . . est-il un seul état pour les malheureuses filles? . . . dans les rangs même plus élevés, les femmes n'obtiennent de vous qu'une

considération dérisoire: leurrées de respects apparents, dans une servi-
tude réelle, traitées en mineures pour nos biens, punies en majeures
pour nos fautes."

Marcellina's aria is an important part of the opera's pattern of
behaviour and attitudes. It comes at almost the only possible moment
for an aria by this character. The musical style is surely deliberate and
just right in style for Figaro's mother—a generation out of date, like
Mozart's own father and mother. Marcellina is saying something that
needed to be said, something that the gentle and inarticulate Countess
would never say. Old madam pedant thinks it at us cheerfully, plati-
tudinously, assertively. Like Barbarina she is accompanied by strings
only. But the key has jumped back yet again to G major; this time, all
the way from F minor. The verbal and musical clichés suggest that she
and Bartolo are well-matched.

The words of her first verse, which echo Ariosto's *Orlando Furioso*
1.5, are simple and—to a twentieth-century ear—unconvincing. "The
she-goat and the he-goat in amity survive. The he-lamb and the little
she-lamb in warfare do not strive; and even the ferocious, atrocious,
angry he-boars—gentle are they to she-boars, they love them as they
are." Animals, like Rousseau's noble savages, often lead an even less
idyllic existence than civilised men and women. But Marcellina's
meaning is clear, her choice of animals judicious. Get on with it, we
think impatiently as the old dear sings it all again. Then she comes to
the point, *allegro*. "But we women of human birth who love you more
than aught on earth are soon accused of perfidy, so hard of heart you
are. We are treated worse than animals, so hard of heart you are."

By a strange compensation Mozart, who is so sympathetic to the
Countess, is less than fully sympathetic to the woman who speaks up
here in terms that apply more to the Countess than to herself. Our
minds are surely meant to go back to the great quarrel in which a
woman who had loved too well (Ah je l'ai trop aimé) was treated worse
than an animal, by a man who behaves as a brute animal would not
behave. Marcellina's aria, by its very banality, is a telling condemnation
of such behaviour. But the last word will remain with the Countess,
the power of whose passionate love is the central theme of the opera.

A last minute concession to singer's pride? Or a proper answer to
Basilio's sneering *Così fan tutte*, an essential counterpart to Figaro's aria
against women, a revelation of essential differences of character? It
may have to be omitted, when the best available singer is a mezzo. But
it can be very effective when sung and played as meaningful parody of
the music of an older generation.

It paves the way for a charming little incident. As Marcellina goes off
to warn Susanna, in comes Barbarina with her lantern and a big basket
of fruit. It is getting darker all the time. Barbarina is excited and cheerful. She is a child, toute entière à chaque événement. Her little recitative
follows Marcellina's G major, not her own previous F minor. She is
looking forward to a tête-à-tête with Cherubino in the left-hand pavilion. She hopes he won't forget for any reason. She had to pay the
horrid steward with kisses for the fruit. It is all as vivid as her recollection of the Count's message in 23A21; as light-hearted as her giggle
in 18B10.

"Oh murder." A large figure looms in the darkness. She runs to the
pavilion and disappears. It is Figaro. Holcroft, in the 1784 English
stage version of Le Mariage, makes a nice point: "Figaro imagines at
first Agnes" (Fanchette, Barbarina) "to be Susan; and, as it is too dark
to see, endeavours to follow the sound of her voice, having entered
while she was speaking."

It is darker than ever. Figaro is jumpy. Silhouetted in the darkness,
we can just see his big cloak and conspiratorial hat. He calls "Who goes
there?" to two figures that grope their way after him. One of the
shadows speaks with the unmistakable elegant sneering voice of Basilio:
"The two you invited yourself." The other shadow speaks with the
familiar vacuous boom of Bartolo: "What on earth are all these dark
preparations?" Figaro, with a melodramatic flourish that is eloquent of
misery, tells them. They are here to witness the happy mating of their
feudal lord and Figaro's loving faithful wife. He has invited Basilio and
Bartolo to help him expose the Count.

It is sometimes assumed that Basilio and Bartolo accept the valet's
invitation, and are in hiding on or near the stage until the Count cries
Gente, gente (28.335). It would be out of character if they did so. Even
in Act One Bartolo never dreamed of vengeance on his social superior.
As for Basilio, he reacts in two ways, both equally characteristic. First
"Ah buono, buono! Oh how amusing, they agreed it without me,
after all." It is typical of Basilio, the calumniator, the scandal-monger,
the malicious pandar, that he should unhesitatingly believe Figaro's
story, thus confirming Figaro's own certainty about it. Then when the
valet has issued his orders—he has to go and make some arrangements,
he will be back in half a moment, if he whistles they are to come
running—Basilio's second reaction is made plain. On no account will
he co-operate with a man whose plan is foolish, dangerous, idiotic.
"There is nothing to worry about. The Count has taken fancy to
Susanna, and she has given him an assignation." "Indeed" asks Bartolo

the conventional "ought Figaro to suffer it in silence?" "But we all have to do so. Why should he be exempted? And if he does try, will it do any good? For in this world, friend, if you take on the mighty you are ninety per cent sure to be worse off than ever, so do not venture."

Don Basilio is a man endowed with elegance, wit, and charm; a man with the dangerous gift of plausibility. He is a professional musician (in a century in which the professional musician was often a menial lackey). He is "organiste, maître à chanter, infatué de son art." Elegance, charm, and musicality are essential to the playing of the andante prelude to his B♭ aria. The musical style of the aria sounds like another deliberate parody (of light descriptive music in Vienna in Mozart's time?). But what a strange, vulgar, terrible self-portrait is conveyed by those innocent bars! In the play Bazile n'est aussi qu'un rôle secondaire. Mozart and da Ponte have painted a bigger, more complex character. Da Ponte in particular had reason to know about the Basilios of this world. He was, by a twist of fate, one of them himself. Basilio is not only a musician, he wears the soutane. Like da Ponte he is an ordained priest without religous belief. His aria has been placed in the darkest and most serious part of the opera; a perfect contrast to the arias of Figaro and Susanna, an important part of the pattern of attitudes to life and love, a splendid prelude to Figaro's lonely cry of despair "Oh, Susanna, Susanna!"

Take on the mighty? "I do not commit such folly, but was once as mad as he; for I found it very jolly to be full of righteous glee. Then I met the Lady Patience." (Listen to the bassoons.) "I abjured a life of pride, of caprices, of aberrations; as a youthful ardour died. We had had a little pleasure." (Listen to the violins.) "We were near a tanner's hovel, and she promised me a treasure, but I first would have to grovel by the carcase of a donkey, of a donkey, of a donkey! Then she said, My dear young donkey." (Listen to the clarinets and bassoons, whose twiddle is so unlike the oboe twiddles of love in this opera.) "My dear young donkey!" (It is all so simple, say the violins.) "I was thrown the ass's hide, and she vanished from my side."

Tempo di menuetto now, and the notes recall part of Basilio's hypocritical B♭ phrase in 7. "Then as I looked at her present in wonder" (a scurrying and rumbling in the orchestra, as the 'cellos go from legato crotchets to staccato quavers) "there was a sudden flash!" (Swish! Woomph! The 'cellos catch up with the second violins and violas, there is a crashing wind chord.) "Crash came the thunder, and then the hail began, with rain in torrents." The hail bounces audibly, the rain pours, the wind blows louder. It dies away; Basilio is coming to the point. Nonchalantly, with off-beat quavers in violins and viola, he tells us "But I was bone dry!" (No! say flute, violins and viola.) "With no abhorrence!" (No! say the instruments, still incredulous.) "Thick was the donkey-skin, I was inside." A thick skin, a thick skin.

"There came another peril then to greet me. Two lions, ravening, sprang then to eat me." (I apologise for doubling the lion, to fit the vocal line.) The orchestra anticipate and accompany the lions with vulgar slides; miaows, with all the vowel sounds of Eliza Doolittle in Shaw's *Pygmalion*. "They were upon me." Violins drool, woodwind and 'cello echo. "They slobbered on me." He comes to the second main point. "What could I do, except hide in my hide?" The crucial words are repeated, and the music becomes more than ever like— why, of course, the campfire sing-song or smoking concert. It is the unrefayned Mozart of the Bäsle letters.

"But at the horrible smell coming from it, appetite waned and the lions had to vomit." How revolting! Exactly. It is the third main point; da Ponte leaves us in no doubt about the *fiuto ignobile*. "And so they went away." We hear them going. "Unsatisfied."

Proudly, triumphantly, Basilio boasts. "Oh yes an immoral yarn; but, Sir, it has a moral." Basilio is fond of morals. "Danger, embarrass-ment, discomfort, and sorrow; you can escape them with an ass's hide." Basilio has lost his illusions. For what? For a patient thick-skinned acquiescence in his own degradation. He knows it to be degradation. He knows about the horrible smell. What could he do, except hide in his hide? He is a willing agent of evil ("Cet autre maraud loge ici? C'est une caverne! Hé, qu'y fait il?" "Tout le mal dont il est capable.") To our generation he seems startlingly contemporary. Is he not belatedly revealed in his aria—a fable as tame and innocent as an animal painting by Goya?

During Basilio's aria total darkness has fallen. We hardly need to see his inevitable departure with Bartolo at the end of the aria; to the château, the bonfire, anywhere in the world except the post of danger and folly appointed for him by a man he hates. Off they go, and we hear Figaro return, full of his thoughts. "Everything is ready. Yes, and the hour, the minute draws near." There is silence—silence so utter that, as every camper knows, and as Mörike knew in *Um Mitternacht*, one suddenly hears the running of a nearby brook.

"A tread, a footfall?" Figaro's heart thumps; staccato quavers for the strings. "Susanna? No, 'twas nothing." The strings have a legato phrase of misery and solitude. "Devilish darkness! So I begin to learn the foolish trade of husband, before I truly am one." The orchestra, and

Abert, have warned us that this is a sentence which matters in the characterisation of Figaro; a man with feelings and courage, a man with sufficient intelligence, or sophistication, to be amused at himself in a stock situation. Figaro sadly recalls that he saw the Count reading the billet doux. She must have given it to him during the actual wedding!

Cherubino grew today from vague love of "*donne*" to sudden premature love of the one (or one-at-a-time!) "*donna*". Figaro loves his "*donna*". He, a man of thirty who has never been sheltered from the world, infers that if she is false all "*donne*" are false. "Oh, Susanna!" That unaccompanied cry (so often gabbled through, because this is only recitative and it is getting late) is perhaps the darkest moment of all. "Susanna!" He repeats it pleadingly and miserably with a soft accompanying chord. He was so sure of her. Never trust a woman!

Commentators say that Figaro's aria (*26*) is a mere *Weiber-arie*, for which da Ponte deserves the blame. In truth, it not only comes from Beaumarchais but is necessary to the dramatic situation. As Emilia said to Othello about Desdemona, "If she be not honest, chaste and true, there's no man happy; the purest of their wives is foul as slander." Women! Women! Women! It may be trite. It may be the too familiar theme of buffo song, and of Macheath in Newgate; the ambiguous groan of pub, club and barracks. But it is as rightly the stuff of song as any other emotion; and da Ponte the philanderer, the friend of Casanova, was expert enough on the subject of women to make something interesting out of "O femme! femme! femme! créature faible et décevante! nul animal créé ne peut manquer à son instinct; le tien est-il donc de tromper?" What else could Figaro be thinking, once he had made the fatal assumption that Susanna was going off with another man on his wedding night? Nor was the wickedness of womanhood a topic outside Mozart's personal experience; for instance, with Madame Weber and her daughters.

If we are disappointed with this aria, we must assume with Walter Legge that not until the end of the nineteenth century (Verdi's Ford and Wolf's Lukas) was it possible for music to take full measure of the feelings of an outraged husband; or that Mozart felt inhibited; or that the singer has not quite risen to the occasion. But don't blame the singer if the build-up (Marcellina's and Basilio's arias) has been omitted.

With a thudding anger, precisely conveyed in the cacophonous scrubbing noise committed by the violins on the third beat, Figaro thinks. "O man, you foolish creature!" It is jolty enough to be the Count's music. "Women are false by nature." The clarinets make it heartfelt. "No longer be so credulous but see them as they are." There is, as Gerald Abraham says, the most subtly bitter and ironical flavour to it all. There is also an analytical quality about the original that makes one think of Stendhal rather than Macheath. "Only a mind enfeebled can worship mortal woman." It sounds like a military march, to begin with; followed by trills that are a caricature of seductive music. "Deluded is the human who praises from afar . . ." (get ready for the list) ". . . the witch who entices you, trill trill, to live in a cage; the mermaid who beckons you, trill trill, to waters that rage; the she-cat who plays with you to mangle you and leave you." There is special venom in the unanimity of voice and orchestra at this point. Could Mozart help thinking of the "false, malicious coquette" Aloysia, who encouraged him, told him he was too poor, and married Josef Lange; the unhappy jealous man to whom we owe one of the few authentic portraits of Mozart? "The beacon that shines for you but only to deceive you" (could Mozart even be sure of the fidelity of his wife Constanze, Aloysia's sister?) "The rosebush to prick you, trill trill, the *vixen* to trick you, trill trill." Josefa, the eldest sister, became the first Queen of the Night; Mozart described her in a letter dated 15th December 1781 as "a lazy gross perfidious person, as cunning as a *fox*." On it goes, getting more buffo-like, more desperate, faster, louder. "No pity they show, no pity they show, no, no, no, no." To quote Gerald Abraham again, Figaro does not put himself forward as the broken-hearted clown. He is Figaro, alone in the darkness, thinking; in words that happen by coincidence to be addressed *ad spectatores*. The rest of the story he spares us, for we all of us, all of us know. But while he waits he repeats the story, in order to show that if the second verse is omitted the list follows naturally from the first verse. As it would be boring to repeat the list in full he gives us the headings with string accompaniment, and tells us each time (with clarinet, bassoon and horn) that he will spare us the rest. He gets bored with this variation, and gives us the remainder of the list in full. "No pity they show, No, No, No, No"; and the rest of the story he spares us but (in case we still do not know) the horns tell us. After such an impressive list of types of villainess, the anticlimax is unpredictable and just right. Figaro, lurking by the willows, does not care a damn about general types. He is worried about Susanna and the Count. (Does his fourfold NO refer to, or modulate to, Susanna?) He has been killing time. He is impatient. A grim sense of humour is keeping him sane as he awaits foreseeable danger, embarrassment, discomfort and sorrow; *without* the protection of an ass's hide.

It is still very dark. We see for a moment, silhouetted against the lighted window of the hall, two women on their way from the château. A third woman hurries up behind them. It is Marcellina. She tells Susanna (who is with the Countess) that Figaro has found out about the rendezvous. Susanna tells the Countess, in an ordinary voice. Marcellina hushes her. Susanna makes an inaudible remark to the Countess. Marcellina goes off to the pavilion.

Susanna raises her voice so that Figaro can hear. "My lady, you are shivering." The Countess agrees, also in a raised voice. She proposes audibly to retire. The two girls are now in the very dark part of the stage, near the looming silhouettes of the willows (pines). Figaro is at present the sole listener to their charade. We hear him thinking. "Lo and behold, the critical moment approaches." He hears Susanna's "If madam does not need me, I will stay for half an hour to commune with nature under a willow." "With nature! With nature!" Poor Figaro; it was a cruel joke. "Half an hour, an hour if you wish" says the Countess, and steps back among the willows.

"How dare the rascal doubt me! I will sing, for the sentry who guards the gate against another's entry."

Susanna sings. It is an episode full of magic and poetry, planned and contrived by Mozart with da Ponte's help. It has no counterpart in the play, nor could it have. Yet it is perfectly in keeping with the play, it tells us a great deal about Susanna, and it ends the phase of despair that began with Barbarina's little song. The deepening darkness has been symbolic as well as real. The real darkness remains, and black despair remains for a while in Figaro's heart; but for us the quality of the darkness changes, as the strings begin Susanna's thoughts with four bars of serene C major. It is *allegro vivace assai*, not too fast; a main consideration being to retain reasonable consistency between the feel of the orchestral and vocal bars. "Very near is the moment, the serene time of yielding in the arms of my adored one." Susanna is unaccompanied, seemingly alone in the dark. Neither we nor Figaro are meant to see her. The quality of her voice and of the orchestral playing are enough.

Four more bars from the orchestra. "Fears, hesitations, I beg you all to cease now. I am joyful, do not disturb my peace now." We are here, we will protect you, say the orchestra. "Oh 'tis a place intended for such lovers! Nature around, above us. The earth waits. The air doth hearken." The violins begin a wonderful arching phrase, magic in the light-headedness of being away from the steady crotchet beat in viola and 'cello. The voice takes over, arching down. "Magical nightfall!"

The voice has another arch, all by itself. "Our stolen joys you darken." Gently the strings end her recitative.

For a long moment there is silence, modified by the slight tinkle of running water. The moon has not yet risen. Darkness wraps a world in stillness biding.

Musingly, lullingly, oboe and bassoon offer Susanna (27.25) a melody. It is a simple-seeming phrase in F major; just the right length for a verse line. With the help of the flute they tell her (27.29) how the melody might end, by tripping off through the upper air to F in alt. It is another simple-seeming phrase, full of the feeling of a midsummer night's dream. Susanna accepts the melody but alters it to suit her purpose.

Deh vieni; come soon, come. Although the words are misapplied by the unhappy sentry, it is of the dramatic essence of this sincere deception that the words should not be misunderstood. Susanna is singing a *canzonetta sull'aria*, a sequel to the letter, a passionate invitation: "Come soon, my only joy, for night is falling. Come, for the hour of love's delight is calling."

There is a tendency for singers and writers to be frightened of the verbal meaning of this irresistible *andante*. There is a familiar near-*adagio*, used by singers with great virtuosity to negate any suggestion of continuity with the tempo of the letter duet. Writers also emphasize the purity of the music, thereby implying that the passion by itself would be too impure for Mozart. It is better not to suggest the passion at all than to suggest it wrongly. But it is better still that we should hear it suggested rightly, unforgettably; as we sometimes do.

Line by line, three bars at a time, the incomparable song proceeds. Line is linked to line by phrases for oboe and bassoon. The vocal line goes deep down, as Susanna pictures the torch of the moon below the horizon. The oboe phrase arches up. A four-line verse ends, and the woodwind trip down and up.

"The murmuring brook, the rustling breezes call you." We are in the dominant; flute, oboe and bassoon complete a C major chord. "Ah so softly they" (the brook, the breezes) "say what shall befall you" (with an unexpected change from long-short to short-long in the lilt of the vocal line). "The cooler grass, the flowers that sway in greeting, all things here invite and bless our meeting."

The strings have been having a gentle pizzicato. At the end of the second four-line verse, the first violins are played with the bow again. In the third verse the vocal line is prolonged. "Come, my belovéd, where deeper shadow closes." Even on a moonless night it is darker beneath the willows; the woodwind trip up to F in alt again. "Come, delay not." The music pauses. "True love is waiting." Up from F go voice and violin, down from F comes viola. "Come for your crown of roses." On the word "crown", at the top of the octave, accompanied by the gentlest of tutti, a woman's voice exults. Up to A, down to C, back to F, down to A. ". . . of roses"; down to F.

Again voice and violin climb. This time bassoon supports viola in the countering downward phrase. The voice stays on F; a sustained living F that oboe and bassoon embellish. "Your crown, your kingly crown of roses." The woodwind trip away. The rose aria, the garden aria, is over.

Figaro has been listening. He assumes that every word and nuance is intended for the Count. He resorts to the Count's favourite cry of perfidy. "Treacherous girl! And so our love was all an illusion. Am I awake or dreaming?" Well may he ask.

At the first performance of Figaro, conducted by Mozart, the Susanna was Nancy Storace, a young singer of twenty. She and her brother Stephen were close friends of Mozart. It has been suggested by Alfred Einstein that she was the one woman of whom Constanze Mozart could have had a reason to be jealous. This is not the place to discuss the tenuous evidence, but musicians can consider for themselves whether they detect personal feeling in K.505, *Ch'io mi scordi di te?*, the musical dialogue between soprano and clavier, written "für Mselle Storace und mich." "We do not know", says Paul Hamburger in the *Mozart Companion*, p. 356, "what were the actual relations of Mozart and the pretty Nancy, but this work is the most mature love-letter ever written in music. The author of the notorious 'Bäsle' letters has grown up. On the rope that stretches between dalliance and death, Mozart's heart dances." Nancy Storace was London-born, with an Irish mother. In 1784 she had married a much older man, John Abraham Fisher. The marriage soon broke up.

Soon we shall hear the good firm scrunch of a low D. It will be the finale, and it will begin in D major because the finale (like the opera as a whole) is going to begin and end in the same key. It is a long way from *Deh vieni* in key and feeling; and the gap is made wider when Cherubino enters singing la la la. It is usually assumed to be the LA la la of *Voi che sapete* in B♭. But Christopher Raeburn assures me that it was probably meant to be the la la LA of *Non so più* in E♭. Either way the boy who took the key to E♭ in Act One now has to get it most of the way back in a much shorter recitative. He does it quickly. "There was a voice." (B♭). "Well, I am going in with Barbarina." (D).

But wait! He sees a woman. It is the Countess dressed as Susanna. "No, it cannot be. Susanna's bonnet! I declare she is waiting for a lover." The disguised Countess leans in alarm into D minor. "If the Count should arrive, all (F♮) would be over."

After the opening chord the feeling of the finale is set by the tune that is given to the violins (with horns chipping in at the end of the bar, "and four and *one*"). The vocal lines have a lesser melodic interest. Soon, thanks to the violins, the finale is like one of those perfect last movements of concerto or symphony, that have been in our heads ever since we first heard them. Yet the music is still hugging the words, still telling us exactly how each character reacts. We still get the best of two worlds; a world of absolute music, and a world of music accompanied by meanings.

Cherubino tiptoes towards the supposed Susanna. "Softly, I will take a forfeit. Opportunity is here." A three-bar cycle is concluded, and begins again with the violin tune. The Countess tells us yet again that there will be trouble if the Count comes; but it is the orchestra, and above all the violins (with a flutter of F♮ in the augmented sixth chord) who convey her anxiety to us. Then the violins chuckle and frolic, like naughty children giving the game away. The sombre half of the Act is over. It is about now that the audience should be allowed to see a glimmer of the moon.

In order to get the full humour of the following bars—in order to enjoy them, as Mozart and the violins so evidently enjoy them—one needs to be vividly aware of almost everything that has happened today to Cherubino and the Countess, separately or together. This scamp is the boy who in the play "dared not dare" to kiss Susanna; the boy who was behind the chair when the Count gave him a free lesson in how not to behave; the boy who had always been timid and well-behaved with the Countess; who has today, perhaps, fallen deeply in love with his one "donna". The Countess is the dignified young godmother who was distressed to learn that the boy had been behind the chair when her husband was setting a bad example; the anxious girl who is so easily flustered; the woman who desperately wants to win back her husband; the Rosina who during Susanna's playful aria became uneasily aware that she could fall in love with her godson.

Imagine her feelings as she hears him say "Netta dearest! Are you dumb now? Do not hide your face but come now." Delightedly the violins give him a new vocal phrase in which to sing "I have caught you, never fear." The horns are so excited that they play semiquavers on their own. The Countess is cross, shocked, anxious. We are told so by off-beat wind chords, by downward violin sweeps, and by the whole inflection and timing of her vocal line. "You so brazen! How amazing! Hurry, hurry, disappear." Cheerfully Cherubino counters with "You tease me! Oh appease me, for I know why you are here."

Here comes the Count. He sees a woman's shape. "There she is, my sweet Susanna." Figaro and the real Susanna watch from the sides of the stage. "There he is, my lord and master." Neither Cherubino nor the Countess notice. "Why adopt a haughty manner?" asks Cherubino. At this outrageous remark, the stage is full of harmonic anxiety—the unanimous thoughts of Susanna, the Count and Figaro: "Ah, my heart is beating faster, for another man is there."

"I will shout unless you stop it" threatens the Countess. "Kiss me, kiss me, my pretty poppet" says Cherubino. ("By the voice, it is the pageboy" think the watchers.) "Oh you put me in a rage, boy" says the Countess. "And why should you not allow me what the Count will have, I swear? So you were flirting!" says Cherubino. Angry thoughts converge on him: "He is shameless, shameless, shameless." "You were flirting" he insists "when I was behind the chair." At last a singer has shared the first theme with the violins; it comes low in the voice and is not very recognisable. The violins are shocked. Four minds have one thought: "He must go at once, I know that this will ruin the affair." It is lucky that the Countess is so angry; or the affair would be ruined already.

Cherubino reaches to kiss the Countess. The Count and Figaro rush forward, knowing that the kiss is intended for Susanna. The Count arrives between the Countess and Cherubino. It is the Count's male cheek that receives a kiss intended for Susanna's lips. The Countess thinks a word-hugging squawk. " 'Tis oh! his Lordship." " 'Twas ooh! his Lordship" thinks Cherubino, disgusted. He slips away to join Barbarina. The Count is preparing to cuff Cherubino. Figaro, arriving to "see what happened there," gets the cuff. He retires ruefully, reflecting that curiosity has been rewarded. The others imagine that temerity (the page's) has been well rewarded. They all chuckle for ten long bars. In the last three bars and in the bar of transition to G major the violins seem to be playfully cuffing Cherubino or Figaro.

Con un poco più di moto the Count begins to court a woman. He thinks it is Susanna. He thinks he is alone with her. He has, he thinks, sent that wretched boy away with a good cuff. It was therefore still dark, but the moon is gradually coming out a little further, to provide the conventional degree of illumination for a romantic scene. Bassoon and first violin resume more or less where they left off in *16*.

The Count is less ardent than in *16*. But he warms up, and the woman encourages him: "I come to do your pleasure joyfully, willingly." Figaro thinks indignantly, disgustedly: "An obliging woman certainly! What wifely loyalty!" The strings spare a moment of jolty unison sympathy for him. The first violins soar two octaves (*28.59*) with an ardent legato phrase for the Count: "Give me your hand, my precious." Away go the violins with oboe help to fetch heartfelt compliance. "With all my heart" says the supposed Susanna. The violins offer Figaro his indignant phrase, but he is beyond indignation. He hears the Count say "Delicious!" He echoes the word in sardonic misery. The Count rejoices in the feel of fingers that "are so slender, with skin so soft and tender." It does not occur to him or Figaro that this sounds like the hand of a lady of leisure. The Count slobbers as he describes the erotic effect of fingers so willingly offered to his caress. The others do not mince their thoughts. "To reason is he blinded, to passion is he minded, 'tis well he cannot see."

Softly and a little shamefacedly the Count pays up in E minor. "Take then, my love, the money. But that is what I owe you, so take this ring to show you what gratitude can be." The Countess replies with one of her less heartfelt vocal lines; an ironical "I am indeed your debtor." But oboe and violin betray her irrepressible love. "I take them, as you see" (still in E minor). "Oh better still and better" thinks the Count "the best is still to be." An amused Susanna thinks the same. Figaro also thinks it; with a very different nuance! The violins continue to frolic.

The supposed Susanna points out that men are coming with torches. The Count, with tiptoeing violins, points cheerfully to the pavilion. "Then come in here with me, my fair! O Venus, we proceed." This is the eighteenth century of *Tom Jones*, which so offended Doctor Johnson. " 'Tis dark in there, I feel." "The darkness is ideal; as well you know I enter for a purpose, not to read." Readers may or may not be amused by da Ponte's text. But the scoring shows that Mozart enjoyed it; and the unison phrase should be played from its opening sforzando in a way that convinces the whole listening audience that conductor and orchestra are enjoying it.

For Figaro it is not a joke (a fact which increases its comic effectiveness). His indignant phrase returns: "Oh she is going after him, more proof I do not need." Susanna and the Countess titter at a better joke. "We have misled them thoroughly, 'tis going well indeed." Loudly, and almost but not quite in unison, the orchestra offer Figaro his indignant phrase again. But Figaro is acting, not thinking. The staccato quavers have become the tramp of his feet. He comes forward, unable to bear it longer. "Who is it?" asks the Count. "Just a no one!" shouts Figaro. " 'Tis Figaro ! I flee" says the woman dressed as Susanna. "Go on, go on then—and wait for me!" says the Count as he goes after her.

More tramping. The music modulates, with an effect like Alice jumping one of the little dotted brooks on the giant chess-board that lay *Through the Looking Glass*. We were watching a crisp West End farce in G major, with one or two lines that probably made the Lord Chamberlain think a bit. Now Figaro is alone for a classical interlude, a depressed soliloquy in the E♭ of *Porgi Amor*. The clarinets take over— we have not heard their characteristic tone-quality since *26*. The violins relax into dreamy downward triplets, legato, three against two. We are invited to contemplate a picture of elegiac tranquillity. For the first time there is moon enough for scenic photography. If the scenery is well contrived, we can enjoy it—now, not earlier.

The barber smatters Latin, as Ben Jonson once said. Figaro, still in the state of mind revealed in *26*, heard the Count saying to the supposed Susanna "O Venus, we proceed." Da Ponte is thinking of what happened to Venus (Aphrodite) in book VIII of the Odyssey. Her husband Vulcan (Hephaestus) prepared a net to catch her in bed with Mars (Ares). Off went Vulcan to Lemnos. Along came Mars. They were caught in the net. The sun gave Vulcan the tip to return. He came, stood in his doorway, and shouted for the gods to come and see. They came, but reacted in a way that the poor lame husband did not expect—with *asbestos gelôs*, unquenchable laughter. "Oh Apollo" said Hermes, "I wish I were in there with her. I would not mind being bound with three times the amount of netting. I would not mind the gods—and all the goddesses—looking on; so long as I was in bed with golden Aphrodite." We in the audience, whether we sit in the cheapest seats or not, are those gods and goddesses; and our laughter need not be quenched by the clarinet blues. Figaro feels lonely, lame, helpless, defeated. Everyone will laugh at him. The Count has won. He will go and catch them (*sforzando*) but—he laughs ruefully at himself—it won't do any good. This 1785 revolutionary has a subtler mind than his *ancien régime* opponent.

The moment of indecision is brief. Suddenly and without change of key the strings bustle and scurry, unhampered by introspective woodwind. Susanna comes forward: "Ah, Figaro ! but hush now." She is disguising her voice, and he takes her to be the Countess—the one person who can help him in his dilemma. He pours out his indignation.

He invites Susanna to catch herself in the act that she has so skilfully avoided. His words—such is his haste—are far from tactful. He is also talking too loudly. She hushes him angrily, in her own voice. "Stay here and I will tell you what my revenge will be!"

It is the most topsy-turvy moment of the folle journée. He was so certain that . . . Now suddenly . . . Whoever it was, it was not Susanna who . . . Er, she is angry . . . In his relief Figaro decides to invite the furious slap which will prove that he is awake, not dreaming. "Revenge? How then? Have you a good solution?" She is thinking how to catch him. Figaro, veteran of the battles of wits in Acts Two and Three, helps her out. "Will you, my lady, will you?" He is guying the Count. Bassoon and first violin guy the appropriate music of seduction. "You see, what did I tell you!" (Susanna addresses the thought to an imaginary confidante.) "Ah, my lady." Figaro lays it on thick. "Here at your feet, my lady" (Bom bom, go the horns) "I kneel and seek a favour." (Horns.) "We may by such behaviour" (Horns) "repay them, I am sure."

These words have a predictable effect on the strings and on Susanna. The first violins can hardly restrain themselves, the second violins race in excitement, the 'cellos bounce. "Oh how my fingers itch for it" thinks Susanna. Figaro's reply is usually supposed to be an aside; it lies low in the voice and is apt to get lost. It should be sung aloud as part of the act: "Oh how my being aches for it." Again we hear them thinking. "I hardly can endure . . ." "She hardly can endure . . ." The vocal lines soars to A♭. At last, after all the hints dropped by Figaro, Susanna thinks of a gambit: "Although you do not love me?" There is an upward orchestral slide between repeated Cs. " 'Twas mute, you were above me." Figaro is inspired, irresistible. A downward slide in the orchestra. "We're wasting time, what say you?" There is a splendid prolongation of the final word into a melisma. "Give me your hand, I pray you" (Bom bom bom) "give me your hand." Susanna thinks it is the equivalent of the Count's "*Porgemi la manina.*" It is not. It is Figaro's sense of humour.

"With pleasure, to be sure." One, two, three, four, five, six furious slaps, to the great excitement of the orchestra. "And this one, and this one!" "She never seems to miss one!" thinks Figaro. Seven, eight, nine. "Mister villain! To show I'm willing." But Figaro only says "Go on, the more the merrier; I love you more and more." His delight is not what Susanna expected. Disconcertedly she says what she thinks of a barber turned seducer. Soon she is echoing Figaro's line. With a final flare of annoyance she soars up once more to that A♭.

The E♭ music draws to a close. A pause, a strong B♭, and we are off with another simple and unforgettable tune. It is a singer's line, dependent on the quality and expressiveness of the voice that sings it. "No more quarrelling, let us agree, dear; for I knew what you wanted of me, dear; I could tell by the voice I adore." Off goes the oboe in affection and trust, though seldom quite able to match what the singer has made of it. "By my voice, dear?" "The voice I adore so." Susanna takes the tune and there is complete understanding between them. It is full moonlight, in which we can see costume and gesture as well as if it were day.

The same vocal line is used by the Count in aggrieved solitary misunderstanding. "I have looked for her all round the garden." " 'Tis the master! Our hearts let us harden!" There is glee in their line. "Hi, Susanna. Where are you? I want you!" So he didn't recognise her. Recognise whom? "My lady!" "My lady?" asks Figaro. "My lady" Susanna assures him. As the comedy soon will be ending, they determine to complete the Count's discomfiture.

The violins oblige with an echo of the Count's hesitant quavers in 16—the *No, no, yes* duet, by now so much parodied. Figaro puts on his act again. This time it is entirely unrestrained. "Yes, my lady, you are my adored one." The Count can learn the foolish trade of husband. "With my wife, sir? And I've not got a sword on!" (Counts should never go into the garden improperly dressed.) Figaro increases the fervour of a scene that is sincere, legitimate, mischievous, and melodramatic. He gets equally sincere and enthusiastic co-operation from the supposed Countess. At last! The Count always believes what he sees. Like an air-raid siren the strings surge upwards, against blaring quaver chords on woodwind and horns. "Oh, the scoundrels, the scoundrels." "Let us hasten away, my beloved, for a love there is nothing to mar." Off they hasten towards the overcrowded pavilion.

Three short chords, and we say goodbye to the B♭ that has been the keynote of so many admirable episodes. For the fifth and last time the music jumps to G. The Count grabs Figaro and shouts for help. Susanna breaks into an undignified run to the pavilion. Figaro puts on an air of complete surprise. " 'Tis . . . the master." The Count shouts again for help. A group of men come running from the bonfire on the terrace; Basilio, Bartolo, Antonio, and the men whom the Countess had seen with torches. "Everyone, come here, support me." ("He has caught me!" explains Figaro helpfully.) "This man has made me look a fool" says the Count "he has betrayed me with a lady you shall see." They are astounded. (Hocquard relates the rhythm of their astonishment with Basilio's "*in mal punto son qui giunto*" 7.16; a "rhythm of ironical discovery".) The Count summons his lady to come out for the due reward of her virtue. With a vindictive little violin trill he hauls out from the pavilion, first Cherubino ("who tries unavailingly to conceal his identity"—Ernest Newman), then Barbarina, then Marcellina. Then and only then does he succeed in grabbing Susanna, dressed as the Countess. Roughly he hauls her out. The little trills have persisted; one for each person hauled out, one for each cry of recognition. Triumphantly the Count points to Susanna and Figaro. "Their doings were shady, my lady and he." Forgive? No. Can infidelity be forgiven? No. Why is everyone taking their side? No, no, no, no, no, NO. Molotov could have made it no plainer. It is a line of Shakespearian grandeur. Desperately, unconvincingly, the Count persists. As Hocquard points out, the first No is too high, on E; the last No is too low, on C. Something is wrong, somewhere.

The Countess has appeared. Unhurriedly—singers have been known to enter on the third beat of the bar or earlier, instead of on the fourth beat—she sings in a perfect legato: "But you will forgive them at my wifely plea." That is all. It is enough. She holds out her hands in mute appeal. Perhaps she shows him with a smile, and a caress of the fingers that were so slender, the ring he gave her. Perhaps she throws Susanna the purse. But these things are unimportant. The music goes into G minor. A naughty but human young husband is discovered to be after all noble-hearted to some extent. Don Giovanni loved every woman and therefore no woman; he was irredeemable. This man cannot resist the undeserved power of his only true asset, Rosina's love. He kneels, in front of the servants. With a tuneful and humble dignity he apologises (in the major again). With an upward sixth from D to B on the last half-beat of the bar he begins "My lady, forgive me, forgive me, forgive me." An upward minor seventh; then questioning anxiety, semitone by upward semitone, fermata by fermata.

She forgives him. The upward interval becomes a simple fifth, from G to D. *Più docile sono*—gentlest of rebukes. "*I* cannot deny *you*, once more I say Yes, once more (what a simple and beautiful turn on the word 'more') I say Yes." Pianissimo, low G. All is forgiven, all is mystical light. The violins sway down from top G, as Susanna swayed down from F near the end of *Deh vieni*. There are three married couples on the stage; Count and Countess, Figaro and Susanna, Bartolo and Marcellina. There are also Cherubino and Barbarina, boy and girl. Antonio and Basilio watch. Antonio is too far gone in drink to notice much. Basilio is too far gone in cynicism to notice anything —except the quality of the singing. But they all share and amplify the beauty of the music with which the Countess forgave. They do not, at their first *sotto voce* entry, intrude on the privacy of that rising interval on the last half-beat. But twice during the next fourteen bars the two heroines, the Countess and Susanna, sing a similar rising interval (now a fourth, up to G) on a last quarter-beat. Twice they all join in. On the second occasion the part-writing becomes more wonderful than ever. Abert and Hocquard relate this perfect page to the purification of Tamino and Pamina, the rhythm of the final chorus of *The Magic Flute*, and the way in which it follows Sarastro's final lines. Hocquard also compares the *In mortis* of the KV 618 *Ave Verum*; he writes of la radieuse nappe sonore, que traversent les prodigieux arpèges lents des cordes.

A moment of rededication is over. The strings quietly voice a thought that was perhaps in Basilio's mind already. As Spike Hughes neatly says, the music is an uneasy question-mark. How long will the contentment last? Something of it may endure passably well (except that Barbarina has no chance of marrying Cherubino—his parents would never consent). There is a drum roll. The opera is back in D major, *allegro assai*. The characters sing: "We were all, yes all tormented by the day's caprice and folly. Now at last we can be jolly. Love alone could set us right. Let us in friendship go dancing and joking. Look, the bonfire needs a stoking." (Antonio is sent off, grumbling, to see to it.) Casually Mozart throws in a final contrast of sound; the rapidly approaching local band. Why? So that "We can hear a merry music" in which the horns of cuckoldry are silent.

I hope I have demonstrated that *Figaro* is worth knowing in detail. It has the sweep and coherence of Michelangelo's design on the Sistine ceiling and wall. But it also has as many particular beauties as the Uffizi gallery; and they all contribute to the effect of the whole. I have had to ignore many musical points, in order to emphasise the musical and verbal points that add up to drama. Yet in performance, if any touch of colour is omitted, or any detail blurred, something goes a little wrong with the focus and perspective of the whole. If a nuance is missed, the truth and humanity of Mozart's vision recede. If too many nuances are missed, we get back to the trivial sketch which Beaumarchais described, tongue in cheek, as "la plus badine des intrigues".

PART III

DON GIOVANNI
(DON JUAN, DON JOHN)

Title: Il dissoluto punito, o sia il Don Giovanni.
Köchel number: 527. *First performance:* 29th October 1787, in Prague.

> I can love both fair and browne,
> Her whom abundance melts, and her whom want betraies,
> Her who loves loneness best, and her who maskes and plaies,
> Her whom the country form'd, and whom the town,
> Her who beleeves, and her who tries,
> Her who still weepes with spungie eyes,
> And her who is dry corke, and never cries;
> I can love her, and her, and you and you,
> I can love any, so she be not true. . . .
>
> For every houre that thou wilt spare me now,
>   I will allow,
> Usurious God of Love, twenty to thee,
> When with my browne, my gray haires equall bee;
> Till then, Love, let my body raigne, and let
> Mee travell, sojourne, snatch, plot, have, forget,
> Resume my last yeares relict: think that yet
>   We'had never met . . .
>
> Wilt thou forgive that sinn, where I begunn,
> Which is my sin, though it were done before?
> Wilt thou forgive those sinns through wch I runn,
> And doe them still, though still I doe deplore?
> When thou hast done, thou hast not done, for I have more.

JOHN DONNE (1573–1631)

DON GIOVANNI

Characters in order of singing

LEPORELLO has been described as the central figure of the opera; the normal and credible human who dreams its absurd events. Are the events so absurd? Let us admit that, as Shaw puts it, "gentlemen who break through the categories of good and evil, and come out the other side singing *Fin ch'han dal vino* and *Là ci darem*, do not as a matter of fact get called on by statues, and taken straight down through the floor to eternal torments." But the characters, normal or not, are grippingly credible. The Don is the central figure, and the Statue (of Anna's father) is a special case. Leporello is neither more nor less important than any of the others.

He is the Don's servant, hanger-on, helper, friend (24.427), foil, critic, compère; the opera's general commentator. He blames the Don: "I swear I was blameless, I was simply led astray. 'Twas my master who did force me, took my innocence away." Because Leporello is a commentator rather than a doer, the same aria (20) contains what are perhaps the most reflective words of the libretto: "What can I say, sir? . . . that not on purpose . . . that in dismay, sir . . . what on the surface was gaily splendid, inside was all dark, will not be mended . . ." He is an active accessory. But he is frightened of the other characters. In one of his spurts of self-confidence (4), he grossly insults Elvira. Later he has his opportunity to "play at master" (1.20–22); dressed as the Don, he is told to "give her four good caresses, speaking to her in my voice; then use your manly charm, persuade her to go off with you somewhere." He gives her four not very good caresses, in crotchet pauses; and begins to acquire confidence—the difficult part having been done for him by the Don. But the Don impatiently interrupts, and Leporello then wanders miserably round the streets with a credulous and willing woman. Meanwhile the Don serenades the maid, disperses the peasants, beats up Masetto and is free to return to the maid. On another occasion Leporello daringly pinches a bottom (5A23). He is less virile than the Don, and frequently finds life too real to be comfortable. "My master bids you dine, sir—'tis his idea, not mine, sir!— this evening as his guest . . . AH, ah, ah, what am I seeing? . . . God pardon me, a sinner! I freeze, I quake, I'm thinner!" But his mind is more usually comforted with phantasies—thoughts of what the Don is doing every day, and safely remote dreams of what he himself would like to do with every woman whom he meets. Note that it is he, not the Don, who talks of "proofs of virility" (*13.250*). He hears the sordid details; which he records and cross-indexes with loving care. He has a girl-friend; whom the Don seduces during *Il mio tesoro*.

DONNA ANNA is not a truthful woman. Shaw imagines her, in old age, taking care to confess more sins than she had committed. How angry she is in *Man and Superman* to find that, despite all efforts to preserve her earthly and heavenly reputation, she has gone to hell. "Oh! and I might have been so much wickeder! All my good deeds wasted! It is unjust." On which, the dead Don explains to her that she had not listened when "fully and clearly warned". *Ma il mondo . . .* she says in the opera; what will people think? (*23.9*). In this respect she is carefully contrasted with Elvira who, when the Don says "Do be quiet! Think a little, there are people all around us; of your reputation brittle be more prudent, have a care" replies "Do not hope for that admission! I have lost all thought of prudence. What you did, and my condition, to them all I shall declare."

Anna's story to Ottavio (*10.25–61*) is at best ambiguous; commentator after commentator has defended her honour without (apparently) having read the text. We shall find that the true meaning is the less creditable one. "In which case" said Newman, offering what he appears to have considered to be evidence of the truth of the story "what becomes of our conception of the noble Donna Anna?" What indeed? Yet our task is to discover what Mozart intended. Let me implore you not to rush to either of the two obvious conclusions. Anna is no heroine. But she is not a mere hypocrite either. To grasp Mozart's idea of her personality we need to pay attention to many things; her *Sturm und Drang* music, her extravagant words, her habit of reverie in Ottavio's presence, her occasional use of *voi* to Ottavio, the characters of Ottavio and the Don, and so on. Briefly, she is an impulsive wilful motherless rich girl.

DON GIOVANNI is the dissolute one (*Il Dissoluto*). In da Ponte's list of characters he is a "young and extremely licentious cavalier". Yet we, like the three famous monkeys, have heard no evil, seen no evil, spoken no evil. Newman, distinguishing between Mozart's Don and da Ponte's Don, describes the latter as "the last poor ineffectual scion of an illustrious race of conquerors . . . Tirso's Don Juan would have refused to sit at the same table with anyone so inefficient; Shadwell's

Libertine would have scorned to be seen raiding the same nunnery in his company."

I am sorry to keep picking on Newman; he errs memorably. But Mozart was not the man to accept a tame Don from da Ponte. The joke has been on us. Mozart's Don is so licentious that he had to be camouflaged. This was done mainly by ambiguities and studied vaguenesses in the libretto. The ambiguities have second meanings that are precise—and lewd. The vaguenesses are at points where precision would have given the game away.

What did Mozart and da Ponte make of this perennial character? A candid, coherent, logical Johnny. His aim in life is to have enjoyed the willing and sufficient response of as many different women as possible. "I, as I sense in me a feeling so extended, wish well to every one of them. But as the women cannot count beyond one, they call my good and natural power deception." "And what a natural power!" says the smirking Leporello "was a power ever more vast or more beneficent?" You see what I mean, about those ambiguities? We are listening to the boastful phallic humour of a madcap young officer and his friend. What has such a man Done?

Luigi Bassi, for whom the part was written (see p. 192) was twenty-two. The Don is not like that smug old bore Casanova, aged sixty-two, who hurried to Prague to pose as what Tamino would have called *Das Original*. Nor is he like the forty-two-year-old Baron Gruner, whom Conan Doyle imagined (*The Case-book of Sherlock Holmes*) as keeping his private lust diary, with full details of about a hundred "souls I have ruined". Mozart's Don is a healthy male animal. He is not just over-sexed. He eats well, drinks well, sees well, has a good sense of smell, is immensely energetic, needs very little sleep. Women respond instinctively to his self-confident presence. He is gay, handsome, wealthy, leisured, well-born, well-dressed, well-mannered; a gentleman in several senses of the word. He has all the advantages, and is a thoroughly irresponsible young fellow. He is therefore out to enjoy a certain ritual. He enjoys it. He ensures that they enjoy it at the time. He is genuinely bewildered that they should be so selfish and narrow-minded as to want to keep him.

Is he then a mere sower of wild oats? What divides Don John from the young John Donne (see p. 145), who became a fairly saintly Dean of Saint Paul's? Not very much, if we accept Shaw's notion of a Don who went to the arduous life of heaven because he found hell so boring. Nor, as Shaw also remarks "is it yet by any means an established fact that the world owes more to its Don Ottavios than to its

Don Juans." The final scene is enough to prove that life can be dull without the Don. Yet Mozart, as usual, remains realistic. Charm can be dangerous. It is easy (and often right) to ridicule the claims of society. Yet many of those claims are the reasonable claims of other people. A hermit, by minimising his claims on them, can minimise their claims on him. But the Don is no hermit. He is a spoiled boy; altogether too untruthful, too lacking in any real consideration for others, too apt to be cruel for the fun of it. In a word he is stony-hearted. Therefore the statue is poetic justice. A John Donne has passionate affairs—fewer than are implied by the verses on p. 145—and then sobers up. The Don is a confidence trickster. He has seduced a woman a day, on average, for five or six years. Elvira, an exceptionally passionate woman, managed to retain his interest for three days. He is therefore behind schedule, so far as the list is concerned. During the opera he makes up for lost time by seducing about half a dozen women in twenty-four hours. His programmes are sometimes too optimistic; but Leporello's strange accountancy is consistent with the entire musical and verbal picture of Mozart's Don, who is too reckless to last long.

THE COMMENDATORE is the only character who, given the right quality of voice, does not have to be a first-class actor as well. He is Anna's father, a staunch upholder of Right and Decency, a Defender of the Faith.

He is not to be thought of as a *comandante*, a commander; the overlap of meaning is too small. The Commendatore is commendable, in this ironic drama, because he dies for the non-existent honour of his daughter. The Italian word *commendatore* means Knight of an order of chivalry. Not every commander get his "K". Not every Knight Commander is a commander.

The part was originally doubled by the singer of Masetto; who had to get out of his statue between *24.554* and *24.603*.

DON OTTAVIO   Any good tenor can make Ottavio's professed love of Anna sound convincing. It is the fatal step towards making nonsense of (a) the part (b) the opera. Ottavio's music, a brilliant parody of conventional tenor love, is meant to be nasty, insincere, complacent, self-congratulatory. Admire my voice. Admire my technique. Admire, above all, my breath-control.

Ottavio is well-born. Anna, an only daughter, has a good dowry and better expectations. A marriage has been arranged. He is on a visit, so that he and his fiancée can meet and get to know each other. By the end of the opera he is beginning to accept (*23A*, *24.726*) that life with Anna will be on Anna's terms: "faithfully your will appeasing, as I should, being so adored." But . . . (see p. 173).

Ottavio's lack of interest in Anna as a person is underlined by his passing interest in Elvira. During the quartet, he is roused to his two most human lines in the opera, "From this place I am not going till I fathom this affair" (*9.50*). By *13.183* she has become *l'amica*. Anna is in passing danger (*13.193*). But Elvira has no fortune, and betrays not the slightest interest in Ottavio. At *19.30* we still find Ottavio telling Anna, calmly and brightly, to dry the tears which *he* dislikes so much. Anna replies, in the finest of her D minor utterances "Let my sorrow have some outlet! For how else may I endure it? Only one thing, only, only death can cure it, only death can bring relief."

Ottavio is insufferable. He lacks Basilio's sense of humour and has an even thicker skin. "Therefore console my darling, *sincerely* sympathise; try, if her tears are falling, to wipe them from her eyes. Tell her I'm hotly burning, lusting for manly bloodshed, and will not be returning save with a hero's prize" (*21*). He returns; without a hero's prize. He lectures her about the will of Heaven (*22A6*); in this case, instant matrimony. She can hardly bear the sight of him. She explodes, and forgets to use *tu*. Ottavio is worried. "Eh? What? You put me off and off, as if wanting to make me unhappy!" At *23A* he has still not taken the hint that she wants to be alone; even after being the witness of a reverie in which she is completely oblivious of his presence—as she almost was, in *2*. At *24.717*, as soon as the Don is dead, his mind turns to a certain *ristoro* (the *remedio* of *18*). "Pray allow me the lawful pleasure I so often have implored." He is a man who deserves to be fobbed off.

Hoffmann said that Anna would never marry Ottavio. Shaw in *Man and Superman* imagines that she married him and became the mother of twelve children. Neither does justice to the ironic realism of the opera. Anna is determined to remain respectable, and has just enjoyed a passionate love-affair with the Don; on sudden romantic impulse, and without what Despina (*Così fan tutte 18A17*) calls "care to prevent the common humiliation of those who trust in menfolk." Will she wait a year? She needs time to simmer down, and to wonder whether she could find someone nicer. She will probably marry Ottavio next week. Just in case. . . .

DONNA ELVIRA   The Don is about twenty-two, at most. Did Mozart think of Elvira as a Marcellina-like frump, clinging to a man less than half her age? Or as a Rosina-like girl in her teens? Or what? A singer who can do justice to the nobility of this part is hardly likely to be in her teens. But Leporello says (*20.53*) that she is a *fanciulla*, a young girl. She has to present herself as awkward, credulous, naïve, stiff-necked, uncompromising, unworldly, very vulnerable—and therefore absurdly young, the *giovin principiante* of *4*. Molière made her a nun. In the opera she finally goes to a convent. She could be a lady of means, strictly brought-up. But her angular and old-fashioned utterances at *3* and *8* suggest the cloistered novice. Her characterisation is further considered in the commentary on *3*, *3A*, *4* and *4A*.

Remember that Mozart is an ironical realist, not a cynic. Other characters in *Figaro* and in the present opera may bluster or prevaricate, pose or caress, fret, jest, mumble, insinuate. Elvira is too straightforward and innocent for such antics. She opens up a new realm of Mozartian irony by *wanting* (and abysmally failing) to mean brave words. Fiordiligi and Dorabella could be her daughters, Ferrando and Guglielmo her godsons. She wants to tear out the Don's heart; she succeeds in talking like a printed book. She wants to be high-minded; she succeeds in being jealous. "He was her man, he done her wrong"; she wants him back. She goes on hoping, even in *24*. She is never more jealous or devoted than when, dazed by the humiliation of *Madamina*, she says "I pray he'll not escape me . . . I'll have recourse to . . . I'll go to . . . I feel inside me nothing left but revenge, fury, retribution". The short concluding secco sections of this opera are invariably important.

✓ ZERLINA was probably a star part for Madame Bondini (p. 158). She is at least as important as the other two women; in some ways, more so. She is a blonde dairymaid with lively eyes. Blonde, because the Don calls her *Zerlinetta gentil* as soon as he is alone with her (*6A2*); his opening gambit with blondes is to praise their *gentilezza* (*4.92*). A dairymaid, because the Don is made to say that her fingers are soft as junket—a good example of the Don's skill in adapting his language to the woman of the moment. Her *occhi bricconcelli* are noted and slyly flattered at *6A17*. Note that she is also abused as a *briccona* (for instance, at *13.322*) by Masetto. He thinks of her as a slut. The flattery and abuse cancel out. *La briccona fa festa*, she likes parties and loves dancing. She is a normal, healthy, flirtatious girl of the type so credibly described by Despina in *Così fan tutte 19*. Her advice to the giggling lasses is "While you whisper of love and of troubles, you should not let the time disappear. You are lasses, your hearts are like bubbles; you are ready for love, I am clear."

Masetto is handsome (*12.2*) and virile, but she could not have chosen a man less compatible in temperament. Their marriage may have its moments. But it will not be the eternally idyllic affair of which she dreams when singing "Here on earth a very heaven nightly, daily, we shall find" (*12.65*). She likes to be admired. He never admires her. She instantly accepts an invitation to the Don's dance (*Si, si, facciamo core, 13.148*). She was mentally there, as soon as she heard the sound of the second orchestra in the distance. But Masetto is a jealous oaf, who can think of only one reason why an attractive woman might want to go to a dance.

She is Masetto's property. He says so publicly. "My Zerlina cannot stay here without me." He is a peasant and a male in the eighteenth century. He is never in any doubt that he owns her. They are not yet legally married (*6A13*). Therefore she can still be swayed by the Don's offer of marriage. But she refers to Masetto, innocently enough, as her husband (*6A5*); and da Ponte tells us that he is her *amante*. Much is explained about the tensions of their relationship, if we assume that the "rough young ploughboy" (*6A10*) had insisted on making sure that she was bringing with her a dowry of fertility.

"*Fosti ognor la mia ruina*, you are what I always thought you" (*6.36*). Her reward for having allowed him a favour is the usual contempt and suspicion. She is thought a slut, easy-going with other men as well. She will always be to blame. He will want to beat her, hard and often (*12*). Yet he responds, despite himself, to her anxiety for his well-being ("Oh you poor man, if he met you, can you guess what he would do", *13.18*). His childish self-pity needs her cheerful mothering and nursing (*17A, 18*). She has a way with her. In his rough way he probably loves her. She will be a valuable property; an energetic mother and housewife, a wife and general molly-coddler. Perhaps he will be prudent enough not to damage the property except when drunk.

Mozart and da Ponte took time and trouble to make a person—warm, rounded, credible—out of the peasant girls who used to flit so titillatingly in and out of the Don Juan saga. Indeed they took even more trouble over this ordinary every-day blonde than over the dignified Elvira or the secretive Anna. Zerlina is less gullible, less dignified, less romantic; above all less secretive. She is the one whose inmost feelings as a woman can effectively be presented on the stage. Elvira was last week's victim, Anna succumbed last night, Zerlina twists our hearts by the detailed truth and credibility of her mixed feelings as she mentally surrenders in daylight, before our eyes, to the rogue who is everything that Masetto is not. An equally credible feminine charm is then twice released on us—and on Masetto, whom she needs.

MASETTO (*Tommasetto*, Tommy) is yet another major character. He must never seem a lesser personality than Zerlina, or an unworthy opponent of the Don. He can be less detestable than Ottavio, but he must be nasty enough to explain Zerlina's dilemma.

Ottavio admires the Don, and is reluctant to think evil of him. Masetto instantly detests him, and suspects the worst. These opposite reactions are evoked by one and the same phenomenon; a man who is handsome, charming, well-born, wealthy, leisured and above all well-dressed. Masetto is a peasant, with a considerable force of personality. He is earthy, narrow, resentful. His relationship with the Don soon develops as a series of contests of wits, will-power and force.

PROLOGUE

Dᴀ Pᴏɴᴛᴇ ᴄʟᴀɪᴍᴇᴅ much of the credit. "I thought that it was time to reawaken my poetic muse. . . . The three renowned Maestri, Martini, Mozzart and Salieri, gave me the opportunity . . . Salieri asked of me only a free translation (of his latest French opera, *Tarare*); Mozzart and Martini left the choice entirely to me. For the former I chose *Don Giovanni*, a subject which pleased him infinitely, and for Martini *l'arbore di Diana*—for him I wanted a gentle subject, suited to his very sweet melodies, which are felt in the soul, but which very few are capable of imitating . . . I informed the Emperor that my intention was to write these three operas simultaneously. 'You wont succeed' he replied. 'Perhaps not' I answered 'but I shall try. For Mozzart I shall write at night and shall account it reading Dante's *Inferno*—I shall write during the morning for Martini, and that will be like studying Petrarch; in the evening I shall write for Salieri, and he shall be my Tasso'. He found my parallel very good, and scarcely had I got home than I began to write. I went to my writing table and sat there twelve hours on end. A small bottle of Tokay on my right, the inkstand in the middle, and a box of Seville snuff on my left. A beautiful sixteen-year-old girl, whom I had meant to love only as a daughter but . . . was staying in my house with her mother who looked after the housekeeping; she came to my room at the sound of the bell, which in sooth I rang rather often, and especially when my inspiration was beginning to grow cool. . . . On the first day, between the Tokay, the Seville snuff, the coffee, the bell, and my young Muse, I wrote the first two scenes of *Don Giovanni*, two others of *l'arbore di Diana*, and more than half of the first act of *Tarar*, a title I changed to *Assur*. In the morning I took these scenes to the three composers, who could scarcely believe that what they read with their own eyes could possibly be achieved; in 63 days the first two operas were entirely finished, and almost two-thirds of the last."

It is a nice story, and may perhaps contain a little more truth than some of the hearsay recollections which we shall consider and discard when we come to the *Magic Flute*. But even a da Ponte does not write a libretto without planning it, or without mentioning the subject to the composer. We can accept that Mozart did not suggest the subject. But it "pleased him infinitely" and the score is evidence enough of Mozart's share in the planning of the libretto.

To appreciate this, we must first recall Mozart's triumphant visit to Prague in January and the early February of 1787. Figaro, as we have seen, was only moderately popular with the Viennese public in 1786. They preferred *Una cosa rara* by Martini (Martin y Soler) and da Ponte. But Mozart had friends at Prague, where Pasquale Bondini (director of the travelling company that performed *die Entführung* at Leipzig in September 1783) was now impresario. The Bohemians were a community of practising musicians, capable of a whole-hearted response to the instrumental brilliance of the *Figaro* score. *Le nozze* was therefore received, at its first Prague performance in December (or late November) 1786 "with an enthusiasm such as only *die Zauberflöte* later knew". The significant admission, that Don Giovanni was less enthusiastically received, is by Niemetschek in 1798. "It is the strictest truth if I say that (*Figaro*) was played almost uninterruptedly that whole winter, and that it completely alleviated the wretched circumstances of the entrepreneur." Like most people who tell us that such-and-such is the strictest truth, Niemetschek was exaggerating, and probably knew it. But a Prague newspaper reported on 12th December that "no piece (so everyone here asserts) has ever caused such a sensation . . . the wind instruments, on which the Bohemians are well known to be decided masters, have a great deal to do in the whole piece. . . ." According to Leopold Mozart, the orchestra and a "company of distinguished connoisseurs and lovers of music" invited the composer to Prague. On 11th January, at noon, Mozart and his wife arrived in Prague. That day he attended a ball at which the dancers "flew about in sheer delight to the music of my Figaro, arranged for quadrilles and waltzes. . . . Here they talk about nothing but *Figaro*. Nothing is played, sung, or whistled but *Figaro*. No opera is drawing but *Figaro*. Nothing, nothing but *Figaro*. . . ." But Mozart had to wait six days before he was acclaimed at a performance of *Figaro*, on 17th January; and we seem only to know for certain of one other performance (conducted by himself) before he left on 8th February. He gave a successful concert on 19th January in the Opera House; the programme included the first performance of the D major "Prague" symphony. He also acquired, no doubt, an impression of the Prague theatres, and of the talents and limitations of the players and singers.

It was in these circumstances that Pasquale Bondini offered Mozart 100 ducats (half the fee that a Rautenstrauch commanded) for an opera to be performed by the Prague company during the following season. A little less than eight months later, on 4th October, Mozart returned with the unfinished score of one of the world's greatest works: *Il dissoluto punito, o sia il Don Giovanni*.

Synopses of earlier stage versions tell us little about the creative excitement with which Mozart welcomed da Ponte's suggestion that it should be an opera about the great seducer. The story was one that everyone knew in outline. Tirso de Molina, a Spanish monk, had rashly created the saga (printed in 1630) of a young Spanish nobleman who seduces women, murders an old man, insults the dead, invites a statue to dinner, and finally sinks through a stage trapdoor into hell. The nobleman, of course, has a servant. The theme lent itself to endless adaptation and improvisation, all over Europe. Audiences loved it. They had their money's worth of seduction and buffoonery, sanctified by an ecclesiastical (and apparently edifying) conclusion. Thomas Shadwell, one of the many writers to offer a profitable pot-boiler on the subject, remarks unctuously in the preface to his *Libertine*: "I hope that the severest Reader will not be offended at the Representation of those Vices, on which they will see a dreadful Punishment inflicted. And I have been told by a worthy Gentleman that many Years agone (when first a play was made upon this Story in Italy) he has seen it acted there by the name of Atheisto Fulminato, in Churches on Sundays. . . ." Goldoni in his Memoirs writes: "Everybody knows the wretched Spanish play which the Italians call *Il Convitato di Pietra*, the French *Le Festin de Pierre* and the English *Don Juan*. In Italy I always considered it with horror, and I could not conceive how such a farce could for so long draw crowds together, and prove the delight of a polished people. The Italian comedians were themselves astonished; and, either by way of joke or from ignorance, some of them used to say that the author of Don Juan had entered into a compact with the devil to support it. I should never have thought of labouring on such a work, but having learned enough of French to be able to read it, I found that Molière and Thomas Corneille had employed their talents on the same subject. I undertook also to give a similar treat to my countrymen, that I might be on somewhat decent terms with the devil." One of the early reviews of Mozart's opera called the story a "monkish farce . . . to which the glorious—if here and there too artful —music by Mozart is about as well suited as Raphael's manner to the ideas of a Teniers or a Calot".

Tirso de Molina was enticing unzealous believers to a mediaeval fabliau-sermon. Molière wrote a study of contemporary manners. Shadwell multiplied the seductions. Goldoni cut out the comic servant and the improbable ending ("In my piece, the statue of the Companion of Honour neither speaks, moves, nor goes to sup in town"). And so on. But in truth none of them made much of it except Tirso de Molina; until the day on which, having been mentioned to Mozart, it "pleased him infinitely".

Mozart was the creator of an Elettra, an Idomeneo, an Osmin, a Blonde, a Belmonte. His Figaro's Wedding had turned out to be a great pattern of characters and attitudes. With luck a Don Juan opera would be simpler, safer, and more remunerative. But think! He would be able to reveal what it feels like, inside, to be the great seducer; or a woman being courted by the great seducer; or a woman who still loves him; or a man who is jealous of him; or a man who half-envies and half-disapproves of him, etc. A triangle . . . two triangles . . . incompatible couples . . . the men nasty enough to explain why the women fall for the Don . . . a handsome young fellow, like the actor/ singer Luigi Bassi (who at age 22 was playing Count Almaviva in the Prague production of Figaro) . . . let's have a good part for Bondini's wife, Susanna in the Prague production ("Sorrows at least depart, the while Bondini sings, the while her roguish art in vocal changes rings") . . . we must keep down the number of characters to a minimum . . . the Don, the statue, three women, three men; seven characters, not counting the statue . . . poetic justice . . . trombones . . . D minor and D major, all the way through . . . a woman a day on average, for five or six years . . . some of them more than once . . . kept him for three days . . . he will have to make up for lost time . . . he needs hardly any sleep, but has a barbarous appetite . . . maximum contrast, please, between each character and all the others . . . episodes and dialogue to bring out character all the time.

Such, I suggest, were approximately the thoughts that da Ponte had in mind, before he even sketched a libretto plan for Mozart's approval. Or perhaps some of them emerged during discussion of the draft plan. The story is a perennial one, and can mainly be worked out from first principles—as John Donne, for instance, worked it out before Tirso de Molina invented Don John. At first sight, the libretto is poor derivative stuff in nice Italian. Look again, and you will see that the borrowings and inventions have a consistent purpose—the revelation of seven contrasted characters. It is a fresh approach; da Ponte's, or Mozart's, or a bit of both. Look closely at the score, and a further fact becomes apparent. The opera, far from being one of the tamest versions of the Don Juan legend, is one of the bawdiest—in the eighteenth-century tradition of *Tom Jones* and *Candide*. The time-scale, which seems at first sight to raise so many insoluble problems, is precise and purposeful—as soon as you look at it the right way. The use of three orchestras in the finale of Act One is a deliberate juggling with different time-scales for the purpose of camouflaging the seduction of Zerlina—*before* she screams. The score contains musical symbols of seduction, and musical clues as to how the libretto is to be interpreted. The language is often riotously improper. There are obvious and very consistent explanations of the oddities about which da Ponte remained so studiously vague. This, too, is in the *Candide* tradition; it is from small oddities of expression (such as "had taken" for "took", in *10.30*) that we are invited to put Two by Two together. We are accustomed to crime detection in prose. This is sin detection; with all the major clues in the music, and plenty of others in the Italian. Can we believe that it was da Ponte who was so bold and original as to create a new genre, in order to solve an artistic problem?

The idea of a Don Juan opera may, for all we know, have been mooted between the two men before the visit to Prague. But let us grant that the idea was probably suggested when (or soon after) Mozart told da Ponte, in February 1787, about the 100-ducat com-mission. Integrated dramatic structures, such as the Don Giovanni score, are not left to evolve as the librettist devotes part of his mind to writing down the words of the two opening scenes. A plan has to be made, vetted for musical viability, modified as necessary, and agreed; *before* the actual writing of the libretto can usefully begin. Mozart had a vivid and realistic imagination; we know this, not only from his other works but from his letters. His vision of seven characters was almost bound to kindle bawdily; and he would soon know, from the feel of the music inside him, that the bawdiness could become intolerable. Μηδὲν ἄγαν, said the ancient Athenians; allow no excesses, be moderate in all things. They were not a safe or moderate people. People who live in one of the creative periods of human thought are apt to need—and, oddly enough, heed—the reminder. We know that Mozart strongly endorsed (because he knew he needed?) the sensible rule that artistic expression should not be allowed to become disgusting (see p. 28). Think of the emotional impact of the D minor opening to the overture to this opera. Imagine such music allied to what he wanted to say about the inner passions of the seven characters, throughout the opera. Remember that there was an active censorship, and that previous dramatists had felt it necessary to make undignified excuses for their Don Juan dramas. There you have the measure of Mozart's problem.

On the evidence of the score Mozart was Don-like in the cool audacity of the solutions that were found to the problem; while da

Ponte was Leporello-like in the alternate zeal and timidity with which he helped to put them into Italian words. None of the on-stage seductions are interrupted until the Don has completed, as quickly as ever, the part of the business which would require unusual skill as opposed to virility. Unusual virility is also stressed. As we shall see, the Don's "score" is three for certain, two probables, and two possibles:

(*a*) Anna, twice, before the curtain goes up.

(*b*) Zerlina, under cover of a three-orchestra trick.

(*c*) Leporello's girl-friend.

(*d*) Elvira's maid, to whom he probably returns after beating up Masetto.

(*e*) the "young and pretty lady" with whom he had a date at his private joy-shop; he probably proceeded with that affair after leaving Leporello to explain matters to Elvira.

(*f*) possibly one of the extras who come on during the quartet ("there are people all around us", *9.68*); by the contrast of *8A1* and *10C6* we are led to ask ourselves whether he took one of them to the joy-shop during *10*.

(*g*) possibly one of the peasant lasses, during the dance which ends at *13.274* after a change of scene.

Elvira is not seduced during the opera; but she is only too anxious to win back the man whom she believes to be her husband.

All this, mark you, in about twenty-four hours. It is that kind of story; told with a lavishness of characterisation that obliged Mozart, after all, to use the apparently un-operatic techniques that he had evolved to solve the problem of putting *Le mariage* into music. Wagner, we may recall, intended *Tristan* to be an easy and short work. Mozart, we may suspect, thought that a Don Juan opera was bound to be more successful than *Le nozze*. In fact his *Don Giovanni* was even more original, even more avant-garde, even more certain to be a box-office flop in Vienna. In Prague, it was less popular than *Figaro*. The producer (Guardasoni) wrote a much-quoted letter to da Ponte: "Long live da Ponte, long live Mozart! Every impresario, every virtuoso must bless them! As long as they live, it shall never be known what theatrical misery means. . . ." But he is thought to have written it before, not after, the first performance. Historical ironies rival dramatic irony. "As long as they live, it shall never be known what theatrical misery means. . . ." Politeness, enthusiasm, wishful thinking, error, lies, cruelty, thoughtlessness, skill, luck; these are some of the things that play a part in life—and therefore in both history and drama.

Anna tells us (*10.29*) that the Don's face was covered by a mantle. For one brief instant she thought it was Ottavio. Then she saw that it was someone else. He embraced her, she resisted; at the third scream he ran.

How long would such an episode take? Fifteen seconds? Half a minute? Perhaps a minute. Now think back to Leporello's F major *molto allegro*. His words (*1.11–19*) were noncommittal. But his music (*1.1–10*) was impatient, if played at the prescribed tempo; and it ended in a splendid *mal dormir* yawn. Mozart was telling us that the Don's visit to Anna, far from being brief and ignominious, had lasted rather a long time. How does a man embrace a woman tightly (*ei più mi stringe, 10.37*) if he is holding a mantle over his face? Who says the Don was wearing a mantle? And what about those screams? The temperamental Anna is a good screamer (*10.1–14*). Yet no one came (*10.39*). How loud were those three utterances in her room? Her first attested call for help is at *1.90*. By then she is engaged in a B♭ major duet with the Don. Musically this section balances the F major section. But the action suddenly dawdles between two swift sections. She called out "People, servants!" Forty-four bars later, someone appeared. Her father. Still no servants. Why not, if she had called for them three times from her room?

You may prefer to suppose that Mozart was incapable of coherent dramatic thought. I maintain that his wickedly precise and quick-witted sense of humour has left us some well-underlined clues that Ottavio did not have. If you expect conventional lyric drama from Mozart in his later operas, you will almost always be wrong. Mozart is not the prisoner of conventions—musical, social, or moral. He uses them, or turns them inside out, to serve some rather surprising dramatic purposes.

A Romeo stays with his Juliet until she says " 'Tis nearly morning, I would have thee gone." The Don, a less romantic character, wanted to keep a date at his *casino* (*2A31*). The word *casino* means brothel, house of ill-fame, house of pleasure. He and Leporello use the word flippantly, man to man, to describe his private "joy-shop".

It is cold, and Leporello has a cloak. But da Ponte carefully refrains from telling us that the Don has a cloak. By the light of the moon we see that he is wearing one of his usual magnificent costumes. When he turns to fight Anna's father he is recognised, and has to kill. He is then in no mood to give Leporello the usual sordid details; he probably feels that he deserves a wash, a snack and a change of clothes before going to the *casino*.

Later, when the moon has gone in, master and servant emerge again. Leporello has by now probably been given full details of the affair which took so unusually long. Being remarkably like you and me, he is amused—and shocked. He tries to lecture the Don. The Don puts him in his place but smells a woman in the dark. He investigates. It is Elvira, the woman who detained him for three whole days and nights in Burgos. She makes a scene. Time passes—it becomes light enough for us to notice that he is wearing a second costume. For future reference he notes a chambermaid, mouselike behind her. He extricates himself and goes off to keep his date—with a significant gesture that leaves Leporello almost speechless with amusement and embarrassment. Elvira is left to face a very cruel disillusion, in the cold light of dawn.

It is an essential part of the characterisation of Mozart's Don that he is a young man of untiring energy. Not later than about ten a.m. he emerges from his palace in (if possible) a third costume. After quickly looking round to ensure that the pestilential Elvira is not waiting for him, he proceeds to patronise a group of peasants who are making the most of a day off ("Very short is a holiday pleasure" 5.48) for the wedding of two of their number. The bride-to-be, Zerlina, is fascinated by a man who is so much richer—and apparently so much nicer—than the rough young ploughboy whom she is about to marry. She cannot resist the Don's offer of a very private "marriage" (in the private wing of his *casinetto*, little home of joy, little hovel; the palace).

Elvira appears. "Run fast and far away, and hear his lies no more; the mouth will you betray, the eyes are lying." She is an old-fashioned girl, with a genuine concern for religion and morality. She believes herself to be the Don's rightful wife. Before she has taken Zerlina out of sight she looks back and sees yet another woman looking devotedly at the Don. It is Anna, who finds 8A15–22 so *much* more romantic and satisfying than 1A15. (Ottavio should also be seen, at this moment, in an ecstasy of admiration for the Don—because the Don dresses so well.) Elvira races back. During the quartet that follows, her dignity is again hurt. Despite brave words she eventually loses heart and goes off with Zerlina to the palace, where Masetto and the peasants have been seeing the more public sights.

The Don politely excuses himself, with the words "Perdonate, bellissima Donn' Anna." They are the words that he used last night when he had to leave her, for his date with another woman. Thereafter:

(*a*) Anna recognises him, by the words and tone of voice. She denounces him to Ottavio and tells her story. Ottavio listens coldly, and is left incredulous—not about what happened last night, but that she can possibly have identified him by his recent words and tone of voice. How could it have been the young cavalier—who dresses so well?

(*b*) Because Anna's fireworks are prolonged there is just about time during *10* and *10A* for the off-stage action described by Leporello during *10C*. (For this purpose no account can be taken of *10B Dalla sua pace*; a later excrescence, grossly at variance with *10A*).

(*c*) We are not told what the Don does. But extras came on stage during *9* ("Do be quiet, think a little, there are people all around us . . .") and *10C6* is strongly contrasted with *8A1*. The Don is naturally resilient but after *8* and *9* any fictional male would at least want a drink. Being the Don, he would want what is meat and drink to him (*14A15*); a woman. It would be a legitimate and amusing (though strictly optional) production touch to let him have his eye on one of the extras. He could then say "Perdonate, bellissima Donn' Anna" with exactly the same meaning and tone of voice as he used last night. Instead of following Elvira he could dally with the extra at the back of the stage during the early bars of *10* which are specifically stated to follow *9A* without a pause; and lead her off (at about *10.10*) to the *casinetto* as a substitute for Zerlina. It would have the dramatic merit of explaining why the Don is so monstrously pleased with himself throughout *10C*.

At the end of *10C* the Don announces his intention of entertaining the peasant lasses for the rest of the day. A ruthlessly unconventional man, he intends the ball to start almost at once. In *11* he issues the necessary instructions. The lasses, who are already half-drunk (*10C21*), are to be given an alcoholic lunch—the *rinfreschi* of *13.296*, tactfully called coffee, chocolate, etc. Leporello is authorised to invite any other women (with or without tenor friend) who may happen to pass the palace. The Don's large private orchestra (a notably more efficient body than the one owned by Mr. Pumpenstempel in Eric Linklater's *Juan in America*) are to perform their celebrated parlour-trick; which consists of getting everyone so confused by a disorderly medley of dances (*minuetto, follia, alemana*) that the Don can proceed *dall' altro canto* with ten girls by the morning. Note the Don's ungentlemanly speed of thought in this aria. Those *presto* quavers will recur, slightly intensified by a change into 3/8 time, when the third orchestra get going; with six bars (*13.461–2*, in the slow-witted and gentlemanly

minuet) that will commit as lewd a D major sin *dall' altro canto* as
4.162, 164, 166; with the usual horn support.

12A4 implies that *11* and *12* are concurrent. The main purpose of the
garden scene is to show an unsuccessful attempt on Zerlina. She turns
pale at the sight of him. But Masetto is watching, and she still has the
sense to resist. So he invites her—and Masetto—to the dance.

Inside, the finale continues—and is proceeding according to schedule,
apart from the momentary embarrassment when Masetto was found
in the niche to which the Don had been going with Zerlina. To lull
suspicion, the Don probably lets Zerlina dance a few dances with
Masetto; while he himself dances (and perhaps proceeds *dall' altro
canto*) with one of the other lasses. Then Zerlina's resistance is syst…
atically undermined; by alcoholic coffee and chocolate, by flattery, by
Masetto's wounding remarks, by the heady sophistry of the hymn in
praise of "liberty", and by a kissing and capering dance with the Don.
The first twenty-four bar Folly, corresponding to bars *439–53*, may
be imagined to last much longer—the whole finale takes only eighteen
minutes on the stage but must surely be assumed to represent the events
of three or four hours. Mozart deliberately juggles with three con…
current time-scales. Zerlina, by now incapable of resisting a skilled
operator like the Don, is swiftly seduced off-stage. She does not
cry out—at first. Then comes an interesting piece of psychology.
She screams in earnest; not, as Anna would, to preserve her repu…
tation.

When women scream *dall' altro canto*, an unwilling Leporello is
sometimes made to take the blame. He told us in *1.13* that he gets no
gratitude or pay for his many services to the Don. Yet there are
occasional compensation bonuses of four or five pounds; a considerable
sum in 1787 (*14A4*). Zerlina by herself might not have dared to
denounce the gentleman in front of everybody. But there are gentry
present. They denounce the Don, and Ottavio even threatens him with
a pistol. Zerlina and Masetto join in.

> Hear the sound of retribution;
> Now, *this very day*, the frightening
> Roar of thunder, rush of lightning
> At your head for all to see.

They do not know exactly what will happen in Act Two. But Mozart
and da Ponte know; and are preparing, as in *Figaro* and *Così fan tutte*,
to conclude the action in about twenty-four hours. The Don is dis-

concerted. But as usual he quickly recovers his confidence. By superior force of character he disarms Ottavio and at once—on his own ground, in his own home, with members of his private orchestra as well as Leporello to support him—dominates the situation. The three women betray instinctive admiration of his handsomeness and audacity by singing his tune. His words, which they do *not* sing, are significant:

> But I do not lack in courage,
> I'll not let you drag me under.
> Though the earth shall fall asunder,
> I from coward fear am free.

Shortly before dusk he is out in the street again, near the hotel in which Elvira is staying. He is wearing yet another suit, with a large white-feathered hat that will show up well when it gets dark. About two and a half hours will elapse before he jumps lightly over the wall into the churchyard. During that time Mozart is consistently concerned to deepen our knowledge of the seven characters.

In *1.20–32* Leporello sang "I wish I could play at master, I wish I need not obey". He now has his opportunity. The two men are made to change clothes, after cracking some phallic jokes. But what happens? The Don, disguised as Leporello, succeeds. Leporello, disguised as the Don, fails. The Don (*a*) gives a particularly dazzling and ruthless display of his powers of courtship with Elvira (*b*) makes a good start with Elvira's maid (*c*) sends off the peasants to beat up Leporello (*d*) takes Masetto away and beats him up, heedless of the possible consequences for Leporello (*e*) returns to the chambermaid and climbs up to her window—why else take Masetto away before beating him up? (*f*) "takes advantage" of Leporello's girl-friend (*21D42*). Leporello, having been presented with an ardent and willing Elvira, becomes ardent himself (*15A30–42*) but—fortunately for Elvira—merely wanders round the streets with her for nearly an hour (*un' oretta circum circa, 20.54*) before arriving in a courtyard with three doors. He tries to get away from Elvira. He cannot get out through the first door because Anna and Ottavio appear. At the second door Zerlina and Masetto block his way. He endures a harrowing half-hour before escaping through the third door.

The moon probably rose during the sextet; it had to be dark after dusk for an hour and a bit, in order to help keep Elvira in bemused ignorance. Equally it has to be moonlit in the churchyard so that Leporello can read the inscription on the statue. The statue had been erected during the lifetime of Anna's father; the inscription had been carved (as in the Gazzaniga/Bertati version) during the day.

By about half past ten the Don is on his way home. He is still not tired. But half a dozen seductions have left him with a barbarous appetite; and the statue is soon forgotten. At, say, a quarter to eleven Ottavio enters Anna's room. By about half past eleven, when the Don is having dinner, Elvira arrives for her final humiliation. At about a quarter to twelve the statue arrives. On the stroke of midnight the statue goes (*24.599*). By about five past twelve Leporello has seen his "friend" (*24.427*, cp. *13.248*) disappear down a smoking hole in the floor. The remaining characters arrive. By about half past twelve they are complacently vindicating the opera's title *Il dissoluto punito*.

Benn (*Mozart on the Stage*, pp. 77–80) prefers to "avoid all difficulties" by spreading the events of a much tamer story over a period of five days.

ACT ONE

<table>
<tr><td>1, Notte e giorno faticar</td><td>8, Ah, fuggi il traditor</td></tr>
<tr><td>1A, Leporello, ove sei?</td><td>8A, Mi par ch'oggi</td></tr>
<tr><td>2, Ma qual mai s'offre</td><td>9, Non ti fidar, o misera</td></tr>
<tr><td>2, Orsù, spicciati presto</td><td>9A, Povera sventurata!</td></tr>
<tr><td>3, Ah! chi mi dice mai</td><td>10, Don Ottavio, son morta</td></tr>
<tr><td>3A, Chi è la?</td><td>10A, Come mai creder deggio</td></tr>
<tr><td>4, Madamina</td><td>10B, Dalla sua pace</td></tr>
<tr><td>4A, In questa forma, dunque, mi tradi</td><td>10C, Io deggio ad ogni patto</td></tr>
<tr><td>5, Giovinette che fate</td><td>11, Fin ch'han dal vino</td></tr>
<tr><td>5A, Manco male, è partita</td><td>11A, Masetto . . . senti un po'</td></tr>
<tr><td>6, Ho capito, Signor, si</td><td>12, Batti, batti</td></tr>
<tr><td>6A, Alfin siamo liberati</td><td>12A, Guarda un po' come seppe</td></tr>
<tr><td>7, Là ci darem la mano</td><td>13, Presto, presto . . . pria ch'ei</td></tr>
<tr><td>7A, Fermati, scellerato</td><td>venga</td></tr>
</table>

IN HIS *Mémoires d'un artiste* Gounod recalls "unparalleled hours, the charm of which has dominated my life like a luminous apparition, a kind of revelatory vision. . . . From the start of the overture I felt myself transported into an absolutely new world by the solemn and majestic chords of the Commandant's final scene. I was seized by a terror which froze me, and as the menacing progression began, with those descending and ascending scales unrolling above it merciless and implacable as a death sentence, I was overcome by such dread that I buried my face in my mother's shoulder, and enveloped in the twofold embrace of the beautiful and the terrible, I whispered Oh mama, what music! this is truly music. . . . Rossini introduced me to purely musical delight; he charmed and fascinated my ear. Mozart did more; to the gratification deriving from the exclusively musical and sensuous, he added the profound and penetrating influence of truth of expression combined with perfect beauty. . . . Everything (for in this deathless work everything may be quoted) put me in that blessed state which one feels only before beautiful things to which the centuries must pay homage, things which are the yardstick of the aesthetic level of the arts. . . .''

D minor . . . D major. We have seen, from a study of the time-scheme, that Anna's story cannot be true. The Don was in her "dusky bedroom" (*camera tetra, 22A*) for some time. Her long story, which is crucial to an understanding of this unusual opera, needs to be examined.

"Night was already well advanced *when there entered, in my private apartments, where I unfortunately had no companion, a man whom at once for the moment I had taken for you, sir.*" What do these words tell us? Her romantic and unruly nature craved a lover. This Ottavio, to whom her father had engaged her, did not seem to be much of a man. But he was a man of sorts; and he was staying in the house. Everything was covered with the little mantle of darkness (as opposed to the big mantle of friendship, *10.22*). She was therefore probably in bed. The figure of a man loomed over her. Who could it be but Ottavio? Even the Don might be surprised at the ardour with which she instantly welcomed him; half the fun and nearly all the skill of his trade was in dispelling initial feminine reluctance.

Da Ponte is careful to make Anna use the pluperfect tense in this sentence. "Had taken" she says; not "took". Mozart, who never wastes crotchets in the middle of recitative phrases, uses one to stress the word "taken". (The only other mid-phrase crotchet in the story is on *vuole 10.34*.) The "entering" and "taking" coincided—at the moment indicated by (a) the ambiguous Italian word *entrar* (*10.28*, cp. *Figaro 28.96*), and (b) a remarkable enharmonic change from a flat key (the romantic Schumannian E♭ minor, outside Mozart's normal key palette) to a sharp key (the dominant of B minor; not far from the Don's D major). The man entered, the woman took. The "extraordinary story" (strange event, *strano avvenimento, 10.23*) has begun. At "for you, sir" the music arrives on B minor with, probably, a remote and chilly appoggiatura (from C♯ to B). "For you, sir", *per voi* (compare the illuminating plural at *22A13*). In the aria, Anna reverts to *tu*. But throughout the present recitative she and Ottavio address each other as *voi*; a grotesquely formal effect, as in *Figaro 13*.

"Goodness! Continue!" says Ottavio. The off-stage affair between Anna and Giovanni is a serial story; To Be Continued. Mozart found da Ponte's little joke so amusing that he accidentally set it to music in its logical place, at the end of phase one. In the autograph score, two bars (the present *10.32, 33*) are scratched out before the present *10.31*. Ottavio has not yet had his cue, which is logically the first sentence of phase two: "But *then*" says Anna "I saw that my man was not you but another." Then, *poi*, a little later, Anna concluded that *il mio*, her surprisingly ardent bedfellow, could not be Ottavio. Let us assume, to make Leporello's impatience plausible, that something like half an hour (*certe mezz' ore*, *Figaro 2A28*) has already elapsed.

Anna is in bed with a *tu* (the Don is still *tu*, at *1.77*; whereas Bertati's Anna addresses him as *voi*). "Silently coming near me, he attempts an embrace. I try to break loose. He holds me closer. I cry out. But no one comes. With one hand on my mouth he stops me using my weak voice; with the other he holds me so close . . . I feel I am conquered." These events presumably followed some such remark by Anna as "*You're* not Ottavio! Who *are* you?" The Don, scenting a more interesting test of skill, coolly responds by embracing her; in a phrase that has the second emphatic mid-phrase crotchet. The quavers rise—*staccato, stringendo, crescendo*—in a G major that hints at the Don's wicked top D (cp. *4.162, 13.461–2*). Anna's vocal *grido* (firm, but not particularly loud) is followed by a crotchet pause. The orchestral *grido* (*10.38–9*) is louder. But no one came—the soft staccato *andante* quavers (cp. *Figaro 26.3*) are more like a heart thumping in silent darkness. Gently the Don places a warning finger on her lips. He proceeds to business; with an embrace, *forte*. She submits in E minor, with staccato quavers still rising to a top D.

"Perfidy!" says Ottavio. (Whose?) "And after that?" The word for "after that?" is *alfine*, *alfin*, which is the word used unambiguously by Zerlina at *6A22*.

"Why then sheer grief" says Anna virtuously "sheer horror, at the infamy attempted, increase my fiery resolution." The Italian word for resolution is *lena*; which can mean "will to carry on". Da Ponte makes us begin to wonder whether there is to be a phase three. The next sentence means something like "By dint of a little wrestling, wriggling and insisting, it came to nothing!" In the Italian, several of the words are not even ambiguous. *Vincolarmi*, binding myself; *torcermi*, wriggling; *piegarmi*, submitting. Many editions read *svincolarmi*, which means *un*binding myself. But that does not account for the astonishing *pie-garmi*; and in any case the reading in the autograph score is *vincolarmi*, not *svincolarmi*. Mozart knew the difference between the two forms— see the commentary on the difference between the libretto and score renderings of the French *à demi démeublée*, in *Figaro 1*. The second half of the sentence, *da lui mi sciolsi*, means "freed myself from him". How is a woman freed by binding herself, wriggling and submitting (with excited-sounding music)? If Anna did all this, she wanted more. If the affair then went no further, the only reasonable inference is that the Don, having had enough, broke loose. It came to nothing. She sounds disappointed. So do the soft string chords. Da Ponte even manages to tell us the words he used: "Perdon*ate*, bellissima Donn' Anna!" They are the words by which she recognises him next day (*9A4*, cp. *10.17*). "Oh dear!" says Ottavio "I breathe again." From what has happened and from Anna's strange behaviour in the rest of the opera we can be certain that she begged the Don to stay, offered to marry him, insisted that he must at least come every night, and implored him to tell her who he was. The *grido* of *10.37*, and the *stridi* of *10.53*, are not even claimed to be cries for help. At 10.55 she calls for help. In context she could easily be making a plea to the Don to save her from having to marry Ottavio. The Don is the last man to accept such a plea, from a silly girl who has already had more than her share of his time. He hurries away. She boldly follows him into the street to stop him. She has become "the assailant, not the assailed".

Leporello has been waiting longer than usual—despite the lack of initial reluctance on Anna's part. When the curtain rises, his F major music could not be simpler or more graphic. Three silent angry strides in one direction. Then the cloaked figure turns abruptly. Three strides and a turn, three strides and a turn, three strides and a turn. A long and profound yawn (*1.9–10*; the orchestral comment on *mal dormir*, *1.19–20*). It would be a legitimate production touch to let Leporello pull out one of his master's pocket watches and read it easily (contrast *21D69*) by the light of the moon. Under his arm as usual (*3A56*) he is clutching a certain *non picciol libro*; the list.

"Must I work all night, all day? Get no gratitude or pay? Then endure the wind and rain, hungry, sleepless, yet *again*!" In such a mood, one exaggerates. But we learn much about Leporello, and about the Don, even from the first four rhyming lines.

As he finishes them the music yawns for him in angry self-pity. Why should he serve such a master? Because Leporello is fascinated, proud, envious. "I wish I could play at master, I wish I need not obey".

The whole feeling of the music changes. Horns share a fine long dis-contented vocal phrase (*1.20*). Oboes and bassoons add a hint of Don Giovanni's characteristic itch (*1.22*). Note the simplicity and sureness of it all. Mozart and da Ponte depict a particular character in a particu-lar situation; while selecting traits which strike a chord in all of us as well. The feeling of the music changes again, as Leporello's unspoken thoughts become warmer, more knowing, self-indulgent. His spoken thoughts remain sardonic. "Oh so nice and oh so honest!" His un-conscious thoughts kindle. "To her room you make your entry; I stay here, a lonely sentry, a lonely sentry, a lonely sentry". The Italian word *galantuomo* means a decent man, a real gentleman. King Umberto was known as Il Re Galantuomo; not because he was of gentle (indeed, royal) birth but because he had a nice character. Mozart and da Ponte are, as so often, using a word to imply its opposite.

"What is that? I hear some people, I believe I hear some people, I think I will hide away." He tries, not very successfully, to hide. With a surge of orchestral anger Donna Anna emerges, having taken the key from F major into B♭ major. Yet her vocal phrase (*1.75*) begins on the low F again, quite softly (an effect often marred because the preceding orchestral phrase is allowed to drown it). She has not yet given up hope of keeping her wonderful heavensent man. Therefore the vocal line and its string accompaniment are aimed at him alone. "I declare, unless you kill me, I will never let you go." She is using the intimate "tu", as she holds one of his arms. With the other arm he is hiding his face, to prevent her recognising him by the bright light of the moon. We see him wearing one of his usual splendid suits; there is no mention of a cloak. He is annoyed, but as usual coolly suits his vocal line to the woman of the moment. "You are mad, in vain you tell me; who I am you shall not know." "Far too noisy!" thinks Leporello; "with fear they fill me, he is in more trouble oh!" At last Anna shouts for help: "People, servants! Oh the traitor!" The Don is getting angry: "Hush, and fear my fury later!" (She will, at *13.201–17*!) "You're inhuman!" she says. "Foolish woman!" he replies. "People, servants!" she cries, at last. "Hush, and fear me!" It is still a lovers' quarrel. At *1.102* comes the first clear vocal *forte*, unaccompanied. "Like a fury I'll pursue you, I am desperate as you see." "Like a fury she'll pursue me! Will she try to ruin me?" thinks the Don. "I begin to wonder if he will not also ruin me" thinks Leporello in an amusing counter-rhythm. And there the action sticks, in an apparently prolix and old-fashioned passage of verbal repetition, until Mozart has finished proving the lady's guilt beyond reasonable doubt.

At *1.134* we return to the terse style in which *Figaro* and most of the present opera is written. The horrified Anna sees her father come out, alone and without servants. She lets go of the Don, and runs into the house.

Age is relative. Anna and the Don refer to her father as old (*10.66, 21D75*); but his voice and behaviour declare him to be a man who has every prospect of keeping Ottavio out of Anna's full inheritance for thirty years. "Assaulting a poor girl! Come, fight me rather" "Go!" says the Don "I do not care to fight a father." He feels some embarrassment; the Commendatore is a gallant neighbour and friend. "A sorry masking of coward flight!" says the Commendatore. "Oh I wish I were more out of sight" thinks Leporello. "Go, I will not fight! No!" says the Don, still with averted face. The Commendatore repeats his taunt higher in the voice. "Pitiful!" mutters the Don. "Draw your sword!" says the Commendatore. "Pitiful!" says the Don again "Why are you asking for endless night?" The Don does not believe all that rot about an after-life. The music is back in a simple and expressive D minor, with many associations. Giovanni turns and is recognised (*conoscerlo*, *10.64*). The surprise of recognition puts the Commendatore at a disadvantage; the vile wretch is his young friend.

The duel is clearly charted in the score (compare *Figaro 15.83–5* and *Così fan tutte 1.36–7*). The first violins begin with a scale; the Don takes and keeps the initiative. The 'cellos and basses reply strongly in the dominant of D major. Tremolo of the inner strings conveys emotional tension. The duel goes on, tit for tat, until the Don puts the Commendatore off his stroke at *1.173*. Giovanni ends the duel with three sforzando jabs of horrid ferocity and power—first violins, flutes, bassoons, horns. The 'cellos and basses recoil. The inner-string tension ends.

"Who will aid me? . . . You betrayed me! . . . Has the murdering sword unmade me? Yes, and from my fluttering body breath of life all fades away." "What a misdeed!" thinks Leporello. "Gross is this deed! I with utter fear am shaking, I'm a-flutter, I am quaking. Ah, what can I do or say?" "Her pursuing fury's falling" thinks the Don (*1.178*; cf. *1.102*). "He in agony is bawling. Yes, and from his fluttering body breath of life all fades away." The instrumental parts are marked *pianissimo*, and the Don's line is marked *sotto voce*. But the long *diminuendo* of the vocal line sung by the Commendatore must surely imply, by the normal rules of musicianship, that the dying man has a good bawling *forte* to begin with. Note his words. In the first agonised cry he has not yet accepted that he is dying. His next thought is one of

horror at the dishonourable betrayal of his trust and friendship—
it is no accident that his first speech as a statue, the following evening,
is at the moment when the Don has similarly betrayed Leporello's
trust and friendship. Note how Mozart has shaped the three vocal lines,
so as to give the maximum opportunity for each set of words to come
through, in one or other of the repetitions. The Don is unusually
subdued. A peasant girl or servant girl exists to amuse him for half an
hour. A gentlewoman has "feelings", to be humoured for a little
longer. A manservant is—well, no more important than a woman of
that class. But a gentleman. . . . Some of the most interesting moments
in these three operas are those in which someone *seems* to be behaving
out of character. Has the Don a conscience? Only in the context which
shows it to be a reflection of his prejudices. The exquisitely sad F minor
is one of mutual self-pity and pity, between gentleman killer and
gentleman victim. But it does not begin slowly or get slower. Just as
the long *diminuendo* means *forte* to begin with, the general quietness is
andante not *adagio*.

The *sotto voce secco* begins in the last fading chord, without a second's
delay. "Leporello, where are you?" "I'm here, to my own great shame;
and you?" "I'm here." "But who died? You, or the old man?" "What
a half-witted question! The old man." We have only to compare the
whole of this opening scene with the Bertati scene (*Vierteljahrsschrift für
Musikwissenschaft, 1888*) to see the superiority of da Ponte's libretto,
in quality and insight. Da Ponte probably had the advantage of having
discussed the dramatic situation with Wolfgang Amadeus Mozart, a
great dramatist. But the charming minor nuances, such as the clear hint
of spiritual death, are surely part of the Abbate's own creative response;
in this case, his response to a trivial passing phrase in the Bertati
libretto. Compare *15A1*, where the dialogue runs as follows: "Well,
what d'you say to that, my friend?" "I say your soul is . . . as stony as a
statue." "Well I'm damned, you're still a half-wit."

Meanwhile Leporello's quicksilver mind is beginning to think of
more important matters. Opening the book, he says "Well done! A
fine brace of achievements! You take a daughter's honour, and kill her
father." The Don remembers his dying friend's reproachful look;
there is a resentful tone in the next significant words: "Well, he had
what he wanted." *L'ha voluto, suo danno*; a more refayned version of
the modern "yer pays yer money and yer takes yer choice". That is
how the Don, too, lived and died.

The travelling inkpot is open, and the quill hovers over the paper;
at entry 1003 (Spanish). Leporello gets little gratitude or pay, but is

incessantly regaled by sordid details. He leers expectantly. "Did Donn'
Anna . . . have what she wanted?" The Don is not in the mood to
allow Leporello his vicarious gratification. "Quiet, you are a bore;
come along—unless you also wish to be hurt!" Leporello cowers:
"I want nothing, my lord, I say no more." Off goes the Don. Leporello
follows.

Anna appears at the door. "Here! My father's in danger! Let us fly
to his aid!" Her fiancé's sword is drawn; to safeguard himself from any
danger. "I am for shedding . . . all my blood *if I have to*. Well then,
where is the rascal?" Ottavio, who took over a hundred bars to dress,
is notably suspicious of the demands made by an emotional and
extravagant girl. Why all the fuss?

"Outside the door here!" says Anna, dragging a reluctant Ottavio
out into the open. At the word "here" she turns—and in the whole of
these three operas there is hardly a passage to match the intense naturalism of her orchestral shock and horror. She sees—not her lover, or her
lover and her father fighting, but the dead body of her father. Her
words strike less of a chord in our twentieth-century soul-substitutes.
"Ah but what am I seeing? A sight, O God, of stark death, before my
very eyes!" More orchestral shock and horror. "My father, my own
father, my own dear father!" Genuine grief, neatly underlined by
Ottavio's surprised and fatuous "Oh sir, sir", is made worse by the
horrid realisation that she is largely to blame. (It is unscholarly to
read into this passage Mozart's grief at his own father's unexpected
death on 28th May 1787. More probably he had the whole dramatic
situation in his mind before then.)

"Ah what a murderous deed was this! A bloodstain . . . and a sword-
wound. . . ." Think for a moment of the picture that she later conveys:
"Remember, remember the wound I discovered! Imagine with anguish
the earth, that with blood was all covered. . . ." Down she goes on her
knees beside him. "His dear face . . . tinted and covered with a deathly
pale grey." She bends down close to the face. "No stir of living
breath!" She touches a clammy hand. "So cold, his fingers?" Compare
2.13–14, and see how simply Mozart conveys the extra agony of "Not
my *father*, my own *father*, *my* dearest father!"; followed, with an
equally inevitable simplicity, by music that tells us (2.37–9), before the
mere words (2.39) can say so, that she is about to faint.

Ottavio (2.44) has had ample warning. But he does not run to
help her, or kneel down beside her, or take a single step towards her.
Blood, a dead body, an emotional girl, extravagant language; most
distasteful. One probably only brought a dozen decent costumes on

this visit to one's fiancée and her father; one cannot bear the thought of staining and creasing good clothes by kneeling down beside her. So one flicks an elegant finger at the servants. They can do what is necessary. Two of them can hold her. Two or three can fetch smelling salts and spirits—a more legitimate request. When she begins to revive, the servants can give her fresh (and unspecified) assistance. In *Figaro 1* Mozart made the point that Figaro was for a moment more interested in status than in Susanna. Ottavio is a conventional person. To kneel beside one's beloved, when she has fainted, is the conventional thing to do. It is therefore particularly significant that he fails to do so. Jeeves would have understood. "The tie, if I might suggest it, sir, a shade more tightly knotted . . . there is no time, sir, at which ties do not matter." Blood, on dirty ground! At such a time even the most conventional act of kindness must be ignored.

Few girls would agree; the romantic Anna least of all. He is *not* kneeling by her. He is saying something fatuous about "fresh assistance". Then the other dreadful thought floods into her mind again. Her father! At that moment—she can hardly believe her ears—Ottavio issues a fresh instruction to the servants. "Go, carry out of her sight the object that is causing the anguish." Here is a new and blinding light on Ottavio's character. He so dislikes the sight of the corpse and is so obsessed by the supreme importance of appearances that he takes it for granted that grief can be cured by taking a dead father's body out of sight. Again, few would agree; Anna least of all. Try to imagine what she is thinking as she sits there, supported by a servant. She hears words which, though they would have been acceptable from a man she loved, or from a man who was at least showing some imagination, are a last straw here and now. "You are my soul's joy, be comforted, take heart again!" In a desperate *allegro* she bursts out "Leave me to die, you are cruel! Go, I am broken-hearted! For he is now departed, who gave . . . this life . . . to me." She is on the verge of tears. Her D minor vocal line is never again *allegro*. At *13.174* it is used by Elvira, *allegretto*. At *19.45* it deepens into the *andante* of "Let my sorrow have some outlet. . . ."

Ottavio pays no attention. He may be dense and slow-witted about some things. But he has now at last put two and two together. Her father is dead! As the motherless only child, she will inherit the whole estate, twenty years or so before schedule. Despite her tantrums, she is transformed before him. She is not a bad-looking woman. Women have never taken him seriously but he is conscious of a certain feeling. Besides, if there is one thing he detests, it is the sight of tears.

He answers her eagerly in the cheerful dominant of F major. "Hear me
—my *sweet*heart—one moment!—look, let your eyes discover your
own, your *dearest* lover, whose thoughts are *all* for thee!" He is all for
her fortune, he is all for her body, he is all for being the licensed owner
of these two desirable properties. Think for a moment of his next
stanza: "See a *husband* and father in me." He hardly pretends to consider her feelings; he is almost unaware that she has any. He takes her
affection for granted: how could she not admire so perfect a piece of
God's handiwork as himself? In his following stanza a man with the
mimimum of sincerity (or, failing sincerity, tact) would have said
"father" or "father as well as husband". He is oblivious of every
consideration except greedy desire to court the orphaned heiress. She,
fresh from the Don's embraces, looks at him with disenchanted eyes.

Dare she send him packing? See *23.9*: "But people . . .", what will
people think? As soon as she realises that she is being courted by this
insufferable man, all her romanticism, all her wilfulness, all her shrewdness and respectability came into play. Confusedly, and with an
infinitely touching ambiguity, she manages to speak through tears.
"Are you . . . my own . . . forgive me . . . a pain . . . that . . . never . . .
would leave me?" With a fraction of her mind she hears the words of a
suitable and respectable husband whom she may need. With the rest . . .

Anna has a habit of reverie in the presence of others. Think for
instance of the *allegretto moderato* of *23*. Berlioz was shocked by
Forse un giorno il cielo ancora sentira-a-a-a (. . . "an incredible run, in
execrable taste") *pieta di me*. "A truly singular form of expression for a
noble outraged woman, to hope that heaven will one day take pity on
her. I found it difficult to forgive Mozart for this enormity. I now feel
I would shed my life's blood if I could thereby erase that shameful
page, and others of the same kind which disfigure some of his work. . . .
Even the epithet 'shameful' scarcely seems to me strong enough to
blast this passage. Mozart has there committed one of the most flagrant
crimes recorded in the history of art against passion, feeling, good taste
and good sense." In other words, even a musician of the stature of
Berlioz had not taken the trouble to think *why* Mozart and da Ponte
wrote *me* instead of the more obvious *te*. Jahn has been condemned for
studying Mozart with the eye of a classical scholar. But classical
scholars are at least taught the unhurrying discipline of textual scholar-
ship, including respect for the *difficilior lectio*.

Today some sopranos still seem puzzled by the reverie in *23*;
on which see p. 210. How many of them have even noticed this earlier
and less obvious reverie? ". . . a pain . . . that . . . never . . . would

leave me? . . ." *L'affano mio, le pene*. At the word *pene*, sorrows, the music completes an apparently interminable modulation into serene F major. The violins twine sensuously. Soft seductive horns, whose tone-colour has been carefully reserved in the background, insist on the key with a long octave chord that we may have noticed—*forte, piano, forte, piano*—when she was quarrelling with her lover. A rogue, a murderer, but—compared with this fop!—a man of real tenderness and charm. She is remembering the Don, with voluptuous affection and pride. She wonders where he is. She hurriedly makes an honest thought of it with "Ah, father, where is he?" "Your father?" asks Ottavio; who is often used by Mozart and da Ponte to underline, unwittingly, what Anna is really thinking.

In the rhetorical pause that follows, the musical texture becomes richer and louder. Through glorious reverie she hears a voice. "Put behind you memories that remind you!" Are the memories bitter? Anna has an unspoken thought; the lush downward seventh, twice. It is a phrase that became one of the clichés of musical romanticism. The unromantic Mozart used it objectively; to help characterise romanticism (the romanticism of his contemporaries, who lived well into the nineteenth century) as one of the elements in his pattern of attitudes to love.

The downward seventh has nothing to do with Ottavio—yet. He tries to intrude on it, with his tactless "See a *husband* and father in me". With an even smaller corner of her mind she manages to remain respectable. "Ah . . . oh, father! My father, where is he?" Methinks she doth insist too much. Ottavio comes out more strongly with his advice. "Put behind you memories that remind you!" Back come the memories. There is nothing bitter about them—*until* Ottavio gate-crashes with the same interval. "See a husband . . . and father." For once the verbal emphases are equal. Then Mozart restores the Ottavian emphasis "See a *husband* and father in *me*!" He kills reverie, ends lyricism. Anna gets angrily to her feet. He wants a wife, does he? Admittedly, she may need a husband. But she is still the wilful Anna. She proceeds to put his alleged devotion to what will obviously be an academic test (unless the Don kills him, too!) In businesslike recitative she says "Swear your revenge, your duty—swear *if you can and will*!" Her look is one of supreme innocence. To humour this unpredictable girl he strikes another elegant pose; in order to swear by innocent eyes and perfect love. "I swear it, I swear it, I swear by virgin beauty, I swear by our love, to fulfil!" Mozart and da Ponte complete the section by drawing our attention, over and over again, to its breathtaking ambiguity. "*A solemn oath*, O Heaven! A time of *cruel notions*! Between *so many emotions*, how can the heart be still?" In compression of dramatic thought, and in psychological subtlety, *Don Giovanni* often outdoes *Figaro*.

Anna, Elvira, Zerlina. We meet them in order of wealth, and they say good-bye to us in the same order (at *24.720–43*).

We began with an Anna scene. Now we have an Elvira scene. It is comparatively simple; Mozart and da Ponte are not exploring the three (or six?) relationships of a woman and two very different men. Elvira's triangle is with the Don and God (*24.741*). Her immediate dramatic function is to provide a relatively simple interlude; with a pretext for the catalogue of past conquests. She, the woman of Burgos, is their chosen representative; because she still loves him. Molière invented her to fill an obvious gap in any treatment of the psychological aspects of a Don Juan saga. Tirso de Molina overlooked her; he was perhaps more concerned to persuade his lusty "parishioners" to confess their current adulteries before it was too late.

We can hardly see the Don and Leporello when they emerge, later the same night. The Don has probably had a meal, while feasting Leporello on the unusually comic and lurid details of his affair with Anna. Leporello has listed Anna. This accounts for the timing and verve of an otherwise rather pointless occurrence of the traditional (and no doubt habitual) lecturing of the Don by his servant. From *2A8* it is clear that Leporello is salving his conscience about his master's women, not about the murder of the poor Commendatore. This time Leporello is so excited and exhilarated that he shouts it into the Don's ear: "Listen, dear lord and master, the life that you have chosen IS VILE AND WORTHLESS". The Don had sworn, even promised, not to be annoyed. But this was going too far. In the Don's Liberty Hall (*13.371–402*) some men are more equal than others. "Your solemn oath?" "To me, an oath is nothing; quiet, or I'll . . ." "I say no more; no, not a breath, dear master."

Having relieved his feelings Leporello reveals that he is eagerly waiting to add No. 1004 (Spanish). He fondles the precious book. The Don is on his way to fetch a young and pretty woman who is expecting to go with him, this night, to the private wing of Liberty Hall; the Joy-shop. But he smells, then sees, a woman's form in the dark. What a sense of smell! And what eyesight! He hides for a moment to spy out the ground. "He's lit already" thinks Leporello.

Elvira is introduced to us in music, through pitchy blackness, without words. *3.1–12* are not a mere prelude, to a singer's solo. They are a slice of Elvira's inner self. Angular E♭ major fury (*3.1–4*) is our first inkling of her—another person who is warm, credible, coherent, and perfectly contrasted with the other six. This girl neither lay awake at nights with prurient thoughts (*10.27*) nor makes roguish eyes at men (*6A17*). In the Italian she says "thou" and "thee" to everyone—this was perhaps intended to sound old-fashioned and pietistic. She is virtuous and rather priggish but has a fine simple dignity of manner and bearing (*9.10–19*). She is also full-blooded (*3.5–8* and the trill in *3.9*). The Don entered her house furtively (*3A12*—no improper double meanings here). By putting on an appropriate act, and by the usual promises and flatteries, he seduced her mind and heart (*3A15*). Being gullible and passionate, the unworldly girl was bowled over by him. By now she only half-believes that she is married (*3A17*) in the eyes of God or men (*3A18*). But she had managed to keep him for three whole days (*3A20*) of blissful belief that she was his rightful wife. Righteous fury has brought her from Burgos, travelling day and night. As a pursuing Fury, she *sounds* more convincing than Anna. "Ah, who will tell me kindly where lies my cruel lord? Whom I adored so blindly, who broke that solemn word! Dear wretch, if I waylay him, he'll make another start, or learn how I repay him by tearing out his heart. I shall tear out that heart . . ." Twelve times she tells us what she will do. Will she?

The Don is interested. "You hear her? A fair lady, by a fickle rogue deserted . . . poor young woman, poor young woman . . . unhappy girl, a comfort will be offered." Orchestral anger is turned into sympathy; and becomes ambiguous, seductive. (Were eighteen hundred of them caught on the rebound?) A coda elaborates Elvira's threat in voice and wind. But the last orchestral word is with the Don, as he utters "Signorina, signorina!"

"Who is it?" The Don and she go close enough to recognise each other in the lessening darkness. "Don Giovanni, you felon, you monster, you foul nest of iniquity!" They are, as Leporello says, admirable descriptions; a good clear proof of how well she knows him. Her home truths go through many keys, and are strictly according to the book. But the dramatic point that Mozart and da Ponte are making is that they fall a long way short of tearing out the heart of a man like the Don. He knows that men like himself are fickle rogues. He said so, only a moment ago. What is life for, but to be enjoyed? Elvira will never hurt him; she is the one who will be hurt, while grimly hanging on to him in jealous indignation. We begin to see what

kind of a man and woman this pair are; just as we saw in 2 what kind
of a man and woman Ottavio and Anna are. It is nearly dawn, on the
day of the Don's undoing. By what he is, by what she is, by what the
others are, the Don's career is coming to its rapid end.

He sees a way out of momentary embarrassment. Leporello can tell
her what kind of a man she is trying to retain. She will listen to any
information about her beloved. Off goes the Don, for his date.
Leporello splutters (3A41–3); more perhaps from admiration of the
Don's audacity than from the embarrassment of finding a way to
explain matters to the lady. "Oh you poor fool, I think you mean to
laugh at my misfortune" says Elvira. She turns to the Don for moral
support. He is gone. "Wretch that I am! Where to? Which direction?"
If she knew, she would follow. If she knew that he was going off
with a young and pretty woman, she would run! "Eh, allow him to go,
ma'am" says Leporello, "he is not worthy of your thought and attention." "Oh, he is evil! Wicked lies, sheer deceit!" "There, there,
console yourself." She is not the first or last of them. "Look here
ma'am"—he walks towards her—"here, at this big and fat book,
already full of the names of his women. Every country, every city, and
every village! Where he has been, there he has met and conquered."
The Don's speed of thought and action (*molto allegro* in the overture,
presto in *11*, three times the speed of a minuet in *13*) is slowed to mere
allegro (C, not *alla breve*; steady and lively; far from fast) for analytical
report by Leporello. But we are in the Don's lusty D major. The Don's
quavers rise arpeggio-like to D; and there is a similar rise, in violin or
'cello, every bar. Leporello's vocal lines rises more slowly. "What you
see, ma'am"—he pushes the open book under her nose—"is a list of
the women that my master has loved in his fashion. It is *my* book of *his*
ruling passion. Look inside it, and read it with me." He turns the
pages, and sniggers. The Don's nimble quavers continue, without
rests; effectively, therefore, at twice the rate. "Here, in Italy, 640."
He turns the pages again. "Here, in Germany, 231." For a third time
he turns the pages. "100 in France, 91 when in Turkey—ah, but in
Spain, ma'am . . ." Leporello basks in the glory of his master's achieve-
ment. "In Spain so far, 1,003." The violins cavort. "Yes, and three."
The rest of the orchestra cavort, as the servant becomes more insolent
to this dignified chit of a girl. "Yes, and three." Elvira, woman of
Burgos, stiffens with wounded pride. She is one of 1,003, one of 2,065.

The Don's quavers march on. "Town or country, married, single;
maid or mistress, here they mingle. Many a baroness or duchess or
princess enjoyed his touches; women all, of every class and every shape

and every age, every age and every class." The violins play a grotesque game with the 'cellos and basses, as Leporello repeats the geographical totals from memory. If you compare *4.71–4* with *4.16–25* you will see that he begins to turn the pages in the occupational or social section of a book that is elaborately and salaciously cross-indexed. The dynamics and musical texture build up to an obviously inconclusive close on the dominant. As if all this were not enough, Elvira is now told about the Don's techniques.

Control of tempo is the main secret of it. The great seducer is the great persuader. To persuade people he goes (like a politician) at their tempo. He is always prepared to court or cajole *andante con moto* (here and in *17*); *andantino* (*15*); or *allegretto* (*16*). Vocal line and tone of voice are also suited to the woman. So are the "nonsenses, charm, and outright lies" of *10C12–13*; the nice things that he says to and about her. While he warms up, he amuses himself by testing the girl's reaction to a stock opening gambit that depends on her colour of hair. Are they fair-haired? Then he will never fail to say "Kind-hearted creature." Are they dark-haired? "Constant ever." Are they white-haired? "Your sweet nature." The music fits each thought and nuance. "Fat in winter if he's chilly; thin in summer, willy-nilly." The music tells of a procession of women, thin or fat. Are they tall ones? They look "striking". The note-values augment into crotchets and minims as the music strikes, and holds, a fine statuesque pose. Then they diminish. "Are they tiny?" The violins have a quick little rising semiquaver phrase, akin to the quaver phrase of *4.131* and *4.150–4*. "Are they tiny, are they tiny, are they tiny . . ., they're to his liking." (Was Caterina Micelli, the first Elvira, tiny?)

The second half of the *andante con moto* classifies them by age, financial position and looks—in that order. "Old? He does not overlook them, he is glad to let me book them." At the words "book them" there is a leering change of harmonic colour. "But for pleasure after dinner he prefers a young beginner"—like the *fanciulla* who is listening. "Weak or healthy, poor or wealthy, is she ugly or a goddess? . . ." Or fat or thin, say the orchestra; they are an unending procession of women. "Is she rich and ugly, or a goddess? If she's wearing skirt and bodice, need I tell you what will pass?" The music is warm; exultant with male victory. When we think of the uses of nuance by Mozart and da Ponte in *Figaro*, and elsewhere in the present opera, we can only conclude that they knew what they were making Leporello say and Elvira hear. Is our post-Victorian sense of humour as strong?

"Need I tell you?" says Leporello. "Need we tell you" say the orchestra. "Need I tell you what will PASS, what will PASS, what will PASS?" It is a gross insult to the virtuous and dignified Elvira. She has not run away. Humiliated in Burgos, humiliated by the Don's little trick a few minutes ago, humiliated by this aria, humiliated again and again during the rest of the opera; she stays, endures, returns. Leporello goes, very pleased with himself. Elvira is left alone in the cold light of day, praying that her man will not escape her. "So this was all he had in mind, when he said that he loved me! Was this the value that he set on my passionate devotion? . . . I pray he'll not escape me . . . I'll have recourse to . . . I'll go to . . . I feel inside me nothing left but revenge, fury, retribution!" So she thinks. Her love becomes desperate—and more jealous than ever.

> The year's at the spring,
> And day's at the morn;
> Morning's at seven;
> The hill-side's dew-pearled;
> The lark's on the wing;
> The snail's on the thorn;
> God's in His heaven—
> All's right with the world!

That is how Browning's mill-girl felt, at the beginning of her one annual day off. And that, roughly, is how the lasses feel at the beginning of the third main scene as they giggle and whisper in a carefree rustic G major (6/8 *allegro*). They are ready for love, it is clear. "It will be, it will be full of cheer, and now it is near, and now it is near." The lads on the other hand look silent and embarrassed. They are ordered about by the irritable Masetto: "You are lads who are silly with leisure . . . do not wander about over here, or there, or here, or there, or here. Very short is a holiday pleasure . . . but for me a beginning is near." Yes, it will be full of cheer. The prospectively happy couple sing "Oh my love let us go and be jolly with some singing and dancing and folly." The Don is approaching, the Don is near. The lasses and lads agree that "It will be, it will be full of cheer, and now it is nearer, and now it is here." The Don is nearer, the Don is here.

" 'Tis as well she (Elvira) has gone away" says the Don to Leporello; "For look here, look, look, what fine young men are these, what fine young *women*!" There might even be one for Leporello.

"Ah, my dear friends, good morning! Carry on with being gay and cheerful; carry on with your playing, my good people. Is someone being married?"

"Yes, my lord, and I am the bride."

"Ah, what a comfort! The bridegroom?"

"I, at your service."

She says "my lord". Masetto omits to say so. He tries to be polite, but his tone of voice is sulky and insolent. The Don comments ironically. Zerlina tries to defend Masetto's kind-heartedness—the quality in which (as she is already well aware) he is most notably deficient. He hears the Don address Zerlina as *voi*, a social equal; himself as *tu*, a social inferior. He can guess what the Don and Leporello mean by offering "protection". He hears himself, with all the other lads and lasses, organised for a tour of inspection of the public rooms of a stately home. He hears Leporello say "Very good, sir". He addresses the Don as "My lord", but mars the effect of this belated servility by the blunt assertion that "My Zerlina cannot stay here without me." The Don really lifts his eyebrows at this; he will quote the words blandly back at Masetto with orchestral laughter at *13.133*. Masetto hears himself reassured by Leporello, the Don, and even Zerlina. "Go, it is nothing, I am safe in his hands, he is a cavalier." Masetto is the kind of man who needs someone to blame. He begins to quarrel with Zerlina. "Oh, and therefore?" "Oh, and therefore I'm not in any doubt." "But what if I am?" "Tut, tut" says the Don "we'll have no arguing. There's nothing more to say, and if you do not go this instant, Masetto, have a care, you will regret it." Note the unusual clash of harmonic wills, between D major (*5A52*) and F major (*6.1*); all the other numbers in this opera follow in the same key as (or next door to) the concluding secco bar.

For the present plot Masetto has to be a nasty man. But Mozart was sympathetically aware of the social and political overtones of the ensuing aria. More openly than Figaro's *Se vuol ballare* it is a document of feelings that smouldered in *ancien régime* Europe. The words are part of the original dramatic conception. The music was written separately, and therefore presumably after the rest of the score; Mozart was perhaps wondering how (and in what key) to do justice to the political part of it, without getting into trouble. Like *Se vuol ballare* (and *Batti, batti*) it is in F major. It is *allegro di molto*, full of the tread of revolutionary feet (*Ça ira . . .*), full of sarcasm. "Very good sir!, I agree, I agree, I can bow my head and go, you have said what you decree, there's no more to say, oh no. . . . You're a lord, you condescend and I need have no concern, for you wish to be my friend; I am slow but I can learn. . . ." It is as splendid—and ineffectual—as Elvira's E♭ major fury.

Masetto devotes the remaining two thirds of his aria to the easier task of hurting Zerlina's feelings. "Little demon, have I caught you? You are what I always thought you! (Yes, I'm coming) You can stay then! All is right and clear as day then! He is free to be a lord, and you a lady in your turn!" Note the grotesque "ride a cock-horse" phrase for strings *before* Masetto sings "he is free to be a lord . . ." He goes, with Leporello; and the key of the ensuing secco line (dominant of D major) makes one wonder whether Mozart had toyed with the idea of yet another D major aria.

The Don laughs gaily. With an appreciative glance at the blonde he says "We are rid of him at last, you dear kind-hearted creature. So now forget him. What do you say, my dear? I did it neatly?" Zerlina, who *is* kind-hearted, is charmed. But her thoughts are with the man who had used rough provocative words to wound her. "My lord, he is my husband." (Is he?)

"Who? That clumsy oaf? D'you think a man of honour, a noble cavalier as I am proud to be, can endure to see that pretty golden face, that look as sweet as sugar, so scolded and ill-used by a rough young ploughboy?" This was the moment at which to deny the accusation. Yet Masetto *had* scolded and ill-used her. So "But, my lord, I have given my word that I will marry him." The admission is significant; it tells the Don (*a*) that she is not yet legally married, and (*b*) that she would otherwise be willing to listen to her new admirer.

"Such a word is not worth a puff of air! You were not made so lovely to be a rustic housewife. Another way of life is assured to those eyes that are so roguish; to the lips of a goddess; to pretty fingers, white and sweetly-scented—you are surely soft as junket, and fresh as roses."

"I would not like to . . ." She does not quite dare to finish her sentence; but the thought is direct and practical. "What would you not like?" "Well, afterwards; to be cheated and left." She reminds him that noblemen had a bad reputation so far as peasant girls were concerned. He changes the subject. "Come on, we're losing precious time; this very moment, I will make you my wife."

"You?" For the Don it is another puff of air, another step in the dance; worldly success depends far too often, not only on going at the right tempo but on simply telling people what they want to hear. Mozart and da Ponte planned Zerlina as the kind of woman who would most certainly respond to the offer. She is being given a last-minute opportunity to avoid being chained for ever to Masetto, whose tastes and outlook are so unlike her own. Would this nice man—the man who *notices* everything—marry her? "Yes I promise." He points deprecatingly to his little hovel, the palace. "There in my own little home of joy!" The word *casino, casa di piacere*, is tactfully softened into *casinetto*. Since *6A21* he has been calling her *tu*; his beloved, not his inferior. "There alone together, yes there, my precious jewel, we'll have our wedding." It is hardly the most plausible of stories. But the Don is already in his most seductive A major. Remember that he is the man whose very voice turns her pale in *12A11*. *Là ci darem* is an intensification, not a beginning. There must be no hint of a stopping at *6A35*. It is a controlled slowing of the Don's quavers into the *andante* that he has chosen for this particular girl. "There, arm in arm, we'll tarry; there you will answer yes; there you and I will marry in half an hour or less." She dare not look at him. Numbly she echoes his vocal line—we saw in *Figaro* that Mozart differentiates *or undifferentiates* unerringly. Her first verse is an aside—even softer than the Don's verse. He is so gentle, so considerate, so unlike Masetto! "I am, I am not willing; inside me, I feel sick; I know it would be thrilling——" Semiquavers mark the moment at which excitement and fright combine to make her vocal line a little independent. "Why do I fear a trick?" The horns join in, with an effect quite unlike the previous gentle use of woodwind to link the Don's words with her own thoughts. "Why, why do I fear a trick?"

"You are supremely pretty" insists the Don, *mezzo forte*. "For Mazetto I feel pity" she thinks. She is still thinking of her rough young ploughboy, more warmly than the oaf deserves. But she is by no means unresponsive to admiring recognition of what she and her mirror know so well. "Therefore be poor no longer!" Not to have to work all day, every day . . . to be a lady . . . to have nice dresses . . . jewels . . . get thee behind me, Satan. . . . "I wish that I were stronger, that I were stronger, that I were stronger." It is a classic example of Mozart's dramatic use of musical repetition, enhancing a punch-line in a way that seems utterly natural and inevitable.

7.30–9 are yet another intensification. The Don's voice is blended with the feminine flute; Zerlina's voice, with masculine bassoon. The section may look like a mere repetition, on the page. But it is varied and recombined; the total effect is by no means the same. The Don is a little louder. Zerlina is a little louder than the Don. Will she, won't she? "I am, I am not willing" she thinks. "There you will answer yes" she hears. "Inside me I feel sick" she thinks. "In half an hour or less" she hears. "*Why* do I fear a trick?" she thinks, with the piercing F♯ of *Figaro 16.55*.

7.40–9 do the trick. The vocal lines overlap, the Don repeats his two main arguments, she thinks for the last time of Masetto. She wishes she were stronger, stronger, stronger, stronger; because she is feeling weaker, weaker, weaker, weaker. "We'll go" he says. "We'll go" he says again, a little higher in the voice. "We'll go" she says; turning to him, and completing the expectant close of the musical section. It is not a particularly joyful assent. "We go, we go, my treasure, to enjoy a harmless pleasure, a love we will not repress." She is succumbing, but needs to convince herself that the pleasure is harmless. St. Paul (Romans VII) would have understood. Inside, she probably knows that the Don is deceiving her. She no longer minds. Desire is winning. Sense and conscience are in disarray. Her response, though not total, is sufficient. Unlike the bored and tired typist, in Part Three of Eliot's "Waste Land", she will enjoy it—at the time.

Having demonstrated the Don's virtuosity, Mozart and da Ponte bring in Elvira to interrupt the proceedings—for the time being. "Stop it, oh stop, you villain! Thank Heaven that I overheard your perfidies. I am in time still, I can save this poor miserable innocent from your barbarous clutches!" "Oh no, oh no, what is this?" asks Zerlina. "Now, Cupid help me" thinks the Don. He is caught between two women; an occupational risk. He mutters to Elvira. "Can't you see, my beloved, I wish for some amusement?" Why should she mind? But he had authorised Leporello to Tell All. "Some amusement! Exactly! Some amusement! Yes, I know all about your cruel amusement!" "But my lord" asks Zerlina "is it true or false?" An extremely pertinent question. "A poor unhappy woman who has fallen in love with me" mutters the Don to Zerlina in reply. "I, out of pity, pretend that I love her. You see, to my misfortune I have a kind heart." Even Anna tells a lie less often.

Elvira explodes, and the Don's wicked D major is threatened by a more orthodox Handelian D major. Each of the characters in this opera lives in a different musical and mental world. Together, their worlds add up to a universe. Of what other single opera, except the *Magic Flute*, can this be said? For forty-five *allegro* bars righteous wrath is heard. Yet the words, and the E and B minor bits, make it a very personal utterance. "Run fast and far away, and hear his lies no more; the mouth will you betray, the eyes are lying. Be taught by my misfortune, for I was led astray; oh learn to feel dismay, for I am crying." Run away . . . his mouth . . . his eyes, his eyes, his eyes. Can we believe this woman when she says (and thinks) that she is no longer in love with the Don? She begins to lead Zerlina to a safe distance. The Don ruminates on his bad luck (compare *Figaro 21A41*): "Why, today, should Satan find it amusing to check my run of peaceable successes? Things are all going badly." He is still somewhat upset by having had to kill Anna's father; and Elvira keeps popping up when she is not wanted.

Enter Anna and Ottavio. They are not yet said to be in mourning. But perhaps Ottavio is more business-like than we thought—he may already have made arrangements for the funeral, and for having a suitable inscription cut on a statue that had been erected during the dead man's lifetime. He is still anxious that Anna should wipe away the tears that he dislikes so much. In order to achieve this, he is even prepared to *talk* about revenge—with the admirably dressed Don Giovanni whom he met recently. "And this was all I lacked!" thinks the Don. "We meet again!" says Donna Anna; "The very man we want! For are you not, sir, a man of courage and generous spirit?" "It remains to be seen what some devil may have told her" thinks the Don. Aloud he merely says: "What a question! But why?" "We are in great need . . . of your friendly assistance." The Don breathes again: "Then command me, my relations, my own parents, my right arm and my good sword—my money, my blood I offer thus, in your service." Anna looks at him adoringly; why could not Ottavio (1A14–15) have made such a handsome offer? The Don asks what is the matter. Back races Elvira. "Ah, so I find you again, treacherous monster!" She turns to the unknown gentlewoman.

The B♭ major quartet, like so many of Mozart's dramatic ensembles, works mainly by contrasting three different points of view. First, Elvira's. "Do not rely, unhappy maid, on one so fit for Hell. I am a woman he betrayed; you'll be betrayed as well." She is wrong, of course. Anna has already been "betrayed"; by her own nature, as much as by the Don. But the music of Elvira's mistake permeates the whole quartet. It is repeated in turn by violins, clarinets, flutes; then used with extra emphasis by Anna and Ottavio, who represent the second point of view: "Heavens! A maiden dignified, with sweet and noble air! Her cheek so pale, her spilling eyes fill me with pity rare." It is another new light on the woman who was going to tear out the Don's heart. In the middle of 8 she was sad. By now she is weeping, in what may perhaps be the saddest B♭ major music that Mozart ever wrote (see Shaw's comment on how it should be sung, p. 23). For whom is she weeping? Not for Donna Anna or for herself but for the Don; who merely decides to pretend that she is mad. His is the third point of view. "My friends, I say with sadness, the girl is prone to madness; perhaps, if you would leave us, I could her mind repair." "Do not believe a single word!" begs Elvira, turning again to Anna and

Ottavio. "She's mad, pay no attention" says the Don. "O stay and pay attention" says Elvira. Anna and Ottavio do not know whom to believe. For eighteen bars (*9.31–49*) they all pay tribute to the power of music to mean what words cannot say. "Oh I cannot describe the emotion, that in me is like wind on the ocean, and through feeling in me is revealing many things that she does not declare." Elvira has slightly different words, and a contrasted line (compare *13.251–72* and *19.131–end*).

"From this place I am not going till I fathom this affair" says Ottavio to Anna; he is almost human for once. "Signs of madness are not showing in her speech or general air" says Anna to Ottavio. "I could go now" thinks the Don "but my going a suspicious look would wear." " 'Tis a handsome outer showing" says Elvira to Anna and Ottavio "but his soul is black, I swear." The two men confer: "She is mad . . .?" "There's no denying." The women confer: "He betrayed . . .?" "It is his nature." "Poor young creature!" says the Don. "He is lying, he is lying, he is lying" says Elvira. "I begin some doubt to share" think Anna and Ottavio.

The Don makes a direct appeal to Elvira, in words that have been quoted on p. 148. She loudly rejects the appeal. By now there are people all around them—Zerlina has probably returned, and other bystanders have collected. Anna and Ottavio, the two original spectators, have words that are too rarely noticed: "He is showing hesitation, he is losing all his colour; what a striking indication of the truth of this affair!" But Elvira is still thinking of the Don; and also perhaps, to a greater extent than she would like to admit, about this further humiliation that he has been inflicting on her. At the end she rather peters out. She goes, still in tears; and takes Zerlina again with her. The Don promptly excuses himself, on the pretext of ensuring that the poor madwoman does not do herself an injury. What he then does, we do not know. But we can guess—see p. 163.

Anna has recognised Giovanni as her seducer: "The final words he spoke, look, voice and manner, they are all and indubitably those of the wretch who, in my apartment . . ." Having studied her story with a candid (or Candide) mind, and having also considered her duet (*2*) with Ottavio, what are we to think of her attitude as the orchestra irrupt so dissonantly, with trumpets? She is mightily confused and upset. She responded to a man, passionately; she begged him to stay; he killed her father; however false he was, she greatly preferred him to Ottavio. It was her neighbour, the eligible young Don Giovanni, all the time! She dare not chase him, as this other woman is doing. So we get, after the story, yet another D major aria; in which her mind is on the Don, while her anger is vented on Ottavio. "You know who was trying to rob me of honour, and left him lying—my father, the father of Anna. Avenge him, says my heart—and your heart, I trust! Remember, remember the wound I discovered! Imagine with anguish the earth that with blood was all covered, if your heart should languish from fury so just!" It is typically high-flown and romantic. Is Anna egging Ottavio on to be killed? She would shed fewer tears over him than over her bold and wicked Giovanni.

Ottavio is left alone. He does not believe that his emotional fiancée can have identified the assailant correctly. He goes off "to disabuse *or* avenge her".

Dalla sua pace is not part of the original plan. It was written for Francesco Morella, who sang Ottavio at the Vienna performance in 1788 (apparently Morella felt unable to sing *Il mio tesoro*). From a dramatic point of view it is better omitted.

The Don approaches with "gay indifference". Things are going well. He learns from a despondent Leporello that the peasants are at the palace. "They are half-drunk already, some are singing, some are frolicking, some continue to drink". Zerlina and Elvira had arrived, accusing the Don of "everything bad that either one could think of." Leporello had got rid of Elvira for the time being. "When I thought that she had blown off enough steam, I politely led her out of the garden, I shut the gate in her face by a nice trick, took away the gate-key and left her all alone out there on the pavement."

"Well done, well done, very well done" says the Don "the affair could not be going better! You have begun it, I will end it myself. I am on tenterhooks, thinking of all those lasses whom I shall now amuse until the evening. See that the girls are suitably dizzy, fill them with fizzy wine at a bar. Out in the street, more girls, if you meet more, bring them along, man, just as they are. Start a disorderly medley of dances—slow minuetting, fast other prances, fine pirouetting—with a hurrah. I in the meanwhile will not be seen, while saying I love them, etcetera, etcetera, etcetera. Ten by to-morrow—I will have had them; you, when you add them, ask who they are." This *presto* frenzy of B♭ major orchestral and vocal energy is Mozart's picture of what it feels like inside to be the young Don Juan. It is also a detailed set of instructions (see p. 163) for the finale.

The next scene is in the garden of Don Giovanni's palace. It is about mid-day. The main gates are locked; so that the peasant lads and lasses are unable to get out. They are lying asleep, or sitting listlessly in groups. The gloomiest is Masetto. Zerlina is pleading with him.

"Masetto! Will you listen! I say, Masetto!"

"Bah, do not touch."

"But why?"

"Bah, what a question! Wicked wench! Ought I to put up with the touches of a hand that has held his?"

"Ah, no, no, do not say it, you are hard, I do not deserve such treatment."

"Baggage! You now offer impudent excuses? You go off with a man, you do it openly on the day I marry you, you put these horns on an honourable peasant, let them laugh at the bridegroom. Oh but if only . . . and you know what they'll say of you . . . I wish I . . ."

"But if I am not to blame? If I was helpless, if I was a victim? What are you thinking? My dear one, do not worry! We did not touch, with tips of little fingers! You don't believe me? Ungrateful! Come here, do it then, half-murder me, do anything rough that will relieve you; but then, Masetto dearest, say you forgive me. Beat oh beat me hard and often; handsome husband, I'll adore you. I will be a lamb before you. Standing here, I shall not mind. Tug my hair off, I will let you. Pluck my eyes out, I'll abet you. I would fondle your dear fingers joyfully, though I were blind. . . . Ah but surely . . . you're unwilling, oh I see you are unwilling! O my love, if I'm forgiven, here on earth a very heaven nightly, daily, we shall find."

Believe it or not, that is what Mozart says in this long warm lulling caress of voice and 'cello. It lulls the male—for about thirty seconds. "Oh and look how you do it! Like a witch, you beguile me. We are weak in the head, and that is certain." The voice of the Don is heard. "Oh Masetto, Masetto, listen, I hear him, it is he, mister cavalier." "And therefore what?" "He'll come." "What does it matter?" "If there were only a place where I could hide!" "Why are you frightened? You suddenly turn pale again! AH! I understand, I understand the whole trick! You're afraid I might even hit on the truth of what took place between you! I will hurry! If he's coming, I will find a place aside here. There's a corner! I will hide here, keeping quiet, watching you."

"Listen, listen! Are you hiding? Oh do not try to hide, Masetto! Oh you poor man, if he met you, can you guess what he would do?"

"Let him do it, let him slay me!"

" 'Tis in vain, he'll not obey me."

"Speak up well, and in my hearing!"

"Some capricious trick I'm fearing."

"I shall know if she's unfaithful, or if what she said is true!"

"Oh how cruel, how ungrateful and how rash a thing to do!"

Enter the Don, attended by four richly-clad servants. He turns to the lasses and lads. "Come, get up, 'tis time for waking! Come, be lively, no evasion! We will all enjoy the occasion, we are here to laugh and play." To the servants he says "Lead them all into the parlour, get them ready for the dancing; there's a bar, so give them all a proper luncheon straight away." The servants know what he means. They are demonic figures. "*We* will all enjoy the occasion, *we* are here to laugh and play."

Zerlina pathetically tries to hide. "If this pair of shrubs were bigger, I could hide, he would not see me."

"Zerlinetta's charming figure! I have seen you, I have seen you, won't you stay?"

"Let me go, it is no pleasure!"

"Stay oh stay, my joy, my treasure!"

"If your heart has any pity . . ."

" 'Tis aflame for one so pretty! I am rich, in yonder niche a fortune waits for you this day."

"That is where Masetto's waiting! He'll be hating me this day."

"Masetto!"

"Yes, Masetto."

"Why hide in there, I pray?" The Don is disconcerted—for a second. He then roars with laughter at the memory of Masetto's defiance ($5A38$). Look at the two violin parts, and the flute part, $13.129\text{--}35$. Hear how the orchestra chuckle as the Don sings "So you and your Zerlina (poor girl, by her demeanour) not long apart can stay!"

"Sir, I remember better."

"I know what would be better" says the Don, changing the subject. And at that moment out of the window comes the sound of the second orchestra playing the *follia*. "The music is beginning, you *both* may come with me."

"Yes, yes, oh yes, we'd better" says Zerlina, who loves dancing. "I think it would be better" say Zerlina and Masetto. "So with the others we will a-dancing go, all three." "You both may, you both may come with me" says the Don. They go, all three.

Enter Anna, Elvira and Ottavio in masks. The dignified Elvira is leading, with Anna's D minor music. "What we shall need is courage, as we shall soon discover if we are to uncover, my friends, his cruel iniquity." Ottavio is impressed. "Our dear new friend I'm heeding, 'tis courage we are needing. Dispel your fear, my dear love, your plain timidity." Anna is pensive. "Oh a narrow pass we're nearing! Oh alas, I foresee violence. Therefore for you I'm fearing, and for our friend and me." The fury of *10* has evaporated.

A window opens and Leporello's voice is heard. "Sir, here are masqueraders. Look, gentlefolk by station." Leporello was wise to check whether his instructions (*11.17–32*) covered gentlewomen. The Don reassures him and appears at the window. "Give them an invitation, tell them they honour me." That handsome face and fine voice declare the gay deceiver. "Tsit, tsit, good Sirs in masquerade" calls Leporello. "And you can answer" say the two women to Ottavio. "Tsit, tsit, good Sirs in masquerade" calls Leporello again. Ottavio replies. "Say what you want, sir." "To dancing, if it please you, my lord invites all three." "Pray thank him for the honour. Come on, my fair companions." ("Twice more" thinks Leporello "can my companion prove his virility.")

But the maskers do not hurry in. They dawdle, during and after a B♭ major trio (*13.251–72*) that is the musical centre-piece of the finale. After two transitional bars (*251–2*) and an unaccompanied bar (*253*), the splendid *adagio* is wind, wind, wind. "Preserve, O righteous heaven, this righteous wrath in me!" Anna is hesitant. She needs assistance from heaven to preserve a wrath that is in any case not entirely righteous. And what about Elvira? In *3*, she was going to tear out his heart. At *3A32* she was thinking of inflicting her own *and* heaven's vengeance. She is becoming less and less inclined to do the job herself. "Punish, O righteous heaven, my man who cheated me." Ottavio sings with Anna. He does not yet believe that Giovanni killed Anna's father; but it's an ill wind . . .

The trio has ended, with several bars of beautiful dreamlike unreality (compare *Figaro 15.308–27* and *15.672–96*). The scene changes and we are in the ball-room, listening to a rousing 6/8 popular dance tune in E♭ major. The lasses and lads have been dancing to it; they are said to be "in the act of" having finished a dance. Therefore *13.273*, like *Figaro 22.1*, is musically a continuation not a beginning.

We last saw the Don at the window (*13.224–7*). As we noticed in the prologue, the events of this finale are spread over several hours. What then, if anything, is the Don supposed to have been doing during the

6/8 hop? Was he dancing? Was he being a wall-flower? Or was he . . .?
At *13.283* he sings "My fair maidens, we'll all have a rest, then"
(thereby implying that the lasses and lads have had several dances).
During the previous bars he is said in a stage-direction to be making
the girls sit. But he hardly needs eleven bars to do so. During bars
273–6 (which equal *280–3*), was he meant by Mozart to be seen
emerging with one of the lasses from the door which Masetto later
breaks down? It is possible, though by no means certain. If so, Zerlina
can be seen finishing the 6/8 dance with Masetto.

Leporello takes his cue: "My fine fellows, I offer refreshment." The
Don and Leporello grin at each other: "We'll return to our follies with
zest, then; we'll return to our dancing with glee." The alcoholic
coffee, chocolate, sherbet and sweetmeats arrive. The Don, we may
assume, gives the servants a slight nod—towards Zerlina, who is the
next objective. She is therefore given preferential treatment, to an
extent that alarms Masetto. "Ah, Zerlina, be careful." He sings it
twice; his soft long wind chords contrast effectively with the 6/8
quaver tune. There could not be a sweeter beginning but how bitter
the ending could be. "You are brilliantly pretty, Zerlina" says the Don;
caressingly, politely. She is delighted—Masetto *never* says anything nice
to her. "You are kind!" she replies. "And the slut seems to like it!" says
Masetto very audibly. "I adore you, Joanna, Sandrina" says Leporello,
trying to imitate (and go one better than) his master. "If 'tis that in
your head, I will strike it!" says Masetto, shaking with fury. "My
Masetto is looking demented!" thinks Zerlina. "Oh how ugly the
ending will be!" She is piqued, as in *5A* and *6*, by Masetto's behaviour.
"Oh you baggage!" he says. "You're a slut, my despair you will be!"
Everyone is looking at him, and at the much-irritated Zerlina. Note
what the Don and Leporello are saying to each other. "Use of brain is
the right remedy." In other words, the time is ripe for a three-orchestra
trick.

First the emotional temperature is carefully lowered. Enter Anna,
Elvira, Ottavio; in a pompous C major. "Come in, you charming
maskers!" says Leporello. "Come in, for you are welcome." The
Italian feminine plural makes it clear that he is addressing the two
ladies, not the gentleman. "Here, everyone is welcome" says the Don.
"Welcome to liberty." "We thank you for your tokens of generosity"
say the three new-comers. The gentry and Leporello praise liberty;
the libertine's liberty, sexual not political. The lasses and lads listen,
bewildered. Zerlina is rather impressed.

The dancing resumes. "Come, we will have more music" says the

Don. He tells Leporello to couple off the dancers. The first orchestra (strings, oboes, horns) strike up a minuet. If you think of the *allegretto* minuets of Mozart's three most famous symphonies, written in the following year, you will see that the present minuet is remarkably slow and stately. It is ideal for Anna and Ottavio; they take the floor and begin the elegant posturing of a court minuet. It is less ideal for the lasses and lads, whom Leporello urges on to the floor when the eight-bar section begins to repeat: "Come, dance and foot it bravely!" "There goes the little farm-girl" says Elvira to the passing Anna. "Oh it kills me!" says Anna; virtuous as ever. It is an illuminating little exchange, and it comes in the fifth bar of the eight-bar section; just where the emotional temperature is raised by going into the dominant. Note that Anna replies swiftly, high in the voice. Ottavio's comment ("Do not show it!") is deliberately contrasted in these two respects.

The minuet continues with an eight-bar counter-tune, slightly richer and more excited in texture. The Don and Leporello are well satisfied. "So all is well, you see!" Masetto overhears and thinks. "So all's well!" Figaro had a similarly ironic comment at *28.88*. Masetto in his turn is overheard. "So keep Masetto mellow!" says the Don to Leporello.

The minuet counter-tune recommences. It is the fourth eight-bar section of the minuet. A second orchestra (strings only) are heard tuning; in minuet tempo, thereby creating the expectation of a second minuet. But *11* promised us a Folly next. "Oh my love, let us go and be jolly, with some singing and dancing and folly!" (*5*). In nearly all the dances of the seventeenth and eighteenth centuries, says the *Encyclopaedia Britannica*, kissing formed a not unimportant part. The present minuet is too grave and formal for that sort of thing. But the traditional minuet, in a rather quicker tempo, was generally followed by the gavotte; which, according to the encyclopaedia, was also originally a peasant's dance (*danse des Gavots*) and consisted chiefly of kissing and capering. The second orchestra are in fact tuning up for the sprightly 2/4 *Contredanse* (or country dance) that we heard through the window at *13.142*. "Not dancing, you poor fellow?" says Leporello to Masetto. "Now I can be your partner" says the Don to Zerlina, who is already more excited than is safe for any girl about to dance with the Don. "Zerlina! Zerlina, come with me!"

The original minuet tune recommences. We are about half-way through, having reached the fifth eight-bar section of the minuet (which is rapidly becoming a bore). Anna and Ottavio solemnly continue. "No, no, I'll do no prancing!" says Masetto. "My friend, we'll go a-dancing!" says Leporello. "No!" says Masetto. "Yes!" says Leporello. The Don and Zerlina dance a Folly. Very probably, most of the lasses and lads are glad to follow their example. The oboes and horns of the first orchestra are beginning to transfer their sympathies to the more amusing dance. There would be no harm in letting a few violins do the same.

The counter-tune recommences; and the underlying minuet rhythm is at once enhanced by a cry from Anna. "I cannot, cannot bear it!" What can she not bear? The sight of the Don dancing with the little farm-girl? "Pretend you cannot see!" suggest Elvira and Ottavio helpfully. She (and we) can see very well that the Don and Zerlina are enjoying their Folly. It goes at the rate of three 2/4 bars to every two minuet bars, twelve bars to every section of the minuet, twenty-four bars to the complete minuet tune and counter-tune (but it begins and ends two crotchet beats later). The third orchestra are tuning. "Dance, man!" says Leporello. "No, no, I will not!" says Masetto. "My friend, we'll go a-dancing!" insists Leporello. "Come, join the rest with me!"

The original minuet tune commences for the last time (seventh eight-bar section). The minuet is now utterly monotonous. Anna and Ottavio continue to dance but their slow-witted gestures are mechanical. By contrast the lasses and lads are having a splendid time. They dance a second Folly, with plenty of kissing and capering. The "disorderly medley of dances" (11.33) is completed when the third orchestra strike up an unusual *Allemande*; a 3/8 "German", of which twenty-four bars coincide exactly with the eight-bar minuet section. (We know it is an *Allemande*, because the Don said it would be, in 11; Dent says it is a waltz, but that is surely even more difficult to believe.) Every violin that can be spared must strengthen the violin line of the third orchestra. The horns of the first orchestra, having supported the Don's Folly, now provide rhythmic energy for the third orchestra. After three crotchets, they belt along in quaver triplets. The third orchestra frolic wildly. "Now come with me, my darling" says the Don. "Let me go!" says Masetto to Leporello; but is danced along. "Ah no! Zerlina!" cries Masetto. "Come with me now!" says the Don, half-pulling her through the door into an adjoining room. "You traitor! You seduce me!" gasps Zerlina as she disappears. The violins of the third orchestra rush up. The bass line of the second orchestra has an extra D for luck (13.459, compare 443). "A seed of ruination!" thinks Leporello, and rushes out. The violins rush up again.

This time they climb the whole D major scale and stay at the top, insisting on the D. To ensure that they are audible, it happens while the first orchestra are silent at the end of the seventh eight-bar section. The last three bars of the twenty-four bar 3/8 dance are neatly linked to the first three bars of its repetition; musically, by a change in the quality of the rhythmic horn support; dramatically, by phallic imagery and the traditional association of horns with cuckoldry. It was for this that Mozart and da Ponte planned the whole finale; for this, that Elvira had to endure the musical clue at the end of *Madamina. Voi sapete quel che fa.* The Don has Done it again. Zerlina has been seduced —quickly, but in imagined minutes rather than seconds. She has not screamed.

The minuet counter-tune begins again, for the fourth and last time; with all the intensity of the musical and dramatic associations that have been accumulating in it. (The pattern is AABBABAB.) The lasses and lads are still happily enjoying their Folly. But Anna and Ottavio are no longer repeating their minuet. With Elvira, they gleefully suppose that the Don has gone too far this time. "Well, well, it is his doing! A noose, for villainy!" Masetto is silent. The wicked fiddles have what looks like the beginning of some more erotic imagery (*13.465–6*); especially when the horns resume their crotchets (*13.466*). Zerlina at once comes to her senses. She calls for help. "Help oh help me, friend or stranger!" In the middle of her vocal phrase the rhythm changes to *allegro assai*. The first (and second) dances are two (four and a half) bars short of their natural conclusions. The third dance is six bars short, or (more probably) has been shortened into eighteen bars. Our attention is focussed on Zerlina, and on the surging struggling harmonies of the *allegro assai*. "Is her innocence in danger?" sing Anna, Elvira and Ottavio. "Ah Zerlina, ah Zerlina" cries Masetto. "Crime astounding!" cries Zerlina; and the echoes rebound. She is scared. Those screams are genuine. The door is broken down. After E♭ major, B♭ minor and C minor there is a half-close on the dominant of D minor. The Don jauntily emerges in F major, blaming Leporello. "Here's the rascal who offended! I'll impose the penalty." Note that, as in *3*, the Don is prepared to condemn his own behaviour. Ottavio draws a pistol and removes his mask. Elvira and Anna also unmask. Zerlina joins in general denunciations of the Don, who is momentarily disconcerted. But he soon recovers his confidence, and presumably either disarms Ottavio or so overawes him that the pistol is put away. In the final *più stretto*, the women sing his tune. (See also page 164.)

ACT TWO

The Don can wheedle his fellow-beings, male or female, to do whatever he wants. He now suits his tempo, tune and tone to Leporello; who has been resolving as usual (compare *10C1*) to leave the Don. "Do not annoy me, do not annoy me! Idiot, I say." says the Don. "Do not employ me, do not employ me! I will not stay" says Leporello. "Listen, dear fellow!" "I go, I tell you." "What have I done, then? Why should you leave me?" "Your sword was fun, then? Nothing to grieve me?" "You are an idiot, for that was clearly merely nearly all done in play." "Oh was it really? I am sincerely sheerly queerly going away." The bully has to repeat his words a little. Then:

"Leporello" "What is it?" "Come here, and let us make peace. Take it!" "How much?" "Four or five pounds." "Oh! Then listen. On this occasion the ritual is accepted. But do not make it a habit, do not think you can seduce men like me as if we were women, by simple force of money." "No more of that, have you had enough encouragement to do again what I tell you?" "Provided . . . no more women?" "Have no more women! Mad idea! Have no more women! For me they're necessities, I need them more than any food I eat, more than the air I breathe!" "Then how, I ask you, can you bear to deceive them all?" "Because I love them all! To be faithful to one alone would be cruel to others. I, as I sense in me a feeling so extended, wish well to every one of them; but as the women cannot count beyond one, they call my good and natural power deception." "And what a natural power! Was a power ever more vast or more beneficent? Come on, what do you wish of me?" "Listen, you saw the chambermaid this morning with Donn' Elvira?" "I? No." "Why then in that case you did not see a thing of beauty. Ah, my dear Leporello, I mean to try my manly

fortune with *her* next. I have decided—'tis nearly dark already—
I will, the more to sharpen up her appetite, present myself to her,
dressed up in your clothes." "What is wrong with presenting your own
self in your own clothes?" "The dress of gentlefolk has all too little
credit left with a girl of that rank. Hurry up! Out of them!" "My
lord, that is no reason . . ." "Enough of that, I allow no opposition!"

They change clothes, in the street below a hotel window; at which
Elvira appears. She believes herself to be alone in the half-light of dusk.
She converses with her heart in A major. Those violins are her heart;
soft, palpitating, young, alive. "Immoral heart, obey me!" Will it
obey? Clarinets and bassoons have a simple rising phrase. Violins tell
us that the immoral heart is excited. She implores it to "beat gently,
calmly, slowly". The clarinet phrase falls, but the bassoon phrase continues to rise. "He's wicked!" Excitement blossoms, in a phrase that
recalls *3.6.* "He would betray me!" The blossom opens. "So banish
sympathy!" That rising phrase becomes more complex and chromatic;
clarinets, bassoons and violins express the sympathy that she wishes to
banish. She tries again with a high A. "O banish sympathy!"

The bassoons throw in an apparently casual phrase for Leporello.
"Hush, sir, 'tis Donn' Elvira! The moment is unpropitious!" "Nonsense" says the Don "it is propitious, stay there for her to see." The
bassoon phrase has been lifted two whole octaves, to be fondled by
flutes and clarinets. A transitional bar takes us into E major; in which
Elvira's heart-tune, repeated by the violins, is joined by a male voice.
"Elvira, I adore you!" Flutes, as well as clarinets and bassoons, have
the original little rising phrase. Her heart pounds. "Elvira, I adore
you!" He's wicked, say the orchestra. But I love him, says her immoral
heart. "Is that the ungrateful villain?" As she sings the words, her
orchestral self knows that he would betray her. She hears him again.
"Yes, here in shame before you, I beg for charity!" (Again the Don
is condemned by his own admission—this time, by answering Yes to
her question.) She sings an aside, and therefore naturally uses the
musical phrase that Leporello and the Don had used for their asides.
"Oh unaccustomed aching . . . I feel it re-awaking!" (with clarinets).
Leporello, trying his best not to look like a scarecrow, is aghast (with
bassoons) as he thinks that "You're mad, if you can listen *again* to
such a plea!"

The melody slides, with a crescendo, into a soft sudden C major.
The Don knows that she is weakening. He can therefore afford to
relapse for a moment into his standard serenade—for use once or twice
daily (cp. *16*) beneath windows. The first five bars are accompanied by

strings alone; and the second violins have a banal mandoline-like accompaniment. "Come down, O joy, O beauty!" Elvira's young heart turns it into poetry. "For now I see my duty, with all my heart I adore you, a penitent sinner see!" The string tremolo tells us that she is angry; but anger is soon modified by woodwind warmth. "That is untrue, you cruel man!" " 'Tis true, I say!" "It is untrue, you cruel man!" He repeats insidiously that it is true. Again she says it is untrue. He insists; and is met by a suspiciously shrill "Untrue, untrue!" The Don takes out a dagger, and points it at Leporello's throat. "Cruel, you kill me!" Leporello, whose sympathies at any given moment are at the librettist's disposal, merely chuckles at the thought of the Don's impending success. "With laughter it would fill me . . ."

"Angel, come here to me!" implores the Don, as the music goes back to its predestined A major. Once more we hear Elvira's heart. A familiar little horn phrase (cp. *Figaro 28.1*) is added, to bridge a widening gap between vocal phrases; after which we are offered three simultaneous sets of thoughts—Elvira's heart, the Don's, Leporello's. In the first two vocal phrases, only her thoughts can (with luck) be heard. "Oh what an evil choosing! I cannot bear refusing!" When she continues, with "Ye Gods, will ye watch over my entire credulity?", the Don's line is contrasted, in a way that helps his words to come through; and there is opportunity at *15.71-2* for Leporello's words to be heard as well. But her thoughts dominate. "Ye Gods, will ye watch over my entire credulity?"

The Don sympathised with Anna's father; and with Elvira herself, in *3*, when he thought she was unbooked. His present emotions are unsympathetic, in direct contrast with what she is thinking. "I hope she's nearly losing! Fine little trick for using! No brain is half so fertile as mine in devilry!" He intends to let Leporello have her.

Leporello has not realised that this is his own opportunity to play at master. His sympathies have veered. "How can he tell her such lies, merely to reseduce her? Ye Gods, will ye watch over entire credulity?" The trio ends with every possible intensification of Elvira's prayer. "Ye Gods, will ye watch over my entire credulity, credulity, ENTIRE CREDULITY, ENTIRE credulity?" Downward bound, she leaves the window.

"Well, what d'you say to that, my friend?" "I say your soul is . . . as stony as a statue!" "Well I'm damned, you're still a half-wit; now pay attention, and when the foolish wench comes, run forward and embrace her; give her four good caresses, speaking to her in my voice; then use your manly charm, persuade her to go off with you somewhere." "But, my lord . . ." "No more arguing." "Yes, but what if I'm recognised?" "She will not recognise unless you let her. Quiet, she's coming out. Hey, be careful!"

"Here I am, take me" she says. "Can I dare to believe that all my sorrow has won back your dear heart? That my Giovanni, beloved and repentant, is now returning to fulfil his obligations?" "Yes . . my darling." He opens his arms to her. She embraces him. "You are cruel! If you only knew how many tears and how many, many, sighs you cost me!" "I, my beloved?" "Yes, you!" She embraces him again. "Oh you poor thing!" he says, embracing her as best he can. "I am truly sorry" he says. "You will not go again?" she asks hurriedly. "No, for I love you." "You will be mine for ever?" "And ever, amen." "My precious man!" "My precious maid!" The jest acquires a savour; he embraces her more warmly. "You my treasure!" she says. "You my desire!" he answers. "I'm aflame for you already!" she says. "I burn to a cinder!" he answers. "He'll scald himself, the rascal!" thinks the Don.

All this is much too slow by the Don's standards. A Juan goes *andante* or *andantino* during the difficult part of the operation; not when a woman is already as ardent and willing as this one. He shoos them away; not meaning to deprive Leporello of his woman (he himself would never be put off by a little thing like that) but because he is impatient to begin serenading Elvira's maid.

Like a good general the Don wins his battles beforehand. He plans coolly and carefully. Above all, he accurately senses what the adversary will think and do. He dazzled Zerlina with wealth and charm. This girl he woos as a fellow-servant, with a 6/8 song that has more than a hint of mere oom-pa-pa in its mandoline accompaniment. The words are an old story, sung with the slightly throaty sensuality of a good crooner. "Look down below your window, oh you my treasure! Look down, and so console my weary sighing! If you will not allow that simple pleasure, before your very eyes you'll see me dying. Your mouth is full of honey, sweet in flavour; for with sugar your body and soul are laden. How long will you be cruel, withholding favour? Show me at least your face, my own fair maiden!"

It works. There she is at the window. He is about to climb to the balcony, when Masetto and the peasant lads appear. "Do not give up, friends, for I am certain we shall find him near here." The Don is seen. "Who is that?" says Masetto: "Why no answer? Cover him, you, with muskets! Who is that?" "I see friends!" says the Don, playing for time. "Are you Masetto?" "The very fellow! And you?" "You do not know me? The servant you saw with Don Giovanni." "Leporello! . . . the servant of that unworthy cavalier-lord!" "Yes indeed; of that confounded rogue!" "Of that man quite without honour! Ah, you can tell me where we may hope to find him. These lads and I, we look for him to kill him." Such a bagatelle, thinks the Don: "Good luck to you, Masetto. No, more than that; for I myself will join you in doing this to a master who deserves it. Listen to me, I'll tell you my intention. Let half of you go down the road, and half of you up there! Go quietly, and look for him—not far away, I swear!" We are in Leporello's F major, for one of the simplest and most inspired arias that even Mozart ever wrote, from the point of view of dramatic expression. Out of context, it means almost nothing. In context, it has everything —atmosphere, excitement, parody, and a double characterisation (the Don playing Leporello, without ever ceasing to be himself); not to mention such lyrical delights as *17.10*.

Casually the Don throws in a portrait of himself. Bassoons trip lightly away in thirds, with a luscious trill that is tossed from violin to oboe. "If man and girl are talking, or in the square are walking, or if beneath a window you hear a lover's greeting, then give the man a beating, a beating, yes a beating!" A vigorously thrashing syncopation of the strings evokes it for us. "My master do not spare!" His master? If he sends them in the right direction, Leporello will be in danger— or will at least have the fright of his life. The Don chuckles, with violins (*17.19–20*). "The hat he will be flaunting is white with handsome plumage; a fine cloak he'll be vaunting, his own long sword he'll wear." The sword (?) is mercilessly stressed.

Again the amorous bassoons trip off, again we hear the trilling violins and oboes. The violin phrase from *17.19–20* comes earlier, when he is thinking of the window. *17.38* sounds like a general reminiscence of *15*. The words "my master do not spare!" are omitted. The Don finds it exceedingly funny (compare *21D8*). Is he thinking of Elvira?

"Be off and do not chatter, chatter, chatter!" He is much too lordly, for a man pretending to be Leporello. But self-confidence has lulled all suspicion. Off go the lads to left and right. The Don turns to Masetto, taking the music momentarily into a sinister subdominant. "And you will come with me!" The next verbal phrase is supported and emphasised in three parallel octave lines. "There's one remaining matter . . ." Woodwind instruments echo the phrase-ending. "As you alone shall see . . . shall see . . . shall see!" The mocking C and A of "shall see", the masterly woodwind embroidery, the sheer audacity, compel our admiration of Mozart and his Don. The aria ends with a longish postlude, during which the Don manœuvres Masetto round one or two buildings, out of sight of the window to which he means to return.

After listening to make sure that the lads are out of earshot, the Don proceeds. "Are we agreed on killing him?" "Undoubtedly". "It would not be enough if we shattered his leg-bones, or his arms at the shoulder?" "No, no, he shall be slaughtered! I'll cut him in a hundred pieces!" "Are you well-armed?" "Good God, yes! This musket, in the first place." He hands it to the NCO (or officer?) for inspection. "And also this pistol." The pistol is also handed over.

"Is that all?" asks the Don. "Is it not enough?" asks Masetto. "Oh yes, 'tis quite enough!" Pocketing the pistol, the Don draws his sword; which he had kept, when changing clothes. Nonchalantly leaning on the musket, he swipes Masetto with the flat of the sword. "Take this, then! This, for your loaded pistol! This, for your murderous musket!" Masetto howls, and calls for help. "Quiet, or I kill you!" says the supposed Leporello. "These, for intended slaughter! These for his hundred pieces, you ill-bred bastard oaf, snout of a mongrel!" He laughs, and saunters off round the buildings. A little later, we see him climb nimbly to the chambermaid's window—an action that is indicated, in da Ponte's innocent-looking libretto, by the otherwise meaningless exit and re-entry with Masetto.

Masetto bellows as loudly as ever. Zerlina conveniently enters with a lantern. "Ow, ow, my head, my poor head, ow, ow, my poor back, my whole front! . . . O God, Zerlina, my sweet Zerlina, help, help me!" "What has happened?" "The villain, the cheating rascal broke all my bones and sinews!" "Then what about poor me?" wonders Zerlina aside. She asks who did it. "Leporello—or else a devil looking very like him!" "You cruel man! Did I not tell you that this mad lusting jealousy would merely, and quite inevitably, get you into trouble? Where does it hurt you?" "Here!" "And where else?" "Here! And also here!" "He has not hurt you elsewhere?" "Oh a little, this left foot, in the left arm, and here the right hand." "There, there, 'tis no great harm, if the rest is unhurt. Come along home with me then, and if you were to promise you'd never be so jealous, I, I would cure your hurts, my own dear bridegroom. Oh yes I would, so if you are good, oh look what fine medicines I will provide." Her meaning is hardly even veiled. A resting-place is found, the C major of this life (Browning, *Abt Vogler* XII). "Natural, human, not bitter tasting; save by a woman they are not supplied. I carry stores for as long as I live, yes, ready to give, yes, when you decide!"

Suggestive words, music that is more than merely suggestive; their combined power was something that Mozart could foresee, clearly enough to make him feel that it must be muted if his vision of seven characters was to be tolerable on the stage. Only a bride and bridegroom were allowed to evoke the feeling as unmistakably as it is evoked in the present aria. "And should you wonder where they all hide, where, how, where and how they all hide . . ." The 'cellos quiver, the horns hold a long chord, the woodwind have a phrase that is the ancestor of *Così 23.56*. "Hear how they beat for you!" She takes his hand and puts it under her left breast. He feels her heart beating. "Feel them, outside!" Staccato semiquavers, from flute, clarinet, bassoon horn. "Feel them outside, here. Medicines fine my heart will provide." Medicines? Her *heart*? Off they go, in search of a secluded place; preferably, nearer than home.

Elvira and Leporello, after wandering around for nearly an hour (*20.54–6*), have reached just such a place. It is a dark outer hall or courtyard, with three doors. By inference (*20A8*) it is in Donna Anna's home. Elvira is still amorous and under the illusion that the dark figure beside her is the Don. Through a window Leporello sees a torchlit procession. He grasps at another excuse. "I see the light of torches . . . coming nearer, my love. Wait here in shadow till they are safely distant." "What are you afraid of, O my much-adored husband?" Leporello hesitates again. Then he remembers that fear is out of character. Hurriedly he tries to sound confident. "Nothing, nothing . . . just a precaution . . . I'll go and see how far away they are now." He is wondering how he can get away from this female. "Stay here, my sweet beloved!" "Ah, do not leave me! I'm alone, alone in darkness, and I feel my spirit fail me. I am frightened! Such thoughts assail me, I shall surely die from fear." Flutes, bassoons, second violins and violas have taken us into E♭ major; for the *andante* section of the following sextet. As usual every little touch of orchestral colour has an expressive meaning. Consider for instance the little shiver of fear that is added in bar 2, the anxious quavers that lag behind the beat in bar 5, the sadly deflated echo of earlier Elvira music in 7 and 8. Note how minutely and sensitively the score brings to life each nuance of the way in which Mozart is feeling the dramatic situation.

"There were three doors, and I need one; yet the more I look the less I seem to find it. Gently, gently. Do I find it? Yes, I find it. Now 'tis time to disappear." That was Leporello, becoming hopeful. But in come Anna and Ottavio, with those torch-bearing servants. They have been to the funeral, and are dressed in deep black for the first time. But now that the funeral is over, Ottavio sees no reason at all to prolong the gloom. In a brightly-clashing D major, he reverts to his sage advice of *8A4-5*. "Dry oh dry your tears, beloved! Weep no more, be tranquil rather. Surely the spirit of your father will be sad at such a grief!"

A semitone away, lies the realm of D minor. "Let my sorrow have some outlet! For how else may I endure it? Only one thing, only, only death can cure it, only death can bring relief!" (A blunt ending on "endure it", *ristoro*, misses the point of having B♭ major on the way to C minor.)

At *19.61* begins another violin figure, drooping and dragging with the anxiety that Elvira and Leporello, for different reasons, both feel. "Where can my beloved be now?" thinks Elvira. "I am lost if she should find me" thinks Leporello. "Through the door that I can see now?" wonders Elvira. She determines as usual to follow him. "Through the door that I can see now, I am gently leaving here" they both sing. They converge from opposite sides towards the central door. Leporello reaches it first. He runs straight into Zerlina and Masetto, who are looking for their secluded place. "Stop, slinking villain, where are you going?" say they, not having recognised the clothes. Anna and Ottavio turn and recognise the hat and cloak. "There's Don Giovanni! How came he here?" "Die for your treacheries! We mean to slay you!" sing all four.

Elvira steps forward. "Pity, I pray you, my husband oh so dear!" It is the maiden dignified, with sweet and noble air; her cheek so pale, her spilling eyes once more create an impression (finely enhanced by the viola line, *19.78, 80, 82,* etc). Her hearers are thrown into indignant confusion. " 'Tis Donn' Elvira, Donn' Elvira, Donn' Elvira! I heard, she said it! What now can I credit?" "Pity, I pray!" "No, no, no no!" they say, striking a resolute violin posture. "We slay!" "Have pity!" "No!" "Have pity!" "No!" "Pity, I pray!" "No, no, no no . . . we slay!" Ottavio solemnly raises his sword (or pistol?). Leporello shows his face; and kneels imploringly. He is not of course wearing a sword; at any side.

"Oh pardon me, sirs, for him I'm taken. I am not he, sirs, she is mistaken, oh do not kill poor me, I faint with fear!" "What? Leporello, a fraud confessing? I'm dimly guessing what might appear" sing the quintet. At *19.125* Masetto is silent; he is visibly wondering who it was that so recently beat him up. At *19.126* Anna falls silent; she can betray a visible agony of jealousy that, if anyone can win the Don back, it is likely to be Elvira. The *andante* section ends questioningly, on the dominant of C minor.

"Many many black forebodings" (thinks Leporello in an agitated E♭ major *molto allegro*) "loom inside my head at present. To escape a death unpleasant is improbable, I fear." The others are also full of forebodings—especially Anna and Elvira, for reasons that converge on a young man who is at present sauntering off from Elvira's maid towards Leporello's girl-friend. "Was there ever a day so stormy?"

Leporello does not trust the strange atmosphere of gloom; or Ottavio's genuine weapon, that droops so ominously. "To escape what hovers o'er me is unlikely; and that is clear!" But Abert, to whose analysis of this sextet I am particularly indebted, points out that Leporello's spirits rise as the would-be avengers grow more despondent. The flute encourages him. There is also a significant plunge on to a chord of D♭ major. "How unheard-of, how bizarre!" sing the others, with a fine florid melisma for Anna. During her held F Leporello sings "How right you are!" on D♭. He is not yet out of trouble. But he is gradually edging backwards towards that third door; while the others begin to be preoccupied with beautiful *sotto voce* singing. (Note that the usual distribution of vocal lines between Elvira and Zerlina looks odd, at some points—one would expect Zerlina, not Elvira, to be singing with Masetto.) The violins have a drooping downward scale figure on behalf of the despondent quintet at *19.168–9*, while Leporello has one of his little upward-moving phrases. After the D♭ interlude, a musical section ends with our attention focussed on Elvira's line (*19.184–92*). Leporello, Anna and Elvira are the three who matter. After the whole section has been repeated, a splendid polyphonic coda breaks out. By now the avenging quintet are resigned to impotence. They leave the Don to Heaven's will—or, as we are soon reminded, to the civic authorities. Off goes Anna in despair.

The other four are still pretty angry with Leporello. In turn, three of them abuse him. First Zerlina. "It was you then, a little while ago, that did so brutally batter my Masetto!" Next Elvira. "It was you all the time, you wicked rogue, you . . . made love to me in place of Don Giovanni!" Next Ottavio. "Dressed as a man of good birth; and with some low-down trick in mind, I'll warrant!" Masetto says nothing. The other three say, in turn: "Allow me, I will punish him!" "No, allow me!" "No, no, let me!" Masetto, the one least affected by polyphony, steps forward. "Let us kill him, all four of us at once!"

Leporello is already near the door. He plays for time, appealing to the better feelings of the three who seem least resolute. "Sir and madams, I implore you, pity me, oh pity me, I humbly pray, I pray. You and they are right, yet I implore you, I kneel before you, I swear

I was blameless, I was simply led astray, 'twas my master who did force me, took my innocence away. Donn' Elvira, you'll allow it, you know how it . . . how he always has his way!" He turns to Zerlina. "Of Masetto, I know nothing, nothing, nothing. This young lady" —Elvira—"will inform you truthfully, clearly; for a whole hour (that, or nearly) she and I did walk this way!" He turns to Ottavio. "What can I say, sir? . . . that not on purpose . . . that in dismay, sir . . . what on the surface was gaily splendid, inside was all dark, will not be mended . . . the doorway . . . the hall, dark . . . if . . . yes . . . that . . . there surely should be . . . that side . . . there would be . . . why yes of course . . . so when I saw it, I ran away. . . ." Once we get it into our minds that the sextet is part of an indivisible dramatic episode— once we forget how lesser composers might have used a sextet—there is nothing particularly strange about the dramatic intention. Those words that Leporello addresses to Ottavio? They may have puzzled old Casanova, whose futile sketch for an alternative version of the aria is printed in Dent's chapter. But they need not puzzle us. By now Mozart and da Ponte were assembling, pretty consciously, a pattern of attitudes to sexual love. A resting-place, the C major of this life? Or something like "th' expense of spirit in a waste of shame", so un-forgettably evoked by Shakespeare in sonnet 129?

> Mad in pursuit and in possession so,
> Had, having, and in quest to have, extreme.
> A bliss in proof and proud and very woe,
> Before a joy propos'd, behind a dream,
> All this the world well knows yet none knows well,
> To shun the heaven that leads men to this hell.

Leporello has escaped. "Stop, stop" cries Elvira. "You are as bad as he!" "I'll never catch that wing-foot!" says Masetto. "Oh the villain!" says Zerlina: " 'Twas an artful escape, though!" Note how the tiniest scraps of secco recitative are in character.

If there is a blemish, it is in the following lines. "My good friends" says Ottavio "after such enormous excesses, I no longer can doubt that Don Giovanni was the impious assassin of Donna Anna's father. Stay in this house for one or two hours to comfort her. I'll have recourse to the right and proper persons. I will in no time have avenged you, I promise. I obey out of duty, compassion, affection. Therefore console my darling, sincerely sympathise. Try, if her tears are falling, to wipe them from her eyes." The opening words read as if they were origin-ally intended to come elsewhere. But in a libretto that is practically flawless at characterisation we should not hurry to conclude that they are nonsense in their present place. For a man like Ottavio, what more disturbing revelation could there be than Leporello "dressed as a man of good birth; and with some low-down trick in mind, I'll warrant"? It was the young cavalier's sartorial elegance, presumably, that made Ottavio disbelieve Anna (*10A*). Now, he suddenly believes her; the alternative of disabusing her would surely now involve too much hard work. Leave it to the proper authorities to sort out this tangle of truth and falsehood. He prefers to send a message to Anna, while preening himself in B♭ major (the key of Basilio's aria in *Figaro*). "Try, if her tears are falling, to WIPE them from her eyes!" Can the others hold a breath as long as that?

Ottavio is aware, by now, that Anna pays regrettably little attention to his reasonable requests about tear-wiping. Silly romantic girl, she likes a hero. So he strikes another posture, with unmuted strings. "Tell her I'm hotly burning, lusting for manly bloodshed; and will not be returning save with a hero's prize." Not bad, eh? A hero's PRIZE! Six whole long bars, that time. Some tenors prudently snatch a breath in the middle. Others manage it unconvincingly. One or two, like McCormack, do it with breath to spare.

By now the Don has seduced Leporello's girl-friend and is ready to jump over the wall into the churchyard. But on 30th April 1788 Mozart composed a *scena* and aria for the "flexible throat" of Katerina Cavalieri (his first Constanze), to be sung at the Vienna performance on 7th May. Unlike the other additions for Vienna, it is worth retaining occasionally on the stage. But we need to crave indulgence for the notion that it can be crammed into the tight time-schedule of the opera (a way out of this difficulty is to regard *21C* and *21D* as happening at the same time).

✓Elvira shivers, with the orchestra. "In what excesses, O Heaven, and in what crimes—what tremendous fearful misdeeds—the wretch is now entangled!" Tremendous, fearful? Forgive the parish platitudes; she is a good and pious woman. "Ah no, the hour comes, with no hope of delaying the divine wrath he deserves. I seem to hear the fatal thunderbolt already, that will strike on his dear head!" We hear it too. "I see, wide open, the deep abyss of Hell." The abyss yawns. It yawns again—but with a sudden B♮ (*21C26*) that crucially modifies her next entry. "Foolish Elvira, what a contrast appears now in your emotions! Why, why should you be sad still, and feel such sorrow? He to me was false, ungrateful; made me suffer a cruel smart. I, abandoned, should find him hateful; yet compassion fills my heart!" As usual, the sense moves easily from recitative to aria. It lacks the bright particularity of the 1787 thinking. But it re-states, clearly enough, Elvira's general place in the drama. She still loves him, after having been deceived. The E♭ major *allegretto* flows finely. At bar *90*, when she has just finished telling us for the sixth time about that cruel smart, the bassoons herald another thought. "When I think of my condition, I am crying out for vengeance; but, if I look at his position, pitter-patter goes my heart."

The next scene is an "enclosed place, in the form of a graveyard". From now on, source-diggers may consult their Bertati again. Much good may it do them—there is all the difference in the world between using a Bertati and responding to a Beaumarchais.

The Don leaps lightly over a wall. "Ha ha ha ha, she was good game. Now let her chase me here! The night is perfect, it is clearer than daylight; just as if it were made for sauntering around and catching women. Is it late yet? Oh, it is not yet two hours from sunset. There's one thing I would like to know—whether it went well; Leporello's affair with Donn' Elvira! He would have to be careful."

Leporello is walking along the pavement outside. His head appears above the wall. We hear a disgruntled thought. "What did *he* care, that I might land in trouble?"

"The very man! Hi, Leporello." "Who is calling?" "But you know, by my voice." "In there, why should I know it?" "What, you rascal!" "Oh, is it you? Forgive me." "What has happened?" "On your behalf, I was virtually murdered." "It would have been an honour to be murdered for me." "One I decline, sir." "Well, well, come in, come in, I have the prettiest things to tell you." "But why are you in there?" "Come in, and I will tell you. The several other stories, of what happened as soon as you had left me, I will keep for another time. Here is the nicest one of all, you'll agree." "About a woman?" "A young girl. She was a nice one, pretty face, fresh and willing, in the road outside here. I go towards her, I take her by the hand, she tries to run away but I say one or two words, and she mistakes me— guess for whom?"

The Don has been handing back Leporello's clothes. Leporello, pre-occupied with valeting and dressing, says "I've no idea." "For Leporello" says the Don. "For me?" "For you." "Oh good, good." "It is she that takes me by the hand now." "Ah, even better!" "She embraces, she hugs me. Dear precious Leporello, my precious, she says. And therefore, I infer, she is one of your women." "Oh damn you, damn you!" "So I take due advantage; but then somehow she recognises who I am, cries out, I hear people, so I speedily leave her, and ready steady go, up over the wall and into this place." "And you tell me it, just like an ordinary story?" "And why not?" "But suppose it had been my wife whom you took thus?" "All the better!" The tombstones echo with a young man's laughter.

Shaw imagines that Anna's father had chased women in his day. But there are Limits. They have been Reached. With three trombones, the dead commendatore remarks (beginning in D minor, and ending in what is presumably an ancient A minor) that YOUR LAUGHING WILL HAVE ENDED BEFORE MORNING. Where the Don or Leporello would use a crotchet, he uses a semibreve. The idea of a slow intoning oracle, with trombones, comes from Gluck's Alceste. But Gluck can offer us nothing like this sudden contrast between speed and eternity. "Who was speaking?" "Oh, it sounded like a spirit from the other world; one who knows you through and through!" "Don't talk nonsense. Who goes there? Who goes there?" The Don draws his sword, prods it between tombstones, and knocks on the tombs to see if they are hollow.

PROFANE SOUL! PRESUME NOT! LET THE DEAD LIE IN PEACE HERE! It would sound flat without his trombones; and, as Shaw at once pointed out, it generally sounds rather flat with them. The second utterance begins a tone lower. The downward melody of the first trombone and first bassoon make it sadder and more menacing than the first. The *adagio*, now in 3/4 time, ends in G minor.

"There, I told you" says Leporello. The Don shakes his head. "It must be someone from outside, attempting a trick on us. I say, look at the statue! It is like Anna's father! Come on, read me out the inscription." "Excuse me! I was not taught by anyone to read or write by moonlight!" The Don waves aside this feeble excuse—Leporello reads and writes The Book by moonlight; and may even be capable of reading watches by the same difficult light. So Leporello is made to read the inscription: "An impious villain brought me to this extreme pass. I await the hour of vengeance."

"How senile, and how laughable!" says the Don. "Tell him I await the pleasure of his company at supper this evening."

"Are you mad?" asks Leporello. "And I think . . . O God, O God, look, he is turning his eyes this way at us, he seems alive . . . as if wanting . . . as if about to speak!" "Do what I say" says the Don "or I will slice you up, and bury you in pieces!"

"Not so loud, sir, I beg! I will obey you. Sir statue of the gentleman who was Donn' Anna's father! My lord, I'm in a pother! I cannot! I cannot say the rest!" Mozart makes us see the statue through the eyes

and mind of a simple flustered man facing reality. Hence the bright
driving E major—marked *allegro*. Hence the brusque orchestral chords
at *22.4*; which, instead of performing the usual job of linking verbal
line to line, almost suppress Leporello's low B's. Hence the pathetic
downward seventh. As Abert remarks, a romantic composer would
have set the scene very differently; with high-flown description of the
dark *genius loci*. It is Mozart's method that can stand your hair on end.

"Go on, I say! Or I prick you, I stick you through the breast!"
The Don's naked sword-point touches Leporello's tunic, and violins
tremble. "How vicious, how capricious!" shudders Leporello, low in
the voice; with violins telling us just how he shudders. "I'm laughing
as I flick you!" says the Don. "I freeze at such a jest" thinks Leporello.
A sophisticated man laughs at a superstitious fool; whose superstitions
we begin to share. The music continues in the dominant. "Sir statue of
the gentleman—although you're made in marble . . . ah, my lord! . . .
noble master! look this way, his eyes are not at rest!" "Die then, die
then!" "Ah no, not so emphatic . . . so emphatic!" For the third time
he opens his mouth to address the statue. No sound comes. For
twelve whole bars the 'cellos and basses are practically silent. There is a
shivering organ-point from the violas instead; on F$\sharp$, here dominant
of the dominant. There are tiny remote whispers of frozen fear in the
violins. "My master bids you dine, sir . . ." Another age elapses.
". . . 'tis his idea, not mine, sir! . . ." Another age. ". . . this evening as
his guest—AAH, AH, ah, what am I seeing? His nod! He was agree-
ing!" "Come, come, you're only jesting" says the Don casually.
"Look this way!" Leporello begs. "Sir, do as I'm requesting!" "And
where am I to look at your request?' asks the Don, looking. "That
marble head you see there . . . did go . . . like this . . . like this!"
Leporello is nodding; and at that moment the statue nods; in full view
of the young man who knows that statues cannot nod agreement.
Puzzling. Some practical joker? Keep cool. The Don addresses the
stone image. "Then speak, sir! (He's too dumb to!) You'll come to
dinner?" YES, says the statue.

"God pardon me, a sinner!" says Leporello "I freeze, I quake,
I'm thinner!" " 'Tis odd" says the Don "but I'm the winner, he says
he'll come to dinner!" "For pity's sake, come, follow!" says Leporello;
"to hurry would be best!" "I wonder what he'll swallow?" says the
Don with a glimmer of scientific curiosity. "I'll come as you suggest";
he has rarely felt so hungry.

The stage has to be prepared for the final scene; Anna needs another
aria; and Mozart has more to tell us about the developing relation

between her and Ottavio. The next scene, therefore, takes place in the *camera tetra*; bed and backcloth, dimly seen through a little mantle of darkness.

Enter Ottavio, twenty-four hours too late. Anna, much shocked, gets hastily out of the other side of the bed. "Come, calm yourself, dear angel" says Ottavio, who has come without a hero's prize; "for we shall soon see that villain punished for his grave excesses." Anna, who had enjoyed some of the excesses, looks annoyed. "We shall soon be avenged" says Ottavio. "But my father!" says Anna. "Oh heavens" she adds; and bites her lip—the fib is dangerously inept this time, since the main professed point of the vengeance was to avenge her father's death. Ottavio kneels across the bed, and takes her by the hand. Smugly, he delivers a lecture. "We should all bow down humbly to the will of the almighty. So breathe again, my dear one, you are free to enjoy now . . . well, tomorrow if you wish, the sweeter recompense . . . of a heart . . . of a hand that . . . of my own tender love. . . ."

It is too much for Anna. Here, of all places! "God, no! How can you, sir? In these moments of sadness . . ." It is the plural again; nearly as chilly as the C♯ and B of the appoggiatura on *10.31*.

"Eh? What? You put me off and off, as if wanting . . . to make me more unhappy. You are cruel!" "I? Cruel?" says Anna with sudden resolution. She'll show him. Women are apt to keep this particular form of cruelty for other women, as in *Figaro 5*; half the pleasure of it is that the victim should know perfectly well, from the outset, that you do not mean what you choose to say.

"Ah, no, beloved . . ." A feline *larghetto* strokes the victim. "Would I enjoy putting far from you a good that, for a long time, I have also desired? . . . but people . . . oh heavens, do not force me to weakness, by seducing my soft heart. Be content, that my love pleads for you always. . . . Do not say to me, my treasure, I for pleasure am cruel to you . . . I, before you? I, who adore you? Well you know that I am true!" The clarinets support her all too plausible story. "Calm oh calm your inner torment!" The violins are far from calm; and we are left in no doubt, by the astounding Mozart, that the torment in question is particular rather than general. "Do you wish my death from sorrow? . . . Maybe . . . maybe God will, some other morrow, on my HEART have mercy too." Maybe. Or maybe not. (Was Berlioz right? See p. 175).

After that, and after four *secco* bars in which Ottavio is shown to have learned nothing, the Don's D major gusto seems simple and wholesome. "I see dinner laid and ready. Players, let me hear you playing. I am rich, I will be paying, therefore let your tune be gay. Leporello, come and wait on me!" "Sir" says Leporello "I hasten to obey." Players play, servants bustle, Leporello supervises and dancing-girls (according to Abert, they derive from a note by Mozart) do a cabaret turn. The Don's musical tastes are fairly low-brow—he knows what he likes; and the players give him a selection of recent hits. Bravo, says Leporello. "Cosa rara!" *Cosa rara, bellezza ed onesta*, by Martin y Soler and da Ponte, was the work that drove Figaro off the Vienna stage in 1786. Mozart is quoting from the first finale:

> *Isabella* O quanto un si bel giubilo,
>   O quanto alletta e piace.
>   Di pura gioja e pace
>   Sorgente ognor sara.
> *Lilla, Gita, Lubino, Tita*
>   Godiamo, su godiamo,
>   E con sincero amore
>   Rendiamo grazie al core
>   Di vostra Maesta

"Do you like the composition?" asks the Don. "It deserves your recognition" says Leporello with casual insolence. The Don is busy: "Ah the soup is truly luscious!" "Oh his appetite atrocious, oh his greedy giant mouthfuls!" thinks Leporello, feeling faint at the sight. "He is looking at my mouthfuls, as if sure to faint away" thinks the Don. "Next course!"

"Coming!" says Leporello. The players strike up a new tune. "Ah good, here is *Litiganti*." The tune is from Sarti's *Fra due litiganti il terzo gode* (Mozart had himself written variations on it, K.460). The words are:

> Come un agnello
> Che va al macello
> Andrai belando
> Per il citta.

"Pour the Rhenish!" says the Don. Leporello pours. "Very smooth; you may replenish." Leporello changes the Don's plate, then goes back to the serving-table. "Oh some pheasant would be pleasant! I will gobble while I may." The Don notices. "He is eating, crafty peasant, while I look the other way."

The next tune is *Non più andrai*. "This is one that I know only too well" thinks Leporello (to the delight, no doubt, of the Prague audience at the first performance).

> You'll not flutter or twirl any more, sir,
> Or make eyes day and night at the ladies,
> Or disturb their repose as before, sir,
> You Adonis, you young knave of hearts.

"Leporello!" says the Don suddenly. "Sir, what is it?" says Leporello with a full mouth. "Rascal, you are not articulating clearly" says the Don. "Sir, 'tis due to belching merely, 'tis impeding what I say!" "You may whistle to amuse me." "Don't know how." "What's that?" asks the Don, turning. "Forgive me!" says Leporello "Your cook, sir, so supremely does he cook them, that I could not overlook them, that I could not keep away."

In bursts Elvira, *allegro assai* (B♭ major, 3/4). After that leisurely *buffo* interlude we are back to the opera's normal speed and intensity. "Here is a final . . . proof of devotion . . . that with emotion . . . I will supply . . . I in this fashion . . . freely forgive you . . . I avow compassion!" "What's this, and why?" The Don gets up, and motions to the players and dancing girls to go. Elvira kneels. "I am not aiming for a reward now, nor am I claiming love in reply!" "Oh how surprising! What do you seek then? If you are meek, then . . ." (he kneels, too) "so too am I." "Ah do not laugh at me, merely for trying!" "Who says I laugh at you? Heavens, but why?" ("I do not laugh at her, I am for crying" thinks Leporello) "My love, what is it?" asks the Don. "Repent, you sinner . . . your perfidy!" ("Bravo!" thinks Leporello) The Don laughs. "Let me have dinner—or would you care for some of this pie?" "In your iniquity wallow for ever, dreadful example of passion unkind!" The Don is unmoved. "Here is to womanhood, here's to the bottle, bolster and glory of mortal mankind!" Leporello is appalled. "She cannot move him! He has a stone heart; or has he no heart, is he blind?"

In tears Elvira leaves. Going out of the door, she screams. She runs back into the room (looking as if she has seen a ghost, *24.683*) and rushes out of the opposite door. Leporello is sent to investigate. He sees, and screams. The Don asks why. "Ah . . . my lord . . . I beg and pray . . . do not go out there, I say . . . that . . . white . . . statue . . . silhouetted . . . ah, dear master . . . I shiver, I feel faint . . . if you saw it, if you met it, if you looked and if you heard . . . bom bom bom bom." "That's impossible, it can't be!" "Bom bom bom bom." "And I shan't believe a word!" There are knocks at the door. "Listen, listen!" says Leporello. "Someone knocking" says the Don. More knocks are heard. Leporello is too frightened to open the door. "Idiot! To undo the knot, so be it, you're afraid, so I will go." He takes a light and goes to the door. Leporello hides under the table. "Oh my friend, I dare not see it, I will hide in here below."

The Don opens the door. There, in unforgettable D minor, is the statue; an overture to damnation. "DON GIOVANNI, YOU DID INVITE ME TO THIS DINNER, TO SHARE YOUR TABLE." Under the table, Leporello shudders. So do we, at the slow words and remorseless music. The Don shrugs politely, and a syncopated violin line soars. "Sir, I thought you'd not be able." The second violins think quickly for him. "But we'll do our best, I know. Leporello, another dinner! Let them bring in, quickly, one for . . ." Leporello, his head half out from under the table, interrupts. "Ah my lord, we're dead and done for!" "Go, I tell you" says the Don. Leporello begins to scramble to his feet. "NO, THANK YOU, NO! FOR THOSE SOULS THAT HAVE EATEN DIVINE FOOD, MORTAL FOOD HAS NO MORE USE OR FLAVOUR. OTHER LONGINGS, AND THOUGHTS THAT ARE GRAVER, OTHER CARES BRING ME BACK HERE BELOW." Minims and dotted crotchets for the voice, a resumption of grandeur in the orchestra. At *24.454* the trombones (with bassoons and oboes) have an eery unison with the voice. Then we hear the full orchestra again; and then (at the words OTHER LONGINGS) ascending and descending scales.

"I am sure I have tertian fever, for my limbs are all out of control!" Leporello's vocal line moves in quick triplets, under broader violin phrases. "Speak and tell me your purpose, your wish, sir" says the Don, with a confident rising bassoon phrase. "HEAR ME, I'M SPEAKING, I DARE NOT BE SLOW" says the statue, intoning slowly on B♮. "Speak, man, speak; I am not deaf, you know!" says the Don.

"YOU INVITED ME TO DINNER. THEREFORE, IT IS MY DUE , SIR . . . COME, ANSWER ME! . . . WILL YOU, SIR, DINE AT MY TABLE?" "Oh no, oh no! No, for he has no time, sir!" says Leporello. Back comes the climbing syncopation, as the Don scornfully rejects the excuse. "I'll not commit the crime, sir, of being mean or low!" Coolly, the gentleman faces his absurd fate. It is easier to die well, in seconds or minutes, than to live well through a long life-time. Many choices become no choice—except the choice of how you face it. You have no time.

"DECIDE THEN!" booms the statue. "I have decided" says the

Don, quietly. "Say to him no, say to him no!" implores Leporello; in what must surely be one of the most memorable short phrases in all opera. Violins, then violas and 'cellos, break out with loud dotted quavers. "My heart is calm and steady" says the Don, "I'm not afraid, I'll go!" There is a hush, as the dotted crotchets resume on a soft G, soon enhanced by wind into a G minor chord. "GIVE ME YOUR HAND AS TOKEN!" (On the word TOKEN the music becomes a roar, with open string resonance.) "Here it is" (The music gathers speed—*più stretto*.) "Oh dear!" "WHAT IS IT?" "You pay a chilling visit!" "NOW YOU HAVE ONE MORE MINUTE" (The duel music, from Act One, resumes—deep-voiced 'cello and bass, thrusting. Because there is no violin to fight back, a downward minor seventh is added—as if an imaginary blade were being pulled out of the Don's body.) "TO SAY YOU ARE REPENTANT!" (The sword thrusts again. The Don vainly tries to free himself, in dotted minims agony.) "No, I am unrepentant!" (Again the pain.) "Go, go away, go fast!" (Again the pain.) The Don is helplessly writhing. "SAY YOU REPENT, YOU VILLAIN!" (A savage 'cello thrust, withdrawn with even greater savagery (downward octave).) "Old fool, I say I will not!" (Again it comes.) "COME, REPENT" says the statue softly; twice, with two more jabs. "No" shouts the Don, each time. "YES!" (For a while, the Don has been louder than his enemy. But the 'cellos and basses now indicate failing strength.) "No!" "YES!" "No!" Leporello joins the statue in imploring the Don to qualify for the mitigated torments of the late-repentant. "No, no!" yells the Don, with the last of his strength. "MY TIME HAS COME AT LAST" says the statue; and leaves the Don to his fate.

Few of us share the particular beliefs of Tirso de Molina. Therefore the final D minor *allegro* is apt to seem tawdry; at any rate, if treated as an excuse for clever visual effects. The dramatic purpose of the section is to show how a previously brave young man, already tortured beyond our comprehension, is reduced to fear. "Suddenly I am tremulous. Suddenly flames are eddying; and oh where are they rising from? From Hell, from Hell with fear!" The initial progression is down, down, down. "No hell for you is too hot" call the demons. "Come, there is worse to fear!" "Who tears my living heart, my soul? Who shakes my every part, my whole? What agony, oh what torture! Oh Hell! And oh what fear!" Leporello watches: "That look of desperation! Those gestures of damnation! What cries, what shrieks, what howlings! I am again in fear!" The flames rise. With the flames (if we are to believe 24.673) rises a demon; still singing "Come, there is worse to fear". The Don is engulfed, and taken down to Hell. As he sinks, he shrieks. Leporello echoes the shriek, as if he himself were the victim. None of it is easy to do—well.

In burst the others, with officers of the law. "Where is that worthless lord? Where is the traitor? To indignation I shall give way." That was sung *allegro assai* in G major by Elvira, Ottavio, Zerlina and Masetto. Anna is given a different comment—while loving flutes and bassoons trip softly upwards in thirds! "Only by seeing him tight bound, yes tightly, my sorrow lightly shall I allay!" What do the psychologists make of that one? "That hope abandon!" says Leporello: "You will not find him, you cannot bind him, he went away!"

"How so? Come, tell us!" "In came a giant!" "How so? Come, tell us!" "I am not wrong, sir!" "Short, sharp and double-quick!" "My story's long, sir, it is too long, sir!" "Quickly! Come, tell us! Double-quick!"

"Flames like an eddy! Careful, sir, steady! Statue to dinner! Stop, or you're in, sir. Down there, the sulphur! Torturing hell-fire! I saw the demon who dragged him away!" It is hardly an articulate version of what happened. Elvira therefore gets confused (the statue was not a demon; and was much too solid to be a ghost). "That was the ghost I met on my way!" The others nod, impressed. "Ah yes, for certain. That was the ghost she met on her way."

Ottavio promptly turns to Anna (the music slows to *larghetto*). "Now that heaven, O you my treasure, has on our behalf taken vengeance, pray allow me the lawful pleasure I so often have implored!" With a bright smile Anna puts him off again. "My beloved, a year for easing grief and pain to me afford!" Ottavio contemplates his fate: "Faithfully your will appeasing? As I should, being so adored?" She agrees, smiling more brightly than ever.

Twenty-eight bars for Anna and Ottavio; six bars for the other four characters. First Elvira. "I will go into a convent; there to die, a nun I'll be." Then Zerlina and Masetto. "We will go back home together, there to feast in company." Finally, Leporello. "I go to a hostelry, there to find a better lord."

The music changes. Leporello, Zerlina and Masetto sing together. They are no longer in character. Emanuele Conegliano—better known to you, by now, as the elegant Lorenzo da Ponte—is speaking. The Italian words play with classical imagery; Proserpine, and Pluto. Like all the classical allusions in *Figaro*, *Don Giovanni* and *Così fan tutte*, they are relevant and evocative (think back to that bit from the Odyssey, in *Figaro 28*).

"Let our Don in Hell belong! What he did was very wrong." They pause, and look at the audience; who in that day and age were in full view of the performers. "There are honest folk before us, we'll repeat in cheerful chorus this familiar ancient song . . ."

The final fugato begins; Anna and Elvira take over. "Here's an end we all shall face." Death is the key, wrote Mozart to his father on 4th April 1787, "which unlocks the door to our true happiness. I never lie down at night without reflecting that—young as I am—I may not live to see another day. Yet no one of my acquaintances could say that in company I am morose or disgruntled." *Presto*, D major, *sotto voce*. Then the others join in. "What if you or I were dying? Have I earned a higher place?" Has Anna? Or Ottavio? Has Elvira, or Zerlina? Has Leporello or Masetto?

Creative delight and a certain premature detachment seem to shine from the concluding bars. "As you from crimes would pardon'd be, let your indulgence set me free. . . ." (Shakespeare was an older man than Mozart, when he wrote farewell lines for Prospero.) Could any musical score, asked Wagner in *Opera and Drama*, be more perfect than Mozart's Don Giovanni? After a hundred and eighty years, can any single score offer more dramatic power, irony and sheer insight? But would enough of it get across—even in Prague, even in the bawdy-minded eighteenth century? Mozart had already passed the brief zenith of his worldly confidence. In December 1791 his young body was deposited in a pauper's grave.

PART IV

THE MAGIC FLUTE

Title: Die Zauberflöte. *Köchel number:* 620.
First performance: 30th September 1791, at the Freehouse (Starhemberg) theatre on the Wieden, outside the walls of Vienna

Mann und Weib ist ein Leib.

MOZART

Allein ich schreibe nicht für die Leser, ich schreibe für die Bühne, dahin verweise ich meinen Herrn Rezensenten

SCHIKANEDER

Go, litel bok . . .
And red wherso thou be, or elles songe,
That thou be understonde, God I biseche!

CHAUCER

As I walked through the wilderness of this world, I lighted on a certain place where was a Den, and I laid me down in that place to sleep; and as I slept I dreamed a dream.

BUNYAN

THE MAGIC FLUTE

Characters in order of singing

TAMINO Christian August Vulpius, brother-in-law of Goethe, was one of the first to tamper with the libretto of this opera. His singularly feeble improvements stirred the librettist to a degree of candour that da Ponte never achieved. In the foreword to *Der Spiegel von Arkadien* (1794/5) Schikaneder insisted on the care with which he *and Mozart* had planned the story (*den Text mit dem seligen Mozart fleissig durchdacht*). I can at last be categorical. The story was exposed in detail, at a formative stage, to a finer mind than Schikaneder's; and that is why, as Goethe insisted, it is more important to see the deep merits of the libretto than its superficial clumsiness. We have seen how the creative and unifying mind of Mozart probably re-thought the characters of the *Don Juan* legend. It is not a matter of spatchcocking, or of adding uncooked ingredients from here and there. Otto Rommel, the weight of whose erudition on old Viennese popular comedy fills a thousand big pages, offers an opinion; he says that the *Magic Flute* is a theatre-poem from two full hearts.

Tamino, *der holde Jüngling selbst* (9B7), is less simple than the adventuring princess-seeker of the ordinary fairy-story or pantomime. He is a timid prince, trying to be brave; he needs, among other things, a brave princess. He is earnestly anxious to become a wise ruler. He is more than prince, he is man—a docile innocent artistic facet of humanity. He is the dreamer of all those symbols and maxims; a young intellectual.

Let us consider him, for the time being, as a walking myth of elementary political philosophy, in his own dream. Hereditary rule settled, or helped to settle, the problem of the claim to power. But hereditary rulers were apt to seem a job lot—good, bad and indifferent. A panacea much favoured by Rational men in the eighteenth century was to educate and train the future autocrat, so that he might be an Enlightened Despot. Consider the local facts as they might appear, early in 1791, to Viennese Masonic friends. A Holy Roman Emperor might be a Mason, and therefore Enlightened; like easygoing Franz I who was admitted at the Hague in 1731 by the British Ambassador, Lord Chesterfield. He might be a woman; like the able Empress Maria Theresa, who so regrettably prohibited Masonry in

1764. Mozart had reason to remember both, with loyal affection (see p. 223). Joseph II, sole ruler from 1780 (when his mother died) until 1790, referred to Masons contemptuously as Schurken. But he tolerated them; it had been a good decade for Viennese Masons, even though Ignaz von Born (long favoured by commentators as the original of Sarastro) had walked out on them in 1786. Leopold II, who was reputed to have been an Enlightened Grand Duke of Tuscany, proved on his succession in 1790 to be remarkably chilly about Masonry —and music. Perhaps the young Archduke Franz, who had been educated with such exceptional care by order of his childless uncle Joseph, would be more sympathetic—he had been living in Vienna, under Joseph's formidable eye, since 1784. Joseph, though unpopular, had been self-consciously Enlightened.

In fact, even Joseph knew that his reckless policies had failed. The new Emperor and the young heir apparent were worried men. In a brief reign Leopold skilfully disentangled himself from the worst of his brother's follies, abroad and at home. But things looked bad, and were getting worse. After his sister's flight to Varennes in 1791, Leopold made a dramatic appeal to the crowned heads of Europe to stop playing politics against each other and make common cause against the protagonists of Liberté, Egalité and Fraternité. (If you want to know how propertied people already felt in England, compare the tone of The Times in 1785 and 1791.) One could see before then which way things were going. The young Archduke (whose tutor, by the way, had been a Graf Colloredo) was busy urging his father to strengthen the police and suppress cabals. People were smelling out the men who might have revolutionary sympathies (remember how Holcroft was indicted for high treason in 1792).

We rub our eyes, therefore, at the breathtakingly naïve rashness of Mozart and Schikaneder. Tamino, who will become Enlightened "*in diesen heil'gen Mauern*", by joining a *Freimaurer* Lodge, is a King's (or Emperor's?) son, only a year or so younger than the conscientious young Archduke whom Joseph had wanted to be "*lebhafter, lustiger— er sollte sich mehr lösen, schwätzen, lachen.*" However, if Mozart borrowed some of Tamino from an impression of the Archduke, he also thought the character out from first principles; and by the irony of history has created a figure that is universal, recognisable, perennially relevant.

Tamino comes from distant Japan, the land of the Rising Sun. Having been carefully educated, he is now doing the Grand Tour to broaden his mind. He seems to have lost his servants and his money, in some kind of Arabian Night adventure. It all happened "once upon a time", several thousand years ago, when one was probably lucky to have a bow and arrow.

Today the problems of human welfare are more complicated. But Tamino now exists in his tens of thousands, all over the world. He is the intelligent young man who "cares". He has a bump of curiosity and a sense of duty. He is prepared to attempt carrying some of the responsibility. He is naïve, and will make mistakes. But he is willing to learn, and go on learning, from experience. He is lucky enough to find the right wife. He plays a musical instrument. He perseveres, and may mature into being one of the people who carry an increasing burden of responsibility. "O Isis and Osiris, let them be duly filled with Wisdom's power. Then, when they walk, do not forget them; let them endure in peril's hour."

Ta-min and Pa-min, says Morenz, were names common in Hellenistic (and later Coptic) Egypt. Ta means *woman*, Pa *man*, "belonging to Min" (for the deity Min see Plutarch *Isis and Osiris* 56). The transposed names, as we know them, appear to create a deliberate association between (*a*) Pamina and Papageno, who are Woman and Man by Nature, (*b*) Tamino and Gebler's *King Thamos* (whose name derives from Plato's *Phaedrus* 274C).

PAPAGENO There were bird-men before Papageno. For instance, Rosenberg's book has an impressive sixteenth-century drawing of a man who has the head and shoulders of a bird—and wears a large birdcage on his back. Old Viennese comedy also had its Hanswurst and Kasperl (affectionately known as Käsperle). But Papageno is a creation in his own right.

"There is no rarer bird than I, I'm always happy ho hi hi." A Figaro is ambitious and politically-minded, a Leporello is sometimes critical or envious of authority, a Papageno is one of life's contented privates, infecting even his NCOs and officers with his own childlike happiness. "The song-bird catcher all do know, yes, young and old where e'er I go." He does an ordinary job—milkman, postman, or on the shop floor of the factory—while whistling or singing to himself. "For I can lay a skilful snare, and with my piping drive out care; and that is why my life is fine, for all the singing birds are mine." He is birdlike. More precisely, he is the *Papagei*-man, the parrot; by the austere Masonic standard of *Verschwiegenheit* he talks too much—as he ruefully realises, at a crucial moment of self-knowledge in *21.441, 2*. He is not scrupulously truthful. But he is a good companion, with a sense of humour;

and there is not a scrap of harm or ill-will in him. He is simple sunny G, F or C major human nature at its best (unlike Monostatos, who is G, F and C major with a large chip on the shoulder).

Note that many of the best Taminos—the durable ones, at any rate —have something of Papageno in them. They have a certain joie de vivre, they seem at ease, they can laugh and relax at a moment's notice. By way of cautionary contrast, consider poor young anxious Archduke Franz, who became the last Holy Roman Emperor. He took on more and more work, refused to be swayed by men like Metternich, became his own Prime Minister, and delegated less and less. At his death, the administration collapsed. He was succeeded by the feebleminded Ferdinand.

Tamino sings "With my two arms (oh the pleasure) to this my hot heart I would press her, and she would be for ever mine." But Papageno is the one presented to us as Man by Nature. "And she would softly kiss me then, were she my wife and I her man . . . I wish I were together with someone, maid or wife; for two birds of a feather find happiness in life. I always would drink well and eat well, I would be of princes the equal, I would in my wisdom live well, I would in Elysium dwell. . . . If none of them love will allow me, the flame will eat up and devour me, but if one would come for a kiss, there soon would be nothing amiss. . . . All very well, that's very funny! If in your bellies love were burning, then even you would women chase. . . . Are we now allowed each other? . . . Will you be my only lover? . . . Think of all our future joys, when the years in sweet succession bring our love a long procession of little tiny girls and boys . . . it is the highest human pleasure when there are MANY . . . to be the blessings of our life as father, mother, man and wife."

Papageno is not always happy. But he lives in the moment—when he is happy, he forgets unhappiness. And he is happy more often than other people; because his wants (apart from the one audacious want, a companion "till death do us part") are limited. He considers that his straw hut—which does not even qualify as an "enclosed building", 2A22—shelters him adequately from rain and cold. Papagena may not agree. But "battling is not my affair, and I do not really care for wisdom, I am an ordinary simple man; sleep, food and drink are enough for me . . . I wish I were in my straw hut, or in the forest; then at least I should be hearing birds all the time." He does not profess to be brave. But he is less of a coward than Monostatos (6A2), finds himself ahead of Tamino (6A), and is positively bold and resourceful when he cannot run away from danger (8.284).

"You shall never know the heavenly pleasures of the initiate" says the Speaker. "Ah well" he replies, "at any rate there are more people like me; just now, a good glass of wine would be heaven enough." He too is universal, recognisable, perennially relevant.

THE QUEEN OF NIGHT and Sarastro lead the opposing forces of evil and good; and have two arias each. But the Queen's appearances, though impressive, are brief. She and Sarastro belong to an older generation, and therefore fall outside Mozart's main stream of young characters—five major characters in *Le Nozze di Figaro*, seven in *Don Giovanni*, four lovers and Despina in *Così fan tutte*. In the present opera, the ones who are presented with sympathy include even Monostatos; but exclude the Queen. She has a plausible-seeming story, but her first aria should be sung in such a way that only a very innocent and earnest young person would fall for it. Tamino is therefore duly deceived. In Act One, Pamina trusts her. *13A* and *14* are therefore a shocking revelation of the Queen of Night as she is, with all civilised pretences gone; a cold, brilliant, selfish bitch.

The part was written for a sister-in-law, Josefa Hofer, whom Mozart had once fondly described as "a lazy gross perfidious woman, and as cunning as a fox". That was in the days when Leopold Mozart was heatedly explaining to his son the "wiles of women" (*11*), with special reference to Madame Weber. Since then, much water had flowed down the Danube. There is a chuckling reference to Madame Weber in Mozart's letter of 8th–9th October 1791: "I am taking Mamma to-morrow. Hofer has already given her the libretto to read. In her case, what will probably happen will be that she will *see* the opera but not *hear* it."

Does the Queen represent a particular anti-Masonic person or faction? "Through deception and superstition she hopes to beguile the people, and to destroy our mighty temple." Surely not the dead Empress Maria Theresa as is sometimes suggested? "Their Majesties received us with such extraordinary graciousness that, when I shall tell of it, people will declare that I have made it up. Suffice it to say that Woferl jumped up on the Empress's lap, put his arms round her neck and kissed her heartily. In short we were there from three to six o'clock and the Emperor himself came out of the next room and made me go in there to hear the Infanta play the violin. On the 15th the Empress sent us by the Privy Paymaster, who drove up to our house in state, two dresses, one for the boy and one for the girl." That was in October 1762. Things were very different at Schönbrunn under Maria

Theresa's third son Leopold. *Così fan tutte*, which had been commissioned by the Emperor Joseph, had its run fatally interrupted by court mourning. 1790 was a year of bleak despair for Mozart. The new régime would be personified (if at all) in the cold figure of a man, Leopold II. I think the Queen is simply a symbol of Evil and Unenlightenment.

MONOSTATOS   Even the wisest of rulers can be let down by a man whom he puts in authority under him. But Sarastro was plain careless (though commendably free from colour prejudice) when he entrusted Pamina to the care of a man who is practically a psychopath. He goes pale at the mention of Sarastro's name (*5A18*, a piece of dialogue that is too often cut). But having threatened Pamina with death, after her recapture, he soon recklessly intends rape (*6.20–31*). For this, he is sentenced to receive seventy-seven lashes on the soles of his feet (*8.493*). The sentence is remitted (*12A8*). Soon . . . "If I could be sure . . . alone, no one looking . . . I might try once more. . . ." Even in this, the most "primitive" and mythological of his great dramatic visions, Mozart disapproved of nasty caveman tactics. Therefore the composer of *Figaro* and *Don Giovanni* presented the relevant aria, with extraordinary power and realism, as a quiet whisper of lust. But there is compassion as well. "Hath not a Jew eyes? Hath not a Jew hands, organs, dimensions, senses, affections, passions? . . . If you prick us, do we not bleed?" Or, as it emerges in Schikaneder's doggerel:

> Others all are free to trifle,
> Kiss them, pet them, nothing lack.
> I the feeling am to stifle,
> Since I am a hated black.
> Do I lack all wishes human?
> I am flesh and blood as well.
> All my life without a woman?
> That would be to burn in hell.
> I will, as a living being,
> Kiss her, pet her, feel delight.
> Moon, forgive what you are seeing,
> I succumb to beauty white.
> White is fair and I shall kiss it.
> Moon, go down if you are wise.
> Or if you desire to miss it,
> You had better close your eyes.

He tries to bludgeon Pamina into assent, by blackmail (*14A*). If he cannot have the daughter, he will look for the mother (*14A22*).

The mother promises Pamina to him but (according to Goethe's Part Two of the Magic Flute) marries him herself. They are birds of a feather.

PAMINA   In the Utopia with which this opera begins and ends, the various hierarchies of the *ancien régime* are reformed or replaced. But lower orders remain; unenlightened men, peasants, women and black men. In Tamino's dream women are Necessary—even desirable by Nature. But they are Other Beings; specialised, irrational, dangerous— "You shall beware the wiles of women! This is the most important law; for many a man, whom sense was dim in, has gone wrong— this he did ignore." Women, because they are women, are more decisively inferior than black men. The three ladies frighten Tamino (*2A67*), and get no thanks for saving his life. They are gossips (like Papageno); credulous (like Tamino); and self-righteous (like Sarastro). Is there a Difference? They are women, and for this crime share the final fate of the two unpleasant characters; an undignified return to the Queen's realm, by what appears to be a kind of underground conveyor-belt.

Pamina is the *Fräuleinbild*, the picture-girl (*6A2, 22, 36, 38, 40*); an ideal woman from a Tamino's point of view. She expresses no independent views on political philosophy or public affairs. "But, mother dear, could I not love him when he is an initiate, as tenderly as I love him now? Father, too, used to associate with these wise men. He was always so happy talking about them; and he used to praise their goodness, their understanding, their virtue. Sarastro is not less virtuous than father." It is a perfect example of the nicest kind of irrationality (*13A15*). She is not even upset when Sarastro tells her, in effect, to "be good, sweet maid, and let who will be clever". "A man should guide your heart's affection" he says. "Without a man, why, any woman steps outside her sphere of action." She is going to be a perfect wife and mother. She is a beautiful princess (*3*), brave and unselfishly loyal (*6.9–17*), virtuous (*6.22–3*, cp. *14A19*), a gentle and sympathetic listener (*6A*) who will also make the right comforting remark at the right moment (*6A45*), exultant at the hope of married love (*7.45–50*), truthful (*8.360–70, 395–406*), ardently affectionate (*8.448, 8.455, 21.279*; she beats him to it, every time—and had not even seen his picture, the first time!). She is also incorruptible (*14A1*).

Being a phenomenon of Nature rather than Reason, she has much in common with the other nice unbrainy character, Papageno. That is probably part of the reason why she is Pamina, not Tamina—an indication of having been born to a lower class in the opera's hierarchy of merit. However, despite lack of the normal qualifications, she earns class-to-class promotion for truthfulness and courage—the exceptional Strength and Beauty of her womanly Nature. She is therefore finally admitted as a sister to honorary membership of the élite club of Wise and Enlightened Men.

Why does she nearly commit suicide? She is a woman who lives for others, and possesses an utterly open *Sturm und Drang* sensibility; *Ach ich fühl's* is the natural counterpart to Tamino's *Ich fühl' es*. She is cursed by a mother who, as she is suddenly forced to realise, does not love her in the least. She is pestered by Monostatos, not for the first time. She is comforted by Sarastro but is still in need of comfort and help. Tamino refuses to speak to her. She has lost everything for which life, to her, is worth living. He says good-bye. No wonder she becomes half-crazed, and fondles a dagger.

Dent found parts of *Don Giovanni* endurable "only if one takes a completely frivolous view of the whole play". That, presumably, is why he also felt it necessary to bowdlerise Pamina's mad scene. She talks to the dagger. "Then you are he with whom I wed! With you I seek a wedding bed. . . . My love, be patient, yours am I, and soon we shall, oh soon we shall together lie . . . I am willing, for the man whom I evermore shall cherish leaves a loving one to perish. . . . This, my mother did provide. . . . Better die upon this metal than in such a sorrow settle. Mother! Through you this will be, for your curse has followed me. . . . Ha, my sorrow's cup is full! False Tamino, fare you well. Yes, I die for you. Oh see, see the dagger marry me!" Those thoughts, with the emotional power of Mozart's music, have all the greater dramatic force because they are sung by Mozart's Perfect Woman, *das sanfte tugendhafte Mädchen* (9B7).

Anna Gottlieb, aged seventeen, was the first Pamina. At the age of twelve she had been the first Barbarina. There is a tear-jerking story that, when Mozart died, she lost her voice and was never able to sing again. The truth, according to Christopher Raeburn, is less romantic; she had a well-documented subsequent career as a singer.

SARASTRO   As so often in this opera, dramatic effect depends on getting *exactly* the right sonority; which in turn depends, not only on having the right voice, but on understanding the dramatic situation. "Sir, do not punish my mother; it was grief at my absence!" pleads Pamina, instinctively protecting a mother whom she now knows to be worthless. "I know . . . all" says Sarastro. "You shall see how I revenge myself on your mother ... she shall return in shame to her home; for in this hall so solemn revenge cannot succeed, and if a man has fallen then love will gently lead. Then two together, hand in hand, can gladly walk to a better land. Within this holy palace, where men in friendship live, no traitors watch in malice, for we our foes forgive. Who does not join us joyfully does not deserve a man to be." We wriggle with embarrassment; the more so, as Sarastro is too often made to sound like the booming bore of the opera. He is in fact a nice fatherly man whom Pamina can trust; as she trusted her own father, whose Sevenfold Sun-Circle Sarastro is wearing before her eyes. Sarastro is too gentle and trusting to prosper in this world. But his Wisdom despises the use of cunning. Sarastro is meant to be Reasonable and Natural, a civilised man with nothing of the Pomp and Solemnity that frame his first two entries. It is significant that, as we shall see, *O Isis und Osiris* was not originally planned as an aria for Sarastro. He twinkles with gentle Mozartian irony, he is as radiantly serene as Papageno—and Saint Francis.

"TODAY, FRIDAY THE 30th September . . ." So begins the original bill of performance, now in the Mozart museum at Salzburg. The words take us back to Vienna, less than two hundred years ago, in 1791. "The players of the Imperial and Royal privileged theatre on the Wieden have the honour to perform for the first time DIE ZAUBER-FLÖTE, a grand opera in two Acts by Emanuel Schikaneder . . . the music is by Herr Wolfgang Amade Mozart, Kapellmeister, and actual I & R Chamber Composer. Herr Mozard [*sic*], out of respect for a gracious and honour-worthy public, and from friendship for the author of this piece, will today direct the orchestra in person."

At least one modern commentator has assured us that Schikaneder knew that the name of Mozart would greatly add to the popular appeal of the work. In fact Schikaneder, who was then prosperous, was taking a big risk by being associated with an impoverished and unentertaining avant-garde composer like Mozart. Some of those present, that Friday night, had probably enjoyed *Die Entführung*; but if they had hoped that this new opera might be another *Entführung*, they were undeceived before the curtain went up. What would the gracious and honour-worthy public make of this new overture? To many people now, it is heaven; which, as we shall see, is more or less what Mozart intended (Utopia, heaven on earth). But at the first performance, the more blasé and knowledgeable members of the audience probably thought it too intense and austere; and were perhaps muttering to each other something like "Oh hell, another *Don Giovanni*." We may doubt whether any of them noticed certain resemblances between this new opera and the music that Mozart had written for *König Thamos* (e.g. the *Maestoso* opening of 2, the "*sanfter Flöten Zauberklang*" of 6, "*Schon weichet dir, Sonne!, des Lichtes Feindin, die Nacht*" in 1). The majority of the audience were probably puzzled and a little resentful. They were simple people who enjoyed simple entertainments. They were perhaps waiting to see what Schikaneder had to offer as a counter-blast to Marinelli's Leopoldstadt production *Der Fagottist, oder die Zauberzither*. *Zauber* this, *Zauber* that—one knew what to expect, and the new Schikaneder show was rumoured to come from *Lulu, oder die Zauberflöte*, a remarkably innocent tale by Margarethe Liebeskind (*née* Dedekind) in the third volume of a recent collection of stories with the general title of *Dschinnistan*.

On 9th October, a correspondent wrote to the *Berlin Musical Weekly* that "the new machine comedy, the Magic Flute, with music by our Kapellmeister Mozart, has been presented at great expense and with much splendour of decoration, but is failing to find the hoped-for applause, because the content and diction of the piece are too poor." So far as the German diction is concerned, the criticism was and is valid—the libretto contains (as Einstein puts it) "a great number of unskilful, childish, vulgar turns of speech". But, as Einstein also remarks "the critics who therefore decide that the whole libretto is childish and preposterous deceive themselves. . . . Not a stone in the structure of these two acts could be removed or replaced, quite apart from the fact that any change would demolish Mozart's carefully thought out and organic succession of keys." There is all the difference in the world between being childlike and childish. Moreover, Mozart and Schikaneder may deliberately have been playing up the more trivial-seeming parts of the great design. There were good practical reasons why they should do so.

Where the Berlin critic was definitely wrong was in his snide remark about the "hoped-for applause". He sounds like a man who had been more sympathetic to the three big Italian operas, and positively preferred opera to be in a foreign language, so that one need not be embarrassed by the libretto. But Mozart was at last offering a major drama that consistently made sense, of a simple kind, in the audience's own language. One can get glimmerings of the meaning of *Figaro* from the stage action. But it is easy to miss the whole dramatic point of *Don Giovanni* and *Così fan tutte* (and therefore, disastrously, to assume that they need cutting). It is no coincidence that the vernacular *Magic Flute* was the one that "broke through" and was applauded—by audiences, if not by critics—from the outset. Mozart was not deceiving himself when as early as 7th October he wrote jubilantly to his wife that "the opera was as full as ever . . . as usual, the duet, *Mann und Weib* (7) and Papageno's glockenspiel in Act One (8.294–326) had to be repeated, and also the trio of the boys in Act Two (16)." This was a balanced and perceptive choice of special favourites by the audience; and the theatre was apparently full of that special, rare but wonderful, hush of attention to the music: "what always gives me most pleasure is the *silent* approval . . . you can see how this opera is becoming more and more popular." On 8th October, the opera was again "performed to a full house, and with the usual applause and repetition of numbers". Audiences reported favourably in street and home and coffee-shop. Even on 7th October, Mozart had already heard from Prague friends (presumably the Duscheks) that they had heard about the opera's success (presumably in a letter from some other friend).

On 5th December, Mozart died. He was perhaps too poor, too weak, too exhausted to have any resistance to disease; he could not stand the relief, the reaction from long stress. But these weeks had been the turning-point towards national and world recognition. His death therefore had news-value, and appears to have clinched matters. Within years, Mozart was a popular composer throughout Germany. Meanwhile, the *Flute* continued its run. On 23rd November 1792 Schikaneder announced the 100th performance, on 22nd October 1795 the 200th performance, on 1st January 1798 the 300th. Like Papageno, Schikaneder was less than scrupulous about exact truth. In sober fact, the alleged 100th and 200th performances were the 83rd and 135th, and there were only 223 performances at the theatre on the Wieden, up to 6th May 1801. Only! And before 1800, by a tally that may still be incomplete, the opera had conquered hearts in fifty-eight towns and nine countries. (*Madamina! Il catalogo è questo* . . .)

As the years went by, myth and anecdote gradually began to provide answers to a question incited by Natural curiosity. How was the opera written? In 1798 Niemetschek knows only that Mozart wrote it for the theatre of "the renowned" Schikaneder, his old friend. By 1804, Jean Baptiste Suard is saying that Mozart wrote it to please a woman of the theatre, who put this price on her favours, from which Mozart contracted the incurable malady of which he died! The woman was decided, presumably by coffee-shop assent, to have been Madame Gerl, who was the first Papagena and wife of the first Sarastro; it did not perhaps occur to the people who spread this rumour that *5.63* and *12.54–69* were meant to apply to *them*.

In 1828 Constanze's account became available, in the biography of Mozart by her second husband, Nissen. According to Nissen, Mozart wrote it "for the theatre of Schikaneder, his old friend" (Niemetschek's sentence, with a significant omission; "the renowned"). Schikaneder, we read, wrote the poetry and thus managed to be dragged along behind Mozart to immortality (a fair point, put in an unfair way). Schikaneder was destitute (untrue). Half in desperation (why?) Schikaneder came to Mozart, explained his circumstances, and concluded that only Mozart could "save him". We are told (on Constanze's authority?) the very words of the one and only (?) conversation: "I? How?" said Mozart. "Write an opera for me, in the taste of the Viennese public of the day. . . . I will look after the libretto, provide scenery, etc., everything that they want nowadays." "Good, I will do it." "What do you want as an honorarium?" "You are destitute? We will arrange matters so as to help you, and so that I am not deprived of all benefit. I give my score to you alone. Give me for it what you wish, but on condition that you guarantee that it is not copied. If the opera is a success, I can sell it to other managements, and that will be my recompense." The gentleman theatre manager (we read) was of course delighted, and concluded the bargain with solemn oaths; Mozart worked hard and wrote fine music, just as that man wanted; the opera was produced, the takings were big, its reputation went all over Germany, and after a few weeks it was being performed at other theatres without a single one of them having got the score from Mozart; who, when he saw that the man was swindling him in this way, merely said "The rascal" and forgot it.

The opera was not produced in any other theatre during Mozart's life; and the account is so unlike the general tone of Nissen's remarks on the opera (e.g. in the *Anhang* to his biography) as to suggest that it records a story that Constanze herself repeated to all hearers, over the years. She prepared the book for publication after Nissen's death, and therefore had the opportunity to ensure that her view had been accurately and fully recorded. She may or may not have had a legitimate grievance against Schikaneder. But no court, and no historian, could convict him on the basis of this story alone. Moreover, one's heart sinks at Constanze's lack of comprehension of how her first husband had for years been setting about the task of writing operas. We know that Mozart loved her. But she seems to have been somewhat inadequate as a companion and confidante. It is obvious why Mozart was receptive to the Masonic view of woman's inferiority. Pamina, the exceptional *Fräuleinbild*, has—shall we say?—certain qualities that Constanze lacked.

There was also a lad named Ignaz von Seyfried. He was fifteen in 1791, and had the good fortune to be (perhaps not more than once or twice) a guest of Schikaneder, at the same table as Mozart. Therefore, as the years went by, he became well-known as an authority on the circumstances in which the opera was written. His account of the matter was written down at the request of G. F. Treitschke in about 1840, nearly fifty years after the events which it purports to recall. If we reflect for even a moment, it will be evident that such an account has little value. Seyfried may be right in saying that Mozart wrote some of the music in the Gerl flat. At any rate, it explains why gossip attributed Mozart's death to a disease acquired from Madame Gerl—human chatter is, if anything, even more monotonously sexual than human

behaviour. And we need not disbelieve Seyfried's assertion that
Mozart also wrote some of it in the famous garden hut, now to be seen
at Salzburg. Neither of these alleged facts matters a hoot, when it
comes to understanding the opera; but they relate to simple things
that could be common knowledge in the circle of Schikaneder's friends.
What passes belief is that Seyfried was trusted by reputable scholars
when he recalls that "the libretto was finished as far as the first finale
when the *Magic Zither* or *Kaspar the bassoon-player* appeared at Marinelli's Leopoldstadt theatre. . . . Perinet had used the same story but
more accurately . . . this did not suit our Emanuel, who soon met the
situation by turning the whole plan round." To put it bluntly, the
fifteen-year-old boy is unlikely to have been privy to what "our
Emanuel" and "our Wolfgang" were planning. Gradually, and for
reasons that need not here concern us, scholars have been forced to
reject Seyfried's version of an alleged change of plot in the finale of Act
One. But the general theory of a change of plot, though no longer
held by scholars who know the opera well, lingers. It is at first sight
confirmed by the libretto; which is presumably where Seyfried got it
from—if he is not simply an echo of other Reasoning citizens.

Human reason, which has its place in the dramatic scheme of the
opera, can be trusted too much or too little. It churns out far more
error than truth—including the error of supposing, fatalistically, that
reason itself is therefore a futile and laughable phenomenon. If used
with care, on the basis of accurate data, reason discovers truth in many
fields; and is also an aid to practical decision. But one often has to begin
—as in the opera—by learning to recognise and discard one's errors.
Let me for instance assure you in the somewhat dogmatic tones of the
Old Priest that the following stories are probably *Zungenspiel*, mere
idle guesswork; (*a*) Schikaneder suggested the opera (*b*) Mozart said
"If we make a fiasco I cannot help it, for I never wrote a magic opera
in my life". (*c*) It was first intended to be a simple setting of some story
like *Lulu*, and later changed to have a Masonic ending (*d*) Mozart had
to rewrite No. *7* five times, to please Schikaneder (*e*) he was unable to
think of a tune for No. *20* until Schikaneder whistled one for him (*f*) he
only wrote the Priest's March because Schikaneder decided at the dress
rehearsal that (as clearly stated in the printed libretto, on sale at the first
performance!) the priests should enter to music (*g*) Mozart had to alter
the Papageno/Papagena duet because Schikaneder called out at a
rehearsal "Hi, you, Mozart, that's no good, the music must express
more astonishment" (*h*) Schikaneder took the credit for words that
were written for him by other men—in Schikaneder's own inimitably

awful style and handwriting (*i*) Schikaneder tricked Mozart into writing the opera, bullied him, enticed him to orgies, cheated him out of his fair share of the proceeds, etc. These are samples of the nauseatingly cheap gossip that by some Gresham's Law accumulated, and went on accumulating, so long as there was anyone who had been near Mozart in 1791, or knew a man who had been in Schikaneder's employment in 1793, or knew a man who knew a man who . . ., etc. Too often, commentators appear to have assumed that they can sift the pile and pick out, by intuition, the bits which are "good tradition". This means the bits *we* like to believe, *we* think plausible; another sure way of reducing Mozart to our level.

A work as great as the *Magic Flute* can survive much misunderstanding. But it is hardly surprising that, as the years went by, performers and audiences began to be affected by all these insidious whispers, portraying Mozart and Schikaneder as mediocre simpletons. Even in Germanic lands, where the prestige of the first great German opera remained high, interest began to wane after about 1860. The French condescendingly "improved" it from the outset—it reached Paris in 1801 as *Les mystéres d'Isis* with a French text by Morel de Chédeville, and music "arranged" by L. W. Lachnith to include bits of *Figaro*, *Don Giovanni* and *Clemenza di Tito*. In England, it was almost unknown. Our second-hand music counters still include evidence that we knew it dimly as *Il Flauto Magico*, one of Mozart's lesser Italian operas. Shaw had to rebuke his readers for assuming that it was "a vapid tawdry tomfoolery for showing off a soprano with a high F and a bass with a low F." But Shaw was presumably considered to be off form that week. Why waste time in denying the obvious? Surely everyone knows that all opera is, very precisely, vapid tawdry tomfoolery for showing off voices? By now the *Magic Flute* is in all probability better loved in Britain and America than even in Germany. But even Dent, who did so much to bring this about, still thought of the story as, in itself, "an agglomeration of absurdities". To which, Brigid Brophy has neatly replied that it is nearly as nonsensical as Shakespeare's *Tempest* (which was, by the way, known to Germans at that time as the *Magic Island*; *Der Sturm oder die Zauberinsel*, translated by Wieland).

One wishes of course that Mozart had lived to write his memoirs, including a judicious and candid chapter about this opera. But "death and despair were all he earned", as he himself ruefully said in a letter to Constanze on the morning of 11th June 1791, reporting that "from sheer boredom I composed today an aria for my opera . . . I got up as early as half past four." He was expecting to lunch that day with

Puchberg, the fellow Mason to whom he wrote begging letters. He
was expecting that someone else would call on him between twelve
and one to "settle up everything". The unknown person never called,
and Mozart missed his lunch with Puchberg. In the evening, "to cheer
myself up I went to the Käsperle Theatre to see the new opera *Der
Fagottist* which is making such a sensation but which is shoddy stuff."
By 2nd July the unorchestrated score of Act One was at Baden near
Vienna. "Please tell that idiotic fellow Süssmayr" (the one who finished
the Requiem, after Mozart's death) "to send me my score of the first
act from the introduction to the finale, so that I may orchestrate it."
On 4th July he is "weak for want of food". The next day he is asking
Süssmayr to "send me Nos. *4* and *5* of my manuscript". On 12th July
"even my work gives me no pleasure, because I am accustomed to
stop working now and then, and exchange a few words with you.
Alas! this is no longer possible. If I go to the piano and sing something
out of my opera I have to stop at once, for this stirs my emotions too
deeply." It was in such a state of body and mind that Mozart wrote
the luminously serene sonorities of this score.

There are anecdotes about numbers of the operas that were written
or orchestrated after July—for instance, Nissen has a nice story about
5, of which (he says) Mozart jotted down the beginning in Prague,
while playing billiards. This presumably implies that he wrote it just
before the first performance of the hurriedly-written *Clemenza di Tito*,
in early September. But we have seen that he was orchestrating it in
early July, and in any case Mozart's own thematic catalogue, which is
better evidence than Nissen, suggests that the entire opera was finished
in July; apart perhaps from the two orchestral items. Nothing is more
certain from a study of the score than that the overture (No. *1* of twenty-
two numbers) was mainly or partly in his head at a fairly early stage
in the work of composition; and the same may apply to the Priests'
March, although neither was written down until on or just before
28th September. The practical point here is that Schikaneder's competent company had time to rehearse the opera properly before the first
performance on 30th September; the items which Mozart put on one
side, in order to get down to the *Requiem* and *Clemenza*, were the two
that his friend Emanuel—playwright, librettist, impresario, producer,
actor and singer—did not urgently need.

History, like a computer, can only produce some of the right answers
if you ask the right questions. Let me propose one or two questions that
have not been often enough asked. Once the two friends decided to
write an operatic defence of Masonry, why did they add or retain

elements of fairy-tale, spectacle and farce? Is it only Schikaneder who deserves the praise accorded by Goethe (*Conversations with Eckermann II* 358) to the author of the libretto for "understanding in high degree the art of working through contrasts and producing big theatrical effects"? Why is it that the libretto plan, though a little less fiercely condensed than *Figaro* and *Don Giovanni*, has the same bold universality —complete with camouflage-trick—as *Don Giovanni*?

"My sole aim" wrote Schikaneder in 1787, in a foreword to *Der Grandprofoss*, "is to work for the box-office, and to see what makes the biggest effect on the stage, so as to secure a full house and good takings." *The Magic Flute* was to be his greatest box-office success. But he could not see into the future, any more than you or I can do today. Put yourself in his place therefore, as you carefully think through, with Mozart, the first sketch of any project which contains a twenty-year-old Masonic prince and sentiments like

> When Virtue, paired with Righteousness,
> The path of Rank shall strew with praise . . .

You would scare away your public. You would be the laughing-stock of any rival impresario. But above all the Emperor would forbid it. You have not yet b—— well forgotten the fiasco in 1785 when the Enlightened Joseph suppressed a *Figaro* version by one of his own handful of supporters—and when you, not b—— Rautenstrauch, were ruined. Trust b—— b—— Leopold? Not likely. Or words to that effect, in Schikaneder's rough south German. No one in authority would be much impressed by the mere fact that the action was supposed to take place in ancient Egypt. The emphasis would of course be on Enlightened Despotism—a respectable theory—instead of on *Liberté, Egalité* and *Fraternité*. There need be no disrespect for authority, none of that *Se vuol ballare* and *Ho capito* stuff. He could afford to make it a nice lavish "spectacular" (the expense and splendour of decoration impressed several critics). Even so, plain prudence would suggest, in this year of grace 1791, that the Message should be as wishy-washy as possible.

Instead of being played down, it was played up. Was it perhaps the composer of *Figaro* and *Don Giovanni* who suggested the essential solution, against all the rules of safe theatre? The plan had to be widened and lengthened so as to "lose" the otherwise too blatant Message by adding almost everything that either of them wanted to say, not only about love but about life. Were it not for the use of spoken dialogue, the opera would be at least as long as *Don Giovanni*. Comedy and farce are thrown in. Some of the most serious and heart-felt messages are sung lightly, or from the mouths of comic characters; or are spoken. It is the musician who was accustomed to work by contrasts, varying his textures, combining grave and gay movements. It was Mozart who expected audiences to follow swift flickerings in and out of seriousness, when listening to *Figaro*, *Don Giovanni* and *Così fan tutte*. It was Mozart who, if Part III of this book is right, camou-flaged his *Giovanni* so that the *giovane* could be *estremamente licenzioso* while appearing tame or *defututus*. In a sense the great design of the *Magic Flute* looks like Mozart's attempt to atone for the naughtiness of *Don Giovanni*; a *Purgatorio* and *Paradiso* to balance his *Inferno*.

An article about the new *Theater an der Wien* in 1803 mentioned the "almost universal rumour that Schikaneder is not the father and actual begetter of his theatrical children." It has been demonstrated, continues the article, "that the *plan and dialogue* (my italics) are his own, and Herr Winter who is also superintendent of this theatre will attest it; for only he, and perhaps he alone, can read Schikaneder's deliberate hiero-glyphics, which he is always the first to receive for copying . . . that Schikaneder did not write all the verses of his operas, however, he him-self does not deny." Note the distinction between plan and dialogue; we have seen that Schikaneder stated in 1795 that he "thought the text (i.e. the plan) right through, diligently, with Mozart". Rommel and Komorzynski have established that the thinking of the libretto is closely related to Schikaneder's life and work; and that the libretto is in his style. We must surely give Emanuel Schikaneder credit for helping to keep the story relatively simple; and for the fact that the dialogue and stage-directions show a most careful eye for visual effect. Da Ponte, for all his talent and charm, was not such an experienced man of the theatre as Schikaneder.

Yet the unity and boldness of the plan proclaim that Mozart exercised a decisive influence in the evolution of the libretto as we have it. Whether or not any of the sketches (p. 252) were in Mozart's handwriting, he could think about each of them without offence, on the pretext of making sure that the increasingly unusual structure was viable from a musical point of view. Once again therefore we can reasonably suppose that the approximate key-plan, with something of the astonishing universality of musical styles (past and present, German and non-German) grew up with the libretto plan in Mozart's mind, before the libretto was written. And who but Mozart saw that the principal tenor's flute not only fitted his own *King Thamos* music but provided a fashionably trivial title? Think of it! They could even drag in bits of those stories from *Dschinnistan*!

Schikaneder, being a practical man, may have assured Mozart that most of the audience would not even notice the serious bits, except as *entr'acte* music. But Mozart had not yet quite lost the illusion that audiences were up to the level of attentiveness and adaptability that is needed (until some patient ass has worked it all out from the score, as I have) to understand his detailed tragi-comedy:

"The ———s had a box this evening, and applauded everything most heartily. But he, the know-all, showed himself to be such a thorough Bavarian that I could not remain, or I should have had to call him an ass. Unfortunately I was there just when the second act began, that is, at the solemn scene (*9, 9AB, 10*). He made fun of everything! At first I was patient enough to draw his attention to a few passages. But he laughed at everything. Well, I could stand it no longer. I called him a Papageno and cleared out. But I don't think that the idiot understood my remark." (Letter of 8th October 1791.)

Mozart worked off his fury by playing a gay prank on Schikaneder (p. 278). He wanted listeners to enjoy and understand it all, gay or solemn, sung or spoken. If his personal friends could not make such an elementary "switch" as this one, in their own language, what hope was there for the Italian operas? Would they hear no continuity in *Figaro*? No sex in *Don Giovanni*? Would they think that *Così fan tutte* is an artificial puppet comedy? Ah well, they were at least enjoying this one. He felt a sort of impulse to play the glockenspiel. . . .

ACT ONE

Overture	*4A, Ist's denn auch Wirklichkeit*
1, Zu Hilfe!	*5, Hm hm hm hm*
1A, Wo bin ich?	*5A, Ha ha ha*
2, Der Vogelfänger bin ich ja	*6, Du feines Täubchen*
2A, He da!	*6A, Mutter, Mutter, Mutter!*
3, Dies Bildnis . . .	*7, Bei Männern welche Liebe fühlen*
3A, Rüste dich mit Mut . . .	*8, Zum Ziele führt dich diese Bahn*
4, O zitt're nicht	

THE FINAL CHORUS praises Strength, Beauty and Wisdom. Here surely, at the beginning of the overture, are the same three values, in the same key of three flats. The two little semiquaver chords are (or should be) lightly played, to enhance the force of the three main chords and the three big pauses; from which a soft violin triplet leads into syncopated chords for violins and viola, against a rising and falling pattern for 'cello and bassoon. The phrase leads on and on. Indeed, the whole of the opening *adagio* is one great phrase—and a text-book example of Mozart's use of expressive contrasts.

Those three main opening chords were played *fortissimo*, by the full orchestra. The trombones, that were reserved until Act Two of *Don Giovanni*, are here used from the outset. The Three Chords must not be confused with the Triple Accord, which we hear in the middle of the overture and at the beginning of Act Two. The Triple (in fact, ninefold) Accord is mainly a monotonous repetition of one B♭ major chord, blown by eighteen primitive and unwieldy wind instruments, the great black horns enchased with gold (*8A, 9A*; only the flutes add triadic D*s* and F*s*). The Three Chords, on the other hand are essentially three different chords, climbing the E♭ major triad—E♭, G, B♭. The Triple Accord could be the rhythm of nine ritual knocks on the door; the Three Chords are a musical pattern.

The other two hundred bars are dazzlingly different. When one is Mozart, the artistic problem calls out its own music; but it is difficult to believe that even Mozart would have written the *allegro* of a *Magic Flute* overture in such fugato, such counterpoint, at the time of *Figaro* (1785–6) or *Don Giovanni* (1787). It is essentially post-1788, after the three last symphonies; in the same class as the finale of the Jupiter symphony.

After this vision of Utopian strength, there comes a human reality—weakness. The music resumes in soft frightened C minor (*1.1*). The first violins have a three-bar phrase (*1.2–4*) that begins by climbing the C minor triad; C, E♭, G. The three-bar phrase is repeated (*1.5–7*). Then tension grows in a long phrase that falls at *1.15–16*. The curtain has risen (not necessarily at bar 1) and we are in what Schikaneder calls a "rocky region"; the realm of the Queen of Night. It is hilly country (*2A10*); and we are told at *3A18* that Sarastro lives "very near our hills, in a beautiful and pleasant valley . . . his city is fine, and well guarded."

Is the Queen's city fine, and well-guarded? The rocky serpent-infested region sounds a little bleak—the wilderness of this world, outside the fertile delta of the ancient Egypt in which the action of the opera is supposed to take place. Here and there, trees are said to grow between and over the rocks. On either side are climbable hills. We must not place too much reliance on the 1795 illustrations; they are from Brno, according to Otto Erich Deutsch. But it is interesting to note that in one of the very early productions (see p. 224) the hills were mountainsides, and the trees poor specimens compared with the ones that grew in Sarastro's valley (p. 224, p. 225). There is one (round) temple—the affluent Sarastro has three temples.

Enter Tamino. He scrambles down from a rock, dressed in a handsome Japanese hunting costume (the reading could be "Javanese"—both are exotic, both imply that Tamino comes from a distant land). He has a bow but no arrows. He is being chased by an angry serpent.

"For a helper, a helper, a helper I cry now! A helper, or else I am lost, and I die now!" Tamino's words climb the C minor triad—it was for this that the violins climbed it in bars *2* and *5*. But where the violins sweep down (*1.3, 6, 19, 22*) the voice ends forthrightly. According to Abert therefore Tamino sings in a thoroughly manly tone, without any effeminate fear (after all, the bravest of soldiers can run out of ammunition). But Abert is wrong, or partly wrong. Think for a moment of Pamina's carefully contrasted entry in *6*. "For this, your life is forfeited!" sings the angry Monostatos. "I do not fear the thought of it!" sings Pamina. Tamino's entry is C minor, breathless, timid, unselfreliant. Tamino faints (*1.40*); is frightened, *furchtsam*, when he revives (*1A*); is told *not* to shiver, at *2A70*; has to be told to arm himself with courage (*3A1*); is startled, and told to compose himself, at *3A19–20*; and prays for courage at *4A*. He *wants* to be brave. He will face ordeals, but with a sinking heart. "I fear no death, I have my manhood, the path of virtue leads me onward! O doors of *horror*, open wide; with happy heart I go inside!" Note the word in italics, and think how delighted he is at the chance of having the brave Pamina with him. With Pamina he will achieve courage and strength.

Meanwhile he is calling for help; human or divine, or both. "A slithering monster of evil is near me! Divine powers, hear me!" Mozart first wrote into the score a ferocious lion (*dem grimmigen Löwen*). But the slithering music (see below) and the original libretto suggest that the serpent was part of the original plan. Auden and Kallman regard the serpent as forces in the depth of Tamino's nature, that he cannot understand or control. Alternatively, the serpent is the hostile environment of our life; and a poisonous beast, of whom anyone might be frightened once it had been roused. Either way the serpent is a symbol of evil (Genesis iii.13–15); and its music, apart from explaining *1.8–14* by *1.24–8*, becomes overtly pictorial. The second violin line continues to shiver with Tamino. But the other strings convey the serpent's slithering ("Upon thy belly shalt thou go . . .") and the rising of its head above Tamino. If Tamino is still standing, the serpent is Fafner-size. But *1.15–16*, and the illustration at p. 224, suggest that early productions thought of Tamino as singing the whole of his first solo in a near-prostrate position, with a large but not colossal snake rearing and swaying to strike. Either way Tamino's ordeals in this opera are nothing to those faced by Pamina; and by Schikaneder and subsequent producers.

"So near, oh so near! So near now is he! Come, rescue me!" By *1.30* (music tells us) the serpent is in position. Tamino's cries, thereafter, are another nice study in Mozart's ability to make repetition credible. Note how the cries broaden, to suit the desperate close. At *1.40* Tamino falls in a faint. At the same time, according to Schikaneder's stage-direction, the door of the temple opens, and out come three veiled ladies. With silver javelins they kill the snake. "Die, monster, die, by us you die!" From the timing of the words, in relation to Tamino's faint, Mozart apparently envisaged that the javelins should be thrown from inside the temple door, before the ladies appear. According to an old tradition, the snake falls into three bits. If so, one of the three javelins misses, or hits the serpent's head. But there is nothing about the three pieces in score or libretto.

After three bridging bars the music settles into E♮ major; with a light parody of heroic music in the wind, and a scale figure in the strings. The ladies are pleasantly surprised at their own prowess. "Oh joy!" With flutes and clarinets, they congratulate themselves. "Our heads are high, our fame is won!" Violin quavers trip down to suit the natural rhythm of their next words. "And he is freed!" Clarinets and bassoons are delighted at the next thought. "Our arms have done this mighty deed!" There is a hint of Mozartian irony here; as if a Prospero-like Sarastro had sent his Ariel to ensure that the Ladies aimed well and threw hard.

Much has happened in sixty-two bars. In the rest of the *Introduzione* (converse of *Finale*) almost nothing happens for over a hundred and fifty bars. Mozart, the composer of *Figaro* and *Don Giovanni*, was restraining his natural speed of thought. Like his own Don, he was adjusting his tempo to the particular audience. I imagine Schikaneder begging Mozart to go at ordinary operatic speed for a change. There is therefore plenty of time to shake our heads if the ladies fail to do justice to the blending sonorities of their parts. But the probable dramatic purpose of the passage is to give a portrait of ordinary womanhood. Pamina is Beautiful and Good, the Queen is Beautiful and Wicked. We do not know whether the three ladies are Beautiful behind those veils (see *2A52-5*). But they sing (and should *act*) like women who are cheerful, frivolous, talkative, sentimental and a little spiteful.

From E♭ major, soft 'cellos and double-basses establish a long and placid subdominant (A♭) passage. Violins curve up to meet the first lady on an F. "So fair, so young, so full of grace" she says, looking at Tamino (who has thoughtfully fainted in a position that reveals his face). Up goes the violin again, for the second lady. "I never saw so fair a face." The violin is delighted; it curves up higher to A♭ and memorably accompanies the third lady as she reveals her special interest and accomplishment. "Oh, painter's joy! So fair to trace!" Flutes and clarinets frolic against viola and bassoon. "Were I to give my heart in fee, for this young man 'twould have to be!" The first and second ladies sing it together; the third lady goes her own way with violin help. The strings trip along (*1.87*); they have a suggestion to make. "O let us to our mistress hurry! The happy message let us carry." The music of "Were I to give my heart in fee . . ." returns; this time bassoons join the violins in backing up the third lady. "Maybe, that one so fair, so kind, can yet restore her peace of mind." Again the strings trip along. Each in turn suggests that the other two should take the message. "Go, take the word of cheer, and I will tarry here." The second lady is at once suspicious, in F minor. "No, you can go away, and I alone will stay." "No, no, it cannot be" says the third lady "the duty is for me." The first lady pouts in G minor "I, I will tarry here!" The second lady insists: "I, I alone will stay!" "I, I alone 'twill be" says the third lady. "I tarry!" "I only!" I'll guard him!" "I!" "I!" "I!"

All good singers act primarily through the voice. But it is sad to see three stodgy motionless forms ignore, even contradict, the 6/8 *allegretto* that follows. The violins still trip, the flutes add a soft twiddle. "I go away?" The woodwind fun is enhanced. "Oh ho I see!" 'Cellos and basses drop out. "Alone with him they'd like to be! No, no, I will not let it be . . ." The music goes into C major for a concluding *allegro* section. Each lady in turn grins happily: "But oh what would I not give gaily, to be beside him nightly, daily, if I could have him all for me, yes, all for me." A *forte* toot from trumpet and drum dispels the dream. "They will not go, it cannot be; as matters are, I'd better go." They pause, and look at Tamino. "Oh youth so dear, so full of charm, may fortune keep you free from harm!" The lines have a charming little oboe copula, with something of the feel of the flute and clarinet comment in *1.78*. "Again we'll meet, I know . . ." The farewell is duly prolonged. Eventually they go into the temple, looking crossly at each other. The door opens for them, and shuts behind them.

Tamino wakes. Timidly, he looks round. "Where am I? Is it fantasy that I am still alive? Or has a higher power rescued me?" He gets to his feet, and looks round. "What? The evil snake dead at my feet?"

We hear the distant sound of a pan-pipe; a stage-direction says that the orchestra accompany it softly, while Tamino thinks "What do I hear? Where am I? What unknown place is this? Ha, a human shape coming down the valley!" He hides behind a tree. The strings—rhythmically, softly, and at a very moderate speed—begin the prelude to a simple 2/4 strophic song in G major. At the end of each two-bar phrase comes a soft staccato horn-phrase, like holiday peasants clapping their hands. Papageno, the man who talks too much (*21.441*), and does not care for wisdom (*10A25*), is about to present another antithesis to the ideal qualities of the overture. He appears coming down a path with a bird-cage on his back. It is a big bird-cage, projecting high above his head. In it are a number of birds. He is himself a bird (p. 193). He is holding the pan-pipe with both hands. At *2.13–14*, after the conclusion of six two-bar phrases in the orchestra, oboes and horns have their brief say. Then he pipes; still at a distance. During the next eight bars he comes closer. At *2.22* he again pipes. This time, the oboe and horn phrase follows.

"There is no rarer bird than I, I'm always happy, ho hi hi; the song-bird catcher all do know, yes, young and old where e'er I go." The orchestra echo a line. "For I can lay a skilful snare, and with my piping drive out care . . ." Oh yes, say the oboes and horns; again he pipes. "And that is why my life is fine, for all the singing birds are mine." He pipes, the oboes and horns follow. A final two-bar phrase concludes the refrain.

"There is no rarer bird than I . . ." Papageno repeats his simple quatrain, and we perhaps begin to notice that the thoughts were meaningful. "I'd also like a maiden-snare, a dozen ruses I'd prepare . . ." The oboes and horns, and the piping, begin to make the pause significant; a certain wistful feeling colours his happiness. But not for long. "In cages of my own design, oh all the maidens would be mine!" Papageno is about twenty-eight (*15A25*); but is still as naïve as the thirteen-year-old Cherubino in *Non so più*.

The third verse is optional. It is not in the autograph score, and was apparently added by Schikaneder during the opera's long first run, to underline the implied dramatic point of the second verse. "And when the maidens all were mine, I'd barter one for sugar fine, and oh the one that I liked best, I'd feed her sugar with the rest. . . . And she would softly kiss me then, were she my wife and I her man. . . ." This time the "oh yes" from oboes and horns, and the piping, are unmistakably significant, a damned quadruple dot in music. "And she would lie in slumber mild, and I would lull her like a child." He pipes, the oboes and horns respond. The orchestra give us that two-bar phrase, loud and clear, for the final time; while Papageno goes to the temple door (and probably takes off his bird-cage, in order to deliver the birds— 6A20).

Tamino comes forward, and takes him by the hand (a symbol of friendliness); having concluded, after earnest and anxious observation, that the native is not hostile. The ensuing dialogue contains a great deal of relevant information, and should on no account be "improved". If it is properly spoken and rehearsed, one should be able to endure a naïveté that is after all, an integral part of the opera. "Hey there." "Eh what?" "Ah friend, you are a jolly fellow—who are you?" "Who am I? That's a silly question. A human like you." Tamino's question is answered at 2A30, just as 2A15 is answered at 2A22. Note the hint, after all, of Égalité and Fraternité. Papageno continues: "And suppose I were to ask, who are you?" "I should reply, that I am of imperial descent." Like young Franz; but Tamino, of course, was merely the wandering Nanki-Poo son of an ancient oriental ruler.

Of imperial descent? "That is beyond me" says Papageno. "You must speak more simply, if I am to understand you." "My father is an emperor, who rules over many lands and many peoples. That is why they call me prince." "Lands? Peoples? Prince?" "Therefore I ask . . ." "Slow there! Let me ask! First, you tell me. Are there lands and people beyond these hills?" "Many thousands of them." "What a market for my birds!" Europe is now a crowded continent of cities and airports. But there are still remote corners in which a Papageno is credible, with his mixture of ignorance and shrewdness.

"Now tell me, what place is this?" "What place?" The question baffles Papageno; he shrugs, and looks round. "In the hills, between bottom and top." "You are right, but what is the place called? Who rules here?" "How would I know? You might as well ask me, how I came into the world." Tamino laughs and the sophisticated listener groans. "What? Do you not even know where you were born, or who were your parents?" "What do you mean? A man brought me up and fed me. He was old but very jolly." "That was presumably your father." "I don't know." "Did you not know your mother?" "I did not. But they once told me that she had been in service, in this enclosed building that belongs to the dark star-flaming queen. Whether she is still alive, or what became of her, I do not know. I only know that I have a straw hut, not far from here, that shelters me from wind and rain." "But how do you live?" "By eating and drinking, like other humans." "How do you obtain it?" "By barter. I catch birds for the star-flaming Queen and her ladies. For that, I am daily given food and drink at her command." He is as far from Enlightenment as a Noble Savage can be. But the picture is vivid and consistent—note the barter, which was also specifically mentioned in the third verse of Papageno's *Eintrittslied*.

Tamino is thinking. "Star-flaming Queen! Suppose it were the mighty lady of night! Tell me, my good friend, were you ever so fortunate as to see this goddess of the night?" "Huh! You are weak in the head, if you ask such a question. Now I do believe that you were born in another land." "I was, indeed I was, dear friend. I only thought that . . ." "See? See the star-flaming Queen? If you come to me with another question as silly as that one, why as sure as my name is Papageno I will shut you into my bird-cage like a silly bullfinch, and take you along with my other birds to the Queen of Night and her ladies, and hand you in. And then, for all I care, they can cook you." A strange man, thinks Tamino. "See?" continues Papageno. "See the star-flaming Queen? What mortal can boast that he has ever seen her? What human eye could see through her black-woven veil?" "At any rate, I am now answered" thinks Tamino. "It is the Queen of Night, of whom my father so often spoke to me. I cannot imagine how I came so far out of my way."

From Monteverdi onwards opera composers have used myth and symbolism. In *Mozart the Dramatist* Brigid Brophy speculates fascinatingly about Isis, the *regina coeli* (Apuleius, *Golden Ass X1.2*) and the moon. I know of no reason to suppose that Mozart (whose thought comes more from life, and less from books) was knowledgeable about the *regina coeli*, except as a term for the Virgin Mary in ecclesiastical vocal music. But the contrast of light and darkness moved him greatly (for instance, in *Don Giovanni*) and he was presumably familiar with the kind of thinking that is contained in books like Sethos, by the Abbé Terrasson. Used with caution, such knowledge can most certainly help to elucidate Mozart's dramatic intentions in this opera.

In the middle of *2A33*, we move to the fourth main section of this dialogue. "And this is no ordinary man!" thinks Tamino timidly: "Perhaps he is one of her serving spirits." He stares at Papageno, who begins to be afraid of him and asks: "Why do you look at me like that?"

"Because . . . because I begin to doubt whether you are human."
"Why?" "By the feathers that cover you, I take you for . . ." Tamino
is moving closer, to touch the feathers. "Not for a bird? Stand back, I
say. I warn you, when I fight anyone, I have the strength of a giant.
(*Aside*) If he does not soon begin to be frightened of me, I shall have to
run away." Papageno is a blustering Aguecheek, so evidently frightened that even the timid Tamino cannot be afraid of him. But Tamino
is credulous and well-brought-up. "The strength of a giant?" He looks
at the dead serpent. "Then were you the one who saved my life, by
overpowering this poisonous snake?" "Snake!!" Papageno looks, and
takes several steps backward. He is shaking with fear. "Oooh! Dead or
alive?" "By your modest question, you want to avoid being thanked.
But I must tell you, I am eternally grateful to you for your valiant
action." Papageno is still panic-stricken at the thought of being mistaken for one of his own songbirds and "caught". He therefore gladly
accepts the chance of letting the stranger persist in this convenient
assertion. "Do not talk of it. We can be glad that, happily, it was overcome." As usual, the step from an evasion to a lie is a small one. "But
how on earth, my friend" asks Tamino "did you subdue the monster?
You have no weapon." "Don't need one! I have a grasp that is stronger
than weapons." "You throttled it?" "Yes, throttled it!" Aside, Papageno reflects that never in his life has he been so strong as today.

With magical swiftness the three ladies appear. Their gestures are a
threat of trouble. "Papageno!" they cry. They are furious. The bird-
catcher is inadvertently stealing their glory. "Aha, for me; look, friend"
says Papageno. "Who are these ladies?" asks Tamino. "Who they are,
properly, I do not know. I only know that they take my birds each
day; and give me wine, sugarloaf and sweet figs instead." "They are
presumably very beautiful?" "I don't think! If they were beautiful,
they would not cover their faces." "PAPAGENO!!" say the ladies.
"Quiet" says Papageno, "now they threaten me. You ask if they are
beautiful? I can only answer that I have not yet seen anything more
charming—now they will be nice again." "PAPAGENO!!!" "What
have I done today, that they are so cross with me? Here, my beauties, I
hand over my birds." The first lady merely produces an elegant
French bottle of water. "And in return" she says, handing it to him "for
the first time, our lady sends you, in place of wine, pure clear water."
"And she commanded me" adds the second lady "to bring you, instead
of sugarloaf, this stone; I wish you joy of it!" "What! Am I to gnaw
stone?" "And instead of the sweet figs" says the artistic third lady "I
have the honour of fastening this golden lock on your mouth." She

padlocks his lips, while Papageno's expressive face and gestures tell us
what the songbird feels. It is an unexpected fulfilment of his horror of
being caged. "You presumably know why our lady has punished you
in this way?" Papageno mournfully nods. "So that in future you do not
tell lies to strangers" adds the second lady. "And so that you do not
in future boast of mighty deeds that others have accomplished" adds
the third lady, more candidly than the other two (who probably
look crossly at her for it). "Tell me, did you overpower this snake?"
asks the first lady. Papageno shakes his head. "Who did?" asks the
second lady. An eloquent gesture tells us that Papageno does not
know.

"It was we, young man, who freed you" says the third lady; to
whom appropriately, a certain work of Art has been entrusted
(perhaps she painted it?) "Do not be frightened" she says. (Of whom?
Of the three women, in whom the thoughts of the latter part of *1* are
very much alive?) "Delight and joy await you. Here, take this painting.
It is sent to you by our mighty queen. It is the portrait of her daughter.
She said, if you find that you are not indifferent to these features, then
happiness honour and fame are your lot. Farewell, until we meet again."
She goes. Papageno has been acting self-pity, and is at present ruefully
showing the French bottle to Tamino. Its shape is more elaborate than
that of any flask of *vin ordinaire*. "Adieu, Monsieur Papageno!" says
the second lady with Versailles grace. She goes. "Don't finish the nice
water too quickly!" adds the first lady; with a good giggle to remind us
that these are still the unenlightened womenfolk of *1.62–218*. She goes.
Papageno looks to Tamino for sympathy.

Tamino has been gazing at the portrait. He has seen nothing else—
and has heard nothing of what the ladies have been saying—since it
was put in his hands by the third lady. Here is a visionary glimpse of
Beauty; something holy, numinous. To make up for more than four
minutes of talk, Mozart begins to paint First Love in the opera's central
key of E♭ major. Two gentle orchestral sighs are touched into life.
Then he uses the warm colour of lightly accompanied tenor voice;
relying on the singer to put his beloved vocal organ at the service of a
nuance of expression which, though poetic, has to be most carefully
pre-imagined, by dropping all worldly sophistication of art and life.
For a singer the clue is to think of Schubert. "Never was a musician so
young" says Capell. "Theocritus and Boccaccio were wise compared
with Schubert, who knew nothing but the rapture and poignancy of
first sensations, the loss of which is the beginning of wisdom. . . ." The
Lied, as a genre, owes much to Schubert's response to this E♭ major

song; an aria which in itself is merely one facet of the many-sided genius of Mozart. Jane Austen preferred sense to sensibility as a guide through life. Mozart, as we know from *Così fan tutte*, would agree. But youthful sensibility must have its due.

"Enchanting picture, full of grace!" Three quaver chords link the vocal lines. "None ever saw so fair a face!" The quaver chords follow suit. They are for clarinets, of course; with bassoons, horns and 'cellos. "I feel here . . ." Tamino has his hand on his heart, without being aware that this is a gesture cheapened by subsequent use. There is unashamed wonder in the leaning semiquaver intervals (for voice, then violins). "I feel here . . ." Tamino feels, feels, feels; but is never ill-bred or extravagant about it. (Is this the music that you expected from that nice little boy in formal eighteenth-century clothes?) ". . . how this goddess true . . ." The word "goddess" stands out briefly on an A♭, with a tutti sfp chord in the orchestra. ". . . has filled my heart with pulsings new." It is the final line of the first verse, and evokes a long serene cantilena. The words have no independent merit, in German or in English. But they define the dramatic and poetic content of the music. If the voice is right, and if the vocal-cum-orchestral expression is right, no verbal deficiency need be found.

Papageno, very Naturally, had the same simple tune for each verse. There is no such simplicity in the musical art used here. The clarinets release one of the new "pulsings" (*3.15–16*), and Tamino tries to put words to it. "I know not how to name this yearning, but oh I feel how I am burning." A richer orchestral phrase increases our expectation. "Is it the fire of love in me?" Love? That unspoken thought was in the first violins. "Is it . . .?" Yes, yes, say the clarinets and bassoons. "Yes, yes" says Tamino. "Of love alone twill be . . . of new love . . . of true love . . . of lifelong love . . . *here* in me." Again he is holding his heart.

Therefore the setting of the final verse is richer in texture. "Oh could I now but look upon her . . . if my two eyes could fasten on her . . . oh I would . . . I would . . . warm and fine . . . what would I do?" Over a long organ point the violins have been surging up (*3.34, 36, 38*) to enrich the vocal line. Strings and wind, with alternate semiquavers, have created an extraordinary excitement. And Mozart has applied his mastery of the broken-sentence reverie; with a whole bar left empty, so that we may ask ourselves what Tamino would do. Commentators tell us that the true love of Tamino and Pamina is mystic not physical. Of course it is physical—and mystic. At *8.455,7* Tamino is slower off the mark than Pamina, but does exactly what the music and words of his aria said that he would. "With my two arms—oh, the pleasure—to this my hot heart I would press her." The phrase ends longingly, on a Dβ. "And she would be for ever mine, mine, MINE, mine!" Two bars later, Tamino is his own shy self again.

He is about to go in search of her, when he is met by the three ladies. They, poor things, are a little agitated—they keep interrupting each other. "Arm yourself with steadfastness and courage, handsome youth! The empress . . . has told *me* to tell you . . . that your future happiness is assured . . . she could hear your words, and how you meant them, she could read . . . the changing expression of your face (tenors, please note!). Yes and her motherly heart . . . has decided to complete your happiness: If this youth, said she, is as brave and resolute as he is tender-hearted, oh depend upon it, my daughter is as good as rescued."

"Rescued? O eternal darkness, what do I hear? The real princess . . . .?" The ladies explain that a mighty evil demon has snatched her away from her mother. It was a fine May morning, and she was sitting alone in her favourite place; the cypress grove, that gives life to all things. Tamino and Papageno listen in horror to a colourful tale. The naughty man (disguised as Sarastro the friend of Pamina's beloved father, *13A12, 13A15*) crept up and . . . Tamino's imagination completes the sentence. He wonders whether she is at this moment being . . . The ladies tell him not to blaspheme the virtue of sweet beauty. He asks where the tyrant lives. On being told, he asks the ladies to show him the way, so that he can slay the wicked man and rescue Pamina. But Mozart and Schikaneder seem to have been in a waspish mood when they planned this section of dialogue. At once the valiant prince is scared out of his skin by a rumbling of stage effects and orchestral sound. The cliffs roll away, the round temple disappears. To the repeated sound of thunder, the scene changes to a splendid hall; in which the queen sits, on a throne adorned with transparent stars. I'm sorry I had no room for Goethe's own sketch of this scene.

After the build-up in *2A* and *3A* we expect something impressive; and that, quite literally, is what we get. "Oh do not show such frightened eyes! For you are innocent, pious, wise." Innocent and pious, yes. But wise? However much sympathy we have with the pleas of a mother who has lost her daughter, this is an opera by Mozart and Schikaneder, and it is their point of view that matters. "You shall beware the wiles of women; this is the most important law" (*11*). The feel of the Bβ major music is unusually cold, the G minor section is artificial, the concluding instructions are brisk. There is less irony in this opera than in *Figaro* or *Don Giovanni*, but Mozart has not forgotten the knack of setting words with an insincerity that should be as transparent as those stars on her throne. "I see in you, dear son, a youth ideal, the sorrow of a mother's heart to heal." The magic flute is presumably useless to her, until she has found an innocent and pious young man to play it. Out of spite, she is determined to get her own back on Sarastro. Out of injured pride, she wants her daughter back. She cares not a scrap for her daughter's feelings and welfare (*13A, 14*).

"Oh I am a woman broken-hearted! I miss my daughter every day!" The *mezzo-forte* Eb and D, carefully marked staccato in the orchestra, cry out to be sung with the sort of sob that would warn any less naïve young man. "With her is happiness departed!" The sob is even more blatant in the oboe and bassoon trill. "A wicked man . . ." She pauses for dramatic orchestral effect. Tamino makes a horrified gesture—we were warned at *3A14* that his imagination tells him what wicked men do. "A man has taken her away!" Tamino, a man who wants to take her away, stands goggle-eyed. The Queen, lifting an amused eyebrow, continues. "I still see her shivers, her poor shy endeavours to offer resistance, to call for assistance!" Being a deity of sorts, the Queen can see a long way (she could see Tamino in front of her temple). But we were expressly told that Pamina was alone in the cypress grove. Do we believe those viola and bassoon blues, those rather obvious violin and 'cello shivers? "I saw it all with harrowed feeling." Another trilling sob. Did she see any of it? "Help, HELP, was all that she could speak. It was in vain, her cry appealing; for my poor armoury was too weak." Despite *6A31*, there is no evidence that Pamina was dragged away, or that she was maltreated in any way except by Monostatos. If you want genuine G minor grief, listen to Pamina's own aria. If you are impressed by this bit of play-acting—well, so was Tamino. By now he is only too ready to do whatever the Queen may ask. She points at him in Bb major (*allegro moderato*). "You! You! You possess the power to free her! You have the power to save a life. When you return—and when I see her—she will become your loving wife." There is much coloratura; sinister, but more dazzlingly impressive than ever. Tamino is left uncomfortable. "Was *this* reality? Or were my senses deceiving me? O ye good gods, deceive me not; unless it is your will to make trial of me! Shield my arm, steel my courage! For such help, Tamino's heart will offer you eternal gratitude!"

The libretto says that the scene-change should now be reversed, so that the quintet can take place outside the round temple. The score is silent on this point. The continued use of Bb major looks at first sight like justification for letting the quintet be sung in the dark hall of illusion, to save time. But it is a gayer, more normal B♭ major; and it is legitimate to emphasise this by visual transformation. As for Papageno, we know from *5.150* that he was on-stage during *3.4*; so presumably he was also present during the Queen's aria. No wonder he remained silent—until the Queen had gone.

"Hm hm hm hm!" Tamino turns, and sees the padlocked lips. "Poor man, you say you are in prison? A tongue is under lock and key? I can but pity your condition, I am *too weak* to set you free." Note the words in italics; Tamino is still an embodiment of *Schwäche*, not *Stärke*.

5.35–77 are in the dominant. The ladies, who went off with the Queen at her beckoning, have returned. "The Queen today is lenient, I may undo your punishment" says the first lady, taking the lock off Papageno's mouth. "For happy chatter I was dying!" bursts out Papageno. "Yes, chatter! But without more lying" says the second lady. "I lie no more, oh no indeed!" says Papageno. "It was the warning you do need" say the ladies (with a private snigger to each other, if we bother to take the quintet in its context). Papageno insists that he will never need the warning; the ladies insist that he will. The strings have a simple rising figure (F, A, C, *5.53*; another triad!), and the five voices join in one of the characteristic "morals" of the opera. "If on their lips all naughty liars had golden locks to keep them good, all vile tongue-wagging black desires would fade in love and brotherhood." Mozart lets the tongues wag hard at *5.63* and *5.71*. Of the five singers, four are confirmed tongue-waggers; there is therefore something particularly amusing in their panacea for the envy, hatred, malice and all uncharitableness that abounded in 1791, continued to abound (see p. 230) and still abound.

Back in the tonic, the first lady gives Tamino an important present. "O prince, I bring this gift for you; the Queen bestows a favour new. This Magic Flute support can lend you, in peril's hour it will defend you." At *21.316–25* we learn that the flute is made of oak, and was cut by Pamina's father, the late King of Day. It is gold-painted. The flute was far from being Mozart's favourite instrument, but here it is made to symbolise the whole power of music. "Herewith almighty are your dealings, you can transform all hurtful feelings. The sick at heart in joy will share, all single folk in love will pair. Oh, the art of music has value more than thrones or gold, for it has power to bring us joy, and a happiness untold . . ." Note that the ladies, as well as Tamino and Papageno, are single folk; and are distinctly sick at heart.

Papageno is shrewd enough to guess what all this is leading up to. The music veers off to G minor. "Now, dear women, to my sorrow I have . . . other business." "Keep the business for tomorrow; for our gracious lady says the repentant liar must go with the prince to find Sarastro." There is work for him to do. That is why he has been let out of his portable tongue-prison. "Not Sarastro! I decline, for I heard your tale so fine! What would happen if he took me, cruelly to pluck and cook me, or to give the dogs a feast?" He wriggles (5.150, etc.) and gabbles (5.155, etc.). The ladies are unrelenting. "The prince will guard you properly, and you his serving-man will be." Papageno is dubious (rightly—6.32, 6A28). Aside, he says what he thinks. "As for the prince, oh devil take him! To me my life is dear. Oh I can tell you I am quaking, I feel death very near."

With a glorious turn to the subdominant, the first and second ladies produce the best magic instrument of all. The horns in Act Two are monotonous ("that damned tune will go on all night" says Geraint Evans—and brings the house down). The Trump of Doom (15A, 17A) hardly counts as a magic instrument, any more than the pan-pipe does. The flute is memorably symbolic. The glockenspiel (defined as a ring of bells that sounds like "wooden laughter") warmed Mozart's heart; and therefore warms all our hearts. "Here, take this treasure for your own." "Oho, what is that ringing tone?" "They are the bells of childhood fable." "But then, to play shall I be able?" "Yes, yes, of course you will, you will." It is the instrument that can only be well played by those who are young at heart.

Tamino and Papageno are now equipped. They have no swords or shields, no helmets or breastplates. But they have flute and glockenspiel. They begin to say good-bye, back in the tonic. The violins add a light phrase (5.193, 195, 199) that we shall later associate with the Three Boys. Then Tamino and Papageno realise that they do not know the way. They ask the obvious question, on the dominant. A long high oboe C steals in, like the G of 8.2–5 and 10–13.

After a pause, the music resumes in the tonic. Clarinets, not yet heard in this quintet, have a long gentle *dolce* phrase. High bassoons help out. Soft *pizzicato* violins (no violas or 'cellos) complete the *andante* texture. "There are three boys, young, fair, good, clever, will hover over your endeavour . . ." It is tempting to let them float overhead, at this point. But Papageno says later (6A26–8) that neither Tamino nor he has seen them. However, the ladies promise that the boys will guide them on their way. "Follow obediently what they say!" The Queen and her ladies are in Sarastro's power, 8.428; they work his will and use his agents. Three ladies and two men say *auf Wiedersehen*. The curtain falls.

Despite the visible change or changes of scenery, the action in the Queen's realm has been swift and continuous. It may be assumed to have taken place in less than two hours, during the early part of the morning. If so, the bleakness of the opening scene could suitably be enhanced by frost; the sun did not shine early into the Queen's valley. But in Sarastro's broader valley the sun is shining (*6A33*). When Tamino and Papageno arrive, it is nearly noon (*6A34*).

5A is about the only section of dialogue that can at a pinch be shortened without much loss. The scene is a handsome Egyptian room. Two slaves carry out a fine cushion and a handsome carpeted Turkish table—to remind us, presumably, of a somewhat similar set-up in the seraglio of Pasha Selim; European slaves, rascally overseer, talk of torture, honest master. The third slave tells the other two that Pamina has run away. "You know master full-belly and his pretty ways. Well, the maiden was smarter than I thought. At the moment when he was sure of having her, she called out Sarastro's name. That shook the Moor. He stood there dumb and motionless. And that was the moment when she ran down to the canal, onto a gondola, and off in the direction of the palmgrove." But she has been caught, and is being dragged back by the ungentle Monostatos. We hear him shout to the slaves. "Bring some fetters!" Then he appears, dragging in Pamina. In G major *Entführung* music, he threatens her with death; duly preceded by worse-than-death. When told about the death, Pamina says that she does not fear it; except for the grief that (she naïvely supposes) will be felt by her mother. When told about the worse-than-death, she reacts with dignity and courage. Being only a woman (how often the thought recurs, in this opera) she has more excuse than Tamino for fainting. "Oh a fair young maid is she. She is whiter far than chalk, though." The unnatural whiteness implies sensitivity. The crude rhyme *Leute*—*Kreide* seems to have distracted attention from the aptness of the dramatic insight; Ignaz von Seyfried, who said (wrongly) that the "prompter Haselbeck had the task of versifying Sch.'s prose sketches", added that verses like *Leute*—*Kreide* were bad enough to be by "Sch." himself.

The trio is only seventy-one bars long, *allegro molto*; and consists essentially of two little duets. In the first, corrupted *Naturmensch* faces perfect woman; as he will again, unforgettably, in *12A* and *13*. His greedy look will be recalled at *8.483–93*. In the second duet he faces uncorrupted *Naturmensch* in their common key of G major. Benn rightly insists that Monostatos and Papageno sing their words rather than shriek: "the music is delicate, and their fear is such as to render them almost speechless". Uncorrupted *Naturmensch* has inadvertently saved perfect woman.

The length of 6A is deliberate and important. The two Ps, Pamina and Papageno, fritter away precious time in friendly chatter. She is revealed as a sympathetic listener. There is much emphasis on the natural humanity that they share. We are told (*6A20, 6A8*) that in all these years the bird-catcher has never seen his employer's daughter. Is he perhaps her elder brother, a Natural son of the far from virtuous Queen of Night? All that Papageno tells us about his mother is that she came from "that enclosed building", where he believes that she was a servant. *Entia non sunt multiplicanda praeter necessitatem*, even in an apparently rambling work like this; and the wine, sugarloaf and sweet figs always seem generous payment for the one or two little birds, barely a mouthful each.

A more important reason for adopting this hypothesis is that it seems to be implied in the dream-duet that follows—*Bei Männern welche Liebe fühlen*. (Note the downward triad of four of the vocal lines.) Here in the opera's central E♭ major is one of Mozart's strongest convictions. The thoughts that it expresses (see p. 27) happen to be, for the most part, starkly and perennially true. Yet they are the thoughts of a married couple; and are sung, with considerable naïveté and to an even simpler accompaniment, by a man and woman who are not in love with each other, or (as yet) with anyone else. There is much in common between them. They both want to be in love, they are both capable of strong feeling. Nature again, not Reason. In this dream hierarchy, as if they were figures on some great Jesse window, Loving Natural Woman and Loving Natural Man stand chastely side by side; sister and brother, hand in hand. They are waiting for The Man and The Woman. As Benn rightly says, "the behaviour of Pamina and Papageno in this duet must be such that it never enters the mind that there is any subtlety in the words they sing, or that they bear any but their face meaning." The words are knowing, the singers virginal—except that Pamina instinctively becomes more and more exultant. "And God saw every thing that he had made, and, behold, it was very good. . . . And they were both naked . . . and were not ashamed." They had not yet eaten "of the tree of the knowledge of good and evil." In Act Two Papageno remains at a (nice) primitive level. Pamina meets Good and Evil—and is nearly driven mad.

There is no more to say for the moment about the glories and miseries of Nature. So the backcloth rises to reveal intellectual solemnity—three connected temples, labelled Reason (left), Wisdom (centre) and Nature (right). It was careless of the early illustrators (p. 224) to omit the colonnades from Reason and Nature to the central quality of Wisdom; this is an opera in which almost everything connects sooner or later. We are not told whether the trees are cypresses (3A10); but they are probably greener and more flourishing than the trees in the Queen's realm. There is a C for bass trombone, muffled drum, bassoons, trumpet and 'cello; with G from alto trombone and trumpet; and the intervening E from a tenor trombone to complete another triad. Then flutes and clarinets sustain an apparently endless high G, and the violins have a tune for the three boy-genii; who now enter, leading Tamino. Each has a silver palm-spray to show that he is on Sarastro's side—see the central stage-direction at the beginning of Act Two. "Your goal is yonder, honest youth; but you must win by manly battling." We can infer from a theatre bill of 29th September 1792 that the three original boys (not named in the original bill) probably included a young girl, Nanette Schikaneder, who was Emanuel's niece and daughter of Urban Schikaneder the First Priest. The desired tone quality is choirboy; the different sonority of sopranos is only to be endured in the last resort, however difficult it may be to get boys who can sing in tune and "compete" with other voices. The boys continue. "So ponder these our words of truth. Be STEADFAST, PATIENT; NEVER PRATTLING." The advice in capitals is punctuated by three trombones, as well as flutes and clarinets in octaves. With a turn into the dominant (and with anxious second violin triplets) Tamino asks, very Reasonably, whether the advice is relevant to his task. "Tell me, my helpers, if you can; may I Pamina rescue, thus?" We are given those Gs again. "To tell you this, is not for us. Be STEADFAST, PATIENT; NEVER PRATTLING. So think of this, be but a Man; then you will win, by Manly battling." Gravely they go. Could these Cherubs ever be like the elegant and worldly young Cherub who said "Oh but I did my *best* not to hear you?" These boys are Bunyan, not Beaumarchais. "Three Shining Ones came to him and saluted him . . . then Christian gave three leaps for joy and went on, singing . . . often reading in the roll that one of the Shining Ones gave him, by which he was refreshed."

8.39–159 are mostly accompanied recitative; the longest and finest that Mozart wrote. Tamino is no longer merely timid and weak. He is docile, well-meaning, petulant, fallible Reason: "They spoke in Wisdom's weighty measure! Oh then may I their sayings treasure!", with the emphasis on the bold word "I". "Where am I now? What do I see? Is this the seat of deity? I see by the Portals, I see by the Pillars, that Hard Work and Knowledge and Art all are dwellers." One can see why Beethoven and others preferred this earnest wisdom to the urbane wisdom of *Così fan tutte*. Already much edified, Tamino breaks into an enthusiastic *allegro*. "Activity is ruler, and Idleness is banned, so there can be no room for Vice in the land." Perhaps we in England are too lazy to qualify. It is a Germanic virtue; wise and necessary, but not a sufficient substitute for the sadder Wisdom that Europe has tried to learn in two world wars.

Now *allegro assai*. "I go to the Gate with a Hope that is sure, my purpose is Noble and Honest and PURE." Galahad and Parsifal were of this opinion. "Then quake, you coward rogue, in Shame." D major has been established. "Pamina's rescue is my aim." Note the old-fashioned cadence at "is my aim"; here beginneth the first lesson.

Tamino goes to the door of his Nature, and is met by a strong bass voice. The last fourteen words of the usual stage-direction are not in the score (Peter Branscombe points out that the score contains rather fewer stage-directions than the libretto, and that those which we do find are mostly shorter than in the libretto). "Go back!" says the voice; our timid Galahad recoils. "Go back? Go back? Then here I'll try my luck." So he goes to the door of his Reason. "Go back!" says another bass voice. "Here too, the call 'Go back'? But here is one other door! Is this perhaps the entry sure?" Timidly, humbly, he goes to the door. This time, he knocks. (Every action, every sight is significant.) The door of Wisdom opens, and an old priest comes out (*not* necessarily the Speaker/First Priest whom we meet in Act Two).

The tempo changes to *adagio*, and the old priest moves through various flat keys, beginning in A♭ major. "Bold youth, where may your purpose reach? What seek you here in sanctuary?" Tamino answers in a confident *andante*; "What Love and Virtue keep for me!" The old priest, shaking his head at the perennial folly of first-year undergraduates, Reasons with him. "Of lofty import are your words; but think, what is their inner purport? Of Love and Virtue, not at all; for Death and Vengeance are your purpose." His slow C minor unison disconcerts Tamino. "But only for the criminal!" he cries. "No evil man here owes allegiance" says the priest firmly. A horrid doubt strikes Tamino—he hurriedly asks if "Sarastro *governs* in these regions!" "Yes, yes, Sarastro governs here." "Not in the temple, Wisdom's hall?" "He rules in Wisdom's hall; in here." "Then it is all hypocrisy!" cries Tamino, on a loud diminished seventh; sounding more tense, and more like an undergraduate, than ever. The violins and violas take the key into B♭ minor. The priest asks "Will you so early go?" "Yes, I will go, glad and free." He is striding off towards the Temple of Reason; but he turns wistfully. "*Never* your temple know!" The stress on "never" gives the game away. He does not want to leave this nice place. The next little phrase, for violins and violas, is perhaps the most poignant in the dialogue. The priest rejoins: "Some closer Reason give! I fear you are misled." Enter oboes and bassoons with strings. Tamino answers crossly (compare the self-assured *8.88–90*) "Sarastro here does live!" Pat comes a *forte* chord of annoyance and bewilderment. "Enough has then been said!" Pat comes another *forte* chord. Tamino is afraid to continue Reasoning.

"As you do love your life" says the voice of the priest, "so tell me (there remain) do you Sarastro hate?" "Yes, ever and again." "Explain to me your Reasoning." "He's an inhuman wicked king!" "Bring proof of this your accusation!" "A weeping woman's information! The grief and woe had bowed her head!" "A woman has you so misled? A woman does little, says too much. Do you, young man, at gossip clutch?" *Verschwiegenheit*, the ability to keep one's mouth shut, was a quality much valued by Masons. Papageno cannot keep his mouth shut, either; but the suggestion is that women are more inclined to talk harm of others. They have no monopoly of it; but they include some of the more blatant practitioners, even today. *Man zischelt . . . man sagt. . . .* Note the cruelly accurate quaver clacking of *12.54, 65* and *5.63.*

"O could you hear Sarastro plead the Reason true of this his deed!" says the priest. "The Reason's plain to any view!" says Tamino. "Did he not snatch, to pastures other, Pamina from her own dear mother?" "Yes, young one, what you say is true." "Where is she, whom the robber took? Upon the blood-red altar slain?" "Dear son, I may not this explain, nor may we open yet the book." "Explain this riddle! Be not loath!" "My tongue is held by duty's oath." "O when will all this darkness vanish?" The priest smiles gently at him, and sings a Wise phrase; in mysterious A minor. "So soon as two go hand in hand, in holiness, to join the band." The phrase initiates a more lyrical passage. It is in unison with the 'cellos, and is strengthened by alternate quavers from the double-basses and upper strings. The priest turns and goes. His grandfatherly reasoning, from the threshold of Wisdom, has already more than half subdued Tamino; who is too bewildered to go on being callow and impetuous.

"Endless is Night!" It is afternoon, in Sarastro's green and pleasant

land. The darkness is therefore symbolic; Tamino is "filled with
virtuous desire for that which we must all achieve with toil and dili-
gence—the tearing away of our human veil of Night, that we may look
upon the holiness of perfect Enlightenment" (9B1). The tenor voice
must imply by tone-quality that Night is ill-will, misery, ignorance,
confusion, loneliness. "When will it vanish? When will the dawn my
eye replenish?" "Soon!" say soft trombones and voices, in an A minor
triad; with 'cellos repeating the old priest's final A minor tune. "Soon,
young one, if at all!' "Soon? Soon? Soon, say they, if at all! Ye voices,
tell me truthfully, is my Pamina alive?" For a third time, the 'cellos
have their A minor tune. The voices assure him that she is alive. "She
lives! She lives! I thank you feelingly. Oh that it lay within my power,
Almighty Gods, in this glad hour to show my gratitude sincere in
music, as I feel . . . FEEL it here." Again his hand is on his heart. Note
that Mozart allows closed vowels on high notes in this opera.

    One of several reasons why the opera is called the *Magic Flute* is that
Benedict Schack (1758–1826) was a good flautist. Perhaps the most
versatile man (other than Schikaneder) in a versatile company, he was
not only a singer-actor and flautist but a successful composer of opera
and operetta. On 30th September 1791, and on many later evenings, he
now transmuted the "feel" of this finale by bringing out his own flute,
on stage. Thus far, the finale has been mainly solemn. But the Magic
Flute's own C major tune secures a dreamlike transformation to
fantasy. Tamino is armed and shielded through life by music (5.80–132).
He was Weakness, then callow Reason. Now he sounds like Orpheus,
to whom the wild animals and birds will listen with joy. One doubts
at first whether he is a sufficiently competent musician. But Mozart is
saying that Tamino, *der holde Jüngling*, is most certainly Artist man—
composer, poet, painter, singer, actor or player of an instrument, etc.
It is another integral part of the vision. Abert dismissed it as a relic
from the *Lulu* tale, and said that it has nothing to do with the immediate
dramatic situation or with the symbolism of the opera. Thus we impose
our own patterns, and conclude that what does not fit them is a blemish.
When we are dealing with a Mozart, we need to discover Mozart's
pattern in which it is not a blemish. Let us grant, if you wish, that every
element in the opera "comes from" some musical or literary source;
and that Mozart was content to use commonplaces. But origins do
not determine value; what matters is how he used the common-places
without which he could have little hope of sharing his vision with us.
"Your tone has power beyond compare, O flute of magic! O my magic
flute entrancing, wild animals with joy are dancing."

Indeed they are; and for this purpose you and I are wild animals too. Give Reason a rest. Here endeth the first lesson. We are back with Nature (and about time!) The birds—Papageno's birds—pipe too.

"Wild animals with joy are . . ." Tamino stops. This frightens the wild animals, and they run away (*8.186*). Note that Schikaneder's stage-direction (*8.160*) appears to be partly out of place. Tamino has been so absorbed in the task of giving proper expression to his joy that he has forgotten Pamina. "But . . . but Pamina cannot share . . ." He yearns into the tonic minor. He calls her name. He plays, and flute tone is magically answered by an even more Natural sound; the pan-pipe. "Ha, that *is* Papageno's tone!" Papageno can only manage the bottom five notes of the G major scale; so Tamino, who had apparently decided that it was time to get down to some scale practice, answers the same simple bird-call. Contact is established. "Perhaps he saw her all alone, perhaps she hither runs on air, perhaps, *perhaps* . . . his tone will guide me there!"

The big moments of this second section of the finale are the pleasantly ludicrous examples of the Natural power of music—magic flute and magic glockenspiel. Between them, everyone is looking for everyone else; we move from the nursery to the in-and-out bit of a pantomime. Tamino hurries off, on the Reason side of the central Temple. In run Pamina and Papageno, hand in hand, from the Nature side. (Somehow Papageno has managed to free Pamina from her fetters.) G major, a male Nature key, is now established. But the brave Pamina is leading. "Nimble running, courage high will defeat the enemy. Let us then Tamino find, or they'll catch us, for they are not far behind!" "Oh where are you?" calls Pamina. "Quiet, I know better" says Papageno. He pipes, and Tamino answers. The two Children of Nature exult. "Oh could any joy be greater? 'Tis Tamino, yes, a friend, 'tis from him the notes ascend. When we meet I'll not be sorry, what a hurryhurry!" Enter Monostatos, mocking their hurryhurry. "Ha! See, I have caught you both! They are bringing iron fetters, you shall learn to love your betters! Shall the Moor allow defection? Bring the method of correction! Come, you lazy slaves, appear!" All is up with Pamina and Papageno, we fear. But Papageno once more surprises us. His cowardice is partly chatter, partly a refusal to go looking for trouble. In an emergency he is often cool and brave. "He who dares, he who dares, of good luck he often tells. Come, you pretty play of bells, let the bells go ringing, ringing; ring, until their ears are singing!" The play of bells is less primitive than the pan-pipe; but more childlike, less cool and intellectual than the flute. It is joie de vivre, gay, skilful, exuberant. We are captivated. So were the first Vienna audiences. So were Monostatos and the slaves. They dance, and sing "This ringing is much like the heaven of joy; I never heard such-like as man or as boy, larala, lala, larala, lala, larala!" Out they go, in marching order. In sophisticated fairy-tale doggerel (and with a folk-type tune that Schubert used in the same key for Heidenröslein), Pamina and Papageno point Mozart's moral. "All good people, verily, need a bell so charming. Enemies would rapidly cease to be alarming. We would live in harmony! Only gentle harmony softens anguish racking; lack we this great sympathy, happiness is lacking!" This is the urbane ironic Mozart whom we met so often in *Figaro* and *Don Giovanni*. "How can you bear to be so light and flippant on a serious matter?" asked Susanna. "Be contented that I *am* light and flippant" said Figaro/Mozart.

We are approaching the third main section of the finale. It is going to be Sarastro's section, the section of Wisdom. But much of the music needs to be played lightly; and this alone should make us wonder whether Mozartian Wisdom is as solemn as we have unwisely supposed. We return to C major with an ironic phrase on trumpets and drums, in Mozart's best anti-militarist mood. Voices are heard. "All hail to Sarastro! Sarastro, master!" It sounds, and is meant to sound, ordinary. "What is this? What is it? I shiver, I quiver!" says Papageno. "My friend, the end of hope is near" says Pamina with equanimity. Mozart and Schikaneder are keeping up the pretence as long as possible. Pamina, who does not trust Monostatos, trusts Sarastro. But her words have frightened Papageno. "I wish I were a mouse—to hide I should not fail—or else a little snail, to creep into my house." His panic is expressed by a squirming unison of voice with strings and bassoons. "My child! What story are we telling?" "The TRUE one, the TRUE one, though we were rebelling!" I am sorry to disillusion you, but this fine and proper affirmation is not particularly heroic. Papageno, and the more naïve members of the audience, may be allowed to keep up the suspense. But Pamina does not need to be afraid that anything dreadful will happen. The truth can safely be told. On second thoughts, therefore, Mozart omitted a few lines in special praise of Truth from the libretto.

Enter a procession, such as one might expect to see in some small eighteenth-century city—colourful, bombastic, authoritarian and inefficient. At the end of the procession come six (twice three) lions, drawing a chariot. In the chariot sits Sarastro; unpompous in the middle of pomp. Pamina goes to him, looking ashamed. She kneels, as F major is established with the new sound of Masonic basset-horns (tenor clarinets, expressive but sombre). "Sir, though my deed was

criminal, and though to do't my will did call. . . ." She looks reproach-
fully at him. "The blame should go to where it lay. The lusty Moor
did try my honour, and that is why I ran away." The music has leaned
into D minor, with agitated semi-quavers for the violins. She is too
polite to say that it is Sarastro's fault for trusting Monostatos. Sarastro
Wisely changes the subject. Never mind, he says in effect; forget that
nasty man, you have won the love of a nice prince, *der holde Jüngling
selbst*. "Arise, be glad, fair maid of honour. I know, I do not have to
ask you—I know, for I your heart can scan—you deeply love another
man." He sounds sad about it (*8.413–14*). Sachs-like, he himself loves
her—which makes it all the more reprehensible that he should have
trusted Monostatos. "To love I do not mean to force you; but cannot
leave you free to go." He sings it again with "BUT . . ."; a classic use,
in any language. Very nice *but* . . . Very well done *but* . . . A pompous
Sarastro usually makes it sound dull.

Pamina reminds him that she wants to go back to her mother. " . . .
who is in my power" says Sarastro gently. Note that the dotted rhythm of
8.429–30 has not yet begun. He is putting out his hand with an amused
smile; as if a little uncomfortable about the certainty of being mis-
represented. The composer of *Figaro* and *Don Giovanni* has a reason for
every little nuance: a Sarastro who boorishly interrupts is unlikely to be
what Mozart wanted. "And you would soon regret the hour if I should
let you meet your mother." It is implied that Pamina has been living for
some months in Sarastro's realm, and would see her mother with the eyes
of a young woman who is no longer a child; as happens in *13A* and *14*.

"I love the very name of mother" says Pamina more emotionally;
"and she is that!" ". . . and a stubborn woman!" says Sarastro quickly;
to the same tune, the same accompaniment and the same dynamics as
8.428 but a tone lower. The violins have a *forte*, not to be anticipated
by Sarastro. "A man should guide your heart's affection; without a
man, why, any woman steps out*side* her sphere of action." The syllable
in italics is, I agree, rather pompous with its diminished seventh; but
also apologetic. See also the prologue and notes on characters.

Enter Monostatos, dragging Tamino. We are back in F major, and
the violin phrase has something of the *Entführung* brilliance of the
Moor's first entry. "O stubborn youth, come here with me, the Lord
Sarastro you shall see!" It is not the Moor's lucky afternoon. "'Tis he!"
cries Pamina (first off the mark, as usual). "'Tis she!" cries Tamino. "Or
do I dream?" asks Pamina. "'Tis she!" "'Tis he!" they cry. "It is no
dream!" says Tamino. Note the plain string chord on "do I" and "is
no"; the voices are thrown into relief. "My arms about him (her) I do

knit . . . though I should suffer death for it!" "Why, what is that, pray?" ask the startled populace. Monostatos reacts in agony. "So unashamed you are? Undo, undo, I say! You go too far!" The proud girl who would not look at him has run into the arms of a man whom she had never met. Because he is white, because he is white! He separates them, and kneels low at Sarastro's feet. "I lie here as your slave, I offer to let the bold young villain *suffer*! The one who dared this deed absurd—who sent this rare and crafty bird to steal away from you Pamina! Alone I smelled a misdemeanour." But Sarastro knows too much. "You know me" continues Monostatos; the slight pause after these three words is to show, by Sarastro's sad shrug, that the Moor's virtuous-sounding story is as good as a confession of what Pamina had told him. "These my probing eyes . . ." says Monostatos; we saw them looking greedily at Pamina in *6*. "Do win for you a handsome prize" says Sarastro quickly (another interruption; intolerably sarcastic if Sarastro is a solemn man). Sarastro turns to his servants. "Ho, give the man his rich reward." "All added wealth is welcome, lord!" says the delighted Monostatos, with another kind of greed in his probing eyes. "Including the seventy-seven, here?" asks Sarastro sadly, tapping the soles of the Moor's feet with a wand. This taps the Moor into F minor. "Oh no! I shall not clap or cheer!" "No need" says Sarastro, "It is my duty clear." The populace applaud. "All hail to Sarastro, the wisest of judges! For he is impartial, the others had grudges." Another back-handed blow at human society; we remember the self-consciously virtuous punishment of Papageno by women who had reason to be cross with him.

"Go, lead these two young newcomers to the place of proof, where all are tried; and let their heads be duly veiled, for they must first be purified!" At Sarastro's command—still gentle and kindly, not pompous—priests bring sacks, and cover the heads of the two men (*not* Pamina and Tamino; see *10A*, cp. *18A*). In a cheerful final C major chorus (*presto*) we are told that:

> When Virtue, paired with Righteousness,
> The path of Rank shall strew with praise,
> Then there is Heaven here on Earth,
> And mortal Men are Gods in worth.

In other words, a humanist Utopia; to be established from the top by fair-minded and Benevolent Despotism. The *Magic Flute* lives as great music, and is one of the greatest of music-dramas. Spare a thought for it, from time to time, as perhaps *the* greatest document of eighteenth-century Enlightenment.

ACT TWO

The curtain rises to reveal a symbolic pattern. Not being a Mason, Viennese or English, I cannot interpret it with certainty. It looks like a kind of mnemonic, and one is reminded of a Revelation. "I, John, was in the isle that is called Patmos . . . and the first voice which I heard was as it were of a trumpet . . . and behold a throne was set in heaven, and one sat on the throne . . . and round about the throne were four and twenty seats: and upon the seats I saw four and twenty elders sitting, clothed in white raiment; and they had on their heads crowns of gold. . . . Here, at a very central point in the opera's plan, there are eighteen elders in white raiment, and eighteen seats. On each seat is a "pyramid", i.e. a multiply triple construction of some kind; and a great black horn enchased with gold. One seat, with the biggest "pyramid", is a central throne. This implies two nines, of which the inner nine is another kind of multiply triple shape:

in which wisdom is central to the whole and to the four innermost triads or trinities; radiant, like a sun. The outer nine would presumably be three threes, disposed like the side of a pyramid to shield the central chamber from profane view:

```
              .
             . .
            . . .
            . . .
            . . .
      .               .
     . .             . .
```

From elementary political philosophy we have moved to an ethical system that would be trivial, or far from trivial, according to the quality of the minds that constructed and used it. Freemasonry, we understand, is "an organised system of morality, derived from divine wisdom and age-long experience, which, for preservation from outer assault and inner decay, is veiled in allegory and illustrated by symbol" (Robbins, *English-speaking Freemasonry*). From this definition, and from the hints dropped in the score, we can infer that there are no surprises in a first identification of the points of such a pattern. We know that Wisdom (a distant quality, difficult to recognise and even more difficult to attain) is central. We know two of the triads of Wisdom. Very approximately, the pattern might be something like this:

Virtue
Tugend

Discretion   Beneficence
Verschwiegenheit   *Wohltätigkeit*

Truth   Beauty   Purity
Wahrheit Schönheit Reinheit

Reason WISDOM Nature
Vernunft WEISHEIT *Natur*

Patience Strength Friendship
Geduld   Stärke   Freundschaft

Craftsmanship   Justice
Klugheit   *Gerechtigkeit*
Hard work   Arts   Forgiveness   Goodwill
Arbeit   Künste   *Vergebung   Menschenliebe*

In this arbitrary reconstruction of Viennese Masonry as Mozart may have known it, the top "three" are the "north door" qualifications for entry and continued membership. Schikaneder's unvirtuous conduct, we are told, may at one stage have led to his suspension or expulsion; did he perhaps go ahead with the project of a Masonic opera to atone, or acquire some overdue merit? The inner square (thank goodness it is not a cube!) is a formulation of values. We all have values, of one kind or another: are yours, or mine, preferable to these? At bottom left are precepts of prudence and self-respect, derived from (perhaps) the craft of masonry. At bottom right are rules for behaviour to fellow human beings; explaining perhaps why Sarastro, having ordered Monostatos to be punished in Act One, dismisses him with a rebuke in Act Two for much the same offence—intended rape and murder.

I digress for a moment to consider a problem of names. Almaviva is Soul-alive, Cherubino is Cherub, Giovanni is Young, Leporello is Timorous Hare, Masetto is Little Tommy, Fiordiligi is Flower of Loyalty, Dorabella is Golden Beauty, Despina the maid is Mistress (in Greek), Papageno is the Parrot Man who talks too much, Sarastro is Zoroaster. Men in three of the operas, women in a fourth; there is a detectable pattern, and a trend towards the use of meaningful names, where possible, for the more important characters. In an Everyman play like the *Magic Flute*, the use of meaningful names or titles is particularly likely. What about Tamino? The name has a startlingly ancient derivation (p. 221). We do not know how it reached Mozart and Schikaneder, and whether it was they or some intermediate source that made the Jungian transposition of Pa and Ta. But I have for some time suspected that the name Tamino was chosen because, in some way, it fitted the obsessively systematic three-patterning of the music and dialogue. Was the name changed from Pa-min to Tamino in order to be TAMino? My guess has been, for the reasons stated in this paragraph, that *der holde Jüngling* is compounded of *Tugend, Arbeit* and *Menschenliebe*.

At the three corners of the diagram therefore I have ventured to put these three qualities. Tamino is an earnest young Reasoner, a Natural lover, a seeker of Wisdom. Papageno correlates the same qualities in a different way; the *Naturmensch* is told (*12A6*) to use his Reason, and has a certain simple Wisdom ("I would in my wisdom live well", *20*). Sarastro, though Wise, is also Reasonable and Natural. The three temples are connected. The persistent emphasis on correlation of qualities implies that correlation is important in interpreting the diagram. Moreover, certain obvious traditional values (Good; Faith,

Hope, Love; Harmony, etc.) are conspicuously missing from it. Why?

Throughout my study of these operas I have been astonished by their unity, their coherence, their correlation of tiny details into intricate wholes.

It is by no means the pattern of dramatic thinking that one expects from a mere diatonic composer, ham-strung by bad libretti and impeded by the traditional divisions of opera into aria, recitative, etc. What made Mozart's superb musical mind suddenly develop a mature mastery of the patterning and resolution of intricate but coherent dramatic conflicts? I have suggested that he learned much from the musical dialogue of Haydn's quartets. I have also suggested that he came of age as a dramatist by wrestling, in the late summer of 1785, with the apparently impossible task of constructing an opera libretto out of *Le Mariage de Figaro*. Was there, perhaps, more to it than this? Mozart, by the late summer of 1785, had been a Mason for some time. It is obvious that Mozart's main positive alteration of the content of *Le Mariage* was to put more emphasis on the idea of Reconciliation. Had his interest in the patterning of dramatic conflicts been brought to maturity by this symbolic diagram of moral concepts? The diagram can easily be completed, in a way that puts the same emphasis on interrelation of items. For instance let us suppose that the three big triangles (tops, lefts and rights of the three outer triangles) were meant to be separately identified, in a vaguely Platonic and uplifting association of general ideas, as follows. The degree of true Nobility, Manliness and Enlightenment would be held to depend on the Reconciliation, Harmony and Love of the Whole; the immortal Joy, Activity and Peace of created mortal Mankind; creative Good. For the purpose of understanding Mozart, it does not matter whether the above guesses are correct in every detail. But if one looks at the structural affinities of the three operas as a whole, some such general correlation is implied, and could account for almost every positive quality that is sung or given orchestral emphasis or spoken in this opera; with the exception of *Standhaftigkeit*, which would perhaps be regarded as the ordinary weak man's first approximation to *Stärke*. Faith and Hope are played down; perhaps they were considered too passive.

Consider now the palm-trees. The tallest are in the centre behind Wisdom. Unless the whole major pyramid can legitimately be inverted, they are also behind the three furthest of the eighteen seats. The trees are silver like the poor man's glockenspiel. The leaves are golden like the prince's flute and the ornamentation of the great black horns. Given the worthy but humourless type of mind that formulates a symbolic patterning of morals (humourlessness has rubbed off onto our idea of Sarastro, through the music of 9 and 10) the golden leaves are presumably fruit; "by their fruits ye shall know them". The eighteen seats are leaf-piles; perhaps accumulations of daily good deeds, on which your conscience can at last sit fairly easily and softly. Darkness is falling (10A), and the eighteen "pyramids" are later identified as lanterns. "How far that little candle throws his beams! So shines a good deed in a naughty world." Portia's words, in the final scene of *The Merchant of Venice*, continue a trend of thought from the famous dialogue between Lorenzo and Jessica; another source more relevant, directly or indirectly, than *Lulu*. A general trend of Masonic thinking is clear. Mysticism, perhaps, for the few who are in practice helped by that kind of thing. For the rest, a formulation of enlightened self-interest; not so much a substitute for the other sincere loyalties and beliefs of Humanity as a practical back-room Man-to-Man attempt to establish their highest common factor. It does not matter in the least, for the purpose of this book, whether Viennese Masonry is True Belief. What matters is that it was clearly a big Human idea; and that Mozart (a Roman Catholic, but one whose setting of the Great Mass in C minor, K.427, got significantly stuck in the Creed) found it exciting. When a big idea like Masonry or Juanism excites a Mozart, big things happen.

Sarastro and the other seventeen priests enter in solemn marching procession, carrying palm-sprays (like the three boys at the beginning of 8). The original intention, as stated in the libretto, was to have the march accompanied by wind instruments. In the event, Mozart added strings. The march ends. After a pause (because a Man thinks before he speaks?—12.132) Sarastro consults the priests, as if he and they were Dean and Chapter in the Chapter House of some great cathedral (or abbey?).

Tamino is reported to be at the North Door; where he is hoping to tear away his human veil of Night. He is virtuous, he can keep silent, he is a doer of good. The priests decide to offer him the hand of Friendship. They raise the ritual horns, and blow the stiffly repetitive B♭ major Triple Accord, *adagio*; as in bars 97–102 of the overture. The actual sounds come from the basset-horns, the rest of the woodwind (except ordinary clarinets) and a fine assortment of brass; horns, trumpets and three trombones. Then Sarastro makes a little speech, in which Night is identified with prejudice, deception and superstition. Tamino, the lovable youth, will help the initiates. At this news the priests blow the Triple Accord again. The Speaker rises, to express doubt as to whether a prince can survive the ordeals. But Tamino is more than prince; he is Human. If he dies he will go to Isis and Osiris and will know the joys of heaven earlier. The Triple Accord is sounded again. The Speaker, appointed by the Gods through the initiates as advocate of Truth, is told to fulfil his holy office by instructing Tamino and Papageno. They are to learn from his wisdom the duty of Humanity —to acknowledge the power of the Gods. The Speaker goes, taking a second priest with him for use whenever both novices need to be lectured.

The remaining Priests gather round the central throne of Wisdom, with their palm-sprays. To the basset-horns, bassoons and trombones of the Triple Accord Mozart adds the mellow beauty of 'cello and divided violas, in a soft four-bar *adagio* phrase. The orchestra is nearly, but not quite, in groups of three instruments. The key is F major. Sarastro sings a famous and moving musical prayer. "O Isis and Osiris, let them be duly filled with Wisdom's power . . ." There are two short verses. In each verse the last and most important line is sung three times for emphasis; twice by Sarastro, and once—gently, briefly, and with greater effect than many a full-length chorus—by the four-part choir of priests. The vocal line and harmony follow the thoughts, embody the thoughts, live the thoughts; because they are Mozart's thoughts. "Then, when they walk, do not forget them; let them endure in peril's hour!" At *10.29* the music rises hopefully into G minor: "Let them their prizes live to cherish!" Then it falls into an F minor region, at a more sombre thought: "Yet, should it be their doom to perish . . ." The music mounts again. "Courage and virtue as you do love, take them to dwell in heaven above." (The immediate context of these thoughts is the preceding prose dialogue.)

Peter Branscombe has pointed out that the original libretto allots this prayer, like the other "O Isis und Osiris" (*18*), to the priests. This probably means that Mozart first intended choral treatment.

The scene changes, and the front of the stage becomes a derelict yard or forecourt of the temple, with the fallen ruins of pillars and "pyramids" among thorn-bushes. Pillars (*9B7*) like pyramids (and thorn-bushes, St. Matthew xiii, 7) are symbolic. Therefore the stage effect is another sharp contrast, like the opening of Act One, after the overture. This is the yard in which, after a visionary glimpse of Wisdom, good resolutions can crumble. The lights have gone out. Darkness, and the distant rolling of thunder, set the stage for ordeals. The thunder may be taken from Sethos, where it represents the underground clanging of doors. But we later learn that the underground chambers of this temple contain the Queen. The less recherché symbolism of bad weather (compare Lear 3.1) is also relevant. Tamino and Papageno are led in by the Speaker and second priest. The sacks are taken off. The priests go, and the two men are left in "frightening" darkness. It frightens them both. But Papageno's uninhibited natural fright is contrasted with Tamino's earnest attempt to "be a Man".

The priests return. Their torches throw a little light on the scene, revealing two high doors through which they came. The doors are in good condition, unlike the collapsed ideals. They project into the forecourt like side-buildings (or cathedral north porches?) and are in ancient Egyptian style. On being questioned, Tamino says that he wants Friendship (from the priests) and Love (from Pamina). He summons up courage to say that he will, if necessary, die for these two things. He refuses the opportunity to turn back. Papageno, the *Naturmensch*, has no desire to search for wisdom or run risks. As bait, a Papagena is mentioned. He is not prepared to run risks, even for her. But he admits that he would like—out of curiosity—to see her. For this he agrees not to speak to her; and Tamino is told that he must not speak to Pamina.

There is something odd and personal about the following duet (*11*). The first verse is general, but with special emphasis on significant words. "You shall beware the wiles of women! This is the most important law; for many a man, whom sense was dim in, *has gone wrong*— this he did ignore." Oboes and bassoons, with strings, help the two vocal parts. Flutes are added at the words "has gone wrong". It is not certain that the *andante* marking in the autograph goes back to Mozart; yet it seems a sensible amendment of the original *allegretto*, especially as it is also *alla breve*. Why emphasize the words, and then gabble them so fast? The second verse is individual, not general. The strings abandon the melody to the clarinets and bassoons. "He saw her finally desert him, his loyalty was merely spurned!" A long-held horn chord has been added. For the next line the violins are more agitated. With woodwind they then rise from *mf* to a substantial *forte*. The words of this line are: "In vain he cried that she had hurt him!" The final line consists of words quoted by Mozart to his wife in the letter of 11th June 1791, after composing one of the arias of this opera: "Death and despair were all he earned". The fantastic instrumentation includes soft divided violas, soft divided bassoons and soft divided trombones; all staccato, and doubling the two vocal lines, which are an opposite of the loving *legato* thirds of woman and man in so many duets. The four final bars for full orchestra repeat the message of the concluding line.

The words are Schikaneder's. The Starhemberg Freehouse Theatre on the Wieden came into his control from his wife, to whom it had been left by Johann Friedel, for whom she left Schikaneder in 1786 (she sent for Schikaneder to come and help, when her lover died!). But the words may have meant little to Schikaneder, and I do not think we need assume that Mozart meant them personally about his relationship with Constanze. Would he have quoted them to her, if he thought of his feeling of death and despair as her fault? He had a big forgiving mind. There may be a little emotion recollected in tranquillity. But what matters is the idea of an unhappy man, and the placing of this idea at the beginning of a long section (11–14) of positive nastiness (like the darkness of the first half of Act Four of *Figaro*).

Tamino and Papageno are left in pitchy blackness again. Almost at once the Three Ladies appear; rising from trapdoors that, from now on, are in fairly constant use. We need not assume that their coming has been willed by Sarastro. But it provides a well-timed test of whether the two men have (a) understood (b) believed what the two priests were saying. "Why, why, why are you in this dreadful gloom? Fie, fie, fie, you will not escape from doom!" The ladies, who are never a mere caricature of Human Womanhood, are puzzled and anxious. The orchestral phrase at *12.9–10* is full of charm, and there is perhaps more self-deception than malice in their first wild allegation: "Tamino, they have sworn to kill you". Then they insinuate to Papageno: "You will not like it either, will you?" Papageno begins to reply: "No, no, that I could not bear . . ." Tamino hushes him. "Papageno, quiet there! Do you wish to lose the battle? Will you thus with women prattle?" "You heard them? Death we both do face!" says Papageno. "Hush, you idiot! Hush, I say" says Tamino. "Always hush, and always hush!" complains poor Papageno (who has the easiest part to make effective).

We are in a brisk G major *allegro*; not so fast as to reduce the words to gibberish. At first sight, it is a light-hearted interlude between 11 and 13. "The Queen is coming here apace" say the Ladies. "She's in the temple, very near." Again Papageno begins to speak, and has to be hushed. Again the charming orchestral phrase. Again the Ladies appeal to Tamino. "Remember what the Queen did see!" Fair enough. But what of this? "And everybody whispers, always, that priests are full of falsity!" The Ladies are tainted by a common failing—the one for which they professed to punish Papageno in 5. Papageno had done no harm. But they believe, and spread, malicious gossip. The violins and violas have staccato tittle-tattle. Tamino, being a priggish young intellectual, says to himself "Wise men do judge without regard to tattle by the common herd!" "And if you swear to join the band, men say that off to hell you go!" say the Ladies. Papageno is horrified. "That, not the devil ever planned! Oh say, Tamino, is it so?" "Mere trash that woman's wit repeats!" says Tamino. "It was made up by hypocrites." The nice orchestral phrase is now identified with woman's wit. "But if the queen believes in it?" asks Papageno. "She too has but a woman's wit" says Tamino. Though lightly uttered, the frequent sentiments of this kind are part of the serious message of the opera. Again, fair enough if applied where the headgear (female or male) fits. We still suffer from trash made up by hypocrites. The least we can do is to be chary of repeating it.

All this has been whispered between the two men. The Ladies are hurt; after all, they saved Tamino's life this morning. But a final, rather coy, appeal fails; Tamino once more succeeds in hushing Papageno. "Then we must leave!" say the Ladies "A shameful matter, for clearly neither one will chat." Soon they are all singing that "a manly man is never weak; he stops to think what he can speak." (It sounds an unlikely sentiment for the Ladies and Papageno; but once more the headgear can fit as praise of those, of either sex, who think before they speak.) The women are about to go, but a final humiliation awaits them. They have desecrated the temple junkyard and are therefore sent to damnation through the trap-doors. They will be back. Their "Oh alas, oh alas, oh alas!" is echoed by Papageno. After his first "Oh alas!" he falls to the ground.

The quintet has taken place in black night; in other words, in an atmosphere of general prejudice, deception and superstition. The two priests return with their torches. Tamino is commended for his steadfast and manly behaviour. "With pure heart" says the Speaker "we determine to continue our journey." Papageno, the *Naturmensch*, explains that he has fainted with fear. He gets up, asks a question—and is told to use his Reason. With sacks over their heads once more, they are led away. There is time for one or more ordeals off-stage before we see them in the hall at *15A*. (What else would they be doing? Waiting is an ordeal.)

The backcloth rises to reveal an idyllic garden by moonlight. Pamina is asleep in an arbour. Enter Monostatos (Johann Joseph Noiseul, who was primarily an actor rather than a singer). He is nimble, for a man who is supposed to have had seventy-seven strokes on the soles of his feet; as he soon tells us, the sentence had been remitted. "Ha, the shrinking flower! For so small a plant, would they threaten to hammer the soles of my feet? And it is only because the day is one of rejoicing that I still tread the earth with skin unharmed. Hm! What was my crime? That I took fancy to a transplanted flower? What man, though he was born in a temperate climate, could remain cold at the sight of her? By the stars above! She can still make me lose my senses. The fire smoulders. It will burn me up. If I could be sure ... alone, no one looking ... I might try once more. What a damned fuss they make about a little love! One small kiss, I thought, might be excused!" He has been looking round, and fanning himself. The soliloquy is not one to be gabbled or mumbled; the early illustrations of this scene, and Noiseul's competence as an actor, are evidence that it was meant to come over powerfully. One small kiss, forsooth!

The music of the following aria, says the libretto, is to be sung and played as softly as if it were coming from a great distance. The words *sempre pianissimo* in the score say the same thing more briefly. The words of the aria are quoted at p. 224. Of the variant German readings of the sixth line, *Bin ich nicht von Fleisch und Blut?* is by Mozart, *Ich bin auch den Mädchen gut* is by Schikaneder. The inner feeling of hot exultant animal lust is created by voice and orchestra—not for nothing had Mozart been through the experience of writing *Don Giovanni*. There is a steady growth of nastiness from *12* through *13* to *14*. Irresponsible and slanderous whispers, impurity and attempted rape, incitement to murder, hellish ferment of revenge, the cold and cruel cursing of a daughter; none are wise or reasonable, all are ugly perversions of nature, all are black as night. The nastier they sound, the more moving will be the kindly and forgiving justice of Wisdom (*15*). (Remember that, as we have seen, *10* may well have been planned as a chorus; therefore Sarastro, like Pamina and Tamino, was probably intended to have only one aria; the placing of which would be planned with special care.)

We come to one of the most important sections of prose dialogue. With a clap of thunder the Queen rises from the centre trap-door. She stands in front of Pamina, and addresses a brief contemptuous "Be off with you!" to the Moor. Pamina, woken by the thunder, cries "Ye Gods!" Monostatos recoils, but his black soul guesses that it is only the unfrightening goddess of night. Seeing that she has already forgotten him, he stands absolutely still. Pamina rushes into the Queen's arms, with a triple cry of "Mother!" as at *6A1*. "Mother, hm?" thinks Monostatos "I will go back a little and listen." He creeps away as far as the edge of the stage. "You can be thankful that I still call myself your mother" says the Queen to Pamina "I only do so because they snatched you from me. Where is the youth whom I sent to fetch you?" Pamina says he has given himself to the initiates. In that case, says the Queen, Pamina is torn from her for ever. The Queen's power went to the grave with her husband, who of his own free will gave the Seven-fold Circle of the Sun to the initiates, while leaving to his wife and daughter only those treasures (such as the magic flute) which were his own to give. "Do not ask about matters that are beyond a woman's comprehension" he had said: "Your duty is to allow wise men to guide you and your daughter!" The Queen's tone of voice is going beyond the reasonable exasperation of a woman at such an argument. "But mother dear" says the unperturbed Pamina "after all that, is Tamino also lost to me for ever?" "Yes" says the Queen "unless you persuade him to run away through these underground chambers before the dawn tints earth. It is the first glimmer of daylight that decides whether he is devoted to you or to the initiates." "But mother dear" says Pamina for the second time; and proceeds with the words quoted on p. 225. This infuriates the Queen. She gives Pamina a last chance. "Do you see this steel? It is sharpened for Sarastro. You shall kill him, and hand over to me the mighty sun-circle." "But mother dearest!" says Pamina, objecting for the third time to the dictates of a mother whom she had always adored. "Not a word!" says her mother as D minor fury begins to sizzle; "for of revenge I feel the hellish ferment. Death, as my heart boils—death and revenge like FIRE about me roar!" These flames are not hot, like the Moor's fanned lust. They are the maximum heat attainable—at about the normal emotional freezing point—by cold black egotism. "Unless through you Sarastro dies in torment, I say you ARE my daughter nevermore!" The coloratura is as dazzling as stars on a winter night. This is not just an aria, it is part of a cruel dramatic dialogue. Think of the effect on a *sanftes tugendhaftes Mädchen* of suddenly seeing and hearing such a mother as she really is: "Oh, I disown for ever, and I destroy for ever, I throw away for ever every BOND of Nature's troth . . . for ever, for ever! . . . unless through you Sarastro bleeds to slow death!" The Queen is a sadist. "Hark, hark, HARK, gods avenging! Hark to a mother's oath!" She hands the dagger to Pamina, and returns spon-taneously to the underground chambers of 13A14. Try taking her to pieces with the tool-kit of moral values from p. 263. When we first met her, she seemed like Truth, Beauty, and Purity—a more impressive person than the ordinary mortals of Act One. Now she is revealed as Unwise, Unreasonable, even Unnatural; and therefore, significantly,

Weak. (Were all the characters constructed, up to a point, in this way?)

Pamina looks at the dagger. "Shall I do murder? Ye Gods, I cannot!" With this dagger she will later attempt self-murder. Meanwhile Monostatos hurries delightedly forward: "So the power is in Sarastro's sun-circle, and the fair Pamina is to kill him to get it! That is all salt in my soup." Improvers of the dialogue almost always omit the turns of phrase, like "salt in my soup", with which Schikaneder prevented the Moor's little blackmailing scene from sounding too corny. "I have your life, and your mother's, in my power. I have only to say a word to Sarastro, and your mother is drowned in the cellar— yes, drowned in the very water that is to purify, haha purify, the initiates." But Pamina refuses to love him. "No? And why not? Because I am black? I understand. Ha, then die." She begs for pity. "Love or die!" says Monostatos, equating love with his sexual pleasure. "My heart is given to Tamino" says Pamina. "What do I care?" says Monostatos. (If you look at it from his point of view, the caveman is at least asking the girl to agree. After the two attempted rapes, he sounds relatively enlightened.)

Sarastro appears. "Lord, you cannot punish me! They were plotting your death, I was avenging you." It is the usual crafty half-truth. "I know all" says Sarastro. "Your soul is as black as your face. I would punish your deed as you deserve. But as the dagger was brought by another—the wicked mother of a most virtuous daughter—you may thank her evil purpose that you are unpunished. Go!" Off goes Monostatos, thinking that "If I cannot have the daughter . . . I will look for the mother." There he would at least find a woman who does not complicate life with silly notions of love and truth.

After the flatward progression of the last three numbers (G, C, D minor) we are finely edified in E major. In its dramatic context, all that *In diesen heil'gen Hallen* requires is scrupulously careful performance of the easy-seeming music. The words are quoted in the note on Sarastro's character. The word *Mauern* appears (compare *10A13*) in the German text of the aria of *Freimaurerei*. The important fourth line of each verse is caressed by a change of vocal rhythm. "Then Love will gently lead." A solo flute shines out for Love, which has been much purified since the days when an oboe twiddle decorated it in *Non più andrai*. Violin thirds (that walked together for a few steps at the end of the second line, where the singer breathes) become a repeated staccato semiquaver B for second violins and violas; from which voice and first violin climb together in unison of low and high, against a quiet counterpoint for second bassoon. The final couplet of each verse is sung three times, though neither the tune nor the instrumentation remains the same.

The next scene is a hall, in which the flying machine can operate. In front are two grass banks. Tamino and Papageno, no longer wearing sacks, are led in by the Speaker and second priest. "You are to be left alone" says the Speaker. "When you hear the Trumpet of Doom, go forward at once." The *röchelnde Posaune* will sound thrice three times. There is no good reason for supposing that this is Schikaneder's clumsy way of referring to the 9A Triple Accord, blown on the great black horns enchased with gold. The word *röchelnde* is meant to be frightening; it means death-rattling. Hence Papageno's excuses, at 17A.

"Prince, farewell. We shall see you again, before you reach your goal." From this sentence we know that the Two Men in Armour, who were not shown separately in the original cast, will be the Speaker and second priest. Once more, silence is enjoined. To Papageno the second priest says with emphasis that "He who breaks silence in this place will be punished by the Gods with lightning and thunder." But you might as well tell a bird not to sing. Papageno is not therefore punished until he is on the verge of breaking the promise he made at 10A44. Meanwhile he has been given water (in a big jug, not a fancy-shaped French bottle) by an old woman who says that she is eighteen years and two minutes old (in other words she was magically created the right age, two minutes ago).

Enter the Three Boys, aloft in their celestial flying machine. They are, perhaps, one of the very special "threes"; something like Reconciliation, Love and Harmony. At any rate, the harmony of the trio is created with a particularly stunning virtuosity, to suit the air-borne triple Ariel "which art but air". Those who are worried because the Magic Flute and Glockenspiel were given by the Queen and the Ladies should remember that the Magic Flute was made (21.316–25) by Pamina's father, who left both instruments to his wife when he died. The Queen and her Ladies were apparently unable to make any use of them. Moreover, the second and third uses of each instrument, including the important use of the flute during the ordeals of fire and water, come after they have been re-given by Sarastro and the Three Boys.

The words of the Three Boys are simple, unselfcentred and practical. They have brought with them, apart from the flute and glockenspiel, a table well piled with food and drink. "Here is a goodly meal for eating, if you do not prefer to fast." Spare a thought for Mozart himself, who was weak for want of food as he wrote this music for us.

"Then if you reach our final meeting, courage will bring you joy at last." This, as they remark in *16.5*, has been their second meeting with Tamino. (Papageno is already one down, and does not achieve the final meeting.) We shall see the Boys holding flowers in the final Utopia. Meanwhile, "Courage, dear Prince! Near is the goal." Although Tamino is growing in moral stature, he is still far from bold. "Hush, Papageno, talking bird, do not say a word."

Tamino will obviously choose to fast. But a prince who was exhausted this morning, and has had nothing to eat all day, is hungry. He looks greedily at the food, and has to play the flute to distract himself. Papageno proceeds to gorge. Pamina, hearing the flute, runs in. Obeying *10A47*, Tamino sighs and says nothing. Pamina is in great need of comfort and help (*16A7*); all Tamino can do is to grieve her more. Does he not love her any more? Tamino sighs. Pamina appeals to Papageno. Papageno has his mouth full, and has not (yet) forgotten what the Boys told him. "Oh, this passes grief, passes death" says Pamina. "My dearest, only Tamino! Ah, I *feel* his love is dying; gone oh gone is all my bliss . . . gone, gone." People have such a capacity for hurting each other that one is asking to be hurt by having feelings at all. But in 1791 Mozart took it for granted that his nice young heroine and hero would be people of an utterly open sensibility. One need not overdo it; Nissen, in the interesting *Anhang* to his Biography, says that Mozart took this 6/8 *andante* rather fast. But the strings remain too stunned to do more than take the simple G minor harmony along in hushed intermittent quavers. "Nevermore will joyful sighing fill my HEART with happiness." That first verse was soliloquy; a natural expression of misery and hopelessness. The bassoon, whose trill mocked the Queen's G minor in Act One, is here sympathetic. The second verse is addressed to Tamino; with flute, oboe and bassoon. "See Tamino, tears are flowing, falling for you fast and free. You no sign of love are showing, so my peace in death shall be." It is more tragic than *Porgi, amor* (the Countess, with her strong love veiled by platitudes, was merely unhappy and depressed; in *Figaro*, only the F minor of Barbarina—Nannina Gottlieb—has a hint of the same desperation as Pamina's G minor.) This girl is not far from suicide. Every vocal phrase is uncannily expressive of the precise thought implied by the words; for instance, the first short phrase, the long melisma for the heart that will never know happiness again, the two equally natural expressions of a thought in *17.27* and *29*, the strangely trusting resignation of *17.31–3*, and the lonely despair of *17.33–6*. She soon finishes, and even the consolation of sung words is denied to her;

all her young despair floods into what is perhaps the finest short postlude of any song ever written.

Can we accept Schikaneder/Papageno stuffing himself during that aria? Pamina sings in misery. Tamino hears in misery. Life, not even noticing, goes on. It is typical of Mozart to welcome, even suggest, contrasts of this kind. Think of Leporello and Elvira at the end of *Madamina*. Think of Alfonso chuckling during *Addio*. "You see, Tamino, I can also keep my mouth shut when necessary!" It was the one time when he could have done good by talking. There is dramatic point in the contrast—and no point in spoiling the splendour of the next number by cutting the dialogue and thus allowing *Welche Wonne!* (*18.5–6*) to sound like an ironic comment on Pamina's plight. We are, I think, meant to be angry with Papageno (who is at his worst during the whole episode) in order to work off our feelings about Pamina; while the Trumpet of Doom blows nine times.

The next scene is in a pyramid vault. Sarastro and the priests are keeping vigil. Two priests carry a large illuminated pyramid on their shoulders; presumably the one from which the Two Men in Armour later read an inscription. Each priest has a transparent pyramid-lantern in his hand. "O Isis and Osiris, joy is dawning! Fade, foul fog of night, in dewy light of morning!" The effect of D major (with full orchestra including trombones, trumpets and horns) is particularly splendid if it comes soon, but not too soon, after G minor. The new sound becomes even more splendid on the word "Joy" if the three-part (TTB) choir produce the right sonority, with a great *sforzando* in the full orchestra. "The noble youth will see new light for living, soon to our service will himself be giving; he will be bold, so pure is he! Soon will he worthy, worthy be." At that moment he is led in. Sarastro congratulates him on being manly and calm so far. There are still two dangerous paths to tread. "If your heart still beats warmly for Pamina, and if you wish to rule as a wise prince, then may the Gods accompany you further." He offers his hand to Tamino and orders Pamina to be brought. There is a hush (of astonishment?) among the priests as Pamina is led in; blindfold, and wearing the same sack as the initiates. This is the first indication that Pamina too is being educated by ordeal. Sarastro loosens the fastening. She looks round. "Where am I? What a fearful stillness! Where is my Tamino?" "He waits for you, to say a last farewell" says Sarastro. "His last farewell? Oh where is he? Lead me to him." "Here" says Sarastro. "Tamino!" she cries, running towards him with open arms. "Go back!" cries Tamino, turning. He knows he could not trust himself to continue obeying Sarastro if she were in his arms. (On no account should the tell-tale words "Go back" be cut.)

The B♭ major trio can sound artificial, after the naturalism of preceding numbers. But if properly managed it is one of the most moving numbers of the opera. Pamina is mainly engrossed in Tamino. Tamino, having turned away, sings in that position until 19.27. Sarastro's opening and closing lines are asides, and must sound and look like it. "Are we to part for evermore" asks Pamina. ("They soon will part for nevermore" thinks Sarastro, benignly.) "You walk a path of deadly danger!" says Pamina, rising above her own misery to concentrate as usual on the worries of another person. "May heaven pity me/him, a stranger!" sing Tamino and Sarastro. "Then you will die, oh I am fearful; upon us both the curse is come!" says she, still giving priority to his problem. "That is no reason to be tearful; the will of heaven shall be done" sing Tamino and Sarastro. At last Pamina seems resentful. "If you did love with my devotion, you would not then so calm appear!" He may look calm from behind, but his face and hands have been looking frantic. He turns. "But I do feel the same emotion! And I am faithful, never fear!" Sarastro sings it with him ("he does . . . he is") but signals to him to be careful, and hurriedly changes the subject: "The hour strikes, you must be starting." From now on, the lovers sing mainly together, but Tamino is looking awkwardly away. "How bitter is the pain of parting!" they sing. "Tamino now is on his way" says Sarastro to Pamina. "Pamina, I am on my way" sings Tamino, an octave higher; and they take the music onto the dominant, with a glorious "Tamino now is on his way?" to Sarastro from Pamina. They are both agitated; Sarastro needs to insist repeatedly that it is time for Tamino to go. Back in the tonic they sing wistfully of lost Peace (which is golden, like the flute, the leaves, etc.). "Ah golden rapture! Rapture fleeting!" ("Until our meeting!" says Sarastro to himself.) The lovers separate and are led away. Sarastro and the priests follow.

The voice of Papageno is heard outside. "Tamino, Tamino, do you mean to desert me completely?" He looks inside the vault. "If I only had the least idea where I am! Tamino, Tamino! So long as I live, I will not stay away from you any more." We infer that he never caught up with Tamino when the Trumpet of Doom blew for the last time. "Just for this time, do not desert your poor travelling-companion." He comes to the door through which Tamino was led away. A voice cries "Back!", there is thunder, a flash of flame comes from the door, a heavy chord is sounded. "Merciful Gods!" He goes back to the door through which he entered. Again he is turned back. "Now I can go neither forwards nor backwards." He bursts into tears like a child. "Am I perhaps to go hungry at my end? Yes, yes. Why did I come?" The Speaker, who has not so far deigned to attend to Papageno, enters for the solemn purpose of telling Papageno that he has failed, and therefore deserves to wander for ever through the dark clefts of the earth, in unending Night. But the Gods forgive Papageno; he is far too happy and harmless a person to be classed with the opera's undesirables. His only punishment is that he will never know the heavenly pleasures of the initiate. Ah well! There are more people like him. Just now, he only wants a glass of wine. Has he no other wish in the world? Not so far. A big jug, brim-full of red wine, rises from the earth. "Oho, that is quick service. Mmm. Wonderful! Heavenly! Godlike! . . . Ha! A very odd feeling round the heart. I should like . . . I wish . . . What do I wish? I wish I were together with someone, maid or wife . . ."

Ideal Masonic Joy (one suspects) would be of the earnest variety. Yet Mozart himself, when depressed at the failure of his "Bavarian" friend to appreciate the solemn scene (p. 237) felt a "sort of impulse to play the glockenspiel". He went behind the scenes. "Well, just for fun, at the point where Schikaneder has a pause, I played an arpeggio. He was startled, looked behind the wings and saw me. When he had his next pause, I played no arpeggio. This time he stopped, and refused to go on. I guessed what he was thinking and again played a chord. He then struck the glockenspiel and said "*Shut up!* Whereupon everyone laughed. I am inclined to think that this joke taught many of the audience for the first time that Papageno does not play the instrument himself." Just for fun . . . But the fun may have been intended to tail off a little. Most scores print the order of verses given in the original libretto: "*Dann schmeckte mir . . . Ach kann ich denn keiner von allen . . . Wird keine mir Liebe gewähren . . .*" But Peter Branscombe has pointed out that Mozart altered the order of the second and third verses. It was altered back by someone (perhaps Schikaneder—one hopes not) who failed to see that Mozart's order gives the better dramatic sense and continuity.

The aria is the second of three uses of the magic glockenspiel. The words are charming, and deserve study; but bring out no new points of importance. The final verse, according to Mozart's order, is: "When beautiful maidens are many, oh am I not pleasing to any? Oh help, anyone that has breath, or I will soon worry to death." The other words are quoted on p. 222.

In totters the old woman. She is dancing (as best she can, with the help of a stick) to the rhythm of the aria. The words of the proper final verse have been taken literally. Papageno capitulates when she tells him that he must marry her or be shut in this pyramid vault for life; with nothing but bread and water, and nobody to talk to. He, the song-bird, is among other things a being who needs freedom, *Liberté*, *Freiheit* ("O welche Lust, in freier Luft . . .") He therefore promises to be faithful to her (so long as he doesn't see a prettier one!) all his life. She turns into Papagena. He is about to embrace her, when the Speaker again enters and takes her by the hand. "Away with you, young woman! He is not yet worthy of you." He drags away a reluctant girl, and orders Papageno not to follow. "Before I agree to stay behind, the earth shall swallow me up!" It does; he disappears down a trap-door, crying "O ye Gods!"

A backcloth drops. The scene is a strip of garden (behind which, the stage is being prepared for the ordeals by fire and water). Clarinets lead a wind sextet as the Three Boys descend from heaven in their special flying apparatus. "Soon, dawn a better light will kindle; the golden sun will rise. Dark superstition soon will dwindle, and rulers will be wise." In these operas Mozart begins and ends the finale of the last act in the key of the overture and the whole opera. Therefore the music sung by three boys with six wind instruments is in E♭ major; and it was probably part of the plan that the libretto should provide Mozart with thoughts of a pre-agreed kind because he had already decided on the key. Here is one of the central statements (in which Mozart substituted *Aberglaube* for the *finstre Irrwahn* of the libretto). "Come down, O peace; of life the centre. Into the hearts of all men enter. There will be heaven here on earth, and mortals will be gods in worth." The thoughts of the concluding paean of Act One are being extended and deepened, in the light of the symbolism at the beginning of Act Two.

The Boys see Pamina approaching. "Oh see that sorrow like an eddy! Let us be there, with comfort ready! She comes! Let us her path pursue, then we can watch what she will do." She enters in C minor (*21.45*), and the eddying phrases of strings and voice confirm her madness. If we remember the exultant coloratura at the end of 7 we see more clearly the force of the longing that drives her to this desperation. For the astonishing words see p. 226. The Boys make fatuous observations, like the chorus of a Greek tragedy. At *21.54* the music is pathetic F minor (emerging briefly into A♭ major when the Boys address her at *21.63*; so that the slurred semiquavers of *21.66–7* can be a striking contrast). Then the Boys intervene, and bring her back to her senses with a change to allegro, and a downward phrase in violins and viola (*21.95, 99*) "If he saw it—yes, your lover—he would nevermore recover: for his love will not grow cold." "What! For me to feel devotion, yet conceal the soft emotion? Turn his face away from me? Why would he not . . . speak to me?" People are sometimes bothered because she seems to have forgotten that he spoke to her in *19*, but it makes dramatic sense that the horror induced by *16A* should be confirmed rather than weakened by *19*. Apparently, he did not even want to say good-bye. He said "Go back!" He kept on looking away from her—at a time when she was already almost out of her mind with suicidal grief, following *17*.

"Though we may not give you reasons, we will take you to his presence, and you will with wonder know that he is for you aglow, and for you through death will go. Come, we take you speedily." Mozart makes Pamina reply with the last of his great dramatic uses of verbal repetition (Pa . . . pa . . . pa is fun but not on a par with this): "Lead me on, that I may *see* him, that I may *see* him, that I may *see* him, that I may SEE him!"

The backcloth rises, and we see two hills. The first hill spits out fire. The other has a waterfall, from which rushing and roaring noises are audible. Each hill has a grating. Through the first grating we see fire with a red-hot horizon. Through the other we see black mist; Tamino is to walk through the water alone, in darkness. The hills are rocky (like the ones in the nearby Queen's realm); each hill has an imposing iron door. Tamino, barefoot and lightly clad, is led in by Two Men in Armour (the Speaker and second priest, *15A1*). Their helmets spout fire. They read out to Tamino the transparent inscription on the large pyramid-lantern, that now stands or hangs high up between the hills near the gratings.

Strings and trombones strike a bare rhythmic figure on C, *adagio*. Flutes, oboes and bassoons turn it into something more tuneful in C minor. In the same *adagio* tempo, a funereal quasi-fugue begins (contrast the feel of the overture's *allegro*). Against its background, in a solemn old-fashioned chorale tune, the Two Men sing "He who will with his earthly burden walk this dark path, made pure by fire, water, air and hard earth, if he of death shall overcome the human fear, he shall from earth climb up to a heavenly sphere. Illumined, he will a fit person be to serve the mysteries of Isis worthily." The words are taken from the German translation of Terrasson's Sethos by Matthias Claudius, published in 1777-8. But they are thought into music by the composer of *Don Giovanni*, as part of his *Magic Flute*. The earthly burden is the human veil of night from *9B1*. The dark path is the path of the ordeals of life ("Then, when they walk, do not forget them; let them endure in peril's hour.") It is a long path; Papageno said "I shall be an old man before the walk is over" (*12A7*). Papageno fell out, and Tamino was left to face the worst alone; fire and water, with the rushing of wind, among bleak hills. Fire, water, air and earth were the four elements of Empedocles. Why? Partly because they do indeed seem elemental to an ordinary human; especially if one is lightly clad and barefooted. Tamino is behaving bravely, from a sense of duty; and is therefore gradually overcoming some of his natural fear—of death, above all things. We noticed at the end of *Don Giovanni* (see p. 216) that Mozart had overcome the worst of his own fear of death; apparently, by the help of Masonic teaching ("I thank my God for graciously granting me the opportunity—you know what I mean—of learning that death is the *key* that unlocks the door to our true happiness . . . for this blessing I daily thank my Creator and wish with all my heart that each one of my fellow creatures could enjoy it." (Letter of 4th April 1787.)

"I fear no death!" says Tamino, with sinking heart. The characters in *Figaro* and *Don Giovanni* often meant the opposite of their words. In *Così fan tutte* they wanted but failed to mean brave words. Here we have a character wanting, and learning, to mean them. "I have my manhood, the path of virtue leads me onward. O doors of horror, open wide; with happy heart I go inside." But he hears Pamina, who takes the music briefly into Db major. "Tamino, stop! With you I go." "What hear I? Pamina calling?" "Yes, yes" say the Men in Armour "it is Pamina calling." He will not have to walk alone. "Glad sound! If she will with me go, then fate can part us nevermore; no, not if death is through that door." For the first time he feels brave. But he remains remarkably childlike. "Am I allowed with her to talk now?" The Two Men, like grown-ups, give permission. Then: "O joy! If we shall meet apace, we hand in hand shall all things face." Again how childlike—and wise. "A wife who fears no death, no pit, is worthy; her they will admit!" Another conflict resolved; by the admission that each partner can try to contribute what she or he may happen to be good at. Timid brainy Tamino, brave unbrainy Pamina. They are a symbol, an illustration. They meet and embrace, as the music modulates. There is a carefully-marked pause. Then in 3/4 *andante* Pamina soars a sixth. "Tamino mine, O joy supreme!" Only a genius writes great music of such simplicity. "Pamina mine, O joy supreme!" It is F major. A pizzicato heart thumps. He shares his problem with her. "Behold the dreadful portal! Within does death abide." She solves the problem. "I will in peril mortal be ever at your side. The leader I will be, and love is leading me." Again the words have no independent merit, in German or in English. But they give the thoughts that Mozart wanted, to help define this part of a coherent vision. Indeed, their straightforwardness suits Pamina; who proceeds to use Tamino's tune from *3*. "With roses love shall strew the path; for thorns have roses, here on earth." We wince when a lesser composer spins one such thought out for five minutes. Mozart gives it three and a half bars; his interest is in a thousand details, and their crowding pattern.

"If you a magic tune will play, the flute shall guard us on our way." The music is still childlike, but becomes mysterious as she and the bassoon tell us a story. "That flute my father ('twas an hour enchanted) from the deepest hollow of thousand-year-old oak did form, in lightning, thunder, pelting storm." The storm is briefly illustrated. "So now, my walking-fellow, play; the flute shall guide us all the way." Again a symbol and illustration. Then the thought is unforgettably amplified in twining quartet music. "We walk in gladness by the might of sounding tone through death's dark night." All of us, not just Pamina and Tamino.

They go through the doors of the hill of fire. The doors shut. As they pass the grating we see them walk through flames. The roar, fanned by wind. A hush. The flute, in long-drawn-out C major. This is the ordeal. The Thing. Odd; one was more frightened beforehand. But how can we? The Thing. One's breath keeps sticking. A tightness. The Thing. Slow, fumbling reaction. A foot shuffles. A muffled heart thumps. The Thing . . . She emerges, leading him. They rejoice. He lifts his flute. They enter. There is a rumbling, as of thunder. The water surges audibly. Go down. Again it lasts an age. Come up. At that precise moment a door opens into the brightly-lit temple; a view that must be (and hardly ever is!) of the greatest possible radiance, with a sense of solemn stillness. "Was e'er a moment such as this? O Isis, this is happiness!" The chorus join in, with trumpets and drums. "'Tis done, 'tis done, you noble pair! You have defeated all despair. Initiation now is yours; come, open are the temple doors." According to Christopher Raeburn, the words *von innen* are not in the libretto or the score; he suggests that the chorus, or some of them, are meant to crowd onto the stage at *21.389–90*, so as to get a bigger effective volume of choral sound.

The backcloth drops, to reveal the strip of garden in which Pamina tried to commit suicide. Enter a breathless anxious Papageno. This G major has an effect quite unlike the G major of 2; but with the same pan-pipe. "Papagena! Papagena! I am here, love! Love-wife, dove-wife! Reappear, love!" Mozart wrote *liebes Täubchen*, then crossed it out and wrote *Herzensweibchen* above the stave. Neither was what Schikaneder had given him. Branscombe comments: "I can think of no better reason than that he wanted to introduce his most character-istic form of address for his letters to Constanze—from 1789 on there are many examples of his calling her his 'HerzensWeibchen' (e.g. 3 July 1791)."

People sometimes feel that this Papageno scene is an anticlimax, after the ordeals. But the structure of the story requires a second and contrasted climax. If the order pleased Schikaneder because it gave him a big moment near the end, why not? We have no right to know better than Mozart how his story should end. Papageno is growing up, belatedly. "'Tis no use! No, I cannot reach her, I am a born unlucky creature. I talk too much, talk too much. I see it quite, therefore I know it serves me right." He thinks of the jug of wine. "After the wine, there came desire." He thinks of the old hag who took pity on him in the pyramid vault. "Then when I saw her, young and fine—my little heart is all on fire, I have an itch here in the spine. Papagena, O my sweet love! Papagena, O my sweet dove!" He pauses for a second, then shakes his head. "As I see my hopes expiring, of this life itself I'm tiring, for to die puts out the fire that in me is raging higher." The music goes into G minor (and thence into B♭ major.) He takes a rope that was coiled round his waist. "Here's a tree that needs adorning." He feels his neck. "I must hang before the morning. My affairs will not go right! Blackamoor world, I say good-night. World, if this is how you treat me, if of my pretty doll you cheat me, I'll go hang, as you shall see. O my pretty, think of me . . . think of me?" "But . . ." He is as human as Fiordiligi and Dorabella; one cannot be taken for granted, one wants *someone*. He grins. ". . . if *one* of them were sorry for a fellow with a worry, then for once I'd let it go. Call out yes, or is it no? . . . No one hears me . . . Not a twitter, not a single twitter. God, you think that *this* is fitter? Papageno, liven up, it is time to drain the cup. I . . . can wait a bit . . . you see . . . I will count out, one, two, three." He counts them, as slowly as possible, with the help of the pan-pipe and a little (not too much!) ad-libbing. Nothing happens. "Very well, it may . . . not be." It is now G minor in earnest; slower, but only *andante* (not *adagio*). His breath chokes in anticipation. "Then, as nothing keeps me, I bid the naughty world good-bye"—and the Boys are heard, taking the music into an *allegretto* C major. "Enough, O Papageno! Use your brain, we live but one life, live it not in vain." ("God will punish suicide!" was the equally familiar argument that they used to Pamina, who is probably more devout.)

Papageno looks at them scornfully. What do these babes know of the desire that he shares with Figaro and the Count, Don Giovanni and Masetto, Tamino and Monostatos? Try the play of bells? "Oh silly I to think of swinging, I'll set it ringing, tingalinging to fetch a fair unfeathered face." Having played it in G major and F major, he now settles for C major—and even the uses of C major in *Figaro* offer no contrast so wide as the difference between 13 and this *alla breve allegro*. "Go, my bells, a-ringing; get the song-bird here . . . bring my songbird here, my bird-wife here." There are times when the dramatist gets his big effect by trivial babble.

(The libretto has lines, mercifully omitted in the score, that are of importance in understanding the view taken of women, not only in this opera but in *Così fan tutte*:

> Komm her, du holdes liebes Weibchen!
> Dem Mann sollst du dein Herzchen weihn!
> Er wird dich lieben, süszes Weibchen,
> Dein Vater, Freund und Bruder sein.
> Sei dieses Mannes Eigenthum!)

When the glockenspiel began, the Three Boys ran back to their flying apparatus and politely helped Papagena—who was there all the time —to get down. The joke was on Papageno, who went on playing. "Now, Papageno, turn around." There follows one of the all too frequent tests of acting ability; comic play during the ritornello. Funny business, in the modern sense, seems to destroy the incredulity and delight of the duet (for the words of which, see p. 222); but the audience are meant to laugh.

"It is the highest human pleasure, when there are many . . ." Off go the two birds, and the music turns for the last time into C minor. The key has come down in the world since we heard it used for the Bachian quasi-fugue and chorale of the Two Men in Armour. But part of the point of it then was to be a bridge from E♭ major to C major. Here it is definitely contrasted to the final E♭ major, just as the *Introduzione* was contrasted with the overture. Tip-toeing staccato stealth, mutual suspicion, fear, unrighteous indignation, destructiveness, malice, vengeance—"Thou art the mighty Queen of Night!"

Suddenly the full orchestra are brought in. Thunder, lightning, storm, says the score. The rest of the usual stage-direction, which has been inserted from the libretto, is a little premature (like the one at *8.160*). What happens at this point is surely the complete extinction of light on the stage: "I sing of *Chaos* and *Eternal Night*". In darkness the benighted ones are engulfed—and the garden backcloth goes up, so that the transformation can take place at *21.820*. It does not have to take place in an instant—light can if necessary grow for five bars. The entire theatre becomes a sun. Sarastro stands exalted; i.e. on a dais at the centre of the "holy light . . . bright effluence of bright essence increate . . . that I may see and tell of things invisible to mortal sight" (*Paradise Lost* III). Tamino and Pamina, dressed in priestly robes, stand on either side of Wisdom to complete a triad. The priests are there, to left and right; in whatever pattern best assists the symbolism of Enlightenment. The Three Boys (no longer in their *Flugwerk*?) hold flowers. Traditionally there is a big *ritardando* at this point. But Mozart's imperiously precise writing gives the effect that he intended; a breathtaking one. *21.820–1* seem to represent a final rapid dispersal of the forces of night. A very slight broadening in *822* and *823*, before the recitative, is perhaps more permissible, so long as it does not overweight them, compared with *820–1*.

"The sunlight of morning has ended the might of rogues and impostors who SLINK in the night." So says Sarastro. Then the choir break in, with an E♭ major version of the C minor phrase for flutes, oboes and bassoons at *21.191*; thus suggesting that the chorale of the Two Men in Armour was always connected in Mozart's mind with the beginning of the finale, and with the end and beginning of the whole vision. "Now your souls enlightened shall *shine* through all night!" The second half of that sentence is given to the sopranos of the choir; whose curving phrase goes back, via the violin phrase at *Figaro 28.430*, to the great G major page of reconciliation (which, as you will remember, was led by the Countess and Susanna). The choral sopranos now hold their note, and the other three parts tell us how gentle and unforgettable is the shining of Wisdom (one of the few really important choral moments in these operas). "Thank, thank, thank our God Osiris! Thank, thank great Isis for Light! The Stronger have conquered, we crown them with Light, O Beauty and Wisdom eternally bright!" O Strength, Beauty and Wisdom of Mozart!

Figaro, a brilliantly plotted *tour de force*, is the delight of every generation of musical people. *Don Giovanni*, a misunderstood masterpiece, has the greatest dramatic power. The *Magic Flute* is perhaps the most beautiful and entertaining sermon ever written. (*Così fan tutte*, with its compassionate but orthodox conclusion, is in form and beauty the most perfect of them as an opera.) My own steady favourite is the one I happen to be hearing—unless, of course, I hear one of the small number of equally great lyric dramas by other composers.

BOOK LIST

BOOK LIST

Primary documents
The Eulenburg miniature score editions of the three operas; or full scores (preferably *Neue Mozart Ausgabe*, when they appear). Variant readings of the words in *Tre Libretti per Mozart*, ed. Lecaldano, Biblioteca Universale Rizzoli, 963–967; and in Branscombe's "Die Zauberflöte: some textual and interpretative problems", *Proceedings of the Royal Musical Association*, 92nd session, 1966, pp. 41–59. The Mozart *Documentary Biography* by Otto Erich Deutsch, in German or English, is essential. The latest and best edition of the Mozart letters, etc., is the N.M.A. edition of the *Briefe und Aufzeichnungen* by Bauer and Deutsch; but see also *The Letters of Mozart and his family*, translated and superbly annotated by Emily Anderson. *Mozart und seine Welt in Zeitgenössischen Bildern* (N.M.A.). The latest edition of *Köchel*. *Annals of Opera 1597–1940* by Loewenberg.

The important literary sources are *Le Barbier de Séville* and *Le Mariage de Figaro* (for instance, in the ordinary little *Classiques/Larousse* edition); and, negatively, the Bertati *Don Juan* libretto available in *Gazzaniga und Mozart* by Chrysander, *Vierteljahrsschrift für Musikwissenschaft, 1888*. The remainder are of very limited importance for understanding Mozart. But the 1776–85 *Vollständiges Liederbuch für Freimäurer* by Scheibe and the 1782 *Vierzig Freimaurer–Lieder* by Naumann are important for the *Magic Flute*.

Commentaries, etc.
Many of the early views and reminiscences are conveniently given in the Documentary Biography (reviews, Niemetschek, Kelly, Da Ponte, etc.). On Stendhal's curious 1814 pastiche *Vie de Haydn, Mozart et Metastase* see *Music and Letters* July 1946, p. 174. See also: 1828, *Biographie W. A. Mozart's* by G. N. von Nissen; 1829, *Don Juan* by E. T. W. Hoffmann; 1842–3, *Nouvelle biographie de Mozart* by Ulibishev; 1845, *Life of Mozart* by Edward Holmes (also 1912, 1932); 1855, *Mozart auf der Reise nach Prag* (based on Ulibishev) by Mörike; 1856–9, *Mozart* by Otto Jahn (tr. Townsend, 1891); 1869, *Mozart-Buch* by Wurzbach; 1885–94, Shaw's notices (now collected in e.g. *Music in London, 1890–4*, and *How to become a Musical Critic*); 1899, *Goethe's Fortsetzung der . . . Zauberflöte*, V. Junk; 1901, *Emanuel Schikaneder* by E. von Komorzynski (popular edition 1948, second main edition 1951);

1902, *Dramaturgie der Oper* by Bulthaus; 1913, *Mozart's Operas* by Dent (second edition 1947, numerous reprints); 1920, *Die Zauberflöte* by Max Pirker; 1920, *Die Zauberflöte* by Waltershausen; 1920, *The Magic Flute* by Lowes Dickinson; 1922, *Goethe und die Musik* by Hermann Abert; 1923–4, *Mozart* by Abert; 1928, *Le Mariage de Figaro* by Gaiffe; 1932, *Mozart und die Königliche Kunst* by Paul Nettl; 1935–7, *Mozart* by Eric Blom; 1935–8, *Mozart Opera Society* notes by Walter Legge; 1937, *Die Zauberflöte* by Paul Stefan; 1938, *Don Giovanni* by Stefan; 1938, *Mozart* by W. J. Turner (second edition, ed. Raeburn 1965); 1938, *Mozart in Böhme* by Nettl; 1939, *W–A Mozart, sa vie musicale*, IV, by Saint-Foix (Vol. V, 1946); 1939, *The legend of Don Juan* by John Austen; 1940, *Mozart* by B. Paumgartner; 1941, *Mozart* by Komorzynski; 1942, *Le Don Juan de Mozart* by Jouve (tr. Earnshaw Smith, 1957); 1943, *Mozart's Dramaturgie der Oper* by Conrad; 1945–8, *Mozart, His Character, His Work* by Alfred Einstein (tr. Mendel and Broder); 1946, *Mozart on the Stage* by Christopher Benn (posthumous); 1948, *The Marriage of Figaro* (Sadlers Wells Opera Book); 1949, *Goethe und Mozart* by Nettl; 1949, *Casanova und seine Zeit* by Nettl; 1952, *Mozart's Le Nozze di Figaro* by Levarie; 1952, *Die Alt–Wiener Volkskomödie* by Otto Rommel; 1952, *Die Zauberflöte* by Morenz; 1953, *Le cas Don Juan* by Micheline Sauvage; 1954, *More Opera Nights* by Ernest Newman; 1955, *Mozart in Retrospect* by A. Hyatt King; 1956, *Glyndebourne Mozart Bicentenary Festival Programme Book;* 1956, *The Mozart Companion* edited by Robbins Landon and Mitchell; 1956, *Die Sieben Grossen Opern Mozarts* by Greither; 1957, *Famous Mozart Operas* by Spike Hughes; 1957, *The Magic Flute* by Auden and Kallman; 1958, *La pensée de Mozart* by Hocquard; 1960 *Mozart und der Tanz* by Nettl; 1960–5, EMI complete recordings, with notes by William Mann; 1963, *Mozart the dramatist* by Brigid Brophy; 1964, *Die Zauberflöte* by Alfons Rosenberg; April 1965, *Mozart's Figaro: the Plan of Act Three* by Moberly and Raeburn in *Music and Letters* (*Mozart-Jahrbuch* 1966, tr. Wallbaum). And much else!

INDEX

INDEX